Praise for *The Whole Brain Business Book*

"Ned Herrmann was way ahead of his time. Long before neuroscience became all the rage, Ned was talking and writing about the mind-body connection and about how we think impacts how we act. He was a pioneer, a genius, and path-finder. Ann Herrmann-Nehdi has done the world a huge favor by updating Ned's seminal work, *The Whole Brain Business Book,* and reintroducing us to the power we each have when we use all of what we're given. This book is rich in ah-ha moments and a treasure trove of practical tips on how to apply Whole Brain Thinking at work, home, and in the community. This is an extraordinary performance, a *tour de force*, and a must read for everyone who wants to apply their whole selves in whatever they do."

—**Jim Kouzes,** coauthor of *The Leadership Challenge* and Dean's Executive Fellow of Leadership, Leavey School of Business, Santa Clara University

"Ned Herrmann and Ann Herrmann-Nehdi know more about the brain than anyone. If you want to function better, this is a must read."

—**Ken Blanchard,** coauthor of *The One Minute Manager*

"Whether you're new to the Whole Brain model, or ready for a twenty-first century update to the classic volume, this book is a must read for anyone with a brain. You will learn how your mind works, how to improve and expand your thinking style, and how to better understand and communicate with the brains around you."

—**Daniel H. Pink,** author of *Drive* and *A Whole New Mind*

"This book delivers on two capabilities that leaders at every level should have: first, to truly know that we all actually process the world differently, and second, to start to really think about thinking itself."

—**David Rock,** author of *Your Brain at Work,* and Director, NeuroLeadership Institute

"We know that being innovative requires a Whole Brain process and team. We also know that we live in a 'whole-brained' world. Whether you want to work smarter or appeal to a broad audience, you have to first understand how different people think."

—**Shannon Loftis,** General Manager, Redmond Games Publishing at Microsoft

"Ann has done a masterful job of updating Ned's original work, by including a contemporary neurological perspective on brain functioning while connecting this to the latest thinking on human performance, interpersonal effectiveness and organizational design. The Whole Brain Model and HBDI are powerful tools for both understanding human behavior and helping everyone to achieve their 'whole brain' potential."

—**Dr. Mark Schar,** Senior Researcher and Lecturer, School of
Engineering, Center for Design Research, Stanford University, and
former Senior Vice President and Chief Marketing Officer, Intuit, Inc.

"I have been in leadership and consulting roles for almost 45 years. *The Whole Brain Business Book* took me to a new place for the first time in over 20 years. The clients I work with create completely new mindsets as a result of exposure to this approach."

—**Mike Packard,** Founder and CEO, TransCat Consulting,
and former Executive Vice President, LensCrafters

"An affirming catalyst to elevate us to the level of engagement we desire most in working with others."

—**Daryl B. Hammett, Sr.,** CEO, Peabody Executive Coaching
and Performance Management Group, and former Senior
Vice President and General Manager, Sears Optical

"In my experience with technical teams in universities and industry, the Whole Brain model provides a first-order engineering approximation to mental diversity that encourages collaborators to empathize nonjudgmentally, thereby enabling them to better leverage their intellectual excellence, spur their creativity, and make pragmatic contributions that really matter to people."

—**Charles E. Leiserson,** Professor of Computer Science and
Engineering, Massachusetts Institute of Technology (MIT)

"We have a much stronger unit with everyone understanding what everyone brings to the table. I use Whole Brain Thinking daily. It has made a difference in my personal and professional life, and I know it has for my team members as well."

—**Brian Wheeler,** Director of Operations, Lastar, Inc.

"Other models are more focused on behavior, so it's harder to have a conversation about problem solving. Whole Brain Thinking is more applicable in the workplace because it's about the way you think and solve problems. It facilitates a good work discussion."

—**Crystal Snoddy,** Head of Delivery Excellence,
International Hotel Group (IHG)

The
Whole Brain
Business
Book

The Whole Brain Business Book

SECOND EDITION

Unlocking the Power of Whole Brain Thinking in Organizations, Teams, and Individuals

Ned Herrmann
Ann Herrmann-Nehdi

McGraw Hill Education

New York   Chicago   San Francisco   Athens   London
Madrid   Mexico City   Milan   New Delhi
Singapore   Sydney   Toronto

1 2 3 4 5 6 7 8 9 0   DOC/DOC   1 2 1 0 9 8 7 6 5

ISBN   978-0-07-184382–9
MHID   0-07-184382–5

e-ISBN 978-0-07-184383–6
e-MHID 0-07-184383–3

The cartoons used in this book are printed with permission from Randy Glasbergen, www.glasbergen.com.

The four-color, four-quadrant graphic; Herrmann Brain Dominance Instrument®; HBDI®; Whole Brain®; and ROI® (Return on Intelligence) are registered trademarks of Herrmann Global, LLC.

McGraw-Hill Education books are available at special quantity discounts to use as premiums and sales promotions or for use in corporate training programs. To contact a representative, please visit the Contact Us pages at www.mhprofessional.com.

My father's excitement about thinking and the brain became the focus of his life's work. I dedicate this book to his legacy and to the millions of people throughout the world whom Whole Brain Thinking has touched and helped as a result.

Ann Herrmann-Nehdi

Contents

For a list of figures that appear in this book, please go to www.wholebrainbusinessbook.com

Preface to the Second Edition

"It's called 'reading'. It's how people install new software into their brains."

Thirty years ago, a high-potential manager sat in a training class at Crotonville, General Electric's world-class corporate university. He listened as my father, Ned Herrmann, then head of GE's Management Education, discussed research that he was developing on how the brain affects day-to-day operations.

Struggling to find the relevance of this information, the manager commented, "Learning about the brain is certainly interesting. But Ned," he went on, "what does the brain have to do with managing?"

An appropriate response? "Well, in your case, everything!"

With the initial publication of *The Whole Brain Business Book* in 1996, Ned opened the eyes of many more managers and leaders around the world to the impact and applications of Whole Brain Thinking for every aspect of business and performance.

I remember vividly those initial experiments he conducted demonstrating specialization in the brain—primarily because they involved wiring me up to an electroencephalograph (EEG) for testing. Such was the life of someone who literally grew up with Whole Brain Thinking.

Since that time, there's been an explosion of new brain research, generating powerful new insights into how we can apply Whole Brain Thinking to drive business results. The process of updating this book has given me the opportunity to translate how each reader can apply this new knowledge in very practical ways to improve his performance on the job and at home, without having to be wired up to the EEG, as I once was.

As I was growing up, I was lucky enough to observe all the ways in which Whole Brain Thinking could be applied, with useful and often breakthrough applications in everyday experiences, from the personal to the professional and every point in between. This updated edition of *The Whole Brain Business Book* captures many new stories and best-practice examples to demonstrate the multitude of ways in which leaders, managers, individuals, and entire organizations can unleash their full thinking capacity and get better results across the board.

In fact, the wide applicability of the Whole Brain concept means that the richness, depth, and variety of these examples have grown exponentially over the past several decades, reinforcing the power and practicality of Whole Brain Thinking in business. There is now a broad community of thousands of Whole Brain Thinking practitioners and business leaders who are taking Ned's elegantly simple yet scientific approach and applying it in ways that even he may not have imagined, giving us a broad array of organizations and functional areas to draw from in this new edition: workplace productivity, strategy experts, organization development leaders, video game developers, sales managers, magazine designers, call center managers, and a host of others, representing nine out of ten of the Fortune 100.

And one other note: you'll see that every chapter includes a cartoon illustrating that chapter's essence. One of the most important things I learned from my father is how effective and brain-friendly humor can be.

Carrying my father's work into the twenty-first century since his passing in 1999 has been a fascinating journey. The business environment has changed in so many ways since *The Whole Brain Business Book* was first published, and so has our understanding of the brain, and how Whole Brain Thinking *can and does fuel business results in every industry*. It was time for an update—to acknowledge the realities of today's workplace and give readers proven and practical new ways to get the most from their most precious currency and most valuable tool: brainpower.

Ann Herrmann-Nehdi

Acknowledgments

When we decided to update this book, we faced an interesting challenge: how to update and reorganize the book to better reflect today's realities and examples while not losing my father's voice and the "soul" of the original book.

I knew we needed a great team to make this happen. I was very fortunate to have the support and creative skills that Marla Lepore provided. Marla's patience, deep knowledge, and fantastic editing skills were essential to the success of the project, and I will be forever thankful to her.

Linda Plante played a significant role, helping the entire team stay on track so that we could meet deadlines and collaborate effectively. We could not have done this without her!

Tracy Sterling brought her great project management expertise to the project, which, combined with her knowledge and extensive experience in Whole Brain Thinking, helped ensure that we delivered a high-quality product with up-to-date, practical, and relevant application content.

I am deeply appreciative of Mohamed Ali Nehdi's graphic design capability, deep knowledge, and experience from working on the first edition of the book. Without it, we could not have provided all the new and updated graphics and data displays. In addition, as my partner in this work and as my husband, he has contributed to our work in Whole Brain Thinking in more ways than I can possibly list. Thank you!

Daniel Stanhope provided important psychometric analysis and concepts for our HBDI data updates, especially the CEO data, which were critical to this project and which I greatly appreciate.

Laura Lovallo Wang and Dale McGowan, along with our manuscript reviewers, Michael Packard and Daryl Hammett, helped to provide invaluable assistance in the final stages of production. Lori Addicks and Michael Morgan contributed stories and examples in addition to serving as manuscript reviewers.

My personal thanks go to all those who contributed updated stories and examples: David Clancy, Ted Coulson, Ann-Louise deBoer, Rich DeSerio, Prasad Deshpande, Manny Elkind, Ayn Fox, Paul Gustavson, Bill Hart, Jay Kayne, Fred Keeton, Lynne Krause, Ed and Monika Lumsdaine, Lewis Lubin, Anne McGee-Cooper, Bob McKown, Tiffany McMacken, Chuck McVinney,

Colin Pidd, Cynthia Radford, Lynn Robinson, Crystal Snoddy, Allison Strickland, Duane Trammell, Chris Webb, and Robert Webber.

Many thanks to Randy Glasbergen for the terrific humor he brings through the cartoons we have included.

Special thanks go to my son, Karim Nehdi, who, as a third-generation leader at Herrmann International, is taking the work to new heights by bringing important new insights and values that also influenced many of the updates we created for this book.

I cannot thank enough my mother, Margy Herrmann, to whom the first edition was dedicated, for all of her significant contribution to this body of work over many decades, which continues today; my sister, Pat, for her terrific proofreading and review of the book; and my sister, Laura, and son, Selim, for their continued love and support.

Finally, my personal thanks to the Herrmann International team and all the HBDI certified practitioners around the globe who continue to provide us with new applications of the concept and are every day helping individuals, teams, and organization drive better results through Whole Brain Thinking.

Ann Herrmann-Nehdi

Introduction

"In an increasingly complex world, sometimes old questions require new answers."

Perhaps you've found yourself in a situation where you've been stuck, frustrated, out of ideas, caught off guard by change, struggling with communication, or challenged by dealing with "difficult" team members, colleagues, or customers.

Or maybe you've wondered:

How do I get my team to be more productive?

How do I grow as a leader in a rapidly changing environment?

What's blocking my organization from implementing the changes we need?

Why is it that we have all the right people and pieces in place, but we just can't seem to get the results we want?

Why isn't my organization more innovative and creative?

What you may not realize is that these kinds of issues often have a common root cause: thinking. And that's why the skill of Whole Brain Thinking, which you'll learn in this book, has become so important.

With the complexity of today's business environment, you and your organization can't afford to be held up by communication breakdowns, poorly functioning teams, or leaders who don't have the necessary vision and agility to cut through the chaos and get results. You can't compete successfully if you're being consistently outpaced by change or stuck in a rut of lackluster ideas. And you certainly can't afford to waste time, talent, and resources.

The challenges are daunting, but this book will show you that the answers are all available to you, waiting to be unleashed. It all starts with thinking.

Every business runs on thinking. The purpose of this book is to provide you with a better understanding of how thinking affects your results *and the tools you need to improve them*, whether you're an individual contributor or leading a team, or whether you're in a small to midsize business or a large global organization. We don't always know how others think, but this book will help you understand the implications of different thinking preferences (including your own) and then show you easy ways to build up your thinking agility so that you can work more effectively with others who think differently and leverage the best thinking around you to avoid costly delays, missed opportunities, and other business risks.

But more than that, you'll rediscover the full power and potential of your own thinking. This book will show you not only how to fully capitalize on your thinking, but also how to break out of your mental defaults so that you can reach new levels of success. In a complex world, that mental dexterity has never been more critical.

In a sense, many individuals and organizations have been taking the long way to results because they haven't adapted their thinking to today's realities. This book will put you on the fast track. As one executive remarked, "If only I had known this years ago. It would have saved me so much time and frustration!"

No matter what your goals are, getting smarter about your thinking will help you reach them faster, more efficiently, and more effectively. This book will help you understand that it's not just *what* you think, it's *how* you think that makes a difference. It will open up your eyes to the full "brain trust" that's available to you and show you how to tap into it and expand your own thinking capacity to optimize what you're doing, get more creative, get more efficient, and get better results.

What to Expect in These Pages

There has been an explosion of information about the brain and business since the first edition of this book was published. But in the midst of all this information—from the plethora of studies and books to the emergence of new "neuro" application fields to the significant research headlines that we read and hear about daily—there remains a need for real-world, how-does-this-apply-and-how-can-I-use-it-to-get-results practicality that is often missing from the more academic discussions and advice. This book keeps the subject down to earth, relevant, and actionable. You won't be reading about complex theories or vague philosophies; you'll be learning practical, proven models and techniques and workable solutions to optimize your performance and improve your business.

The Whole Brain Business Book explores the core business issues that organizations in every industry and of every size and geographic scope are dealing with today. It's divided into sections that answer the following questions:

1. How does my thinking affect my performance, and how can I become more of a Whole Brain thinker?
2. How do I use my whole brain to better harness cognitive diversity: to manage, lead, collaborate with, communicate with, align, and influence people with different thinking preferences?
3. How can I be more agile, strategic, and effective as a leader in today's complex world, and what can I learn from how CEOs think?
4. In an actionable, practical sense, how do I unleash creative and strategic thinking to drive innovation at an individual, team, and organizational level?
5. What steps can I take to continue to learn, grow, evolve, and develop my thinking?

You can read the chapters in sequence to get the full view, or you can dive into a specific chapter or section that focuses on a burning challenge that you're currently facing. Along with a multitude of real-life examples from companies, products, and people that you will immediately recognize, you'll get specific techniques you can use to strategically focus your organization's thinking directly on your key business challenges, or to expand your own thinking skills in individual performance areas. Each chapter concludes with a snapshot summary of key points along with next-step tips to help you put the concepts into action.

The Power of Whole Brain Thinking: A Growing Legacy

This edition of Ned Herrmann's groundbreaking book on the application of Whole Brain Thinking to business is rich with anecdotes from Ned's remarkable journey from management development at General Electric to pioneering researcher, author, and thought leader in the field.

Ned Herrmann died in 1999, but his legacy continues. The concepts, foundation, and spirit of the original edition, including Ned's unique voice, remain, augmented with up-to-date cases, new applications, and new business issues that have emerged over the past several decades. Examples of the payoffs of Whole Brain Thinking are abundant in the business press, and the benefits have been applied successfully in the world of academia as well. Colleges and universities like Wharton, Stanford, and MIT are using these concepts in engineering, executive education, MBA programs, and a variety of innovative programs. In corporate learning and development, an entire discipline of Whole Brain application, design, and delivery continues to grow in nine out of ten of the Fortune 100 and a wide range of small and midsize organizations across the globe. This fully updated book builds on the now decades of concrete examples provided by the team that is carrying on the work today, led by Ned's daughter, Ann Herrmann-Nehdi, and recently joined by his grandson, Karim Nehdi. The result is proven tools that you can *put to use immediately,* without needing a PhD in neuroscience.

Around the world, thousands of professionals are applying Whole Brain Thinking across a wide range of applications, from the classroom to the boardroom. Every day, they are proving Ned's conviction: with better thinking comes better results.

It's your brain—learn to use it better than you ever have!

The Whole Brain Framework

ELECTRONICS

"Can you recommend a GPS device to help me avoid the dead-end streets and locate the shortcuts on the Road to Success?"

CHAPTER 1

Every Business Runs on Thinking

CHAPTER HIGHLIGHTS

> Because every business runs on its thinking, optimizing thinking is the key to better performance and better results.

> The more we learn about the brain, the more relevant these concepts are to every aspect of your business, your own career, and your professional growth.

> With Whole Brain® Thinking, your business will have an improvement process that does for people and the organization what Lean did for manufacturing and Agile did for technology.

> More than 30 years of research stand behind the concepts, examples, and stories you will be reading about in this book.

My first full-scale research activities on brain function caused quite a stir at the GE Management Development Institute at Crotonville in the mid-1970s. Ironically, most people couldn't see how the brain was connected with my professional work in management education. Compared to what we now know about the brain, we were pretty much in the Dark Ages. In addition, most business cultures were so steeped in analytical, logical, and safekeeping modes of thinking that they not only resisted the idea of "Whole Brain" Thinking, but also didn't see why they needed to recognize, acknowledge, and apply the more interpersonal, imaginative styles of thinking that existed within their organizations but were often buried.

Whether it was explicitly articulated or not, the typical response that I seemed to be getting back then was some variation of a basic question:

"So what?" So it's probably fitting that each chapter in this book ends with a section entitled "So What?" Why does it matter that we have different preferences for different kinds of thinking? What does creative thinking have to do with business success? Why should I care about this when I need to make my numbers, deal with complex issues, rally people around a new mission and strategy, and keep people engaged and performing at their peak?

When it comes to running a business, *so what*?

> Almost all men
> are intelligent.
> It is method
> that they lack.
> —F. W. Nichol

What Is Whole Brain Thinking?

Applying Whole Brain Thinking means being able to fully leverage one's own preferences, stretch to other styles when necessary, and adapt to and take advantage of the preferences of those around you to improve performance and results.

The answer is simple: every business runs on thinking. If you want to continually improve and reach new heights in an increasingly complex world, you have to understand the impact of thinking and take advantage of all the thinking potential that you have. For my own company and for all businesses, a more conscious Whole Brain approach to business is a necessity, not an option, for these primary reasons:

If thinking is the fuel that drives business, we need to understand how the brain works in order to deal with change effectively. Are you dealing with the same kinds of problems, opportunities, and work environment that you faced five years ago? Or even a year ago? Change is happening so fast that it's not uncommon for most businesspeople to be coming up against challenges and issues that have no precedent on an almost daily basis.

This level of change requires you to fully leverage all the mental muscle you have in order to move away from resistance and seek out new thinking. When you can engage the kind of specialized thinking that is more inclined to embrace novelty, you'll be better able to make critical decisions after the facts have run out. To compete effectively in a world characterized by change, everyone has to be able to function using all of the brain's different modes. This has never been truer than it is today.

Mentally diverse heterogeneous groups produce more creative, effective solutions than do similar-thinking homogeneous groups. This isn't an altogether new thought. The saying "two heads are better than one" has been around for a while. We just didn't have research to explain it or a way to measure it, manage it, and describe it, which is what the Whole Brain Thinking concept allows. We now have the research that demonstrates why we need all the diverse thinking in our organizations working together if we are to get the best results, particularly as the challenges we face keep getting more complex. The good news is that most organizations have those cognitive differences within their ranks; they just have to know where to seek them out and how best to leverage the diversity.

With greater thinking diversity comes a unique challenge: heterogeneous groups are often much harder to manage. Classic management approaches no longer apply—they're too constricting, and therefore they're usually counterproductive. To manage these diverse groups, leaders need to be more like translators than like traditional taskmasters. The upshot: if we're going to tap the power of the Whole Brain team, we have to learn Whole Brain ways of managing.

Certain modes of thinking will increasingly dominate an organization as it matures unless the leadership applies Whole Brain Thinking to consciously cultivate and encourage the breadth of thinking that is necessary for ongoing success. We tend to hire, coach, promote, and otherwise reward in our own image. It's natural to be drawn to those who think the way we do. It's easy. We have our own shorthand. But if we limit ourselves in this way, we're missing the other perspectives and mental frames of reference we need in order to solve complex problems and find more innovative solutions. All that single-mindedness will lead to stagnation or worse. In the face of increasing complexity and intense competition, companies won't be able to survive over the long term if they don't deliberately look for, develop, and leverage the full spectrum of thinking.

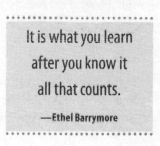

It is what you learn after you know it all that counts.

—Ethel Barrymore

As you read this book, you'll discover that the way you communicate, learn, make decisions, plan your work processes, choose your career, deal with customers, manage people, allocate attention, and handle every other aspect of your business performance is rooted in how you prefer to think. Imagine how much you'll be able to accomplish—how much more productive, more focused, and more flexible you'll be—once you understand and know how to use all your thinking to your advantage.

The Brain Has Everything to Do with Business: How to Put It to Work

EXERCISE: Answer the following critical business questions to learn more about how understanding your thinking can help you improve your learning and your performance and to discover which chapters can help you most in that effort:

Career aspirations: Think of a person you know who is a "misfit" in his career. How does that impact this person's effectiveness?

_____

_____

To learn how a person's thinking patterns make him or her a better "thinking fit" for particular positions, refer to Chapters 4, 6, and 10. Read Chapter 3 for insight on how you can work smarter and align your work and competencies.

Communication: When was the last time you had a communication misunderstanding or mishap? How much time and energy did you lose?

_____

_____

Chapter 8 shows you how to build communication bridges to save time and effort, make the most of all the available talent in your organizations, and encourage people to bring their best thinking to the table.

Corporate culture: How flexible is your corporate culture in these times of constant change? How does inflexibility get in the way of success and agility, and what impact does it have on innovation?

_____

_____

Read about how leaders can keep their corporate culture agile, especially for dealing with change and preserving innovation vitality, in Chapters 15 and 19, and learn how best to deal with disruption and reorganization in Chapters 17 and 18 .

Creativity and innovation: How might creativity help you and your organization better adapt and grow? How often do you feel creative at work? How innovative are you?

_____

_____

Refer to Chapters 21 through 23 to explore real examples of how an organization can establish a climate for creativity, build a creative team, and manage that team to unleash greater personal and business potential.

Customer relationships: How well do you really know your customers?

_____

_____

Read Chapter 13 for stories and examples of specific ways to connect faster, create stronger partnerships, and establish more mutually beneficial relationships with both internal and external customers and stakeholders.

Cognitive diversity: Do you leverage diversity or get frustrated by it?

_____

_____

Learn how to get optimum results and a competitive advantage, rather than frustration, from cognitive diversity in Chapters 5 and 7.

Job design and productivity: Are you as productive as you could be? How about your team? Your organization?

_____

_____

Chapter 10 explores how work and jobs can be designed to gain 20 to 40 percent in additional productivity.

Managing: Do you ever get frustrated with employees or peers who need to change their behavior but aren't doing so? How well do you manage, motivate, and engage them?

_____

_____

Managers can significantly improve the engagement and management of those they work with by understanding and aligning thinking. Learn about managing, motivating, coaching, and delegating with thinking in mind in Chapters 7, 9, and 11.

Planning: Is your planning more strategic or more operational?

_____

_____

Discover what differentiates strategic planning from operational planning and how to make sure you have enough of each when and where you need it most in Chapter 16.

Teamwork: Think of a time when you were on a high-performing team. Why haven't all of your team experiences been like that?

_____

_____

In Chapter 12, you'll find data-based approaches to building and developing the most productive teams, and how a manager and his or her team can better relate in terms of their thinking.

Leadership agility: How well do you and your leaders truly expand leadership capabilities to prepare for the future?

_____

_____

Read what competencies twenty-first-century leaders need, considering the growing complexities and uncertainties of the business world and the ongoing, rapid pace of change, in Chapter 14, and discover how CEOs think and lead in Chapter 20.

Learning and growth: How easily do you flex your thinking to meet the demands of the world around you?

_____

_____

Learn how to stretch your thinking, see past blind spots, and become more entrepreneurial and adaptive in Chapters 24 through 26.

Every organization has a wealth of thinking diversity within it, but only those that know how to access and apply that diversity will fully benefit from it. The good news, as this book will show you, is you don't have to be a neuroscientist to do it.

From improving mentoring at the U.S. Naval Command and developing the next generation of global leaders at IBM to creating a widely popular new video game at Microsoft Game Studio and coming up with killer marketing ideas at Brown-Forman, leading organizations around the world are applying the Whole Brain Thinking system to outthink, outpace, and outperform the competition. You'll read many of their stories in these pages and learn what you can do to apply the same concepts to your challenges. Their examples are both a reminder and proof that no matter what kind of business you're in, the most successful businesses run on Whole Brain Thinking.

With this book, you'll have the background and the tools to start putting your own whole brain to work.

SO WHAT?

> Now more than ever, the brain has everything to do with business.
> The brain is complex, but its application to business shouldn't be; it should be relevant, practical, and easy to use.
> By recognizing, adapting, and applying all the thinking resources available in your organization, you'll be able to improve every aspect of business and performance.
> Because every business runs on thinking, the ones that can optimize that thinking will have a distinct competitive advantage.

© Randy Glasbergen
glasbergen.com

VETERINARY CLINIC

GLASBERGEN

"He's a mixed breed. Part red balloon, part yellow
balloon, part green balloon, part blue balloon."

CHAPTER 2

Making Sense of Thinking: A Practical Organizing Principle for Business

CHAPTER HIGHLIGHTS

> Through the power of understanding your thinking and how others think,
  you will develop new insights that can have a profound impact on everything you do.
> The Whole Brain Model identifies four quadrants of thinking preferences,
  providing an easy-to-understand, practical, and visual metaphor for the
  specialized thinking clusters of the brain.
> Whole Brain Thinking is the key to applying what we know about the brain
  to business.

This book is going to get you thinking about better ways to use your brain, but first, I want you to think about something else: the way you listen to music.

When you have a choice in the matter, how often do you go for the random option and just listen to whatever happens to come along, whether it's rock and roll, country, classical, or talk radio?

More likely, you have favorite artists, stations, genres, or playlists that you've programmed in, and those are the ones you go to when you have the choice. You have access to a world of options across all the different styles, but you save and return most often to the ones you like best.

Maybe your playlists are strictly rock music because that's your strong favorite, or perhaps you have more eclectic tastes, so you've programmed in a combination of Top 40, classical, and oldies stations. Or maybe, because you prefer a wide variety of genres, you're always scanning and reprogramming your selections. No matter what they are, your preferences affect the way you listen to music.

So what does all this have to do with the way you use your brain? Our preferences affect what we access most.

Whole Brain Thinking helps you understand your thinking preferences. At the core of Whole Brain Thinking is the Whole Brain Model, a metaphor for how we tend to use our

> The greatest thing by far is to have a command of metaphor.
>
> —Aristotle

brain and, more important, how our thinking works. The model is based on brain research I initially conducted using EEG equipment, along with observable evidence and, later, psychometric validity studies. In the Whole Brain Model, thinking falls into four preference clusters that we each have access to as follows:

The A quadrant: The Analyzer. Logical thinking, analysis of facts, processing numbers

The B quadrant: The Organizer. Planning approaches, organizing facts, detailed review

The C quadrant: The Personalizer. Interpersonal, intuitive, expressive

The D quadrant: The Strategizer. Imaginative, big-picture thinking, conceptualizing

These four different clusters can be thought of as your thinking system, comprised of four different thinking "selves." You have a team of these four thinking selves available to you, yet if you're like most of us, you probably prefer some of these selves over others. Like a sports team, you have some of the selves "in play" more frequently, while others sit on the bench.

After learning about Whole Brain Thinking, a senior executive at a Fortune 500 company made an insightful comparison between the way we use our brains and the way we listen to music:

When it comes to music, each of us can and does tune into our favorites whenever we like. If we don't listen to a given station or genre very often, we may forget it's there, or it may take us more effort to get to it, but it is there, and it's there for us to access.

Herrmann's four-quadrant model of how the brain works helps us get a read on what "favorites" we may have preferences for in our ways of thinking. While we all have access to all four quadrants, some of us have a very strong preference for one quadrant, while others have stronger preferences for two, three, or even all four quadrants. It's not right, it's not wrong; it's just different. And just because we prefer certain thinking "favorites" over others doesn't mean that we can't access all of them.

As you read through this book, you will begin to get an understanding of what your preferred "stations" are.

It was during my career at General Electric that I developed the Whole Brain Model and the Herrmann Brain Dominance Instrument® (HBDI)®, an assessment tool that quantifies the degree of a person's preference for each of the four thinking preferences. More than 2 million individual HBDI Profiles are part of the ongoing research that provides the data upon which the conclusions of this book are based.

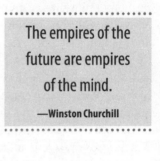

The empires of the future are empires of the mind.

—Winston Churchill

I designed it with a goal of helping business-people solve business problems and be more effective leaders, while also answering many of the questions I'd had about myself over the course of my life and career.

What "stations" or "playlists" are the favorites in your thinking and work preferences? Go online to www.wholebrainbusinessbook.com for access to the HBDI Assessment.

In this chapter and the next, I will share my personal story of the brain-related research that is the basis of HBDI and the metaphorical Whole Brain Model, the organizing principle of how the specialized systems of our inter-connected brain—and more important, the resulting day-to-day thinking preferences—work. As you read through the chapters that follow, think about how the events of your life have been influenced by your thinking preferences and the thinking preferences of those around you, and ultimately, how that shapes your worldview.

This story of my journey may help inspire your own self-discovery.

Research on Creativity Led Me to the Brain

Although a traumatic midlife illness put an end to the performing and singing that I had done since my college years, this unfortunate reality had a silver lining: while I was recovering, I was able to unleash my latent artistic creativity. Though I had always wanted to draw and paint, I could never get past my feelings of inadequacy and self-doubt. When I was bedridden by my illness, I reached the point where my self-imposed barriers were replaced by boredom and frustration. My wife bought me an inexpensive paint set. I selected a scene and started, then chose another and another. It seemed that suddenly I was able to draw and paint, and ultimately even to sculpt! Over the years, I produced hundreds of paint-

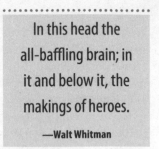

In this head the all-baffling brain; in it and below it, the makings of heroes.

—Walt Whitman

ings and sculptures, won numerous awards, and sold most of my work. I was employed full time by GE as manager of management education, but painting and sculpting had become my second occupation.

I was often asked how I had uncovered this creative talent, and I wondered: Was this available to everyone? My professional interest in learning, combined with my newly discovered talent, motivated me to research and understand the nature and source of this creativity. And then I had the perfect opportunity to pursue this interest further. The Stamford (Connecticut) Art Association, of which I was president at the time, asked me to moderate a panel on the nature and sources of creativity. As I did research on this subject in preparation for the event, I discovered how the brain plays the central role in our ability to be creative. While this concept may seem obvious today, the revelation was like a thunderclap of instant understanding at the time. Creativity was mental, and our ability to control our creative flow could come through understanding the brain. This personal Aha! was shortly followed by a second: if there was something about creativity that could be discovered from the brain, then clearly there was important information about our learning process as well. Again, these conclusions, which seem so obvious now, were considered breakthrough concepts at that time.

The "Right-Brain/Left-Brain" Trap

My continued research about the brain and its connection to creativity and learning led quickly to the work of Roger Sperry,[1] who had shown through his experiments that the brain was divided into two hemispheres that were specialized in function. Robert Ornstein[2] was also writing about the psychology of consciousness in terms of the specialized brain. Numerous experiments carried out by these researchers and others provided convincing evidence that the brain was indeed specialized and that the differences in specialization were located in each half-brain. It wasn't long before this idea that the brain was made up of just two specialized hemispheres had become part of the popular lore of the day (a misconception that still lingers today, in fact).

At the time, Paul MacLean[3] of the National Institutes of Health had developed the triune brain model, which allocated the specialized functions of the brain based on human evolution—that is, the human brain developed sequentially as the reptilian brain (or the brain stem), then the limbic system, and finally, the neocortex.

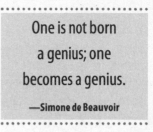

One is not born a genius; one becomes a genius.

—Simone de Beauvoir

All of these researchers were making significant contributions to our knowledge of brain functioning. Sperry's research, for example, shows that although the brain is massively interconnected and works as a whole, specialization exists, and different parts of the brain serve different purposes. The premise of specialization was a crucial finding. However, the focus on the left/right dichotomy became oversimplified and completely overlooked the notion of the whole, including other brain systems, most notably the limbic system, as highlighted by MacLean's model.

Even today, you probably still hear the familiar right-brain/left-brain descriptions of the brain. The world has had a long love affair with dichotomies: right/wrong, good/bad, sweet/sour, up/down, right/left. Separating something into just two categories is a simple, easy, and satisfying approach to categorizing differences. The problem is, this simple dichotomy falls short of accurately describing the way the brain actually works.

While the brain is indeed specialized at the neuronal level, the specialized neurons have relevance only as part of the neuronal network, which functions through the interconnectedness of these neurons. Thus the oversimplified left-brain/right-brain notion betrays the very essence of our brain's design, which relies on interconnections between specialized areas to function, because it implies separateness. The brain is, by design, whole.

When it comes to business, being able to access and leverage the whole brain is the biggest and most important challenge we face, especially as we're dealing with more complexity, greater uncertainty, and rapid change. The good news is that our interconnectedness allows for it. Let's take a closer look at that interconnectedness and why it is so significant from a business standpoint.

The Whole Is More than the Sum of the Parts

The limbic part of the brain is a relatively small, complicated structure that is divided into two interconnected halves, each nestled within one of the cerebral hemispheres (see Figure 2-1). While somewhat primitive compared to the neocortex of the cerebral hemispheres, the limbic cortex is neural, synaptic,

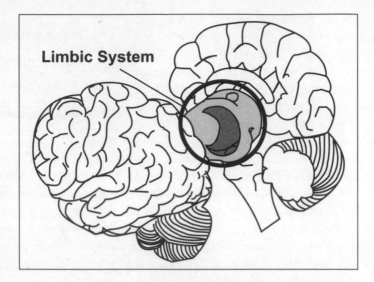

FIGURE 2-1 The limbic system. The cortices of the limbic system nestle in and underneath the cerebral cortices.

and chemical, and therefore capable of thinking in the same way as its cerebral cousin. However, at the time of my research, its role had been basically either overlooked or ignored.

My own experimentation and my analysis of MacLean's and Sperry's work led me to combine elements of the two separate theories into a four-part model representing the interconnected yet specialized *whole thinking* brain. This four-quadrant model serves as a powerful metaphor for the brain and an organizing principle of our thinking preferences (see Figure 2-2): there are four thinking preferences that are massively interconnected and function as a whole, with the idea of quadrants being used to differentiate the different clusters of specialization that I have discovered from my research.

The more work I did, the more I realized that it was the *interconnectedness* of the different specialized clusters of neurons in the brain that really mattered. Understanding the thinking parts of the brain was part of the process of this discovery, but *wholeness* was the ultimate takeaway. Thus, the name Whole Brain Model captured that well.

In fact, one of the best ways to think about the brain is as a network. Think about the Internet: without a connection, any single point cannot function, and the greater the number of contact points available, the greater the viability and flexibility of that network. There are major routers, or nodes, where many

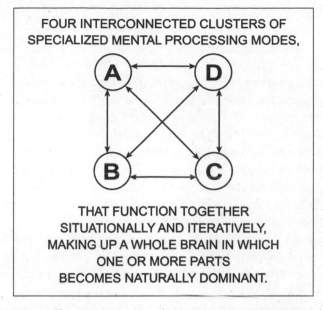

FOUR INTERCONNECTED CLUSTERS OF
SPECIALIZED MENTAL PROCESSING MODES,

THAT FUNCTION TOGETHER
SITUATIONALLY AND ITERATIVELY,
MAKING UP A WHOLE BRAIN IN WHICH
ONE OR MORE PARTS
BECOMES NATURALLY DOMINANT.

FIGURE 2-2 The organizing principle. Herrmann's organizing principle, the basic premise behind his metaphoric model of brain function, defines what is included when speaking of the whole brain.

of the connections converge, and those can be bypassed if one of them fails. At a very high metaphorical level, the brain's "plasticity" or malleability works in much the same way, adjusting over time as the needs of the system change while still maintaining connectedness.

The brain naturally seeks patterns and organizes around patterns. Through hundreds of millions of interconnections, the working brain provides pathways for specialized activities, which often involve many different areas of the brain, to take place. Although my initial research and creation of the Whole Brain Model was inspired by the idea of a mapping different specialized areas in the brain, I came to realize that understanding our preferred patterns of thinking was more relevant and important than determining location, so the model is entirely a metaphor. It became clear that because of the inherent way the brain is designed, no specialized location ever works in a vacuum, so function became more important than location. But placing the quadrants in the four positions helped people understand the concepts and use them easily and quickly. The circular display represents the whole thinking brain, which is then divided into four conscious modes of knowing, each with its own set of behaviors demonstrably associated with it.

A common misconception in the left-brain/right-brain trap is that our thinking preferences result from *one single physical part of the brain* being more connected, stronger, preferred, or more active. This is *not* the case. Thinking requires activation of multiple specialized, complex networks that are shaped by experience and become stronger over time. Further, these richly interconnected networks "learn" by adjusting the degree of interconnection, strengthening or pruning it as needed over time. A great example of this is an unused skill that you might have developed at an earlier time in your life but have since completely stopped using. It might be a foreign language, a sports activity, or a work skill. When those areas cease to be used and activity is directed elsewhere in the brain, they still remain, but they are not as strong as they might once have been. When you reengage those areas, like picking up a musical instrument that you played years ago or a language that you have not spoken for a very long time, you can almost feel the struggle to reconnect those weaker links. If you practiced over time, you could regain your acuity, but doing so would take effort and conscious mental activity. In contrast, those skills that you have continued to use over the course of your life are more solid and better connected—and you can feel that as you engage in those activities.

By understanding and describing these preferred thinking networks in the brain, we can quantify their relationship to one another in the form of this four-quadrant model (see Figure 2-3) and the implications that the quadrants have for our day-to-day thinking and behavior.

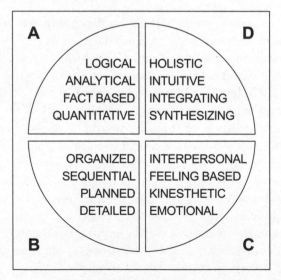

FIGURE 2-3 The Whole Brain Model.

Specialized Thinking and Preferred Patterns

Throughout this book, we'll be exploring the implications and applications of our preferred patterns of thinking in business, including the ways in which a person's thinking preferences affect his or her behaviors, interests, decision-making processes, communication style, and all other aspects of performance. But first we need to define preferred patterns.

One of the easiest ways to understand the concept of preferred patterns (what I originally called "brain dominance") is to use an analogy to our preferred, or dominant, hand. If you are right-handed, your right hand and arm will

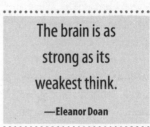

> The brain is as strong as its weakest think.
>
> —Eleanor Doan

develop to a higher level because they're used more frequently. The situation with the specialized thinking preferences that we each have in the brain is similar. Through increased use as a result of our preference, certain patterns of specialized thinking come to be preferred over others, developing to a higher level than the nonpreferred patterns. And as they develop over time as a result of our life experiences, those patterns become evident from the mental preferences that we exhibit. Try this: take a pen or pencil in your nondominant hand and write your full name. Can you do it? Most certainly yes. Is it awkward? Probably. Could it be developed with more practice and concentration? Certainly, but motivation and conscious effort will be required if you are to engage differently from your norm.

From Dominance to Preference

The HBDI assessment, which I referred to earlier in the chapter, measures degrees of preference for each of the four quadrants. Here's a little background on how it and the Whole Brain Model were developed.

> If everyone is thinking alike, then somebody isn't thinking.
>
> —George S. Patton

The Whole Brain Model is the product of numerous studies using electroencephalographic (EEG) data from the brains of test subjects responding to a battery of psychological tests and performing specific activities. The electrical activity that takes place in the cerebral hemispheres can be measured by placing electrodes around the scalp. However, this technique cannot be used to measure the electrical output from the limbic system, as it is located too far below the surface. (These tests were conducted prior to the introduction of positron emission tomography, or PET scans, and subsequently magnetic resonance imaging, or MRI scans, which have given researchers a chance to see the inner structures of the brain at work.)

Despite this measurement limitation, the results of these studies combined with other subsequent research provided enough information to allow me to build a scaffolding for the thinking style clusters, the architecture of the organizing principle just described. Although some of these experiments were carried out at GE's Management Development Institute at Crotonville, it became very clear early on that wiring up GE managers and executives with EEG apparatuses was not a practical method of gathering data for the development of my model. What was needed was a *metaphorical* model, one that would metaphorically represent the highly interconnected yet specialized thinking clusters of the human brain to allow for quantification of an individual's relative preferences for specialized thinking across one or more of the four quadrants of the model. Thus was born the Herrmann Brain Dominance Instrument (HBDI). The month was August 1979. The place was GE's Management Development Institute, where I hosted the first Whole Brain Symposium.

Years later, the metaphorical Whole Brain Model continues to provide a useful and valid basis for determining thinking style preferences leading to application—in other words, their impact on how we interact with the world.

Ann Herrmann-Nehdi on What We Know About the Brain Today

Since the first edition of the *Whole Brain Business Book* was published in 1996, our understanding of the brain has continued to advance while confirming the initial findings of the late 1970s that the 100 billion neurons in the brain are indeed specialized. The findings of this new research have also underscored the tenets of my father's initial studies, reinforcing the point that he emphasizes here and addresses more specifically in Chapter 4, "What You Need to Know So You Can Grow." The degree of specialization in the brain affects how we think and what we pay attention to. We do not function with "half a brain," as the terms "left-brained" and "right-brained" imply. In fact, the brain's very design gives us the opportunity to think in terms of *and* instead of *or*.

Technological advances since the 1990s have also opened the door to faster and more in-depth research than was possible when the early studies were conducted. As he mentions here, to perform his initial experiments demonstrating specialization, my dad wired people up to an EEG for testing. I know this firsthand: as an adolescent, I was among those early test subjects. Today's much less invasive technology has enabled us to learn significantly more about how the brain works.

The wide range of diagnostic devices now available to us can monitor brain activity in new ways. In addition, open-source projects such as the Whole Brain Catalog are enhancing our ability to view the brain in depth and find solutions to even the most complex challenges in brain research through cooperation and crowdsourcing. This project provides rich 3D views that allow researchers to zoom in, out, and around structures deep in a multiscale spatial framework of the mouse brain. The Human Connectome Project,[4] funded by the National Institutes of Health, is an ambitious effort to map the neural pathways that underlie human brain function, with a goal of acquiring and sharing data about the structural and functional connectivity of the human brain. The BRAIN Initiative[5], which was announced by President Obama in April 2013, is expected to teach us even more about brain function, with $300 million in public and private investments dedicated to supporting innovative technologies that will help researchers uncover the mysteries of brain disorders such as Alzheimer's, schizophrenia, autism, epilepsy, and traumatic brain injury.

Research conducted by Daniel Goleman[6] (the author of books on emotional and social intelligence) and others has led to new insights into how people are affected by the chemistry and design of the brain. As acclaimed author and Harvard researcher Clayton Christensen[7] points out, from this research, we know that "people learn in different ways—some of this is encoded in our brains at birth; other differences emerge based on what we experience in life."

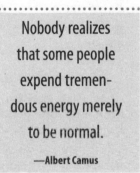

Nobody realizes that some people expend tremendous energy merely to be normal.

—Albert Camus

Yet in spite of 2,500 years of continuous study and research on the brain, there is still a lot that we don't know. It is often reported that our knowledge of the brain doubles every 10 years; the recent explosion of new research, technology, and methods means that we may be learning much more, much faster, but considering the complexity of the brain, it's unlikely we will ever know everything about it. In any case, the good news is that the brain continues to receive such well-deserved attention. The explosion of neurological research has also give rise to healthy "neuroskepticism," much of which I agree with. What will be most critical in coming years is dealing with the "one study syndrome" that provides insight so narrow that it is not generalizable.

My father was ahead of his time. His early research into the specialized brain that functions as a whole through the massive interconnectedness of the physical structure helps explain how we develop our thinking styles over time, and of course how those thinking styles affect every aspect of our lives, especially in business. In that spirit, this book is focused on *what matters most about our gray matter.*

> Research and technology continue to advance our understanding of the brain, which changes almost daily. To discover the latest relevant developments in brain research, go online to www.wholebrainbusinessbook.com.

SO WHAT?

> The popular left-brain/right-brain dichotomy is too simplistic and incomplete to serve as a model of how we think and learn. The massive interconnectedness of the brain's design is evidence of our *wholeness*, not our *separateness*.

> The Whole Brain framework evolved from initial EEG testing at GE combined with experience and research in a business setting; this gives it a practical workplace context, in contrast to other models or psychological constructs.

> Creating a metaphorical model of the four thinking preferences of the brain facilitates the application of current knowledge of brain function and serves as an organizing principle that emphasizes wholeness.

> The natural phenomenon of dominance between paired structures of the body, like handedness, applies to the preference patterning we develop in our thinking as we use our brains throughout the course of our lives, and is the basis of the theory of the preferred thinking patterns that we measure in the HBDI.

"No, we're just learning how to divide.
When you get to business school,
you'll learn how to divide and conquer."

CHAPTER 3

Getting Smart About Work: Your Thinking Preferences, Your Competencies, and Your Career

CHAPTER HIGHLIGHTS

> The secret to productivity is understanding how your preferences affect your work choices.
> Preferences, the focus of this book, are different from competencies, but the two are linked.
> A preference and a lack of preference are of equal impact and importance.
> Work-aligned preferences can make work feel satisfying and stimulating; lack of preference alignment can make work feel draining or uninspiring.
> The Zone of Preference exercises provides a quick understanding of your mental preferences and how they relate to your competencies and competency development.
> The Herrmann Brain Dominance Instrument (HBDI) Profile data provide useful information about typical preference patterns across occupations, which can help you better understand how aligned you are with your work.

As head of management education at General Electric, I felt that my job was to put GE ahead of its competitors by improving manager development and by providing managers with a business-focused problem-solving approach they could apply and benefit from immediately. I believed we could move in that direction by revamping our management courses and learning programs based on new learning about brain function, but we soon realized we simply didn't know enough about our learners' thinking and learning styles—how they preferred to learn and process information. To do what we wanted, we needed an accurate mechanism for measuring preferences that was more workplace-friendly than wiring people up. That's why I created the Herrmann Brain Dominance Instrument.

While the HBDI doesn't measure brain-wave activity in the thinking structures, as my initial EEG research did, it does provide measurements of mental preferences, even more useful, which in turn can be easily interpreted and translated into quite predictable behavior outcomes in the workplace. When you combine that insight with tools to help you develop Whole Brain Thinking, your ability to better leverage your potential grows exponentially. The insights the data provide will help you better understand your preferences and their impact on your world.

> Knowing others is intelligence; knowing yourself is true wisdom. Mastering others is strength; mastering yourself is true power.
>
> —Lao Tzu

Our degree of preference for each of the four thinking modes can be determined by our relative attraction to or aversion for the descriptors found in each mode, which are groups of mental processes that have some commonality (see Figure 3-1).

One helpful way to see the business implications of thinking preferences is to think of them in the context of the organization itself. In every organization, there are different people playing different mental or thinking roles.

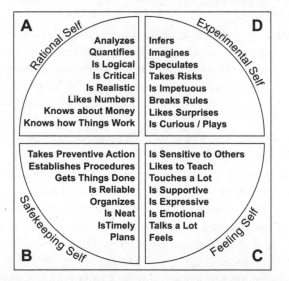

FIGURE 3-1 Our four different selves. The Four Selves Model characterizes specialized modes of the Whole Brain Model in the form of selves that we act out in response to everyday situations.

All are critical players in the overall success of the business, but their preferences shape both their perceptions and what they naturally gravitate to, the information that they "allow in" and what they filter out.

When you look at the Four Selves Model (see Figure 3-1), what functions in business do you think show up in the A quadrant, with its preference for logical, analytical, fact-based thinking? What functions probably fall into the B quadrant, focusing on organized, sequential, detail-oriented work? How about the feelings-based, intuitive C quadrant? And what jobs fall into the domain of the D quadrant, following a more imaginative, risk-taking approach?

Let's look at four managers to see how this plays out in the workplace. Amanda is the finance manager at her company. She is courteous and polite, but she is always focused on business and tends toward the more directive side of management. The human resources staff often gets complaints that Amanda's style is too hard, with an emphasis on the facts and too little attention to individuals' feelings. When asked the question, "What can we do to increase our bottom line?" she says, "We need to upgrade our systems so we can increase our capacity, speed, and overall return on investment. Although we'll have to make an initial up-front investment, we'll be able to save time, reduce staff, and eliminate the overtime and additional employment expenses that are eating into our profits." She has data sets, calculations, and spreadsheets to back up her statements.

Brent is the manager in charge of production. For him, efficiency is paramount. His department follows a comprehensive manual of procedures that he himself developed. No deviation is permitted. Making sure that everything runs according to plan, safely, and on time is everything to him, so he tends to be impatient with ideas and methods that deviate from the norm. When asked, "What can we do to increase our bottom line?" he says, "We need to stick with the basics—orderly, reliable processes that have been tested and proven to work. Holding everyone accountable to the documented schedule and procedures we have in place is critical."

Catherine is the manager in charge of customer relationships and service, helping customers with any questions, complaints, or requests. She says her job isn't just about making sure that customers are satisfied, it's about making sure customers "feel loved." Those on her staff appreciate that she is a great listener, someone who's always willing to be a sounding board when they need advice or just want to vent, but sometimes they're not so clear about her specific goals and expectations. When asked, "What can we do to increase our bottom line?" she says, "We need to engage our customers as well as our employees on a deeper level so that they will feel more connected to what we do and know how much we value them. It may mean offering more freebies and perks, but the long-term payoff will be worth it."

David is the manager of creative services. He has a knack for thinking up very imaginative, almost unheard-of ideas, but the real reason he is a leader is that he excels at anticipating important trends before anyone else does, and he is good at conceptualizing innovative promotion and marketing ideas that others can flesh out. Because he prefers to act on his gut instinct, he sometimes overlooks small but critical details. When asked, "What can we do to increase our bottom line?" he says, "We need to be more on the 'bleeding edge' of our industry if we want to stand out. What's the next big thing? We have to be there before the competition even thinks of it, and that means we can't get keep getting bogged down by overengineered processes and procedures."

These managers give you an idea of possible managerial styles for each separate quadrant of the Whole Brain Model. (See Chapter 7 for further detail on different management styles.) Keep in mind that in an attempt to delineate purely A, B, C, and D styles, extremes of the norm are given. People with a preference for a single quadrant represent only 5 percent of the HBDI assessment data, and even those with a strong preference for one quadrant have and use the other three less-preferred quadrants. In fact, most managers—and most people in general (95 percent of the HBDI database)—prefer two or more quadrants.

Understanding the Individual Quadrants

Even though most people don't typically work within the individual quadrants in isolation, the easiest way to get a sense of each quadrant's influence, as well as the relative compatibilities and incompatibilities among preferences, is to take a look at each of them separately. Each of the following descriptions of the individual quadrants shows one of the four selves in isolation so that you can better understand and differentiate them. As you read, think about which of these quadrants most apply to you.

The A-quadrant self favors activities that involve analyzing, dissecting, figuring out, solving problems logically, simplifying the complex, and getting facts. It uses phrases like, "Time is money," and relies on logic based on certain assumptions, combined with an ability to perceive, verbalize, and express things precisely. The A self will calculate risk and won't move forward if it is excessively high. Argument is more important than personal experience, facts trump intuition, and emotion is to be avoided. The A self's abilities to generalize from the

specific and verbalize those generalizations make it an ideal technical problem solver, but because it lacks attention to emotion, it tends to
appear cold, aloof, and arrogant. "A-only" solutions, while logical, will
often be impractical because they ignore the very real barriers of (for
example) dealing with human inertia or fixed attitudes. Their logic will
chain them to the ground, because they won't make the creative leap
required to set a new direction.

**The B self is very detailed, structured, solid, and down-to-earth, with
no equivocation or ambiguity**. B onlys bear a number of similarities
to their cousins in the A quadrant, but there are significant differences.
For the B self, efficiency is about making sure things are done on time
and correctly, down to the last detail. There are no shortcuts. The A self
devises formulas, while the B self tests them. The B self has little patience
with or respect for the intellectual complexities that the A self finds so
compelling. When you want to get things done, and when perfection
in detail is critical, the B self is the answer to your prayers. The B self
will focus on one thing at a time and get it right the first time. However,
because the B self shows little room for intuition, ambiguity, and emotion,
others tend to view it as domineering, controlling, small-minded, boring,
insensitive, and antisocial. Its ultimate desire is for order and dependabil-
ity, to preserve the tried and true, even though that may ultimately defeat
progress.

**The C-quadrant self is highly participative and team-oriented, and
considers people to be the most important aspect**. When the mood
of an individual or group changes, the C self is immediately aware of
this and responsive to it. Not in the least linear in functioning, the C
self has little time for logic or theory. Experience is reality, goals mean
nothing if they violate human processes, and personal satisfaction is
the prime measure of success. Because of its faith in groups and its
openness to each person's contributions, the C self tends to be viewed
as agreeable, nice to have around, and supportive. But it can be flaky,
undisciplined, overly sentimental, and impractical because it refuses to
deal with facts, goals, time, and money. Most of what the C self talks
about is hard to verbalize, so connection and flow become more important than content. Others can become frustrated by the unfocused,
continual talk.

The D self is intuitive, holistic, adventurous, and risk taking. It speaks
in metaphors and thrives on the excitement of new ideas, possibilities,
variety, incongruities, and questions that sound obvious but actually go

the heart of the matter. The D self tends to be a true visionary, in the best sense of the word, but often has trouble working with others because it's largely nonverbal and has difficulty explaining things or putting concepts into words. Lacking the C quadrant's need to connect, the D self doesn't want to slow down to the speed that's necessary for everyone else to catch up, and it doesn't want to spend energy on developing structure. The D self dislikes structure, words, and logic because it feels that all of these get in the way of the flow of ideas and energy—as does the here and now, whether it's the B self's details and procedures or the C self's emotional grounding.

As you can see, these are the extremes of the four quadrants. You are a combination of the styles and most likely prefer more than one quadrant. Looking at the "selves" preferences individually, however, shows how each has both advantages and disadvantages, strengths and blind spots. All of them are necessary in business, and together, they make up the universe of thinking style preferences (see Figure 3-2) in an organization. You can also begin to see how your own thinking preferences influence what courses you enjoyed most in school, your career choices, and how you work best with others to get things done.

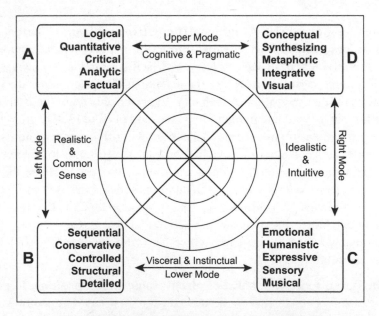

FIGURE 3-2 The universe of thinking styles. An overview of the universe of available characteristics across the Whole Brain Model.

Preference Is Not the Same as Competence

A preference for a given activity and the competency required to perform that activity are not the same thing. I can do bookkeeping very well (competency), but I don't like it (preference). Some people love to sing but can't carry a tune. Preference is a matter of attraction; competence to perform a given task comes through training and experience. Competence can be developed to reasonable or even superior levels whether or not the person is attracted to the task (necessity can be the mother of competency). But true expertise and world-class competence are achieved almost exclusively in our areas of preference.

> Such as are your habitual thoughts, such also will be the character of your mind; for the soul is dyed by the thoughts.
>
> —Marcus Aurelius

That being said, preferences commonly are correlated with competence because people tend to do best at what they like best. We willingly repeat, and thus reinforce, those tasks that we feel good about doing and that we can star in. It's more difficult and less fun to strive for competence in activities that we'd rather avoid. As applied in business, our thinking patterns lead to the development of preferences, which in turn influence our interests, which most often lead to the development of our competencies, influencing our career choices and ultimately the work that we do.

A good way to separate preferences and competences is to think back to a time when you were in school and studying a subject that you really, really loved. In my case, it was physics and music. The boundless energy and interest that you felt for a favorite subject would be more like a preference. Having that interest did not necessarily mean that you automatically developed skills and competencies—just that you were interested and that your mind engaged easily and tended to be energized when you were involved in that type of activity.

When we talk about these kinds of activities in relation to work, we're referring to the ones that are so interesting, so stimulating, and so pleasurable to do that you would select them for these special attributes over other work that was offered to you. They may not be the easiest activities to perform, but in all cases, they are more satisfying and fulfilling, and therefore, the ones you would select if you were given a choice. This is the kind of work that doesn't require constant external rewards because doing the work is reward in itself.

• *Take a moment to think about what work activities satisfy you most.*

On the flip side, think of a subject in school that you really disliked. For me, it was chemistry. Although I had grown up in a family of chemists and was "expected" to follow in their footsteps, I struggled to get engaged or perform in my chemistry classes, and this affected my ability to develop competencies. Maybe you hated math. You may have developed a competency in basic math, but a considerable amount of energy and motivation were probably required, especially for any advanced math courses. The experience is similar to your professional life when your work requires you to perform activities in those areas that you prefer the least. While we can and do develop competencies in areas of lesser preference, this often requires more effort or energy than developing skills in an area of greater preference.

- *What work activities do you enjoy the least that require the most motivation and energy?*

Having now read the descriptions of the different thinking preferences, you are probably guessing what areas of thinking you prefer to "live" in. The following exercises will help you further understand your preferences and how they correlate with your competencies, your performance, and ultimately your career choice.

Put It to Work:
Working Inside and Outside Your Zones of Preference

Exercise A: Write down the subject that you liked least in school. Now imagine that you have been offered a highly lucrative opportunity that will require you to put everything else on hold and do nothing but work related to that subject for the next two years.

- What are your first thoughts upon hearing this?
- Would you take the opportunity?
- If your life depended on it, *could* you do the work?
- If so, what would be required for you to complete the project successfully?

Exercise B: List the key tasks that are required of you in performing your current job.

_____

_____

_____

- Circle those that you enjoy the most.
- Place a checkmark next to those that you have an adequate level of competency to perform well.
- Now underline the activities that you don't enjoy or that you enjoy the least.

Think about ways you can modify your current role to better accommodate your preferences and career goals. Keep in mind that the work that you don't enjoy or that does not represent a current competency typically represents a learning opportunity, which often requires motivation!

> **If you love what you do, you will never work another day in your life.**
>
> **—Anonymous**

These kinds of exercises help you begin to uncover clues to your preferences and also to see how competence and preference, while different, are linked. You *can* work outside your zone of preference, but it will take an enormous amount of effort and motivation. If you are drawn to work that focuses on the human connection and being sensitive to people's needs, you may find it uncomfortable to make decisions based on cold, hard facts. However, aspects of your job may require it, so you learn how to do it. People often describe this process of developing competencies in areas of lesser preference as building a muscle that feels totally unpracticed and underdeveloped, just like working out at the gym. Working within a zone of preference, on the other hand, may also be challenging, but you won't feel as if you're operating from a place of total discomfort. "This is going to be a challenge," you might think, "but I won't hate the ride."

As you consider the activities you are stimulated by—the ones you really love—and those you dislike, you can begin to see a more complete picture of your mental preferences and how they affect your work and your career choices. There are no right or wrong answers; it's just that you are more energized by certain kinds of work and more drained by others. The things that stimulate you are usually in strong alignment with your thinking preferences.

In addition to the letter and descriptors of the quadrants in the Whole Brain Model, each quadrant has its own color (A, blue; B, green; C, red; and D, yellow, as seen on the book jacket flap) that provides an easy-to-remember association. The following description of several colleagues and their relatives working together in a business also includes the quadrant colors.

John loves activities that involve analysis and logic. When presented with a decision or idea, his motto is, "Just the facts." This is representative of the A/blue-quadrant thinking preference. But John also finds other kinds of activities stimulating as well. He is attracted to B/green-quadrant activities such as clear procedures, and he likes to keep his office organized. He also enjoys experimental D/yellow-quadrant activities like seeing the big picture and coming up with ideas and new ways to solve problems. However, he finds C/red-quadrant activities, such as taking time to consider the impact of his decisions on people or being sensitive to interpersonal issues, much more draining and requiring of effort.

Susan, however, finds that she is equally stimulated by work in the orga-nized green (B) and interpersonal red (C) quadrants, and that she dislikes activities that fall into the rational blue (A) or experimental yellow (D) quadrant. The reverse is true for her husband and daughter, who are entre-preneurial and technology-oriented, are highly inspired by experimental and feeling work elements, and don't enjoy organized or analytical work elements.

The more scientific among you would gravitate toward activities in the A and D quadrants, while those of you who are interested in manufacturing things, selling real estate, or doing social work would probably prefer activi-ties that fall within the bottom half of the Whole Brain Model—the B and C quadrants (see Figure 3-3).

And then there will be a few of you who are stimulated by work tasks within each of the four quadrants. This more distributed selection is typical of CEOs, general managers, and executive assistants, to name a few—people whose jobs demand a broader understanding of the wide world of thinking preferences.

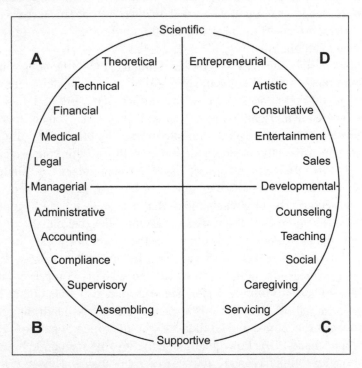

FIGURE 3-3 Representative occupational categories. The array of professional occupations shown across the Whole Brain Model.

The exercises and discussion in this book do not attempt to provide a sophisticated and validated assessment of your thinking styles, of the sort that the HBDI provides. However, they will reveal the *general trend and direction* of your preferences. The HBDI will pinpoint your thinking preferences, and the resulting profile report will provide more detailed data about how you prefer to think and how you can apply this information to your personal and professional life. In the meantime, the following section provides an overview so you'll be able to interpret the references to the HBDI throughout the book.

Get a full report on your preferences. For access to the HBDI assessment, go online to www.wholebrainbusinessbook.com.

How to Understand and Apply the HBDI Thinking Preference Data

In order to grasp the meaning of all the thinking style trends and patterns you'll explore in the examples in this book, you should know what the HBDI Profile is, what it indicates, and how to interpret the examples of HBDI Profiles so that you can apply this work to your own needs. While you do not need to have your HBDI to understand or apply Whole Brain Thinking concepts, you'll find that the HBDI Profile grid is an effective method of displaying and describing the degrees of preference for the quadrants when you apply the concepts to yourself and those you work with.

The HBDI, which millions of people around the world have completed, charts your location in the world of thinking style preferences and was designed specifically for use in business. It can be used to describe individual preferences as well as a wide variety of mental processes, from team operations and customer viewpoints to corporate culture and branding.

> No one who learns to know himself remains just what he was before.
>
> —Thomas Mann

The results of the 120-question HBDI are revealed in a profile displayed on a four-quadrant grid that emulates the four principal thinking structures in the brain. In the east (left)/west (right) positions are those preferences that are more rational and structured (left) and intuitive and holistic (right) ways of thinking. In the north/south positions are those ways of thinking that are referred to as upper (north) and lower (south). The upper modes consist of cognitive and intellectual ways of thinking, and the lower modes encompass visceral, and instinctive ways of thinking.

The four-quadrant display on the left of Figure 3-4 is an example of a typical HBDI Profile. The model in the middle is the Four Selves Model, which describes the coalition of our thinking selves in a more behavioral way. The model on the right is the Whole Brain Model, which is the conceptual and structural basis of the profile grid.

Remember, the HBDI displays mental *preferences*, not abilities or competencies. However, as we discussed earlier, there is a strong relationship between preferences and competencies in that one typically leads to the other (see Figure 3-5).

As you review the typical occupations displayed in Figure 3-6, keep in mind that a preference for a particular thinking style and an avoidance of another style are of equal consequence and have equal impact on an individual. Your preference(s), particularly a very strong preference, will typically be associated with the work you most enjoy. In contrast, a lack of preference or an equal avoidance in a quadrant implies dislike for some or all of the work elements in that particular quadrant. Being stimulated by work is highly motivational and often represents a state of self-actualization.

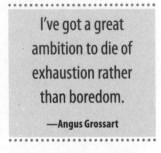

I've got a great ambition to die of exhaustion rather than boredom.

—Angus Grossart

Being repelled by it is highly demotivational unless you have a very specific incentive and drive to pursue that work. For these reasons, the HBDI Profile is quite predictive of a person's potential acquisition of competencies and engagement in work. You will tend focus your energies and efforts on building competencies in the areas you are attracted to mentally. Figure 3-6 is a partial universe of profiles and likely occupations.

360s and Preferences

The 360-degree assessment is a tool that many companies have used for measuring behaviors as part of the process of building a learning and development plan. But can individuals build the *right* developmental plans without understanding how they and others think? One of the challenges with the way 360s are often conducted is that they are done out of context—without taking the thinking preferences of both the rater and the person being rated into account—and we know that the brain misinterprets data it receives out of context. If the rater is focused on organized B-quadrant activities like timelines and detailed procedures, that is what she will tend to pay most attention to, and the ratings will reflect that orientation. This doesn't mean that someone with a D-quadrant experimental mindset isn't getting things done correctly and on time—he might just be using a more unconventional approach to get there.

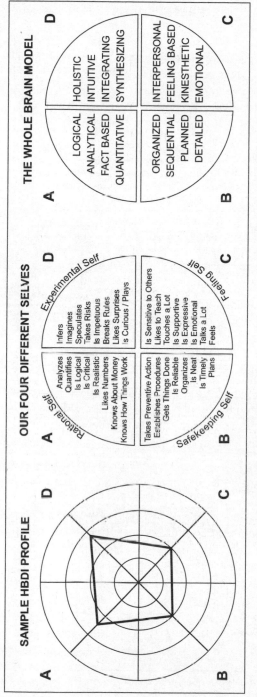

FIGURE 3-4 HBDI Profile grid, our Four Different Selves, and the Whole Brain Model. Three major elements of Whole Brain technology: the HBDI Profile, the Four Selves Model, and the Whole Brain Model.

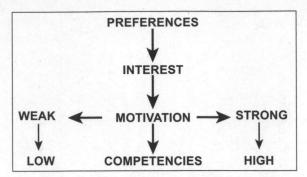

FIGURE 3-5 Relationship between preferences and competencies and all the phases in-between.

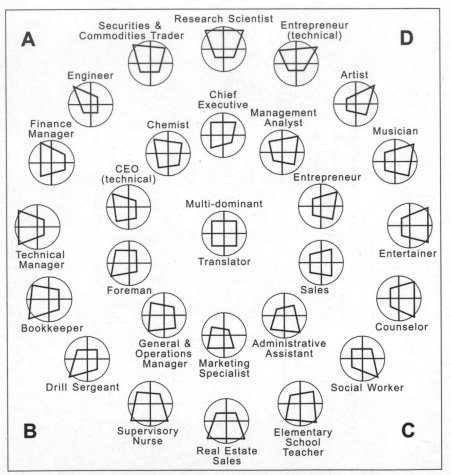

FIGURE 3-6 HBDI pro-forma profiles of the mentality of representative occupations. Categories of occupations and HBDI pro-forma profiles of each.

Since examples of visual profiles and numerical profile codes are used throughout this book, it is necessary to know enough about what they mean to interpret these references in the remaining chapters. Refer to the key in Figure 3-7 as you read through the following Put It to Work exercise.

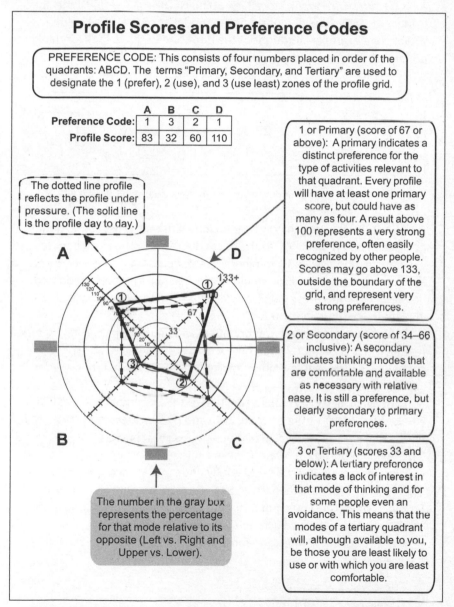

FIGURE 3-7 HBDI Profile interpretation guide. The key to reading the HBDI Profile grid.

Put It to Work:

Guess Who's Who

As you read the following story, look at the HBDI Profiles for insights that explain the behaviors described. These guidelines will also be helpful as you explore examples throughout the book and begin to look for thinking preference clues in yourself and others for greater insight.

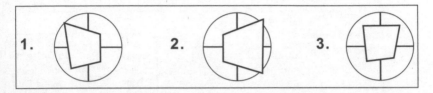

FIGURE 3-8 The three different players in the story. Guess which one is which.

Trish and Frank could hardly bear to sit next to each other at the monthly association board meetings. As the board discussed proposed actions to increase membership and retention, all Frank would listen to was quantitative analysis; if there was none, he wouldn't consider taking action. In addition, he wanted to know every detail in advance, well before anything could be implemented.

Trish, on the other hand, was brimming with ideas for increasing member retention and engagement, but her "data" were qualitative. She spent much of her time talking with members and knew intuitively what they needed and wanted.

Trish felt attacked by Frank's constant requests for data and details. Frank found Trish's desire to brainstorm and discuss ideas at every meeting to be self-serving and a waste of precious meeting time.

The board president, Maria, felt like a referee, constantly blocking and tackling the frequent disputes. She fully understood each perspective and tried to "translate" between them. She was torn, because she knew that both had value. She could jump from brainstorming to data discussions easily, which sometimes frustrated the other board members.

Meetings became more and more tense until everyone began to hate the meetings!

1. Guess Who's Who:
   - Which profile is Trish's?
   - Which is Frank's?
   - Which is Maria's?

2. Look at the shape of each profile and identify the quadrant with the most prominent preference. Under normal, everyday circumstances, this quadrant will be the direction of that person or group's preferred mode of thinking.
   - What would be Profile X's preferred mode? How would that show up in behavior? What about Profile Y? Profile Z?
3. Look for the second-most-preferred quadrant of the profile. If the first and second both have strong scores, the combination of the most- and second-most-preferred quadrants results in a preferred *mode*, such as left, right, upper, or lower.
   - What second-most-preferred quadrants or modes do Trish, Frank, and Maria most prefer?
     - Trish
     - Frank
     - Maria
4. Look for the least-preferred quadrant. Often the lack of preference for a particular thinking style is just as important as the strong preferences. A strong preference indicates the likelihood of a person's being stimulated by a particular style, while the absence of preference, particularly if it is a score of 33 or less, indicates the possibility of an individual's having a strong dislike for that style. In many cases, both of these conditions are visible to family members, colleagues, and friends.
   - How are the lowest preferences affecting the working relationship between Trish and Frank?
5. Look for strong preferences in opposing quadrants, such as B/D and A/C. These profiles often represent internal conflicts as individuals make decisions or react to everyday situations. For example, in the case of the B/D profile, a person could be on the one hand imaginative, holistic, and risk taking and at the same time detailed, traditional, or organized. In other words, such a person has one foot on the accelerator and the other foot on the brake.
   - Was this type of profile present in the board? How did it help or hinder the challenge?
6. Look for profiles that are very balanced, with relatively equal scores in all four quadrants. Such a profile represents a relatively equal distribution of preferences and therefore a balanced distribution of interests, skills, abilities, and competencies. This is extremely rare. Only 3 percent of our database of individuals has a primary preference in all four quadrants.
   - Who has the balanced profile?
     - What challenges does this profile present for the individual?
     - Were there any advantages?

In all cases, the profiles displayed in this book represent actual data, whether they are those of an individual or a group average. *Note:* When profiles are labeled "pro forma," the data are inferred by applying a diagnostic technique based on the Whole Brain Thinking framework.

> Nothing about ourselves can be changed until it is first accepted.
>
> —Sheldon Kopp

SO WHAT?

> There is a strong relationship between the styles of thinking you prefer and the competencies you acquire and enjoy most.
> The HBDI profiles an individual's mental preferences across the four quadrants of the Whole Brain Thinking Model, providing a useful means of understanding how preferences affect the person's work effectiveness.
> Hundreds of business occupations have been profiled, and norms for those profiles are useful to evaluate and better understand the mental demands of those professions—and your own.

"The key to success is the one that locks the bathroom door. That's where I do my best thinking!"

CHAPTER 4

What You Need to Know So You Can Grow: Becoming a Whole Brain Thinker

CHAPTER HIGHLIGHTS

> Your thinking style preferences develop and change.
> *Situational wholeness* is the key to improving your personal effectiveness.
> Thinking preferences influence your decision-making style; using a Whole Brain Thinking approach improves decision-making results.
> Knowing your mental preferences and your mental options is essential to achieving full development of self.

Just a few weeks before he was supposed to take the SAT, Karim, who is left-handed, was in an accident that injured his left hand. Not only was he unable to hold a pencil in his dominant hand, but he was also unable to reschedule the test. This was his last chance to take the SAT that year. Karim did the only thing he could do in the situation: he spent the weeks leading up to the test date practicing filling in bubbles on a sample answer sheet with his right hand.

For someone like Karim, who had spent his life developing strength and comfort using his left hand, practicing with his right hand was like building a brand-new muscle. He couldn't remember a time when he'd had to put so much mental energy into the physical act of writing. But no matter how unnatural and exhausting it felt to him, he was highly motivated to make it work. When the test day came, he used his right hand and got through it.

Unless you're one of the few people who are truly ambidextrous, you probably don't think about which hand you'll use when you write; you just do it. After a few million movements based on a proclivity for right or left, you've developed a lifetime of handedness preference and skill. In a different but analogous sense, your mental patterns, or dominances, have also developed into preferences that have become competencies. You go to them by default because they require less effort and are more comfortable, and as a result, you've strengthened them through repeated use, just as you would a muscle.

But there will be times when the situation will require you to go outside the comfort zones of your preferences. Like a left-hander writing with his right hand, it will probably be challenging, but if you're motivated and deliberate about it, you *can* do it. And the more you practice it, the more effective you'll be in *any* situation.

But first, you may be wondering, how did your preferences develop to begin with? Are they permanent? Can they change?

The Development of Preferences: It's Nature *and* Nurture

Are we on a genetically programmed path that is determined by our genes and chromosomes? The answer is, "No, but. ..." We are, I believe, a product of both nature and nurture, and for most of us, it is the nurture aspect that predominates in determining who we are and who we can become. That is a message of hope! If we were limited to only our genetic inheritance, there would be no opportunity for each of us to develop into our own unique person. Little, if any, of the learning that takes place during our maturing process would have any effect. We would be the product of our genetic inheritance and nothing else. I don't think there is a person alive who would accept that as an accurate description of who he or she is. It's not nature *or* nurture that determines who we are; it's nature *and* nurture. The basic building block of our adult self is the DNA of our inherited genes and chromosomes, but that's only the beginning. From that foundation, we can each become the architect of a unique, emerging human being.

My research into the brain leads me to believe firmly that the grand design is to be whole—that the normal, ordinary, everyday brain is specialized and interconnected in ways that position it to develop as a balanced, multidominant brain that is capable of accessing and using all of its mental options. Since the Whole Brain Model was originally developed, the findings of numerous scientific studies, along with the musings of a variety of writers and thought leaders, only bolster this notion. However, our data on millions of individuals suggest that a small percentage of people end up being that exquisitely balanced. In the more typical case, as we mature mentally, we develop preferences for particular modes of processing.

> One of the saddest experiences that can ever come to a human being is to awaken gray-haired and wrinkled, near the close of a very unproductive career, to the fact that all through the past years he has been using only a small part of himself.
>
> —Orison Swett Marden

These preferences emerge from latent patterning in our brain that leads to preferred characteristics that begin very subtly but are reinforced and grow stronger through daily use. As we respond to life's learning opportunities, it's natural that we learn to go to our strengths first, because they tend to win us praise and other rewards. As our behavior is positively reinforced, this further entrenches our favored pattern of performance, which, in turn, leads to ever-increasing praise, and therefore an intensified preference! This performance-praise feedback loop can turn a small difference in specialization into a powerful preference for one cognitive mode over another.

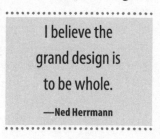

I believe the grand design is to be whole.

—Ned Herrmann

During the early stages of the maturing process, we really don't know any better. By the time we are able to understand the consequences of this strengthening pattern development that's becoming dominance, like handedness, our thinking patterns have already been established. Our mental preferences become mental defaults.

As we saw in Chapter 3, some of our mental patterns may develop into such strong preferences that they have led to competencies in particular ways of thinking. We have become very good at language, or we have developed impressive math skills, or we are exceedingly organized. We can accurately sense the feelings of others, or we are always coming up with new ideas. These early competencies arising out of preferences can lead to a path of similar mental processing clusters that affect our development.

Change and growth can follow the pursuit of our interests. As our interests develop and expand, they can result in enormous changes in our mental capacity and range of thinking. If we assume that the whole spectrum of mental options is preloaded into the developing brain, then the opportunities for growth and change are limitless (see Part 5 for ideas on growth.)

The life experiences that produce change can also build walls that prevent change from taking place. Learning environments that limit rather than stimulate, or parents who refuse to allow a child to pursue his or her interests, not only thwart development but also erect barriers that foreclose on whole domains of thinking. Teachers who present information in ways that serve their own learning style deny learning to others who learn differently. Suffice it to say that the normal person has built into his or her brain a full set of mental processing options that can be accessed and applied if life's circumstances don't get in the way. At birth we have the *wiring to be whole*, and we can become more so by taking more complete charge of our own development.

Put It to Work

Figures 4-1 and 4-2, on the following pages, contain exercises to widen your comfort zone of mental preferences at work and at home. Take a moment to identify at least one activity in each figure that you might never normally pursue, and try it! Note how your thinking is affected, as well as your level of motivation and energy. How might this be a process that you could adapt the next time you get frustrated with something that does not come naturally?

On Being Whole-Brained

Should you aspire to a Whole Brain profile, that is, a profile with four strong primaries, one in each quadrant? Should your goal be a perfectly balanced 1-1-1-1? (For more information on the HBDI preference codes, see the HBDI Profile Interpretation Guide in the appendix.) The answer is a clear *no*. The world would be a dull place indeed if everyone faced life's variable situations and decisions with such an equally distributed array of mental preferences.

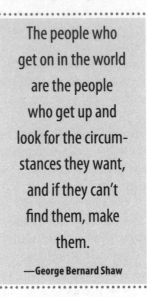

What should be everybody's objective is to be as *situationally* whole-brained as possible. This means that you continue to have the advantage of primary preferences that provide you with a leading response to everyday situations, but you are not *limited* by those preferences. You have a much broader spectrum of mental options available to you, options that can be accessed because you know of the existence of your situational capabilities, and you have practiced using these options to a sufficient extent for these secondary modes to represent competencies that you can count on. Because you have equal access to all four quadrants, when the situation calls for a given type of mental function, you can give it your best response. This is the skill of Whole Brain Thinking.

Make no mistake about it: there is an advantage to having strong primary preferences. Because of these preferences, you have developed interests that have led you to competencies, which represent your mental strengths. In a given situation, that's where you look first for an answer or an appropriate response. In most cases, you don't have to stop and think about everything you do. You go ahead and do it.

> The people who get on in the world are the people who get up and look for the circumstances they want, and if they can't find them, make them.
>
> **—George Bernard Shaw**

A

Activities to engage in, learn, and conquer to better access and develop A-quadrant thinking:

- Find and download a productivity app and use it for one week.
- Read and understand a complex budget, annual report, or financial report.
- Study the operating system you use on your computer tablet or phone and find a tool that would enhance your job.
- Calculate your salary per minute/second.
- Conduct a statistical analysis of a current work issue or challenge.
- Using a spreadsheet, do an analysis or budget report for your team, department, or project.
- Clearly define your work goals for next quarter in terms of the return on time and investment.
- Break down an unresolved decision into logical parts.

D

Activities to engage in, learn, and conquer to better access and develop D-quadrant thinking:

- Go online once a week to seek out new trends that could affect your organization.
- Redecorate your workspace; add creative objects, color, and art.
- Sketch out a "logo" for your job.
- Set aside time for idea generation and think of at least one "crazy" idea per day.
- In your "mind's eye" (with eyes closed), imagine your organization ten years from now.
- Set up an "ideastorming" session on an important issue and listen to all the ideas.
- Conceptualize a new program or product for your organization.
- As you make your next decision, pay attention to your intuition and make the decision using it.

B

Activities to engage in, learn, and conquer to better access and develop B-quadrant thinking:

- Find and download an app to track your daily activities with precision for one week.
- Clean up and organize your filing system, inbox, and workspace.
- Create a "to-do" and "not-to-do" list and check off items when done.
- Arrive on time at work or for appointments all day, then all week.
- Read the policy manual to learn a specific detail you were not aware of.
- Plan out your next project in as much detail as you can and follow through with it in a timely way.
- Create a highly detailed job description.
- For each decision, be more safekeeping by clearly writing out all of the consequences before taking action.

C

Activities to engage in, learn, and conquer to better access and develop C-qadrant thinking:

- Use an app or your calendar to remind you to spend at least 15 minutes per day getting to know others personally.
- Offer to mentor or coach a coworker on a company project.
- Ask for feedback to be more aware of your nonverbal communication and how to make it friendlier; e.g., smile more, make better eye contact.
- Look for ways to make your workspace more inviting and comfortable.
- Come up with an idea for a fun, "people" event and make it happen.
- Practice spontaneously recognizing another employee in a way that is personal and meaningful for them once a week.
- Make a decision completely based on team consensus.

FIGURE 4-1 "At work" activities to help you develop and access your less-preferred modes.

A Activities to engage in, learn, and conquer to better access and develop A-quadrant thinking:

- Find an app that will help you in your financial planning to calculate how much money you will need in 15 years.
- Find out how a frequently used machine or device actually works.
- Take a current personal problem situation and break it down to analyze it into its main parts by stating "how to" _____ "in order to" _____ as many times as you can.
- Analyze the rationale for a recent impulsive decision you made (e.g. purchase)—how could you have made a better decision?
- Declare your target net worth in 15 years and develop a quantitative formula to get there.
- Start or join an investment club.
- Engage in some logic games like Sudoku or find others online.
- Spend time programming and/or setting up a new tech device or appliance.
- Practice playing 'devil's advocate' on your latest idea or decision.
- Analyze how much time and money you spend annually on all of your leisure activities.

B Activities to engage in, learn, and conquer to better access and develop B-quadrant thinking:

- Find an app to better manage and organize your and your family's activities.
- Make a complex recipe or assemble a new appliance or household item following instructions to the letter.
- Develop a personal budget for the next year and maintain it.
- Prepare a detailed personal property list or family tree.
- Reorganize your apps, kitchen, or home office according to categories.
- Select a favorite hobby and look for ways to add more structure and discipline.
- Review your bank statement or credit card statements weekly for errors.
- Clean up, sort through, and organize a "junk drawer," tools, or any "messy" part of the house.
- Be exactly on time all day, and every day for one week.
- Organize your picture files, deleting those you don't need and tagging them so you can easily find them.

D Activities to engage in, learn and conquer to better access and develop D-quadrant thinking:

- Fly a kite with the same excitement a child would have.
- Invent a gourmet dish and then prepare it.
- Play with clay and discover its inner meaning.
- Take a 15-minute "theta break" before getting out of bed.
- Drive to "nowhere" without feeling guilty.
- Take a regular activity you do (commute, workout, etc.) and change it up.
- Create a personal logo or mandalla.
- Spend a day taking photographs and create a montage or slide show.
- Allow yourself to daydream.
- Imagine yourself ten years from now.

C Activities to engage in, learn, and conquer to better access and develop C-quadrant thinking:

- Find a local or online group to meet with regularly around a passion, hobby, or volunteer project.
- Go dancing and/or try dancing without moving your feet.
- Practice mindfulness: take a 10-minute break daily to relax, breathe, and let your feelings "bubble up."
- "Love" something in nature: a pine cone or any other natural thing.
- Expand your musical playlist and listen frequently to take a mental break.
- Allow tears to come to your eyes without feelings of shame or guilt.
- Experience your own spirituality in a nonreligious way.
- Play with (your) children the way they want to play.
- Start a journal where you express your thoughts and feelings through writing.
- Discover things others (friends, family, children) have taught you, and find ways to thank them.

FIGURE 4-2 "At home" activities to help you develop and access your less-preferred modes.

As a case in point, over the years I have developed an uncanny ability for long-range planning. I have been able to conceptualize 5-, 10-, and 15-year goals and make them come true. It is less natural for me to devise short-term goals and develop detailed plans for achieving them. However, because I have become keenly aware of this difference in mental preferences, I have developed a competence and discipline in short-term planning that I use whenever I have to. In earlier times, I would have concentrated on the long-range thinking that came naturally to me. Now that I know I have an available option, I am able to access and apply short-term planning competencies, including dealing with excruciating detail. I do it when I have to because it's useful to me. I don't do it when I don't have to because it doesn't stimulate me and I tend to find it boring. The point is, now that I know what my mental options are, I am able to be much more situationally whole. Knowing my preferences and my mental options positions me to supplement my existing competencies with needed situational competencies. The same could be true for you. In Figure 4-3, consider a day in which you need to analyze the performance data for a key product, work on finalizing the details of next year's budget, hold a one-on-one coaching session with an assistant, and play around with some ideas for the new marketing campaign. All of these modes are situationally available to us all, and it may be more difficult to access the mode that is least preferred.

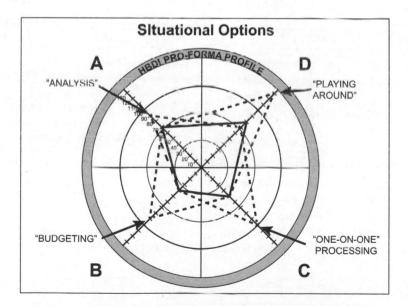

FIGURE 4-3 Situational options chart. The use of each specialized mode is available to us situationally.

Seeing Things from the Viewpoint of Our Least-Preferred Quadrant

Each of us is a coalition of four different selves, but we prefer to use one or more of those selves compared to the others. All HBDI Profiles are made up of most-preferred and least-preferred thinking modes.

It is interesting to group people together on the basis of their most-preferred and least-preferred thinking modes. When those in the group have the same most-preferred mode, they can typically reach an easy consensus on subjects that fall into the domain of their thinking preferences. However, this is not the case when people are dealing with least-preferred thinking modes. When people are grouped together on the basis of their least-preferred quadrants, the group is *heterogeneous* in terms of primary preferences and *homogeneous* in terms of nonpreferences. Unless you give its members a special assignment in their common area of least-preferred thinking, they will exhibit the behaviors of a diverse group and therefore will have difficulty in achieving consensus. Since there is a shared lack of preference for a particular mental domain, there is an opportunity for group learning to take place. For example, using communication as the theme for an assignment, we will group people together on the basis of their least-preferred quadrants and then ask them to play the role of reporters at an accident scene (see Figure 4-4).

A FACTS	FUTURES D
"Once again . . . forensic science, using the undeniable facts of blood type, fingerprints, and spectrographic analysis of paint fragments, proves beyond a doubt . . ."	"This accident demonstrates the lethal combination of drunk driving and faulty car design. These two issues are national in scope and deserve urgent congressional attention if future generations are to be adequately protected . . ."
"At 3:30 pm, Thursday, April 9th, in the 1200 block on Seneca Avenue just outside Perkins Elementary School, a black, brand-new 4-door Toyota sedan traveling at 50 mph in a 25 mph school zone . . ." B FORM	"Tearful, screaming mother attacks the cowering suspect as irate police officers hold off an angry mob at the terrifying scene of a mangled school bus and the accident's bloody victims." FEELINGS C

FIGURE 4-4 Examples of four reporters' views of the same accident. Each one represents a different quadrant viewpoint.

They are asked to interpret the accident through the stereotypical perceptions of reporters who don't like to use a particular quadrant in their perceiving and writing about an event. Let's take the C quadrant as an example. If we group together four or five people who don't prefer to think and write in C-quadrant language, but require them to do so for this assignment, they will typically develop an extremely stereotypical version of a C-quadrant newspaper story. It will be filled with emotion and people issues. They will enjoy doing it, and it will be a hilarious experience. But the important outcome is that they will learn a bit about how to perceive an event in C-quadrant terms and how to write about it using C-quadrant language.

The exercise in least-preferred thinking quickly reveals that the stereotype in the C quadrant is *emotionality*. In the A quadrant, it is *facts*; in the B quadrant, it is *details*; and in the D quadrant, it is *off-the-wall future "stuff."* Even though the stereotypes are ridiculous in the extreme, the assignment provides practice in thinking and writing in ways that these individuals *almost* never use and typically disregard when those who *prefer* to use these modes would do so in a business situation. Walking in the shoes of the people who prefer the things that we least prefer provides an instant wake-up call to the need to pay more attention to what others are saying, and to have more respect for the way they are saying it. Since we are living in a composite Whole Brain world, and since the reality of any multifunctional group is the diversity of its thinking and therefore its perceptions and language, it is essential from a communications standpoint that we increase our tolerance and understanding of what people who are different from us are saying. (See Chapter 8 for more on improving communication through Whole Brain Thinking.)

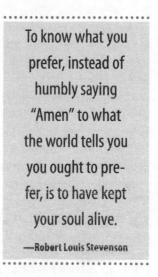

> To know what you prefer, instead of humbly saying "Amen" to what the world tells you you ought to prefer, is to have kept your soul alive.
>
> —Robert Louis Stevenson

How Mental Preferences Play Out in Decision Making

Decision making is a common business area where your mental preferences play out, and where you can learn to draw on the strengths of your preferences and tap into your four selves to be more effective.

Over the years, your decision-making processes will have developed a consistent pattern that is grounded in your preferences. Strongly A-quadrant-oriented thinkers, who prefer facts, become very rational when there are facts upon which to base a decision. When there are not any facts, their decision process is less effective. B-quadrant-oriented thinkers are looking for details. They don't want to make a mistake, so they will delay a decision until they are confident that they know everything there is to know and that there will be no surprises down the road. Without the benefit of careful, deliberate consideration, their decision process is less effective.

The C-quadrant decision process is based not only on a strong preference for preserving relationships, but also on a general avoidance of the analysis of facts and figures. Therefore, the C-quadrant decision process is largely intuitive and more focused on people issues. The D-quadrant decision process is different from the other three quadrants in that it is inclined to be variable: sometimes bold, assertive, and daring, and at other times impulsive and spontaneous.

Because so many businesspeople have double and triple dominances, there are decision styles that are combinations of these single-quadrant styles. The double-dominant A/B left-mode style, for example, has a need for both facts and details, for both logical analysis and step-by-step processing, whereas the double-dominant right-mode style combines the relationship-oriented, intuitive processes of the C quadrant with the more variable, bold and daring, and sometimes vacillating style of the D quadrant.

The double-dominant upper style (A and D) can be thought of as the scientific approach to decision making. It's a potentially synergistic combination of logical, analytic, rational processing and bold, daring, and frequently imaginative ideas. An exemplar of this style might be Captain Kirk of *Star Trek*. The double-dominant, B-quadrant/C-quadrant lower style is more typified by a supervisory nurse's decision-making style—structured, procedural, and conservative, yet highly people-oriented. It is sensitive but careful, spiritual but traditional, with lots of detail but a deep concern for human values.

Double dominance in the B and D quadrants is a more perplexing style. This can make it feel as if the decision maker has "one foot on the accelerator and one foot on the brake," alternating between risk taking and safekeeping, or between big, bold, daring alternatives and conservative, high-security options. The double-dominant A/C profile also exhibits internal confrontation between two very different preferences—on the one hand, the strong A-quadrant preference for rational decision making, and on the other, an equally strong preference for feelings, relationships, and people issues. Businesspeople for whom

> To grow as human beings, to guide our conduct, we also look for universal principles: absolute values.
>
> —Keshavan Nair

this is the everyday decision-making style shuttle back and forth between a consideration of facts and a consideration of human relationships. They typically agonize over their decisions that are hurtful to people.

Whole Brain Decision Making

Just as our preferences affect how we focus and what we focus on when we're making a decision, our areas of lesser preference can become blind spots. Those who have strong A- and B-quadrant preferences may fail to recognize the "people" consequences of a decision, or they may be so risk-averse that they stagnate because they always choose the "safe" option. People who have strong preferences in all quadrants, on the other hand, often analyze well but don't make decisions at all. Ultimately, there are no "good" or "bad" ways to make a decision—only consequences! Your goal should be to manage the consequences of your thinking preferences effectively.

As a result, situational wholeness is especially useful when it comes to decision making. Each of the different quadrants offers different strengths and adds value to the decision-making process, so when all quadrants are considered, we will arrive at a better overall decision.

> Those in the know get it done the way it has always been done, stifling innovation as they barrel along the well-worn path.
>
> —Janet Rae-Dupree

The Whole Brain Decision-Making Walk-Around (see Figure 4-5) is a tool to help ensure that we "walk around" the four-quadrant model, asking

A DO WE HAVE ALL THE FACTS?		HAVE I SEEN ALL THE HIDDEN POSSIBILITIES? D	
Approaches	*May overlook*	*Approaches*	*May overlook*
• Abstract	• Feelings	• Imaginative	• Details
• Data based	• Synergistic	• Forward looking	• Practicality
• Theoretical	opportunities	• Risk taking	
WILL I BE IN CONTROL?		HOW WILL I AFFECT OTHERS?	
Approaches	*May overlook*	*Approaches*	*May overlook*
• Organized	• Alternative	• Emotional	• Facts
• Conservative	solutions	• Interpersonal	• Planning
• Procedural	• Novel ideas	• Intuitive (feelings)	
B	• Big picture		C

FIGURE 4-5 Whole Brain decision-making walk-around.

appropriate questions regarding each aspect of the mental processes involved. For example, have we done a rigorous consideration of the facts? Have we examined the details in the chronology of events? Have we factored in all the people issues and dealt with relationships? Did we take a big-picture view of the entire situation, and have we factored in the future that is appropriate to our conclusion?

The decision-making model provides a discipline to the process that requires a step-by-step consideration of each quadrant-specific aspect of our decision process. Several round trips provide an even better chance that all major aspects of the decision situation have been dealt with. A better decision should result.

Put It to Work

Take a moment to think about a decision that you recently made, ideally a big decision that did not have the outcome you desired. Look over the Decision-Making Walk-Around and analyze which quadrants you paid most attention to. Which did you overlook? How might the decision have been affected if you'd used a whole-brained approach?

Intuition and Pattern Seeking: Shortcut or Trap?

Sometimes we make decisions without elaborate thought. Going with our gut, or relying on intuition, allows us to make decisions quickly. We don't need to discuss the decision at length; instead, based on how we feel about the decision, we just go ahead and make it.

Intuition is a natural process, and once we understand it, we can use it more effectively. As with all mental skills, we can develop our intuition over time. It requires allowing our unconscious mind to come up with the answer rather than processing it consciously. There are other ways the brain works to make the decision-making process faster for us, but sometimes these shortcuts are traps. Designed to be highly efficient, your brain is a pattern-searching machine. It's actually lazy. Whenever you encounter a situation or an issue, your brain looks to see if it has "seen" this before, and if it has, it activates that part of the brain. This is why you may have already arrived at a decision in your head before a colleague has even finished describing the situation. That efficiency has a downside, though, because it gets in the way of our ability to take our thinking to a new place. This type of cognitive bias was called "the curse of knowledge" by Robin

Hogarth, and it has been explored in many contexts, including in Chip and Dan Heath's book *Made to Stick: Why Some Ideas Survive and Others Die*.[1] You can sidestep the curse of knowledge by tricking the brain with novelty and mind-shifters that are often called "mind hacks."

As an example, recent research has shown that people who speak a foreign language can reduce their inherent decision bias by thinking about the decision in the other language. "A foreign language provides a distancing mechanism that moves people from the immediate intuitive system to a more deliberate mode of thinking," wrote Boaz Keysar,[2] professor of psychology at the University of Chicago. This forces the brain to move to a more logical and conscious process, thereby eliminating the frequently instinctive emotional decision bias.

You can create this same effect even if you don't speak a foreign language. Try stepping into the shoes of another role or another person whom you know. This intentional shift will engage your brain to better decipher the issue at hand from a different perspective and bring it to mind consciously. An easy technique is to visualize your living room and imagine what an interior designer might notice about it. Next, imagine what a thief might notice. How about a housekeeper? A real estate agent? This simple activity demonstrates how easily we can get in touch with other viewpoints. The mere process shifts our thinking.

Our mental defaults can become mental blind spots and potential roadblocks to our truly arriving at the best, most balanced decisions. The good news is that we can learn to override these defaults, but it requires understanding and remaining aware and mindful of our mental process so that we can manage *it* rather than having our mental process manage *us*.

Your Preferences and Job Success

What about in our day-to-day work? Our strong primaries often represent work activities that stimulate us, and our lower preferences almost always represent work activities that drain us. When people aren't stimulated by the work they are doing, they drop out of the game. They become selectively blind and deaf to the discussions and activities that are taking place in their areas of avoidance. If a person has avoidance in one of the quadrants, and a large percentage of the work he or she has to do falls into that quadrant, then the likelihood of job success is enormously reduced.

What Motivates You?

Just as having a preference for a type of work doesn't mean that you'll necessarily be good at it, you may also discover that you have skills and competencies in activities you don't particularly like. Career progression and work opportunities bring a full range of competency options into view, and as part of this process, many people realize that although they have performed well at certain tasks and jobs, they didn't really like them. The link between preferences and competencies helps explain why money isn't the primary motivator for most people at work. As Frederick Herzberg's[3] seminal research showed, negative environmental factors such as low pay can be demotivating, but the reverse isn't true; instead, he found, people were motivated by interesting work, challenges, and increasing responsibility. In his book *Drive*,[4] Daniel Pink reiterates this point, identifying autonomy, mastery, and purpose as the three elements that motivate us. Like many researchers and experts today, Pink warns against the "carrot and stick" management methods that rely on money as the key motivator, explaining that not only are they ineffective, but they can do more harm than good.

Occupational mismatch, in which a person is assigned to work that does not fall into his or her area of preference, can produce very poor results. Take, for example, a financial manager who has a super-primary in the A quadrant and a preference in the C quadrant that is so low that it is clearly an avoidance. Because much of the mentality of financial work falls in the A quadrant, this person will typically perform well on all of the logical, analytical, quantitative aspects of the work, but he or she will often be selectively blind and deaf to the people aspects of his financial assignment. This person might be described as a "cold, heartless number cruncher" as a consequence of that avoidance. The finance job typically requires much more than just the ability to deal with numbers effectively. Therefore, this person's avoidance in the C quadrant could seriously limit his or her ability to perform high-level finance work because, in most cases, it requires interest and competence in dealing with human resource issues. (See Chapter 9 for more about occupational "misfits.")

Check this out yourself. Think about your coalition of preferences. Are they equally distributed, or do you have some strong attractions and possibly a few turn-offs? Go back to Chapter 3 and review the exercise in which you listed the tasks in your current job and underlined those that you dislike or like the least. Reflect on the consequences of those underlined words for the work you do and the way you do it. There are several action steps that you might consider. The first is to eliminate as many of these tasks as you can from your work assignment by delegating them or seeing if you can reassign them to a more appropriate person. But because this isn't always possible or realistic, the second step is to begin to make friends with them. Do them in service of your preference. You might find that when you view the work elements you don't like within the context of their contributing to the work you are highly stimulated by, you'll be more motivated to handle them. It's all about mindset.

SO WHAT?

> Who we are, what we do, and how we do it are the result of both nature and nurture.
> In most cases, nurture is the primary influence. This is a message of hope. We can change things if we want to.
> Interesting work that stimulates us is the most powerful influence on our mental preferences.
> Situational wholeness should be the goal. Knowing your preferences and your mental options positions you to supplement your existing competencies with the situational competencies that you need.
> A person's *lack of preference* can be as important to his or her job performance as the strong preferences that qualified him or her for the job.

"I'm trying to find a hacker who can get inside my husband's brain and tell me what's on his mind."

CHAPTER 5

Expect Difference, and Then Take Advantage of It!

CHAPTER HIGHLIGHTS

> Hard data support the finding that the preferences of the world's population are equally distributed across the four quadrants of the Whole Brain Model.
> Any organization of more than 100 people is likely to have thinking preference diversity available to it.
> Leaders of such companies typically do not lead on the basis of the full diversity of thinking in their workforce.
> Every ethnic group, on average, has a balance of thinking preferences represented. When the preferences are combined, this balance will show up as a Whole Brain profile.

The event was an American Creativity Association conference. Ann and I had our presentation prepared, and we knew what activities we wanted to conduct during the workshop. But at the last minute, just before the attendees began streaming into the room, we had an idea: What if we divided the participants into two groups, on the two sides of the room—one composed only of male participants, the other only of females? Would that affect the activities and how the participants completed them? The group dynamics? The outcomes?

There was plenty of grumbling when we instructed the attendees to split up by gender. It was as if we were blatantly violating the rules of political correctness. "What are you trying to prove?" they wanted to know. "Are you implying something?" The truth was, we didn't know for sure how much difference we would find between the male group's creative interactions, processes, and outcomes and the female group's. After all, they were all members of a creativity association, so as a group, they had a lot in common.

The first thing we asked them to do was to work together within their gender-specific groups and answer the question, "What is the most important thing for you to accomplish, the ultimate goal of creativity?"

When they presented their results, Ann and I were stunned.

We knew from brain research that there are differences in the physiology of the brains of males and females. For example, while the human male brain is larger on average than the average female brain, the neurons in the cortex of the female brain are packed closer together, and female brains possess more neurons than male brains. There are other physiological differences that scientists are continually discovering, and our own data consistently shows a difference in thinking preferences, with males tilting more toward the A quadrant and females tilting more toward the C quadrant (see Figure 5-1). This data difference between males and females holds true around the world.

Yet even knowing all this, we were still shocked at how plainly the differences manifested themselves behaviorally in our workshop. In answering our

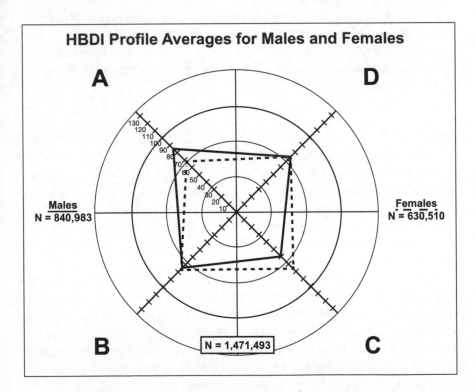

FIGURE 5-1 Male and female profile averages from the HBDI database.

first question, about their approach to creativity, the males overwhelmingly talked about creating a unique, tangible thing—building "stuff" with a specific outcome. The females, on the other hand, talked about the environment and helping people, producing the conditions for creativity, making changes that would affect people in a positive way, and doing something important. Neither of these answers was "right" or "wrong," and in fact, both are essential. But the interesting thing was how neatly their responses aligned with our data, even down to the few outliers in each group—a factor that also shows up in our research. (For more on creative thinking, see Chapters 21, 22, and 23.)

> **Men and women see the world differently—it makes sense that their approaches to creativity would be different as well.**
>
> —Ann Herrmann-Nehdi

Again, these were people who, on the whole, had a lot in common, specifically a passion for creative thinking. But for all their similarities, they still experienced things differently based on their gender.

One of the reasons I wanted to share this story with you is that it's a good introduction to the idea of difference. Difference is everywhere, and one of the most obvious differences is that between male and female.

How do you start to deal with difference, particularly when it comes to thinking? In their article "Putting Your Company's Whole Brain to Work," published in the *Harvard Business Review*, Dorothy Leonard and Susaan Straus[1] put it succinctly: "Start with yourself. When you identify your own style, you gain insight into the ways your preferences unconsciously shape your style of leadership and patterns of communication."

The previous chapters focused on your own thinking preferences and how they play out. But of course, you aren't an island; in work as well as in your personal life, you're going to be interacting with other individuals, and that means you're going to come up against thinking preferences and patterns that are similar to yours and others that are different from yours to one degree or another. It's often easier to work with someone whose thinking preferences are like our own. It's as if we are operating in our own shorthand, and such people instantly seem to

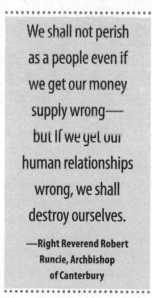

> **We shall not perish as a people even if we get our money supply wrong—but if we get our human relationships wrong, we shall destroy ourselves.**
>
> —Right Reverend Robert Runcie, Archbishop of Canterbury

"get" us. But it's not always possible, or even likely, that you'll be surrounded by people who prefer to think the way you do. In fact, difference is more often the norm.

Thinking Across the World

Taking it a step further, one of the things we've learned from the data we've collected is that not only can you expect differences, but you can expect *balance*: organizations, ethnic groups, and any group of a large enough size will have a balanced distribution across all four quadrants of the Whole Brain Model. One way to put it is that the world is a composite Whole Brain Thinking distribution.

Our hard data from around the world demonstrate this finding conclusively. Studies conducted in the United States and in many countries have a common theme. If the sample size is large enough—1,000, 500, 250, or even as low as 100—the composite of individual HBDI Profiles represents a highly diverse but well-balanced distribution across the four quadrants of the Whole Brain Model. This is true in all parts of the world. Figure 5-2 shows some sample composite profiles.

CEOs are always surprised by the balanced data representing the composite of their employees. They often think their organizations have a tilt to one side, often reflecting the mental preferences of the leadership team or the culture of the company. As a result, they aren't managing or leading their companies on the basis of the composite Whole Brain reality of their organizations. Their leadership and communication styles have been either tilted in one direction or too confined for the global nature of the thinking and learning styles of their employees.

I estimate the costs of business leaders holding wrong assumptions about the mentality of their human assets at hundreds of millions of dollars in lost profits resulting from misalignment in expectations, jobs, training, communication, and leadership.

Can you imagine the difference in performance that would result if companies were managed in a style that is in alignment with their human resource assets? If we now widen the lens to include not only their own organization but also their customers and the general public, the implications become even more profound. Leaders must now rethink their external assumptions as well as their internal practices, particularly if they are in consumer-oriented businesses.

Think of all the content creators today. If they're looking for the broadest readership possible, how could the editing be modified to make that happen? Widening the lens even further includes the composite Whole Brain reality in

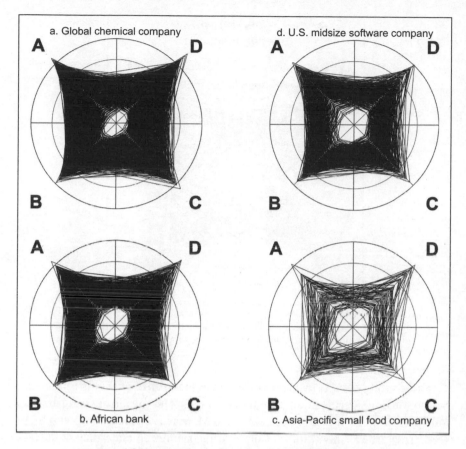

FIGURE 5-2 HBDI composite profiles of organizations from around the world: (a) Global chemical company, (b) African bank, (c) Asia-Pacific small food company, (d) U.S. midsize software company.

educational institutions. It stands to reason that if the student body is a composite Whole Brain, then that should also be the case for the faculty and the curriculum. In contrast to the data on the students, however, many learning institutions still don't have a composite Whole Brain faculty or a composite Whole Brain curriculum.

A striking example is the freshman class of a large midwestern university. The composite average shown in Figure 5-3 represents approximately 500 entering freshmen in the School of Engineering.

This extraordinarily well-balanced composite was a shock to everybody, with the exception of the dean of engineering, who intuitively knew that there was a mismatch between the faculty and the students and that this condition would lead to extremely adverse consequences.

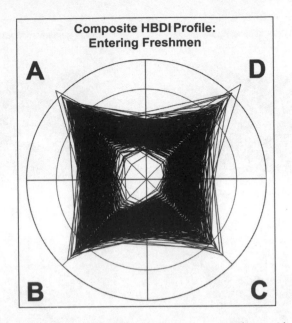

FIGURE 5-3 HBDI composite profile of freshman entering a large midwestern university engineering program. Note the whole range of mental preferences.

Shown in Figure 5-4 is a composite average profile of the faculty of the School of Engineering, alongside the average profile of the entering seniors four years later, as provided by Edward and Monika Lumsdaine's[2] research. As you can see, the average profile of the entering seniors emulates that of the faculty. What you don't see are all those who failed to make the grade, transferred to another school, or dropped out because of unsolvable frustration. Those who didn't make it to graduation were predominantly C- and D-quadrant thinkers. Could they have been successful if the faculty members had recognized this and appealed to a broader spectrum of thinking styles in their teaching methods and approach?

I think this example of an engineering school could be duplicated in most of the colleges and universities around the world. To compound the tragedy, even when those responsible know that they have been holding the wrong assumptions about their students or their employees, they often do not commit themselves to changing what they are doing and the way they are doing it. There are some exceptions, and these champions of human resource development will someday be recognized for their achievements.

Our worldwide database is so far-ranging that readers could pick their own categories and the answer would be essentially the same. What are the thinking preference characteristics of a particular ethnic group, for example? When

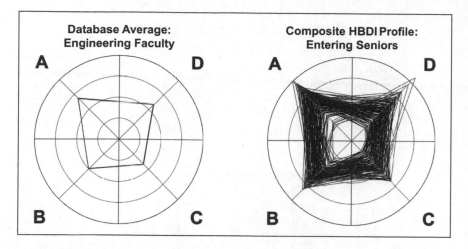

FIGURE 5-4 HBDI database average profile of engineering faculty and the HBDI composite of entering seniors at a large midwestern university.

separate composite profiles are developed for each identifiable ethnic group, on the average, they produce a composite Whole Brain; there is essentially no difference in brain dominance preferences between populations of whites, blacks, Hispanics, Native Americans, and Asians.

Thinking preferences, of course, do not equal intelligence. An individual's HBDI thinking profile describes the degree of that person's mental preferences in each quadrant. There are an infinite number of discrete profiles for the world as a whole and for each ethnic group. A study of our database a few years ago showed that when those individual profiles are assembled into a composite whole and averaged, the result is a 1-1-1-1 balanced profile. (For more information on the HBDI preference codes, see the HBDI Profile Interpretation Guide in the appendix.) The composite profiles for the different ethnic groups and the world in general from our study are shown in Figure 5-5.

While these profiles are not a measure of intelligence, they are a measure of competency potential. The composite Whole Brain distribution for all ethnic groups taken together suggests that the distribution of competency potential is similar within each ethnic group.

I believe that in each ethnic group, there is an equal potential for such occupational aspirations as pilots, physicians, nurses, teachers, social workers, technologists, scientists, stockbrokers, engineers, police officers, musicians, entrepreneurs, researchers, and managers. These are, of course, only examples, because I could fill the book with examples of specific occupations.

From a business perspective, it is important to note that occupational choices cross national and cultural boundaries. The HBDI Profiles of airline

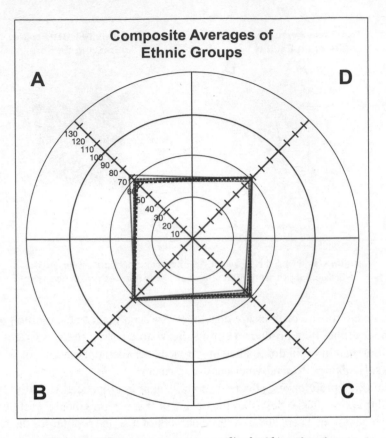

FIGURE 5-5 HBDI composite average profiles for African American, Asian, Caucasian, Latino, Native American ethnicities.

pilots are approximately the same regardless of their ethnic or cultural background. The reason is that the work requirements are the same for airline pilots from India, China, Japan, Germany, France, Mexico, Brazil, Australia, and the United States. The same is true for nurses, pathologists, or engineers. The more rigorous the professional requirements, the more likely it is that the profiles of occupational colleagues will be similar. The reason, again, is that the work requirements are approximately the same regardless of the culture or the ethnic population. Remarkably, the same is true for CEOs, with a few slight differences based on region, as described in detail in Chapter 20.

In the idealized, and I believe attainable, world of the future, businesses will be able to find every capability they need in the composite of candidates representing all ethnic groups, cultures, and genders. Acquiring competence will be up to the individual, regardless of which group he or she is from. Designing jobs to take advantage of available competencies and aligning workers with those jobs is up to the managers of the business.

Thinking Differences at Home

When people want to improve their dealing with differences in the workplace, I often tell them that they have the perfect opportunity to practice over breakfast. In working with thousands of people over the years, we've asked them where they think the preferences of their partner, spouse, or significant other lie, and anecdotally, we can say that opposites attract—at least in first marriages. On the other hand, couples in second and third marriages, as well as unmarried couples who are living together, are generally more similar in their thinking preferences. Perhaps the unmarried couples think so much alike that they don't feel the need for a formal contract. And maybe couples in their second and third marriages have figured out that they just don't want to work that hard anymore!

Male and Female Brains at Work

Let's go back to our participants at the creativity conference for a moment. We know there's a mental tilt in the direction of the A quadrant for males and the C quadrant for females, and we saw this play out in the workshop—but so what? What are the implications and consequences of this in the workplace?

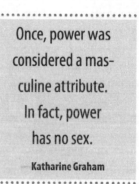

Once, power was considered a masculine attribute. In fact, power has no sex.

Katharine Graham

In terms of work that people really love to do, there is a pretty even distribution across the occupational options, with the exception of those jobs that require strong competencies in technical, numerical, logical, analytical, or diagnostic work, which are more heavily tilted toward males. In contrast, the kind of work with a heavy C-quadrant orientation is primarily relationship-based, requiring competency in understanding feelings and interpersonal transactions. Many men are uninterested or actively dislike—and as a result, haven't built up competencies in—handling the sensitivity and patience required in these kinds of jobs. There is ongoing research exploring the differences in the structures of male and female brains that may one day more fully explain the physiological reasons for the way these differences play out. But the differences are there, and they show up consistently.

But then, of course, there are women who "think more like men" and men who "think more like women." The reality is that, given any kind of career options, men and women will sort themselves out into jobs that align with their interests and thus their preferences.

Women in STEM

There has been a concerted effort to create opportunities and encourage more women to take part in the traditionally male-heavy STEM (science, technology, engineering, and mathematics) disciplines. An integral part of these educational programs has been a focus on teaching approaches, specifically using methods that are proven to engage *all* students. I agree wholeheartedly. If we want to build confidence and encourage people to pursue all sorts of educational opportunities and career paths, we need teaching and learning methods that appeal to a wide range of learners.

The Benefits of Gender Balance

For all their grumbling at the outset of the creativity conference workshop, a funny thing happened after the groups got over the "political incorrectness" of being separated along gender lines: they started having fun. They were laughing and joking, there was lots of lively discussion, and they were really enjoying themselves. It was easy to work in these gender-aligned groups.

But there are important differences in male and female thinking preferences that would argue for gender-balanced teams as the most effective generally, and particularly when creative problem solving is involved.

Examining the characteristics that typify male thinking and female thinking can lead to only one conclusion, and that is that a creative team leader wants both. It has been demonstrated over and over that teams made up of people with diverse thinking styles produce more creative solutions than homogeneous teams. In fact, for most tasks in today's environment, any team leader will benefit from thinking diversity. (In Chapter 12, we will discuss more of the specific research and business examples that demonstrate the power of diverse thinking in teams.) I can say flatly that it is not possible to create the optimum Whole Brain team with only one gender involved. The differences are both subtle and profound. You cannot get to where you want to be mentally without having both males and females involved in the process.

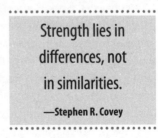

Strength lies in differences, not in similarities.

—Stephen R. Covey

Over the years, my organization has had many opportunities to test out these conclusions. In all the workshops that we offer, there are opportunities for team interaction, and although it is our objective to build gender-balanced, diverse, heterogeneous teams, sometimes the logistics of a particular workshop don't allow for that ideal combination. Therefore, we have the opportunity to observe relatively similar or homogeneous teams, both in thinking style and in gender, as they undertake creative workshop assignments. Homogeneous teams of either gender tend to reach early consensus and settle too quickly on what prove to be mediocre conclusions. In comparison, gender-balanced, diverse, heterogeneous teams not only consume all the time allowed, but also ask for additional time and almost invariably produce the highest, most imaginative creative results.

When I ask each team to describe its team process, the members of the homogeneous teams of either gender talk about the smoothness of the team interaction, the relative speed with which they decided what to do, and the ease with which the team roles were assigned and carried out. The members of the heterogeneous teams of either gender talk about the difficulties of team interaction, highlighting the struggle they had in deciding on a plan of action—for example, carrying out of the individual roles and the difficulty of putting those roles together to make a unified presentation of the results. The gender-balanced heterogeneous teams experienced similar difficulties in time management and independent role development, but in most cases, they had such a superior grasp of the team's conclusions that the team members could contribute independently yet synergistically.

Some business cultures and industries claim that they don't have the necessary balance of genders to be able to form gender-balanced heterogeneous teams. One of the reasons they don't feel that they have the correct balance is that they are overlooking a large number of employees whom they don't feel qualify as potential team members. Many people who hold this view are missing the point. It is not the organizational level of a potential team member that qualifies him or her, but rather the quality and style of the person's thinking. Since most organizations are, in fact, a composite Whole Brain, most of them do in fact have the balance of genders and styles required to form all the teams they would ever need.

Twenty-First Century Research Confirms the Importance of Gender Balance

Years ago, when Ned Herrmann originally proposed that gender-balanced heterogeneous teams would be more creative and effective, the idea seemed reasonable to most people, but was challenged by others who felt that it was too politically correct or too difficult to prove. At last there is research that substantiates this premise.

Coauthored by MIT, Carnegie Mellon University, and Union College researchers, the study sought to better understand how groups perform and, more specifically, what might facilitate or hinder that performance: "We set out to test the hypothesis that groups, like individuals, have a consistent ability to perform across different kinds of tasks," says Anita Williams Woolley,[3] the paper's lead author and an assistant professor at Carnegie Mellon's Tepper School of Business.

"Our hypothesis was confirmed," continues Thomas W. Malone, a coauthor and Patrick J. McGovern Professor of Management at the MIT Sloan School of Management. "We found that there is a general effectiveness, a group collective intelligence, which predicts a group's performance in many situations."

The researchers found that groups showing greater "social sensitivity," which entails perceiving others' emotions effectively, performed better than other groups, especially those that were dominated by one person. This social sensitivity factor was greater in groups with more women— which can also be substantiated by our data showing that women overall tend to have stronger preferences in that domain.

I have gotten mixed reactions to our gender-related research over the years. Some women find it offensive to imply that they are using their brains differently from the way men do. The facts and research prove, however, that women *do* use their brains differently, and that there are important consequences that emerge. Our differences can in fact be an advantage, as this research demonstrates.

Difference does not imply better or worse, right or wrong, but it may make our group process feel more annoying or cumbersome. Bringing together different preferences and styles into a group process may be inconvenient and require greater facilitation skills, but the fact is, when you can harness those varied styles effectively through Whole Brain Thinking techniques, you will get better results.

—*Ann Herrmann-Nehdi*

Put It to Work

Take a moment to identify four people in your personal or professional life who seem to have a strong preference for one of the four quadrants, so that you have one person each for A, B, C, and D. Now imagine that you have been asked to lead the team working on a special project that could be very career-enhancing for you. Your team is this group of four individuals.

- What is the good news about this group?
- What would be your greatest challenge?
- How could you most effectively be a "translator" across quadrants so that all ideas are heard and the differences are leveraged?

Same Thinking Preference Competitiveness

We've talked a lot about difference in this chapter, but what about those who think similarly to us? There can still be challenges. While people with strikingly different thinking preferences often have difficulty understanding each other, those with very similar thinking preferences can become competitive with each other. What is happening here is that while the people's thinking preferences are nominally very similar, there are some minor differences that could be just enough to give Person 1 a slightly different perception of a given situation compared to Person 2. This somewhat different perception could lead to, "We both have pretty much the same understanding, but my way is better than your way."

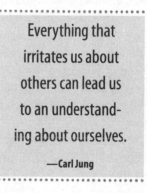

Everything that irritates us about others can lead us to an understanding about ourselves.

—Carl Jung

Here's an example: two individuals with strongly rational (A/B quadrant) thinking preferences are developing a strategy concerning this year's sales plan for one of their industrial customers. Two of the defining characteristics of rational thinkers are logical processing and analytic processing. In this example, Sam prefers both, but he is more logical than analytical. Marie also prefers both, but she is more analytical than logical. They team up to work on the same problem, with one tilting toward analysis and the other tilting toward logic.

Sam, the sales engineer, says that the customer has purchased 500 of the same motor every year for the past three years, and therefore we should project a minimum of 500 for this year.

Marie, the inside sales support engineer, says yes, but her analysis shows that the orders came in distinct cycles, with the majority coming in the second and fourth quarters, and this affects the manufacturing cycle. And what if the customer doesn't order in the fourth quarter? This could adversely affect year-end results. Sam counters with the logic of a three-year track record. Marie argues that analysis has uncovered a buying pattern that could affect future business. They struggle to reach agreement on an issue where they are both partly right.

This form of thinking preference competition seems to favor the A/B left mode, but it can also take place in the upper mode, often in scientific research or an R&D lab. For example, two R&D physicists who share an A/D profile are working together to design a much thinner version of their core product. The person with rational preferences proposes a research study of all the known designs as the first step. That would be the obvious logical thing to do. In contrast, the physicist with experimental preferences would much rather play around with different combinations of existing components to determine which criteria contribute most to thinness. That would be the more interesting and creative way to start the task.

In this case you have two individuals, both with double primary preferences in the rational A quadrant and the experimental D quadrant, but with different mixes. One favors rational thinking a bit more than experimental, and the other favors experimental thinking a bit more than rational. They are clearly on the same track, but one sees a faster route to the finish line than the other. They argue about which approach will produce quicker results. Again, both are partly right, but each feels strongly that his approach is best.

As they work through their individual solutions to a problem, I can see these two people becoming quite competitive about which approach is best. It is likely that either the logical or the experimental approach would ultimately produce a solution, but because both of the people involved are aware of both approaches but favor one, they are often inclined to be quite competitive about the one they prefer.

The C/D right-mode and B/C lower-mode quadrants may be somewhat less susceptible to competition because people favoring these quadrants seem to compete with themselves rather than with others. They are also inclined to be softer in their approach and more attentive to their relationships. In contrast, people with the more pragmatic-oriented thinking preferences in A and D are more sharp-edged and assertive and less concerned with interpersonal relationships. Damn the torpedoes—full steam ahead!

My purpose in citing these examples is not to suggest that competition in thinking preferences is bad. In fact, competitive approaches can lead to better decisions and better solutions. My purpose is to suggest that there are consequences to pairing people with similar profiles. Most people would assume that, since their thinking preferences are so similar, two such people will be entirely compatible in a team situation. With these observations, I'm suggesting that the assumption of compatibility might be premature and that, in some cases, similar but not precisely the same thinking preferences could lead to vigorous competition. The leadership challenge would be to keep this competition healthy and synergistic rather than hostile and combative. The manager has to establish a climate that fosters interaction between members of an organization on the basis of creative added value.

SO WHAT?

> Difference is the norm, so expect it and prepare for it.
> Hard HBDI Profile data from many companies, organizations, universities, schools, conventions, and other groups around the world clearly demonstrate that the world in general, and the business world in particular, represents a composite Whole Brain distribution of preferences.
> Most organizations have a sufficient gender balance to provide appropriate candidates for gender-balanced, diverse, heterogeneous teams. Organizational level should not be the criterion for team selection; rather, it is the style and quality of thinking that should be the determining factors.
> Differences within the same thinking style preference can lead to competitive ways of accomplishing the same work task, which can add value if managed appropriately.

CHAPTER 6

Getting More Satisfaction from Work: Why "Smart" Is Relative

CHAPTER HIGHLIGHTS

> Since our perception is influenced by our thinking preferences, just having good eyesight and hearing doesn't guarantee that you actually hear and understand what is intended.
> Intellectual smartness is only one kind of intelligence; different kinds of intelligence can be mapped against the four quadrants.
> Different occupations have unique mental requirements, which result in specific occupational norms.
> The more aligned the worker is with the work, the more satisfying and fulfilling the work will be.

As a student at Cornell, I noticed that the engineering students had crew cuts, carried slide rules, and talked in technical terms. They wore mostly sweaters and windbreakers. Meanwhile, across the quadrangle, students in the Arts and Sciences College had longer hair, wore sports jackets with leather patches on the elbows, and talked about literature and economics. There were many more women on that side of the campus. The music department was even more obviously different. Here there were also more women than men. The clothes were loose and comfortable and often colorful. The students lounged around and sang or listened to music, and the buildings were converted Victorian houses. There were ivy-covered buildings on the arts quadrangle and steel, concrete, and glass buildings in the engineering area.

Those early observations, made so long ago, continue to hold true today. Our thinking preferences continue to be a consistent basis for human behavior and provide clues about how different we are. Hardly a day goes by when there isn't an excellent example of preference evident in the behavior of characters on television, in the movies, or, better yet, in real life.

A Company Chairman and President
Discover Their Differences

The sponsor of my management presentation in Seattle some years ago invited me to have breakfast with the chairman and the president of a local company that was important to him. During a lively breakfast conversation, I could see that these two men had sharply different views on any given topic, and their nonverbal reactions provided exclamation points to their words. Their eyes flashed as they interjected opposing views.

These two men, along with the 100 others who attended the meeting, had completed the HBDI Assessment prior to the session and, unbeknownst to them, had been assigned seats based on their profiles. In fact, the first tables in each of the four rows were small groups representing the extremes in each quadrant and therefore served as demonstration tables for my workshop (see Figure 6-1).

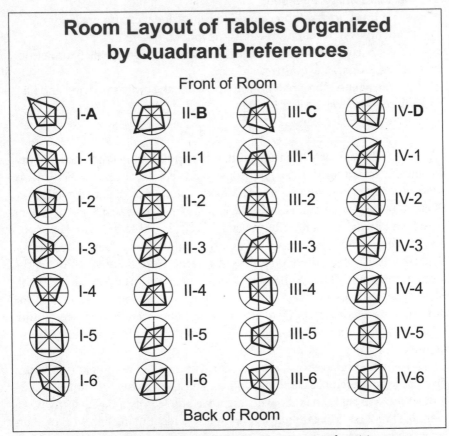

FIGURE 6-1 Typical layout for a presentation where groups of participants are seated according to their thinking preferences, based on their HBDI Profile results. (Room layout of tables organized by quadrant preferences.)

I knew what the chairman and president did not: that they had opposing profiles and had been assigned to the A- and D-quadrant demonstration tables.

I excused myself from breakfast early in order to get ready for the presentation, and therefore I was in a position to observe these two men as they entered the room and were directed to the opposite front-row tables. I watched as they proceeded to their tables and, before sitting down, looked at each other and conveyed by their expressions some understanding of what was going to happen. They had been at each other's throats for 15 years, and maybe they were about to find out why.

Early in my presentation, I conducted an exercise in which individuals revealed their work preferences, similar to the exercises in Chapter 3. At each of the 28 tables were seated three participants with very similar profiles, although each table had a different tilt. As the individuals determined their work preferences and then shared them with others at the same table, they discovered that these were highly homogeneous groups. I then had the four front-row demonstration tables reveal to the entire audience what work they really loved and were energized by.

As it turned out, the chairman and the president were the spokesmen for their respective tables. The president, who was also the chief operating officer, represented the logical, rational, analytic A-quadrant table. The chairman, who was the founder and CEO, represented the holistic, intuitive, risk-taking D-quadrant table (see Figure 6-2). As each of the two made his diametrically opposite comments, they were looking at each other, and I had the distinct feeling that the source of their 15 years of arguments and differences of opinion and frustration was being revealed.

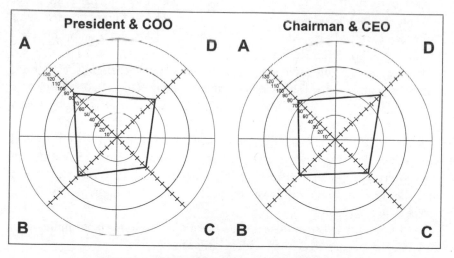

FIGURE 6-2 HBDI Profiles of two corporate officers: the president/COO and the chairman/CEO.

After the session ended, they approached me and admitted that they now knew they had really missed the boat. They had not taken advantage of their differences of opinion in terms of getting more viable or creative alternatives, but rather had frustrated each other for almost their entire relationship. They had both been adding value, but they could have been very much more effective as CEO and COO if they had taken advantage of their mental diversity. For me, and for the workshop participants, it was a memorable public demonstration of the consequences of our thinking preferences in a work setting. For the two men, it was the beginning of a true partnership.

What Our Senses Miss

Most of us who have reasonably good eyesight would assume that we are seeing the world the way it really is. If our hearing is as good as our eyesight, we are also convinced that we hear everything the way it is intended to be heard. In fact, our senses aren't always so accurate. It is much more likely that what we are seeing and hearing is based upon our perceptions, which are biased by our thinking preferences.

How many of us have wondered about a course we took, a job, a relationship, or an event that didn't turn out the way we wanted it to because we just didn't seem to "get it"? We've overheard numerous people say, after understanding their thinking preferences, "Oh! I see. Now I understand why I flunked algebra." Or one married partner, upon seeing the couple's very different HBDI profiles plotted together, will say, "Oh! You think differently from me. Gee, I thought you were doing that on purpose just to irritate me!" Or a parent writes in and says, "It's amazing. Now I get it. My son is not weird. He's just different. So *very* different from me."

In fact, we are all unique, and that is why each of us is different—*and normal* just the way we are. The "aha moments" that happen during this discovery process are a frequent outcome of understanding your thinking preferences by means of the four-quadrant metaphor.

We're designed to take it all in, but we don't really, and then we're surprised when others don't "get us" or align with our thinking. In fact, the first step in your ability to appreciate difference is having an understanding of your own gaps, because then you will have context for understanding why a different perspective is so important.

And as we'll explore in this chapter, there are also important implications for work alignment and dealing with misalignment.

Relative Smartness

Henry Mintzberg, PhD,[1] an expert on management and a professor at McGill University, wrote a classic article in the *Harvard Business Review* in which he raised several questions. The first of them was, "How can some people be so smart and dull at the same time? How can they be so capable of certain mental activities and at the same time be so incapable of others?"

When I read the article, I remember saying to myself, "My God, I think he's talking about me ... but he's also talking about my staff, my boss, my family, and all my friends." Although all of these people were successful in what they did, not one of them was equally "smart" across the entire brain spectrum. We were all smart and dull at the same time. He was talking about everyone!

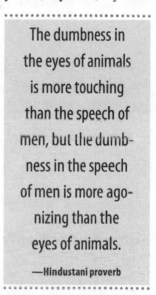

The dumbness in the eyes of animals is more touching than the speech of men, but the dumbness in the speech of men is more agonizing than the eyes of animals.

—Hindustani proverb

I believe thinking preferences provide the answer to Dr. Mintzberg's questions. We have established preferences in our thinking, which in turn lead to interests that, when pursued, can establish competencies in that discrete domain of thinking, while at the same time a neighboring domain remains relatively dull. For example, an individual whose preferences and interests lead to comprehension and ability in algebra, which is linear processing, may be relatively incapable of understanding solid geometry, which is visual and spatially oriented. This example illustrates how two forms of math can involve two completely different methods or thought processes. This is true of other disciplines as well—chemistry versus physics, painting versus sculpture, bookkeeping versus financial analysis. The reason is that these are two separate mental activities in which a person can have highly varying competencies.

Look at the model of "smarts" in Figure 6-3 and find those areas where you either excel or fall short.

Note that "intellectual smarts" falls into one quadrant while other types of smarts, such as "street smarts" and "emotional intelligence," fall into completely different quadrants. Intellectual smarts is the category that IQ attempts to measure, but as we are gradually realizing, there are ways of being smart that go beyond just the intelligence factors measured by IQ tests. One of the important researchers in this area, Harvard professor Howard

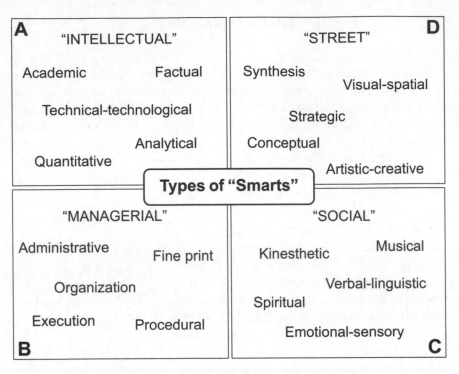

FIGURE 6-3 Types of "smarts" across the four quadrants.

Gardner,[2] describes this as the theory of multiple intelligences. According to Gardner:

> The theory is a critique of the standard psychological view of intellect: that there is a single intelligence, adequately measured by IQ or other short-answer tests. Instead, on the basis of evidence from disparate sources, I claim that human beings have a number of relatively discrete intellectual capacities. IQ tests assess linguistic and logical-mathematical intelligence, and sometimes spatial intelligence. ... But humans have several other significant intellectual capacities.

He goes on to describe musical intelligence, bodily-kinesthetic intelligence, interpersonal (social) intelligence, intrapersonal intelligence (understanding of self), naturalist intelligence, and others. Although somewhat different in design from the concept of Whole Brain Thinking, Gardner's research and that of others, including Daniel Goleman's[3] work on emotional, social, and ecological intelligence, is helpful in understanding that these different kinds of intelligence make up, as Gardner puts it, "the human intellectual toolkit."

The Shortcomings of IQ Tests

I have a personal problem with IQ tests because by their very nature, they attempt to measure only a very narrow spectrum of what I am referring to as "smartness." I recall that the U.S. Armed Services routinely test for IQ and apparently provide the results to branches of the service that are interested. In my own case, I had signed up for flight training, but I was wooed by the Quartermaster Corps because it had latched on to my IQ scores and felt that I could be a bigger success in dealing with war material, such as uniforms and shoes, than in being a fighter pilot.

I was energized and excited by flying; I had no interest in messing with a warehouse. So I ended up in India with the lowest rank possible—an unassigned (but highly trained electronics expert) private. When my contingent arrived at the remote camp that was our final destination, we were lined up for a welcome by the commanding officer, a regular army captain. His first words were, "Can any of you boneheads fix a radio?" Every one of us was smart enough to know that you didn't volunteer. After a minute of total silence, the captain said, "Can any one of you fix *my* radio?" After another minute of silence, I raised my hand and said, "Yes, sir. I can." And the captain said, "Step forward, Sergeant." For my initiative, I was rewarded a promotion on the spot. Thus began an impromptu but award-winning career in the Army Airways Communication System.

To Appreciate "Smarts," You Have to Understand Differences

Your assumptions about what is smart and what is dumb are the result of your preferences, but in reality, every quadrant has something to contribute. If you don't get the idea of relative intelligence—that there are different ways of being smart—then you won't be able to recognize why you should respect the ideas of others.

For example, many organized, traditional businesses often hire on the basis of intellectual smarts, whereas independent, informal businesses frequently thrive on the kinds of smarts that fall into other quadrants. If organized business had a good way of hiring and applying all the different intelligences, the

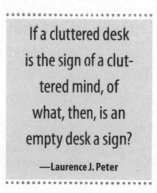

If a cluttered desk is the sign of a cluttered mind, of what, then, is an empty desk a sign?

—Laurence J. Peter

chances are high that those companies would be more successful. But people with the other kinds of smarts appear to be dumb when they are scrutinized through the bureaucratic filters of the typical business hiring process. This is exacerbated by the keyword approach used by many organizations to sort résumés.

Often, what we consider "not smart" is really just a huge blind spot created by our preferences. My classic example of this involves a friend who confessed that he didn't understand his son John and had given up trying to parent him. He was frustrated by John's behavior, didn't like John's friends, was embarrassed by the way John dressed, and was depressed about John's poor performance in school and his apparent lack of any career direction. He further stated that it wasn't just him—the entire family reacted about the same way. They thought John was weird, and they just didn't get him.

My friend, who was very familiar with my work, asked if I could administer HBDI Profiles to his entire family. First, I processed the individual assessments for each of them. Then, to compare the shape of each family member's profile to those of the others, I generated a composite of the entire family member's profiles together (see Figure 6-4).

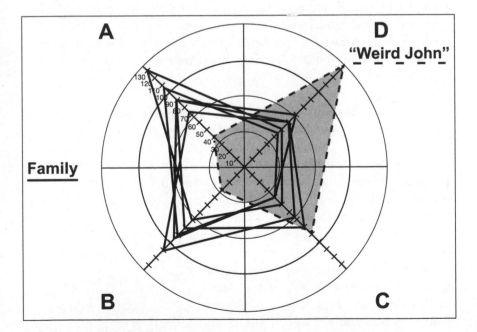

FIGURE 6-4 HBDI composite profile of a family with one member falling outside of the predominant mental preferences of the family culture.

The composite revealed quite dramatically that John's thinking preferences were the exact opposite of those of the rest of his family members. The contrast of the predominant "smartness and dullness" of the family with John's was dramatically apparent to everyone. My friend finally realized that John wasn't abnormal, stupid, or a problem child; he was simply *different* from the rest of his family. As a matter of fact, from John's perspective, it was his family that was weird, not him.

When he saw the profiles, the father said, "Oh, my God, what have I done?" At that point, he realized that he had been critical of John for not having the same interests or talents as the rest of the family. When the family gathered around the kitchen table, looking at each other's profiles, one of John's brothers looked at him as if he were meeting John for the first time.

A year or so after this incident, John married his girlfriend, of whom the family had approved throughout their relationship. Guess what? The bride's profile matched the rest of the family's average profile, and thus a new cycle of understanding differences was started, which is a requirement in all types of relationships if they are to avoid misunderstandings and be successful.

The Quadrants, in Fiction and Real Life

Often scriptwriters create characters of a certain type to make a point. These are frequently consistent with extreme quadrant preferences. For example, Mr. Spock in the *Star Trek* series was so rational that he was established as a nonhuman from another planet in our universe. Spock's mentality was contrasted with that of Dr. McCoy, a medical doctor who was so empathic, caring, and nurturing that he was too good to be true in the real world. Spock is an example of someone with an extreme A-quadrant preference. What he needed to do, he did well. Dr. McCoy exemplifies the strong interpersonal and caring qualities of the C quadrant.

In the real world, we don't generally see such extremes, but you may already be thinking of well-known leaders and businesspeople who could fit into different quadrants. In the A quadrant, for example, you might find Adam Smith, Henry Ford would be in the B quadrant, Jenny Craig might fall primarily in the C quadrant, and Steve Jobs would be in the D quadrant. See Figure 6-5 for HBDI pro-forma profiles of other interesting and famous people.

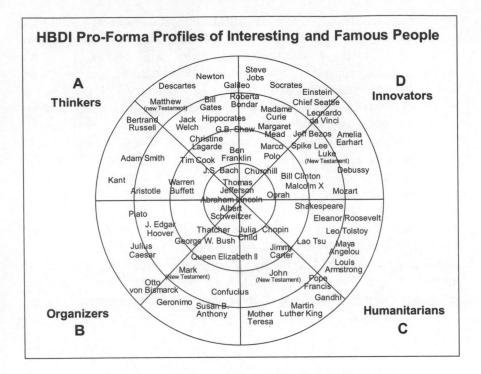

FIGURE 6-5 Preference map of HBDI pro-forma profiles of interesting and famous people.

Signs of Preference in the Workplace

I encourage you to seek out examples of thinking preferences in action in your own workplace. Take a break, wander around the office area, and notice the differences in the different workspaces. As you do so, think about the individual who owns each workspace and assess the degree of alignment between how that workspace looks and the everyday behavior of its occupant (see Figure 6-6). Chances are, clues abound!

For example, here is Mary's desk, and it's neat as a pin. Mary is the administrative assistant who prides herself on being highly organized and punctual. She is fastidious in her dress and appearance. Her workspace is just outside Bill's office, which is covered in paper. The surface of his desk is not visible. The windowsill has become a bookcase, and the guest chair is stacked with reports, as is the top of the filing cabinet. Mary tries to keep Bill's desk neat and orderly, but Bill complains about his papers being somewhere other than

FIGURE 6-6 Alignment between workspace and occupant's behavior. The picture on the left depicts a staff member with a very loose, unstructured work style. The one on the right illustrates someone who prefers working at a clean, orderly desk.

where he put them, so she has given up on trying to categorize his work logically. Mary cannot tolerate her desk being messy, whereas Bill is far more interested in the project he is working on than in how his office appears. Regardless of what others think, though, Bill has his own system that works for him.

Both Mary and Bill are very good at what they do, but it's clear that their preferences influence their priorities. The HBDI Profiles of Mary and Bill are in good alignment with the appearance of their workspaces. Mary's profile has a strong lower left B-quadrant preference. Her need for order and to work only on the project on her desk is quite visible. In contrast, Bill's profile is heading in the opposite direction, toward the upper right D quadrant. Bill works on several projects at a time, and therefore needs to have all his materials out in front of him. He has no need to clean off his desk at the end of the day.

If you venture into the finance area, you will see that a high percentage of the desks are neat and orderly, even though there are some papers and reports on most of them. If you look closely at the papers, you will see neatly organized spreadsheets and reports, and if there are any notes, the writing is typically quite legible, with small, precisely formed letters and numbers. The need for unquestionable accuracy in this area of the company is obvious in the work styles of the staff members.

Whenever you encounter an office or cubicle with lots of paper "stuff" on the desks and numerous surfaces, it probably belongs to someone whose job requires simultaneity, creative thinking, and a nonstructured environment. Cleaning up and being neat is less important than addressing the task at hand. Sometimes, cleaning up gets in the way of such people's work because it doesn't come easy to them. They are working just as hard, but differently.

There is a lot of common sense involved in these clues to thinking preference. It is rare to find a major discontinuity between a person's workspace and his or her thinking preference profile unless he or she is working in an environment where a clean desk is mandated. This is true not only of individuals but of functions such as finance, sales, marketing, R&D, legal, advertising, engineering, manufacturing, and human resources. And this is where we start to see implications in terms of how well someone is aligned with the work he or she performs and, in turn, the person's overall level of work satisfaction.

Occupational Norms

There is a strong relationship between our preferences and the kind of work that energizes us—the work that we love. In this section, I will report on the distribution of high-frequency occupational profiles of general interest.

In looking over our HBDI Profile database and analyzing occupational choices, it became clear that there are norms involving mental preference and occupational choice. For example, the engineering profession (see Figure 6-7) has a distinct tilt toward the A quadrant. The degree of tilt is determined by the type of engineering; chemical engineering is the most strongly A-quadrant-preferred occupation within the broad engineering profession.

The finance profession (see Figure 6-8) also has a strong A-quadrant tilt, and the actuarial occupation is the most strongly A-quadrant-oriented within the finance function.

Business managers (or general managers) as a whole represent a multidominant occupation for both males and females (see Figure 6-9). This is probably because the work requires that breadth of thinking.

Foremen in the manufacturing function have a strong B-quadrant preference, as do finance clerks, bank tellers, and record keepers (see Figure 6-10).

Moving next to double-dominant lower (B/C) profiles, we have administrative assistants as the most common occupation preferring this duality. General office clerks are also in this group. Homemakers often share this strong dual B- and C-quadrant preference (see Figure 6-11).

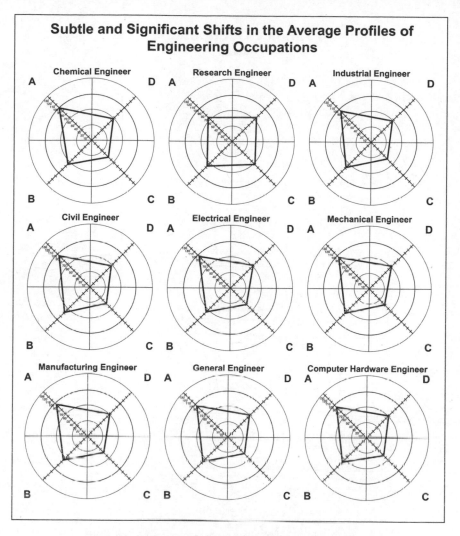

FIGURE 6-7 A continuum of engineering profiles. HBDI profile norms for the nine types of engineers, displayed in a continuum from most A-quadrant to most B-, C-, and then D-quadrant preferences.

The database norms clearly identify the nursing profession as a very C-quadrant-oriented occupational group (except supervisory nurses, who are double-dominant B/C). Social workers, professional volunteers, and teachers share in this preference, particularly elementary school teachers and school counselors (see Figure 6-12).

As we continue in a counterclockwise manner to identify occupational preferences, we come to the double-dominant C/D-quadrant right mode.

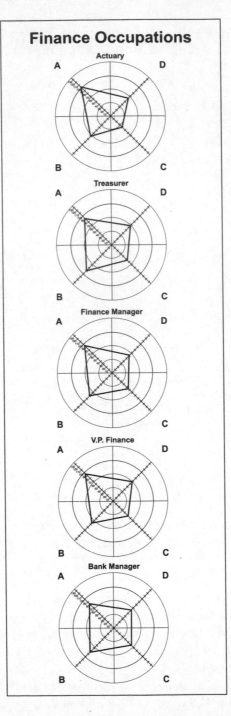

FIGURE 6-8 A continuum of HBDI profiles of financial positions.

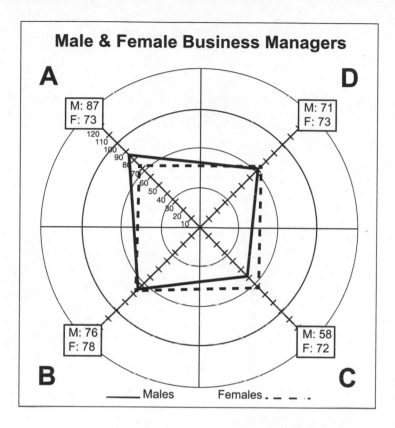

Male & Female Business Managers

A

D

M: 87
F: 73

M: 71
F: 73

M: 76
F: 78

M: 58
F: 72

B

C

———— Males   Females · — — ·

FIGURE 6-9 Averages of business managers' HBDI profiles, showing differences between males and females.

Here we have many ministers, counselors, psychologists, and social workers (see Figure 6-13).

In the D quadrant, there are artists, graphic and interior designers, art directors, and entrepreneurs (see Figure 6-14).

Among those with the double-dominant upper (A/D) profile, we find scientific occupations, such as research and development, and particularly members of the physics profession (see Figure 6-15).

This brings us to the multi-dominant profiles with three or even four primaries (see Figure 6-16). Chief executive officer is a prominent occupational category. (For more on the CEO data, see Chapter 20.) Other four-quadrant occupations include project coordinators, directors, and managers of customer service. The number of occupations is small, since only 3 percent of the total database is quadruple-dominant profiles.

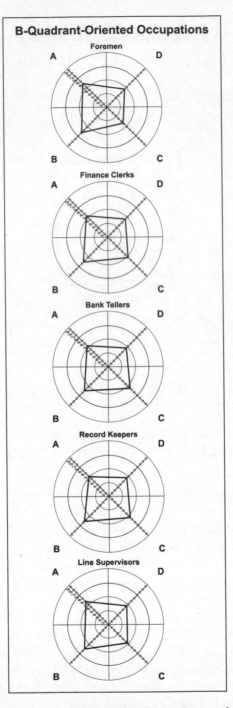

FIGURE 6-10 Example of HBDI profiles of B-quadrant professionals.

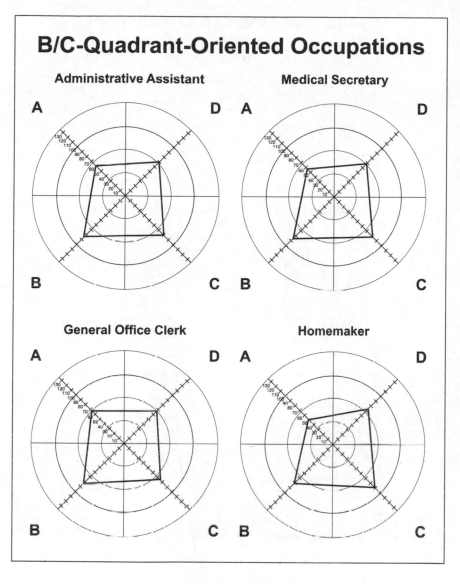

FIGURE 6-11 Examples of HBDI profiles of typically lower-mode
(B- and C-quadrant) professionals.

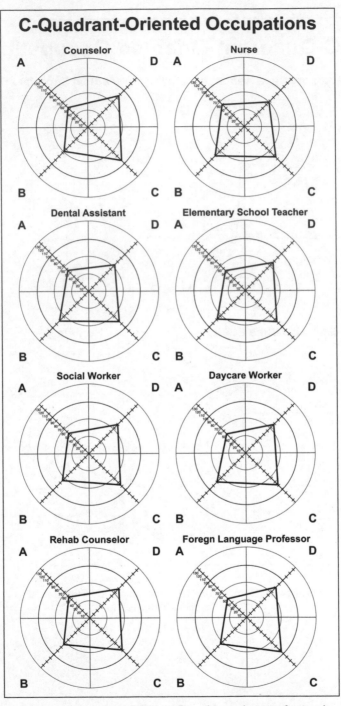

FIGURE 6-12 Examples of HBDI profiles of C-quadrant professionals.

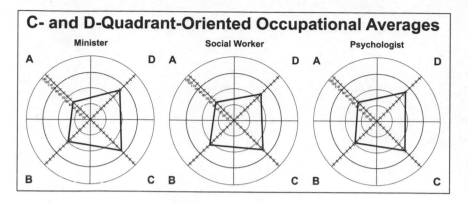

FIGURE 6-13 Examples of HBDI profiles of right-mode (C- and D-quadrant) professionals.

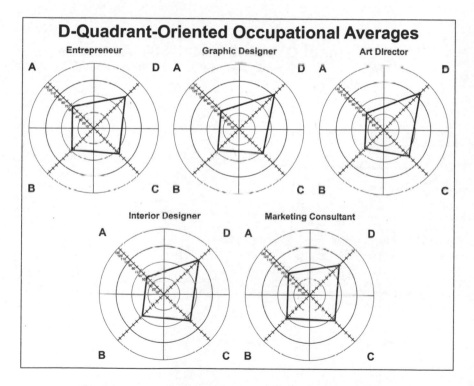

FIGURE 6-14 Examples of HBDI profiles of D-quadrant professionals.

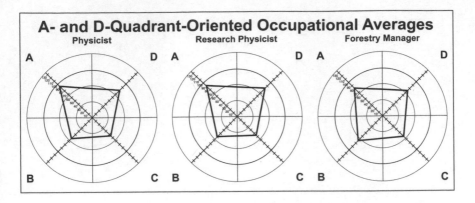

FIGURE 6-15 Examples of HBDI profiles of upper-mode (A- and D-quadrant) professionals.

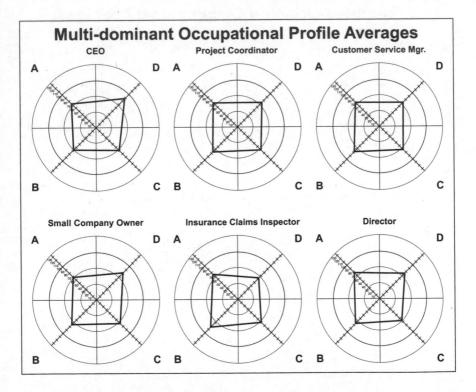

FIGURE 6-16 Examples of professionals with preferences in all
four quadrants: A, B, C, and D (1-1-1-1 HBDI Profile).

Alignment Leads to Greater Satisfaction

It's important to recognize that part of the occupational norm data in the database is influenced by people who occupy positions that are not in strong alignment with their preferences. Therefore, there will be engineers who don't share the A-quadrant-oriented norm, but are still survivors in the engineering profession. And there will be graphic artists who don't share the general strong D-quadrant preference. However, our experience in working with these people is clear: those who engage in this occupation work *differently* from those who constitute the typical norm, those who are in strong alignment with the mentality of the work.

It is also clear that those who are not in alignment with the job norm typically have a significantly lower level of satisfaction and fulfillment in performing the work. In many cases, they are individuals who are trapped in work that is not entirely suited to them, but since they *can* perform that work with reasonably satisfactory results, they continue to occupy that position and receive the economic rewards—even though it is not the ideal work for them to do (unless, of course, they took on the assignment exclusively for learning and stretch and then failed to move on).

Generally speaking, when we look at the database, we find that the highest satisfaction comes from those who have a strong alignment between their mental preferences and the mentality of the work that they are assigned to do, and the corollary is also true. The lowest satisfactions come from those who are misaligned, *unless they are intentionally looking for stretch and challenge in that specific assignment.* The conclusion is obvious: the best of all worlds, from the perspective of both the company and the employee, is to have the highest degree of alignment possible between the worker and the work.

Put It to Work

Ponder this issue for yourself. There is enough material in this book to give you clues about yourself and about your work. Diagnosing your degree of alignment will help you answer questions you may have about your own career.

Does your work provide the basis for energizing you?

If not, what adjustments can be made in your work assignment to improve alignment?

In the worst case, what other jobs are out there that would have the alignment characteristics that would lead to job satisfaction and fulfillment?

In the final analysis, work should be satisfying and fulfilling. It's never too late to make the necessary career changes to achieve that end.

SO WHAT?

> The closer the alignment between an individual's mental preference and the mental requirements of the job, the more likely it is that the individual will achieve job success and satisfaction.
> Nonalignment of job candidates with those occupational norms will significantly reduce the likelihood of the candidates achieving full job satisfaction and fulfillment, unless the individual is looking for a mental challenge.
> The best of all worlds for the company and the employee is to have the closest alignment that can be achieved between the worker and the work.

Where Thinking Meets the Bottom Line

GLASBERGEN

"We need to focus on diversity. I want
you to hire more people who look
different, but think just like me."

CHAPTER 7

Becoming a Thinking Manager: How to Get Results from Cognitive Differences

CHAPTER HIGHLIGHTS

> Most management frustrations have the same common root: a difference in thinking styles.

> Managing cognitive diversity effectively is a key to handling the complexities of business today.

> Management styles result from thinking preferences and avoidances that are shaped by life experiences.

> Most thinking styles are the result of combinations of preferences; therefore, management styles cover the entire range of thinking-style options.

I t was a one-day annual divisionwide program with a fairly typical agenda: the senior manager was going to kick things off with a 15-minute introduction, and then my part, covering Whole Brain Thinking, would follow over the next 6½ hours. The day would conclude with a 15-minute wrap-up by the senior manager.

The group of 800 people had assembled—I had seated them on the basis of their thinking preferences (see their composite profile in Figure 7-1)—and the senior manager began his introduction. He spoke mostly of business facts and numbers, discussing how an analysis of the current issues and objectives provided a solid rationale for their attendance at the session. As he welcomed me to the lectern, he emphasized to the audience members that their participation today would help them achieve the critical business outcomes that the company needed.

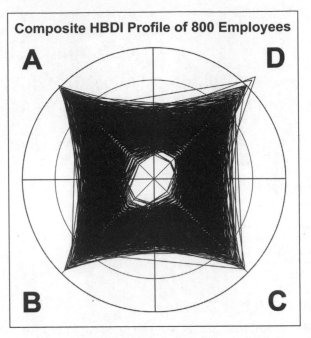

FIGURE 7-1 Actual HBDI composite profile of 800 employees in a major U.S. corporation.

Over the course of the workshop, I asked a variety of questions, getting responses from each of the four corners of the room representing different thinking perspectives. For example, they answered questions about the kinds of work they loved to do and were stimulated by versus the kinds of work they hated to do and were drained by. Gradually, a pattern began to emerge, one that the participants picked up on as well: the people in the different corners of the room were reacting very differently to the same questions.

After my 6½ hours of Whole Brain Thinking was over, the senior manager returned to the lectern and delivered his concluding remarks. His closing comments couldn't have been more different from the morning's introduction. He spoke of the business objectives, but he also talked about how the learnings from the session were going to help them all manage risk and get things done more effectively, how the activities they had worked on together provided a foundation for more cohesive teamwork and awareness of one another's needs and strengths, and how they now had a better appreciation for the possibilities and new ideas they could try out to reach their goals.

Why the stark contrast from the morning's strictly business-focused introduction? The senior manager had cancelled our planned lunch, and now I knew why: he told me that observing the session had been a huge "aha! moment" for him. While the A quadrant was most comfortable for him and was the way he preferred to communicate, he realized that by always doing so, he was failing to connect with three-fourths of his employees. He rewrote his concluding remarks over lunch to appeal to the entire group, not just those who thought the way he did. We can all learn from his example.

Think of all the different kinds of management issues an organization faces:

- Employee performance
- Job design
- Job placement
- Management communications
- Team selection
- Organization design
- Workforce planning
- People management
- Project, task, and time management
- Rewards and recognition

Now imagine trying to optimize the management of these issues with a thinking-style preference that's limited to only one or possibly two quadrants. Most managers of business functions epitomize their occupation, and as we saw in Chapter 6, different occupations have distinct thinking preference norms. But the work required at the managerial level—whether or not it involves managing people—is rarely confined to one or two thinking styles. Particularly as the business environment becomes more complex and unpredictable, it is nearly impossible to be effective without being able to use the full range of thinking styles—not just your own, but the diversity of thinking around you as well.

> Power is given to you by others. It is not yours; it is in trust with you and it is a great responsibility. Power is to be used for the benefit of those whose trustee you are.
>
> —Mahatma Gandhi

The essence of management in today's knowledge worker era is all about becoming a "thinking manager," someone whose primary focus is on the ability to diagnose and respond to the thinking needs of those being managed, including people, projects, and tasks. This is also the essence of managing yourself. Many of the biggest frustrations that managers face on the job can be traced back to their thinking styles, and specifically, differences in thinking.

Managing Cognitive Diversity

One of the "hot button" issues that organizations have faced for many years is diversity. When investigating the subject further, with sources that have included human resources professionals, operating managers, senior executives, and major publications, I've found that age/generation, race, gender, culture, and disabilities are typically the aspects of diversity that they're referring to.

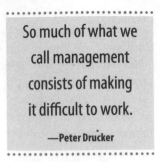

So much of what we call management consists of making it difficult to work.

—Peter Drucker

Diversity is more than that. These sources, and many others in business, are too often overlooking what I consider to be the most significant and the most positive aspect of all—cognitive diversity, the differences in thinking-style preferences.

In Part 1, I explained that the business world is a composite whole brain. That means that organizations are made up of an extraordinarily balanced array of thinking-style preferences. Logic tells us that this level of thinking diversity would occur in companies with more than 10,000 employees; however, our data clearly establishes that this diversity is also true of business organizations with 100 employees and, in many cases, with fewer than 50 employees. It is highly likely that your company's workforce is made up of a balanced distribution of thinking-style preferences. The question to ponder is whether this diverse workforce is managed in a way that takes advantage of its potential productivity.

Financial balance sheets list assets and liabilities as a way of understanding the current status of the business. These are important measures that need to be taken into account; however, the typical balance sheet is incomplete. The most vital asset of most businesses is not money, bricks and mortar, proprietary technology, or the products manufactured. Today more than ever, it is the human resources, and the thinking they bring, that represent the current and future engine of the business. As many human resources executives can attest, this asset is often undervalued and taken for granted.

Human resources is the vital asset that goes home every night and must come back in the morning if your business is to survive and grow. In today's environment, this asset is primarily made up of knowledge workers, and this is true even for those businesses that have a large manufacturing component. In these highly competitive and complex times, production workers need to work smart; therefore, the mental demands of the work are greater than ever.

So how do we manage this vital resource? We can start by understanding the value of its diversity at a significantly high level of sophistication. As one operations manager put it, after discovering the mental diversity within his team of direct reports: "I'm amazed at how many previously untapped resources I have."

I once was asked, "What does the brain have to do with managing?" In the context of cognitive diversity, I can reframe the question as follows: "What does having a workforce with a balanced array of thinking-style preferences have to do with managing?" My answer is: "Everything." That's why the characteristics and aspects of thinking preferences discussed so far affect all of the typical management responsibilities. Recognizing, managing, and getting the benefit of the company's cognitive diversity is essential to managing a successful business today.

For example, in many business situations, creativity is the element that makes the difference between success and failure. It can be *the* make-or-break competitive advantage, since we know that creativity is mental, and mental diversity is a key to the creative process. Business leaders who understand the significance of diversity in the creative process can take advantage of their organization's potential by forming teams that are made up of people with different thinking-style preferences. As we will see in Chapter 12, heterogeneous teams are the ultimate weapon in the race toward creativity.

Taking full advantage of the mentally diverse human assets requires a quantum leap in management understanding and competence. It changes the management game. No longer is any single style, whether it be authoritarian or participative, visionary or a master of execution, good enough to optimize business results. Multiple thinking approaches, situationally applied, are required to take full advantage of the richness of human resources. These highly diverse, high-potential, vital assets are already in place. You don't have to recruit them. You just need to understand them in order to make more effective use of what's already there.

> The best leaders are apt to be found among those executives who have a strong component of unorthodoxy in their characters. Instead of resisting innovation, they symbolize it—and companies cannot grow without innovation.
>
> —David Ogilvy

A Whole Brain Analysis of Management Styles

Just as our thinking preferences influence our competencies and the kinds of work we're attracted to, they are also embedded in our management style. As we engage in work that is consistent with our mental preferences, we will gradually develop a personal style of working that is visible to others. Just as our mental preferences carry over into our daily work habits, they also carry over into our management styles, because we are viewing the world through the lenses of our personal mental preferences. For example, management tasks such as problem solving, determination of work assignments, interpersonal relationships, communications, and budget preparation, as well as other work elements, will be thought about and carried out on the basis of an individual's preferences *and* his or her existing competencies. When this emerging style is affirmed by good results, the managerial behaviors are reinforced and can be difficult to change, especially if the style is in alignment with the surrounding management culture.

Not only are management styles influenced by the work we're attracted to, but they can also be recognized by the work we really dislike. It is not uncommon for our areas of "dullness" to be more obvious than our areas of smartness. That's the primary focus of many 360-degree assessments.

For illustration purposes, in the following segment I will describe various managers based on the distinct management styles associated with each of the quadrants. These are extreme examples! I hasten to say that only 5 percent of the people we have surveyed since the introduction of the HBDI assessment have thinking preferences that are focused on a single quadrant. In general, every person, even someone with a strong preference for one quadrant, actually represents a coalition of preferences that includes each of the four quadrants. So as you read through the descriptions, keep in mind that only a small percentage of people would actually exhibit a quadrant-specific style.

The examples demonstrate how easily our mental preferences can dictate our management style when we have no training or intervention that helps us change that natural progression. In the absence of feedback, a person's style begins to harden and become more and more unchangeable. And if the manager works for a senior manager who has the same style characteristics, those characteristics will tend to become additive and begin to form a management culture. Since seeking out those who are like us is

> The goal is not to be a master of one or all styles, but to gain an awareness of all the styles so that you can honor your strengths and cultivate situational smartness in your areas of dullness.
>
> —Ned Herrmann

a normal human characteristic, managers often hire in their own image. This natural process tends to reinforce an organization's management style.

People will perceive managers with distinct style characteristics on the basis of those work elements that *they are stimulated by*, as well as those elements that *they are drained by*. But it doesn't have to be that way. The obvious virtues of each quadrant's preferences and competencies can be packaged in other combinations, particularly when there are no significant avoidances that make it difficult for the other quadrants to actively contribute.

Our management style, like our personal preferences, can be enriched, broadened, or further focused. Figure 7-2 reviews how each management style may appear by quadrants and modes. The goal is not to be a master of one or all of the styles, but to gain an awareness of all the styles so that you can honor your strengths and cultivate situational smartness in your areas of dullness.

Herrmann Management Styles Matrix

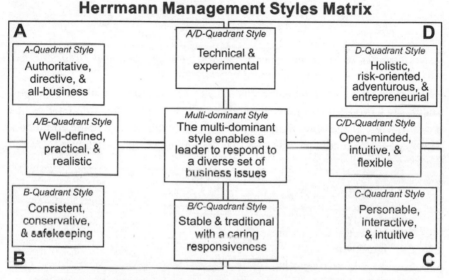

FIGURE 7-2 The Whole Brain Management Styles Matrix provides an overview of how each mode and quadrant may focus.

A-Quadrant Alan

Alan is one of those managers who is completely focused on the task at hand. An engineer, he is extremely comfortable with concrete data such as output records, engineering specs, mathematical formulas, and technical terminology, to name a few. He tends to gravitate toward the information side of the job (what is to be produced, tested, and analyzed) as opposed to the "management of people" side of it, but his employees always know where they stand and what's expected of them because Alan doesn't mince words; he's concise, directive, and all business (see Figure 7-3).

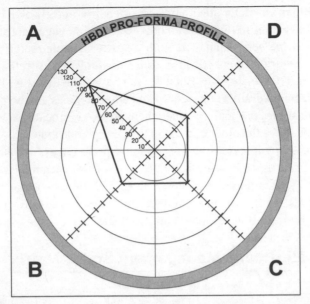

FIGURE 7-3 The A-quadrant management style HBDI pro-forma profile.

He is happiest when he can focus his energy on thinking, processing, and analyzing a problem, as opposed to talking through solutions to problems. As a result, some of the other managers in the organization have made comments like, "Alan is so analytical. He never shows any emotion whatsoever."

How the A-Quadrant Manager Processes Everyday Business Activities

- Gathers facts
- Analyzes issues
- Solves problems logically
- Argues rationally
- Measures precisely
- Understands technical elements
- Considers financial aspects

This reaction isn't surprising. With his strong A-quadrant preferences, Alan is living in a rational, technical world where most things can be explained in logical, analytical terms. When he was promoted to manager, he continued to view the world through these same A-quadrant preferences; his style as a manager carries over his already strong factual orientation. Unless opinions are backed up with factual evidence, he does not consider them important. Alan isn't interested in small talk with his staff or chatting about what they did over the weekend. The only time he truly enjoys talking with others is in the process of analyzing and defining the facts and in debates on the best equipment, methodology, and combination of people to produce the desired result.

Because Alan has little preference for expressive, interpersonal, emotional, feeling-oriented modes, this absence of preference is a visible factor in his style. In fact, it translates into an active avoidance of those C-quadrant "interpersonal" preferences, which is now becoming the predominant style characteristic that others notice. The result is that some people consider him to be a cold-hearted, nonfeeling sort of person who cares only about his technical equipment and proving his theories.

B-Quadrant Ben

Ben, the company's quality manager, has a reputation for being a stickler for details. With his traditional and conservative style, he's far from being the flashiest one in the room, but he is headstrong about striving for safety and quality at all times. Ben is great at structure and at developing policies and procedures, and he expects others to be that way, too. Accountability is important, and that means following the rules and making sure that every point needed to meet deadlines is covered. Recently another manager suggested a change in the quality process on the rationale that it might improve the product in the long run, but Ben was very much resistant to the idea. It would put the company's timelines at risk, and besides, this is his area. Order and lines of authority need to be clear, and they need to be respected (see Figure 7-4).

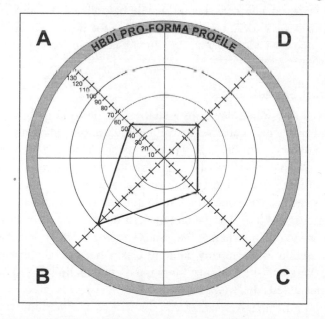

FIGURE 7-4 The B-quadrant management style HBDI pro-forma profile.

How the B-Quadrant Manager Processes Everyday Business Activities

- Finds overlooked flaws
- Approaches problems practically
- Stands firm on issues
- Maintains a standard.of consistency
- Provides stable leadership and supervision
- Reads the fine print
- Organizes and keeps track of essential data
- Develops detailed plans and procedures
- Implements projects in a timely manner
- Articulates plans in an orderly way
- Keeps financial records straight

As a quality manager, Ben oversees work that has to be performed on the basis of documented procedures and strict schedules, with rigorous attention to detail. However, other managers, and sometimes even members of his staff, view his managerial style as being purely time-clock-driven and "nose to the grindstone." They get frustrated by his rigid adherence to the rules and his unwillingness to explore different options. It's not that Ben has no interest in human resources or new ideas, but ultimately his style is productivity first and other concerns second. This has created issues for Ben in his collaboration with others and created the perception that he is intransigent, overly tactical, and somewhat stubborn.

C-Quadrant Casey

To employees who want to both grow in their careers and find satisfaction in their lives, Casey, the company's learning and development manager, is their staunchest advocate. She believes that the business's human resources are its primary assets, and therefore, she fights for policies, programs, and an organizational climate that support employee development. Her team members appreciate that Casey includes them in major decisions and makes them feel a part of things, and they like the fact that her door is always open when they need someone to talk to, whether the issue is work-related or personal. In fact, people throughout the company come to Casey because she is such a great sounding board, and she is known for being a great facilitator and coach, giving well-considered advice (see Figure 7-5).

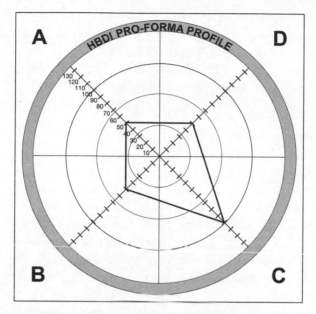

FIGURE 7-5 The C-quadrant management style HBDI pro-forma profile.

Casey has been working on a new values program for the organization. She feels strongly that values are a key element in building an engaging corporate culture.

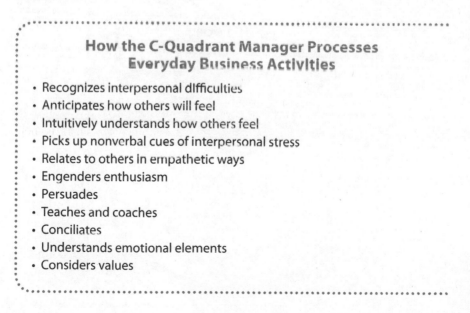

How the C-Quadrant Manager Processes Everyday Business Activities

- Recognizes interpersonal difficulties
- Anticipates how others will feel
- Intuitively understands how others feel
- Picks up nonverbal cues of interpersonal stress
- Relates to others in empathetic ways
- Engenders enthusiasm
- Persuades
- Teaches and coaches
- Conciliates
- Understands emotional elements
- Considers values

Casey enjoys face-to-face interaction. She likes to pick up on the nuances of body language and express herself fully so that everyone understands where she's coming from. But she is disappointed that many of the other managers don't seem to recognize her business value. They say she's too "soft" and focused on "fluff." In fact, many of the managers tolerate her as a necessary part of the business, but don't really view her as an equal partner.

D-Quadrant Danielle

Danielle manages graphic design for the company. A creative and strategic thinker, Danielle is considered by many of her peers to be a resource for new ideas and innovative approaches. Her office is filled with a variety of toys, art books, paper samples, and drawings and doodles, some half completed. Other managers see it as impenetrable clutter, but Danielle says that she wouldn't be able to work effectively without it. She likes to take risks and keeps trying to push the company out of its tried-and-true, traditional image and branding, but she has trouble getting other managers to see what she sees. She feels they're too literal and get too hung up on the details and therefore keep missing the bigger picture.

Danielle says that some of the most valuable time she spends with her team is in free-flowing brainstorming sessions. She'll often have what she calls a "lightbulb" moment, stopping the team in midproject to switch directions and try out a new idea. To other managers, it sometimes seems as if the pursuit of an idea is more important to her than actually finishing something—and sometimes she would agree with them (see Figure 7-6).

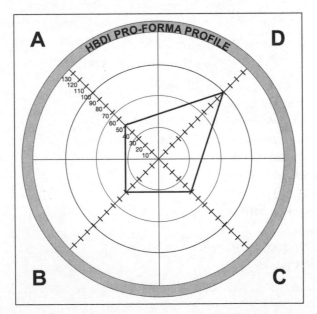

FIGURE 7-6 The D-quadrant management style HBDI pro-forma profile.

How the D-Quadrant Manager Processes Everyday Business Activities

- Reads signs of coming change
- Sees the "big picture"
- Recognizes new possibilities
- Tolerates ambiguity
- Integrates ideas and concepts
- Bends or challenges established policies
- Synthesizes unlike elements into a new whole
- Solves problems in intuitive ways

Structure and time constraints make Danielle uncomfortable. She doesn't want to feel hemmed in by process or detail. Occasionally, this becomes a problem for her team members, who feel a bit lost without clear goals, but overall, they enjoy the open, fun-loving culture she has created for their group. She's even started an annual tradition where the team members decorate their offices in a specific theme and dress in elaborate costumes to match.

Clearly, singular-style approaches have their limitations. And it can be useful to understand the management responsibilities that benefit most from each of the four quadrant styles. As you reflect upon your responsibilities, review Figure 7-7 for examples of tasks that "pull" on your thinking in each quadrant.

> The world will belong to passionate, driven leaders—people who not only have enormous amounts of energy but who can energize those whom they lead.
>
> —Jack Welch

Combination Styles

The A- and B-Quadrant Management Style: Practical and Realistic

The combination of the A- and B-quadrant managerial styles—the double-dominant left—can be overwhelmingly powerful because the main characteristics of this left-mode style are "hard" rather than "soft." Managers with this combination of preferences have frequently supplemented their competencies with an MBA degree. This provides an overlay of financial measurement on top of other functional competencies such as law, engineering, or manufacturing and increases the relative "hardness" of the style (see Figure 7-8).

A
- Knowledge transfer
- Research
- Value analysis
- Reengineering
- Dealing with legal issues
- Presenting factual arguments

D
- Long-range strategy
- Generating new ideas
- Providing a "big-picture" overview
- Coming up with inventive solutions
- Keeping up with trends
- Creative problem solving

- Operational analysis
- Tracking information and bookkeeping
- Logistics
- Managing projects and deadlines
- Error checking
- Improving and documenting

B processes

- Team and group activities
- Facilitating idea sessions with others
- Customer interaction and troubleshooting
- Coaching and mentoring
- Helping employees with concerns or issues
- Dealing with emotional issues   **C**

FIGURE 7-7 Examples of management responsibilities that benefit from different styles.

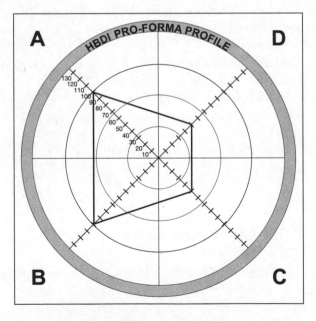

FIGURE 7-8 A combination of A- and B-quadrant management styles in an HBDI pro-forma profile.

The C- and D-Quadrant Management Style: Open-Minded, Intuitive, and Flexible

Just as there is a combination left-mode style that includes the A and B quadrants, there is a combination right-mode style that includes the C and D quadrants. The profile 2-2-1-1 is among the most frequent in business and is seen in many organizations that are more service-oriented. (For more information on the HBDI preference codes, see the HBDI Profile Interpretation Guide in the appendix.) The C/D right-mode style is people-oriented, open-minded, and inclined to be idealistic (see Figure 7-9). Managers of organizational development, for example, would

> People ask the difference between a leader and a boss. The leader works in the open and the boss in covert. The leader leads and the boss drives.
>
> —Theodore Roosevelt

probably fall within the C/D style, which is strong on employee involvement, self-directed work teams, customer service, and a stimulating work climate. Employees who work under this managerial style are often more involved and have more freedom than those who work under an A/B left-mode style.

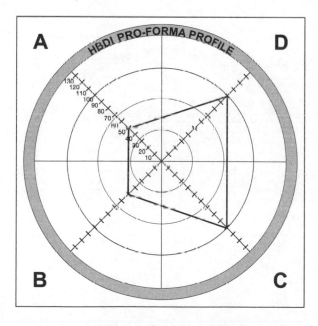

FIGURE 7-9 A combination of C- and D-quadrant management styles in an HBDI pro-forma profile.

There are two other combination styles that frequently show up: the upper-mode style, made up of the A and D quadrants, and the lower-mode style, made up of the B and C quadrants. Some describe the upper mode as being more in your "head" and the lower mode as working more from your "gut."

The Upper, A- and D-Quadrant Management Style: Combining Technical and Experimental Thinking

The upper style is characterized by relatively equal preferences for both the A and D quadrants (see Figure 7-10). These two quadrants represent strikingly different modes of thinking, with the A quadrant being strongly logical, analytic, and rational and the D quadrant being equally strongly conceptual, intuitive, and imaginative. This style combines technical and experimental thinking and is therefore the primary style for scientists, inventors, and research and development organizations.

Like the left-mode and right-mode styles, the A/D style usually lies between the two quadrants that make it up. However, the upper style can be strongly tilted toward either A or D, and you can easily tell the difference. An A-oriented R&D operation would be scientific, serious, and strongly business-oriented. In comparison, an upper style with a strong

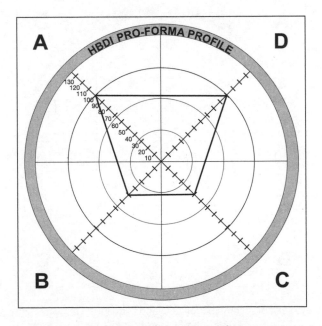

FIGURE 7-10 A combination of A- and D-quadrant management styles in an HBDI pro-forma profile.

D-quadrant orientation would be highly experimental and motivated, but loose and open.

People who exhibit the upper style often get "lost in their work." Imagine a physicist working on a complex problem: it's heady stuff, with frequent insights and technical, scientific breakthroughs. People with these preferences get a lot of internal rewards from the work they do without always having to depend on rewards coming from the managerial bureaucracy. Often this style is recognizable by what it lacks—a groundedness in the security-minded and people-oriented qualities of the lower quadrants.

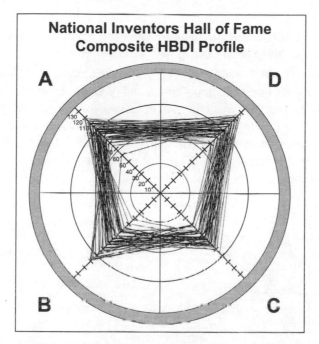

FIGURE 7-11 HBDI composite profile of National Inventors Hall of Fame members.

A study of the members of the National Inventors Hall of Fame shows that an A/D-dominant profile is clearly the preferred profile among its members (see Figure 7-11), and the same has been shown to be true for members of the Lawrence Livermore National Laboratory, which has most recently been known for being a center of supercomputer research. The same double-dominant pattern describes the R&D departments of many major corporations. The technologists who design and develop computer chips and apps share this same average profile and therefore function with the same preference characteristics.

These populations of inventors, scientists, and technologists are strongly male-dominated, often because of the occupational tilts of those roles that typically submit patents. In 2013, the journal *Research Policy* published, "Why Are Women Underrepresented Amongst Patentees?" by economists Jennifer Hunt, Hannah Herman, Jean-Philippe Garant, and David J. Munroe.[1] They found that 92.5 percent of all U.S. patents are held by males. Fifty years ago, that percentage was over 97 percent male. Let's hope the upward trend for females continues!

The Lower, B- and C-Quadrant Management Style: Combining Traditional Stability with Caring Responsiveness

The double-dominant B- and C-quadrant style is quite different. This is a style that combines orderliness, tradition, ritual, and productivity with a strong people orientation, sensitivity to feelings, a preference for team participation, and involvement (see Figure 7-12). It is strongly service-oriented and considers employees, customers, and the community to be high-priority stakeholders. A supervisory nurse embodies this style of management. Social work departments, elementary schools, and department stores like Nordstrom's, with their

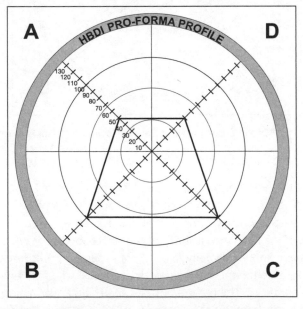

FIGURE 7-12 A combination of B- and C-quadrant management styles in an HBDI pro-forma profile.

strong customer/community orientation, are also prime examples. This style tends to favor the status quo and doing what's right for the company and the individual. It has a strong production orientation, but not at the expense of the people involved. A strong loyalty often accompanies the lower style. As with the upper style, whether the emphasis is on one quadrant or the other depends upon the individuals and the prevailing management culture.

The Multi-Dominant Management Style: Able to Respond to a Diverse Set of Business Issues

A multi-dominant management style is one that can readily access all four quadrants and apply the features of the different styles in situationally appropriate ways. To be able to make use of the multi-dominant style, an individual must be able to access the four different styles on a relatively level playing field. Think of a four-quadrant, four-mode pool of style options that the multi-dominant person could draw from as situationally required: eight discrete styles as just described (see Figure 7-13). While the multi-dominant style could be available to any manager in any function, those managers who have work requirements that involve all four quadrants are the ones who are most likely to apply it. The CEO has traditionally been the individual who most benefited from and needed to rely on a multi-dominant approach, but increasingly managers at all levels and across functions are requiring a more flexible and

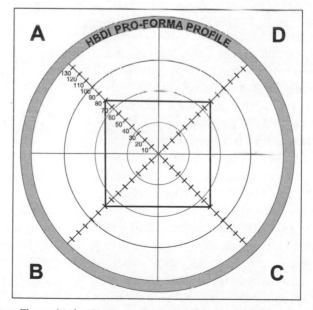

FIGURE 7-13 The multi-dominant management styles in an HBDI pro-forma profile.

agile style to manage effectively in a complex, constantly changing business environment.

Being situational is the key requirement for the full application of the multi-dominant style. By this I mean having the ability to apply the quadrant-specific style characteristics. For example, a manager who deals with a financial issue with his or her team can greatly enhance the outcome by not only drawing on an analytical style, but also incorporating organized, interpersonal, long-range, strategic, and expressive thinking styles. Contrast this with a manager who is limited to just an analytical style.

Another example would be a human resource development manager who is trying to effect a culture change by implementing an effective cash management program but is limiting his implementation style to the confines of a participatory humanistic approach. In this example, the absence of the structured, organized B-quadrant style, the quantitative, logical A-quadrant style, and the integrating-synthesizing D-quadrant style seriously minimizes the likelihood of success.

Being an effective practitioner of the multi-dominant style requires having the opportunity to apply it frequently enough for an appropriate array of competencies to be developed. Managerial and leadership positions that have a high frequency of multi-dominant opportunity are becoming more commonplace across functions; some examples include plant manager, general/division manager, project manager, multifunction team leader, executive assistant, and, of course, chief executive officer. The daily, weekly, and monthly inbox of people in these positions can be so wide-ranging that flexibility of style options is a real advantage, if not a necessity. Since only 3 percent of the population has primary preferences for all four quadrants, being *situationally whole-brained* is the viable solution. This means that those styles that are not our most preferred need to be available for timely application in situations that could benefit from such a style.

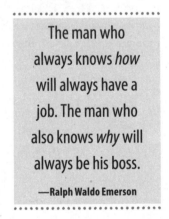

The man who always knows *how* will always have a job. The man who also knows *why* will always be his boss.

—Ralph Waldo Emerson

There is something to be said for consistency, but managing in only one style can be limiting if the situation requires shifting to a style that is more effective. Consider an individual whose work requires effective management behavior in a budgetary situation with finance, a design review session with engineering, deciding on appropriation requests from manufacturing, reaching a decision on the architectural plan for the new headquarters building, responding to the recommendations of the art selection committee for the main lobby, and conducting the annual employee utilization review with the human resources representatives from each of the major functions. These multiple events are scheduled to take place over a three-day period. Now consider for a moment the range of management styles that could be applied to maximize the success of each separate event.

Now think about a single situation that could benefit from the ability to flex your style: coaching or mentoring. When you understand and adapt to the styles of the person you are coaching or mentoring, you'll be able to connect with him or her more quickly and work together in a way that ensures both of you are really heard, understood, and focusing your time and energy where it matters.

The advantage of style flexibility is clear, whether the position is that of a project manager, the head of a multifunctional division, or chief executive officer. Being situational is similar to "rising to the occasion" as the situation demands, even though the experience base is not equally distributed, and even though your preference for managing your way through each unique event is not equally high. Being able to switch back and forth among styles eventually allows for the acquisition of the competencies to meet each different need.

Put It to Work

Take a moment to identify a person who is different from you and challenging for you to work with. Now suppose you want that person to take a specific action, one that he or she most likely will not want to take.

- Using the tips provided in Figure 7-14, how would you need to flex in order to convince this person to take the desired action?
- What language would you use?
- How would you prepare?

Throughout this book, there are quadrant walk-around models that are designed to achieve Whole Brain results. By forcing a walk-around of the four quadrants, these models help diagnose whether the attributes of each quadrant have been factored into whatever domain the model is addressing. Applying this walk-around concept to management styles can help us determine which style is most appropriate, whether it be in a staff meeting, in dealing with a customer complaint, in running an annual meeting, or in dealing with the media. Figure 7-14 provides tips for shifting your style.

In general, the most flexible situational style is the one that will produce the best results from any organization, with the caveat that, whatever the style, the needed competencies required by the business must be available to meet daily business needs. Style alone cannot produce bottom-line results.

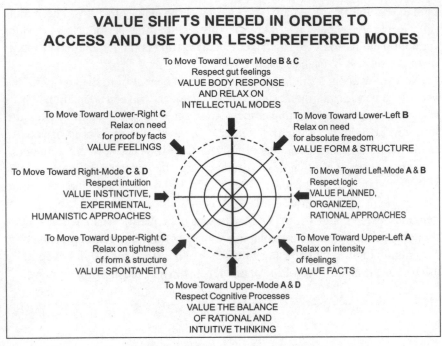

FIGURE 7-14 Tips for shifting your style.

SO WHAT?

> Cognitive diversity is a valuable but often overlooked and underleveraged resource in business.
> Since the world of management is made up of all combinations of preferences and avoidances, all possible management styles are present in the business world.
> Style flexibility contributes to managerial effectiveness.

SOMETIMES I GET TIRED OF BEING THE ONLY SMART PERSON AROUND HERE!

GLASBERGEN
© Randy Glasbergen

CHAPTER 8

Communicating Across Thinking Styles: How to Break Through the Mental Static

CHAPTER HIGHLIGHTS

> Effective communication is fundamental to the success of business processes.

> Differing thinking preferences contribute to the success or failure of communication processes.

> Alignment between communication pairs can range from effective to very ineffective.

> We experience the world around us as enhanced or filtered through our profile of mental preferences.

After a five-year search for a building site, my wife, Margy, and I finally found what we considered to be the ideal place to build a home that would serve as our residence and our headquarters: Lake Lure, North Carolina, at a resort complex now called Rumbling Bald Resort. After settling on the Oregon architect Lou Bruinier to help us design the house, we scheduled a date for him to fly out and view the site.

The morning of the site visit was a perfect September day in the mountains. I led Lou along the pathway skirting the ridge to a clearing on the mountainside that provided a breathtaking view of the lake, the valley below, and the surrounding mountains. The architect was visibly moved by what he saw. He just stood there, drinking it in.

"Well, Lou, what do you think?" I asked. Without turning to me, he answered, "What a place to build a home. What a place to live forever. I feel like I'm doing God's work. Thank you for the privilege!" He then took out his sketchbook and entered the first lines of his design.

About a year later, with Lou's plans ready, we began the search for a builder, and eventually landed on Grover Wilson, the local "Sultan of Homes." I took him up to the building site, and just as it had been at the time of Lou's visit, it was a perfect September day. After Grover looked out at the view and around the site, I asked him, "Well, Grover, what do you think?"

After a minute, he turned, peered at me, and said, "Oh, I've seen a lot worse than this."

Another year went by, and while we were in the process of arranging for a construction loan and mortgage, I invited the banker up to the mountainside to inspect the building site. Once again it was a beautiful September day. He made his way along the same path that Lou and Grover had walked along, taking care not to snag his three-piece suit or scratch his briefcase on the brambles. Once we arrived at the spot, I posed the same question I had asked the others: "Well, Jack, what do you think?"

Jack looked me straight in the eye and said, "Ned, you'll never grow corn on this land."

I had tried to anticipate his response, but this was beyond my imagining.

How different is the view from each of our different thinking preference perspectives, and how different are the meanings we attribute to the words we use to describe those perspectives. The old saw that the Americans and the British are two peoples divided by a common language applies to those of us with dissimilar thinking styles as well. We assume we get what the other person means because we use the same words, but that's not necessarily the case.

> After all, when you come right down to it, how many people speak the same language even when they speak the same language?
>
> —Russell Hoban

The Dialects of the Brain

There is hardly a single topic that is more fundamental to the business process than communication. And there is probably hardly any process that is more susceptible to failure than the everyday activity of businesspeople talking, writing, and somehow signaling to each other. People have vastly different perspectives and attach different meanings to the words they use to describe those perspectives. In fact, differences in thinking preferences can be so great that they create separate and distinct "languages" or dialects. We may be using the same vocabulary, but the dialects assign different meanings to the words and use them to describe worlds seen from vastly different perspectives.

In essence, we are experiencing the world around us as filtered through our profile of mental preferences. Where we have strong preferences, it's as if we're seeing and hearing things close to the way they actually are. In our areas of lesser preference, on the other hand, we're likely to be partially blind and deaf. And in our areas of avoidance, most of us don't see or hear accurately at all.

If we built a continuum of communication success, the high point would occur between two individuals with nearly identical profiles and equal experience in the same profession. At the opposite end would be a pair with opposing profiles, where each person's preference is the other's avoidance and where they hold entirely different levels of experience, such as an A-quadrant insurance company actuary and a C-quadrant kindergarten teacher.

Figure 8-1 shows that the most effective and least difficult communication takes place between people who have the *same quadrant* preference and are in the same occupation. These two people are on the same wavelength, so to speak, and words are likely to mean the same thing to each of them because of their similar preferences and occupations.

Somewhat more difficult and less effective communication takes place between two people whose profiles are in *compatible quadrants*, such as the

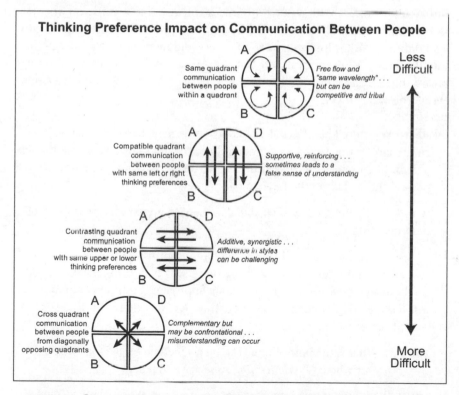

FIGURE 8-1 Communication continuum: communication between those with different thinking styles. The impact of preference on how easy or difficult it is to communicate.

left-mode A and B and the right-mode D and C. The next lower level of communication success occurs between individuals representing *complementary quadrants*, such as A and D or B and C. These complementary quadrants represent interconnected specialized modes in the brain that are able to relate to each other in ways that often lead to creative thinking outcomes.

> You cannot speak of ocean to a well-frog, the creature of a narrower sphere. You cannot speak of ice to a summer insect, the creature of a season.
>
> —Chuang Tzu, "Autumn Floods" (4th–3rd c. BC), tr. Herbert A. Giles

The most difficult end of the communication continuum is where opposing quadrants are involved in the transaction, such as the B and D quadrants or the A and C quadrants. To see what I mean, read the following dialogue between Walter, the vice president of advertising at a large corporation, and John, the creative director.

The conversation begins when John walks into Walter's office with a portfolio under his arm and a smile on his face. Behind his large desk, surrounded by imposing office furniture and traditional décor, Walter looks up as John enters and then stops, about eight feet into the office. Without changing his expression, Walter remarks, "I wasn't aware that we had an appointment, John, but you look as if you have something you want to say."

JOHN: Yes, I do. I need to tell you about some new developments on our campaign for this year's new product line. As you know, we've made such a departure in the new designs that we've been struggling with how to present these ideas in the fall campaign.

WALTER: OK, John, but keep it short. I've got to prepare for an important meeting upstairs.

JOHN: Great. So, Walter, I think I had a breakthrough this morning just after waking up. As I was lying there slowly coming awake, it suddenly dawned on me that our previous approaches to this campaign missed the main concept of the new line. As I lay there mulling that over, I began to see...

WALTER: What is the point, John? I'm on a schedule here. Don't take me through your whole *Good Morning America* sequence.

JOHN: Well, I felt it was important for you to know where the idea came from and how it evolved.

WALTER: You know me well enough to know that all I'm interested in is the end result—not all the hokey stuff that leads up to it.

JOHN: Yes, I know that, and I don't want to take time away from your important work, but this seems like it's a crucial campaign, so it needs not only your approval but also your support in making it happen.

WALTER: John, get on with it.

JOHN: OK, so, the central concept is that instead of featuring individual elements of the product line, what I think we ought to do, and what came to me when I was visualizing this, is a large-format piece showing the whole product line, with visuals showing how each separate product is related to each of the products in the line. We could also create a great animated video that I think would attract some attention.

WALTER: OK, that seems obvious. So what's the big deal?

JOHN: Well, the vision I had for our marketing strategy is oriented toward the whole system rather than the product pieces, and that's why the campaign needs to be expanded to a global approach rather than focused on the parts.

WALTER: Well, we've done pretty darn well around here talking about the parts! Our customers are used to it. I don't see why we should risk a new approach when you look at the successful track record we've had for the past few years. And it's not like our competitors are talking about the whole system. Before we go sailing off into the blue, I'm going to need some hard facts that support such a costly shift.

JOHN: Well, I haven't really gotten to the issue of cost yet, but it seems to me that we have a good chance of bringing this thing in at the same cost and with greater impact.

WALTER: John, I've told you time and again that there are certain ground rules for bringing things to my attention. The first is that you have a complete presentation, starting with the cost of the project and the breakdown of the critical elements, especially with anything new like an online video. Second, that you have a schedule showing the beginning, middle, and end of the project. Third, that you have sufficient copies of these support materials available so I can have other members of the staff check them out too, and fourth, that you make an appointment in advance.

JOHN: Yes, yes, Walt, I know the ground rules, but since this is a hot idea, I thought we could make some quick sketches and preliminary layouts to show you while the idea was fresh. That way we can take advantage of the possible time saved by making a quick decision to go in this direction. Take a look at these layout sketches . . .

WALTER: John, you know I can't do that without the rest being prepared. Aren't you listening to me? When you're ready to present your advertising campaign in a way that factors in the costs and the time to accomplish the task, I'll gladly give you more time, but until then, I'm not available to discuss it. So get cracking!

When the differences in thinking preferences and work requirements are both severely out of alignment, effective communication is least likely to occur. And when it does succeed, it is the result of intense focus and motivation on the part of the people involved. They really want to make it work.

Put It to Work

Read over the dialogue between Walter and John twice, and then answer the following questions:

- Both Walter and John are making "valid" points from their quadrant perspectives. What quadrants are represented in their communication approaches?
  - Walter
  - John
- What quadrant(s) does your own communication most reflect? Are you more technical, precise, and to the point (A)? Detailed, thorough, and step-by-step (B)? Expressive, informal, and personal (C)? Or big picture, conceptual, and imaginative (D)? (See Figures 8-3, 8-4, and 8-5 for more clues.)
- What quadrants do you overlook most in your communication? Do you overlook facts, data, technical aspects (A)? Details, structure, and consistency (B)? Expressiveness, eye contact, and interpersonal sharing (C)? Or metaphorical, imaginative, holistic language (D)? (See Figures 8-3, 8-4, and 8-5 for more clues.)
- Walter and John are not really communicating well. Think about a time in which you experienced a similar situation.
  - Which quadrants were you overlooking most?
  - What challenges did you encounter as a result?
  - Did you ultimately get the results you needed?

Now identify some specific changes you can make in your communication approach to better meet the needs of your listeners so that you get what you want from the communication. *Refer to the models provided in this chapter, which describe the different communication styles and implications across the Whole Brain Model.*

The Male-Female Communication Chasm

From our database, we can conclude that men and women are, on average, equally strong candidates for experiencing difficulties similar to the B/D communication situation between Walter and John, but typically involving an A/C disconnect. That's because, statistically, more men prefer the A quadrant and least prefer the C, whereas more women prefer the exact opposite (see Figure 8-2). I believe this to be the root of what has been described as the "Men are from Mars, Women are from Venus"[1] syndrome (among other books that have been written on this topic). The fact that these differences contribute to the attraction between men and women increases the likelihood that a lot of relationships will be stressed or actually ruptured because of the inherent communication difficulty brought about by the combining of opposing quadrants. Both at home and in the workplace, this provides the opportunity to first understand these differences, then to find value in the complementary nature of these differences, working to bridge the gap and leverage those differences by communicating more effectively.

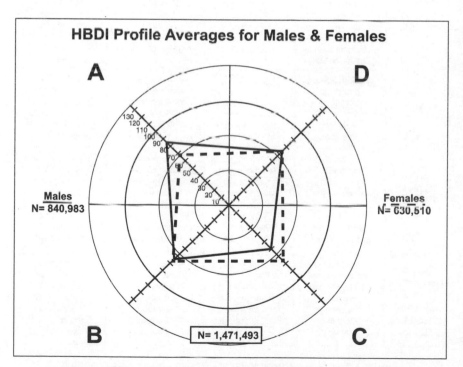

FIGURE 8-2 HBDI profiles averages of males and females in current database.

It is easy to see how specialized jargon can develop around occupational choices and mental preferences. I believe this tends to increase the likelihood of misunderstandings taking place between people with different preferences working in different occupations.

Figure 8-3 helps explain the differences in processing modes on the basis of the four-quadrant model. In this case, the four quadrants are shown as vertical columns, with the horizontal rows indicating key descriptors, occupational choices, and examples of typical phrases used. So where Walter, with his strong preference for B-quadrant thinking, responds best to well-structured and well-articulated approaches and talks about playing by the rules, John is frustrated by what he sees as Walter's "one-track mind" and lack of imagination. On the other hand, while John, who prefers D-quadrant thinking, talks about the long-range big picture and the need to innovate on existing

Differences in Processing Modes

	A Upper Left Blue	B Lower Left Green	C Lower Right Red	D Upper Right Yellow
Descriptors	logical factual rational critical analytical quantitative authoritarian mathematical	technical reader data collector conservative controlled sequential articulate dominant detailed	musical spiritual symbolic talkative emotional intuitive (regarding people) reader (personal)	intuitive (regarding solutions) simultaneous imaginative synthesizer holistic artistic spatial
Skills	problem solving analytical statistical technical scientific financial	planning regulatory supervisory administrative organizational implementation	expressing ideas interpersonal collaborating writing teaching training	integrative visualizing causing change conceptualizing generating ideas trusting intuition
Typical Phrases Used	"Tools" "Hardware" "Key point" "Knowing the bottom line" "Take it apart" "Break it down" "Critical analysis"	"Establishing habits" "We have always done it this way" "Law and order" "Self-discipline" "By the book" "Play it safe" "Sequence"	"Teamwork" "The family" "Interactive" "Participatory" "Human values" "Personal growth" "Human resources" "Team development"	"Play with an idea" "The big picture" "Broad-based" "Synergistic" "Cutting edge" "Conceptual" "Blockbusting" "Innovative"
Typical Derogatory Phrases (Zingers) Used by Others	"Number cruncher" "Power hungry" "Unemotional" "Calculating" "Uncaring" "Cold fish" "Nerd"	"Picky" "Can't think for himself" "Unimaginative" "One-track mind" "Stick-in-the-mud" "Grinds out the task"	"Bleeding heart" "Talk, talk, talk" "Touchy-feely" "A pushover" "Soft touch" "Gullible" "Sappy"	"Reckless" "Can't focus" "Unrealistic" "Off the wall" "Dreams a lot" "Undisciplined" "Head in clouds"

FIGURE 8-3 Differences in typical processing modes for each quadrant.

approaches, bouncing ideas around to arrive at a solution, Walter says that John is undisciplined and unrealistic.

It doesn't have to be this way. Once we understand how different preferences are influencing our own and others' communications, we can adapt to the different dialects of the brain. It takes awareness and conscious effort, but the payoff is worth it.

Communicating in a Whole Brain Way

The challenge for business managers is to find ways of communicating with diverse employee populations that ensure the *intended communication* actually takes place, regardless of differences in the way people perceive. When the intended communication is significant, it is necessary to design and deliver it in ways that allow understanding to take place in all four quadrants. My experience clearly demonstrates that the use of illustrations, videos, graphics, examples, stories, and metaphors, when added to the more traditional forms of communication, greatly enhances the likelihood that the intended meaning will be conveyed to a wide range of people.

The fail-safe assumption is that the population you'll be communicating with will be mentally diverse. Therefore, I recommend delivering each significant communication point in all quadrants and modes if you want to be sure

> Precision of communication is important, more important than ever in our era of hair-trigger balances, when a false or misunderstood word may create as much disaster as a sudden thoughtless act.
>
> —James Thurber

that everyone "gets" what you mean. When information *must* be understood as intended, there is no option other than to employ all quadrants and modes of the Whole Brain Model in delivering that communication.

An easy way to do this is to apply the four-quadrant Whole Brain Communication Walk-Around Model (see Figure 8-4) to the significant points of the intended message. This is a problem-solving process that forces you to review the intended communication in each of the four quadrants, ultimately helping you avoid future problems that arise from miscommunication.

Suppose, for example, that a company president has just drafted a statement for the corporate newsletter. Her first key point is: "It is our strategic intent to double this business in the next five years." She wants to be sure people understand her intended meaning, so she tests her draft statements by eliciting new

Communication Walk-Around

A	D
• Does it use facts? • Is it quantified? • Does it show clear analysis? • Is it to the point? • Is it logical?	• Does it look at the big picture or overview? • Is it visual and colorful? • Does it use metaphors? • Does it look at the future? • Is it conceptually sound or clear?
• Does it provide details? • Is it in sequential order? • Is it neat? • Is it in a recognizable, "appropriate" format? **B**	• Does it use experiences that relate to the audience? • Does it use examples to illustrate the point? • Is it helpful and user-friendly? • Does it acknowledge emotional issues? **C**

FIGURE 8-4 Whole Brain Communication Walk-Around exercise. "Walk around" each quadrant to diagnose your communication style and/or prepare your next important communication.

reactions from each of the four quadrants of the Whole Brain Communication Walk-Around Model:

Quadrant A possible reaction: "Double the business in the next five years? Just what did she intend to convey: Double the sales? The profits? The number of employees? The total assets of the business?"

• By asking herself questions about the factual content of the proposed statement, the president realizes she has to be more precise in her language. What she really means is that the strategic intent is to double the *revenues* of the business—specifically, to grow from $2 billion to $4 billion in annual revenues.

Quadrant B possible reaction: "The draft statement does not address the organizational implications of doubling the revenue. Does she mean that this is to occur without any increase in infrastructure or staff on the basis of the same organizational arrangement?"

- The president discovers that she has failed to build into the statement her intention to create three new strategic business units to achieve this doubling of revenues.

Quadrant C possible reaction: If the president includes a reference to three new business units, the reaction could be: "What might that do to our culture, and does this mean that we will be doubling the number of employees as well? How will it affect the morale of the existing employees? Our customers?"

- The president's statement must stipulate or strongly imply that the strategic intent is not to double employment to achieve a doubling of revenue, nor to double the work of each employee. The significant increase in market focus should allow the doubling of revenue to take place with minimum increases in numbers of employees and extra workload for current employees.

Quadrant D possible reaction: "The initial draft statement limits the strategic intent to five years. Does she mean that we don't plan to grow after five years? Is there no longer-term vision or outlook?"

- In reality, the strategic intent is to grow the business indefinitely, and doubling revenues in five years is just the first of a series of milestones stipulated in the long-range plan. The statement needs to add how this strategy is part of a 15-year vision.

The benefit of the Whole Brain Walk-Around process is that it forces a quadrant-by-quadrant review of intended communication. After completing the walk-around, the president can now see that she will have to modify her draft statement if she is to convey what she intends. For example, she may want to revise it as follows:

"The strategic intent of the first five years of our long-range plan is to double the revenues of our business by reorganizing into three strategic business units, which will provide the level of market focus that will allow us to achieve this goal with minimum staff increases and infrastructure changes."

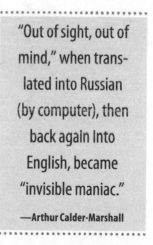

"Out of sight, out of mind," when translated into Russian (by computer), then back again into English, became "invisible maniac."

—Arthur Calder-Marshall

To make sure that everyone understands her message, she should incorporate a visual presentation that graphically depicts the growth plan and provide a handout that documents her statement and stipulates when and what kinds of organizational changes are needed. Addressing the C quadrant, she should offer to answer any questions or concerns or to meet on an individual basis if the changes directly affect an individual, and to help prepare key leaders to do so as well.

How Each Quadrant of the Whole Brain Model Communicates

An additional tool to help improve the communication process is the four-quadrant model of how communication takes place, shown in Figure 8-5. There are communication options for each quadrant that are characteristic of the type of thinking employed by individuals holding those preferences. Increased awareness of these differences aids the communication process by enabling people to listen more purposefully to what they hear and say what they mean more precisely. Improving communications does more than just relieve personal frustration; it means that things can move more quickly with fewer mistakes and missed opportunities.

> No one would talk much in society if he knew how often he misunderstands others.
>
> —Johann Wolfgang von Goethe

I doubt that anyone would argue about the importance of effective communication. In all aspects of business and personal life, communication among members of a team is near or at the top of everybody's list of contributors to success. We can also include the family here, since in many ways the most successful families function like a team.

How the Brain Communicates

A UPPER LEFT	UPPER RIGHT D
• Uses facts to illustrate points • Very matter of fact • Expresses emotions abstractly • Appears to display little or no emotion regardless of the situation	• Asks questions that lead to other questions: Why? How? • Speaks in phrases • Stops in mid-sentence • Abstract—uses metaphors and colorful or lyrical words
• Asks questions that have answers: Who? What? When? Where? • Speaks in sentences and paragraphs • Completes sentences and paragraphs • Very concrete in speaking	• Face is animated—eyes flash, etc. • Uses expansive nonverbal gestures • Uses stories to illustrate points • Talks out loud or to self to learn
B LOWER LEFT	LOWER RIGHT C

FIGURE 8-5 Each quadrant communicates differently.

Whole Brain teams, which are made up of individuals representing all four quadrants and all four modes, present a particularly difficult communication challenge. Taking into account the models in this chapter, think about the communication struggles of an eight-member team whose members are all unique in their preferences, and whose preferences, taken together, represent a balanced distribution of all the quadrant characteristics. There is a strong possibility that each team member is communicating more effectively in his or her area of preference, less effectively in his or her area of less preference, and perhaps not at all in his or her area of avoidance. This means that in the ideal Whole Brain team situation, there are communication patterns of highly variable effectiveness on any given discussion point. Team members who understand this reality will ask questions if they don't understand or will offer paraphrasing or embellishment of their principal points as they are offered, using

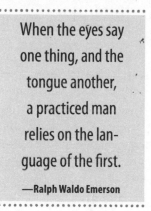

When the eyes say one thing, and the tongue another, a practiced man relies on the language of the first.

—Ralph Waldo Emerson

phrases such as, "By that I mean …," "For instance …," "This illustration will explain what I mean," "This page of the handout explains what I mean," or, "Here's a metaphor that shows what I mean."

It takes a savvy team to engage in this kind of interaction, but it's a requirement when you consider the reality of team communication needs given differences in perception. When Whole Brain team members learn how to express themselves in ways that are true to their thinking style but sensitive to other members' styles, the chances are good that the team will be highly effective. See Chapter 12 for more on Whole Brain teams.

SO WHAT?

> Effective communication is fundamental to successful human interaction and very susceptible to failure in business, family, and social situations.
> Communication processes are typically filtered through an individual's screen of mental preference, causing occasional "blindness and deafness."
> The challenge for business managers is to maximize the *intended* communication by applying Whole Brain communication to a diverse corporate organization.
> There are several tools and models that managers and Whole Brain teams can quickly apply to diagnose and greatly improve their communication processes and outcomes.

CHAPTER 9

Getting Work Done: Motivating, Delegating, and Managing in All Directions

CHAPTER HIGHLIGHTS

> The mental compatibility between employees and their work provides an important link to understanding motivation issues.
> The quality of the manager/direct report relationship greatly influences the effectiveness of their communication, and therefore the delegation process as well.
> The degree of alignment between the manager and the employee is a determining factor in the level of delegation success.
> These factors have implications in terms of what you can expect from your direct reports as well as how you can use these insights to "manage up" effectively.

A Supervisory Case: Solving a Performance Problem

Mary Frankel is an employee benefits manager in the HR department of a Fortune 500 company. She has a dozen benefits specialists reporting directly to her, and she feels that eight of them are responding very well to her supervision. They appear to understand the work, and she can trust them to perform their duties as assigned. Their performance reviews all range from satisfactory to excellent.

But Mary has severe problems with the four other benefits specialists, and she is frustrated because she cannot seem to get them to perform to the standards she has set. After a number of attempts to solve these performance problems, which primarily concern accuracy, timeliness, and completeness of reports, she decides to administer the HBDI assessment to the whole group to see if the resulting profiles will give her a clue as to what the performance problems are.

From the HBDI Profiles, shown in Figure 9-1, Mary learned that the eight high performers are very homogeneous in their thinking styles, with a

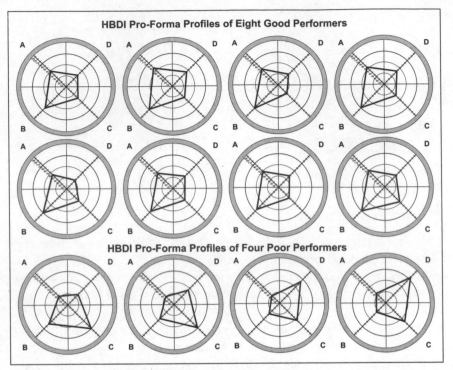

FIGURE 9-1 HBDI pro-forma profiles of good and poor performers on the team.

strong B-quadrant tilt. Of the remaining four, two are strongly C-quadrant, one is double-dominant C/D, and the fourth is strongly D-quadrant. Mary's preferences are strongly tilted toward the B quadrant.

The job description of a benefits specialist is as follows:

- Administer the company's benefits program in strict accordance with Benefits Bulletin 101-A.
- Keep detailed records of all transactions with employees, including correspondence, verbal discussions, and benefits claims.
- Enter all activity into the computer database on a daily basis so that it is available for verification at all times.
- Provide summary reports quarterly and annually.
- Performance will be evaluated on the basis of the company's Zero Defects Program.

Mary looks at the four profiles that are radically different from those of the homogeneous group of eight and says to herself, "Oh, now I get it. I've got four people whose preferences are significantly different from the preferences of those who are performing well, and therefore they seem to be badly out of alignment with the job specs." This confirms her hunch that if these profiles are so different from those of the people who are doing the job the way it should be performed, there must be a good commonsense explanation.

Mary does a quick review of the key descriptors and work elements data of the group of eight and the group of four and comes to the conclusion that none of the four low-performing employees exhibits the common preferences of the eight who are performing well. These include strong preferences for highly detailed, organized, procedural, administrative work activities. As a matter of fact, the profiles show that two of the four have such low preferences for these types of work activities that perhaps they even avoid them altogether and may not have the requisite skills. Further review shows that three of the four have strong preferences for the interpersonal aspects of the job, and their personnel files indicate complimentary feedback from employees who had made visits to the Benefits Office. It is clear that these three specialists take a personal interest in the employees' transactions.

The profile of the fourth benefit specialist is diametrically opposed to that of the eight who are doing their jobs well. This specialist seems more interested in changing the rules than in complying with them. She likes to invent solutions to employee problems. She often overlooks missing pieces of needed information and writes little notes indicating that through verbal discussion, she is satisfied with the employee's submission on the various benefit forms. It becomes clearer and clearer to Mary that this person is really marching to a different drummer and is not properly assigned based on the work requirements for this job. Although she *can* perform, it requires great effort—and is this really the best use of her skills and talents?

A Matter of Preference or Competence?

As we discussed in Chapter 3, although preferences are commonly correlated with competences because people tend to do best what they like best, preferences and competences are not the same thing. Just because the four team members aren't performing well doesn't necessarily mean that they don't have competency for the job or can't be successful in it. What it does mean is that there is a lack of alignment between the responsibilities and requirements of the job and how the person prefers to think and approach work. For this reason, it's not surprising that their performance is lagging and Mary is struggling to resolve the situation. These employees are swimming against the tide of their natural preferences.

Mary decides to take a deeper look in the hopes that she can uncover the nature and extent of any job alignment problems. She gives each person with performance problems a chance to write a description of the job as he or she understands it and then to write a description of the job as he or she would like to perform it.

A Benefits Specialist's Description of Her Existing Job Responsibilities

As a benefits specialist, I see my job as administering the company's benefits programs and explaining them to each employee with whom I come in contact. My job requires me to keep detailed records of all transactions involving the people I work with, and to enter all transactions into the computer on a daily basis. I am supposed to send in summary reports each quarter and at the end of each year.

—*Benefits Specialist A. J. Anderson*

The Same Benefits Specialist Describes How She Would Like to Perform Her Job

I would like to perform my job quite differently from the way it is written in my job description. I understand the need for detail, but the reporting requirements limit my ability to deal with the actual problems that employees have. They always want to talk about their personal issues. They want to be heard. I don't feel that this is my job responsibility, but I would like it to be, since I notice that in those cases where I do listen, the problems seem to lessen or disappear. I don't like the detailed, "mechanical" aspects of my work as laid down in the job description. I really dislike paperwork. I would much rather listen and be helpful. I am good at that. That's what my employee cases seem to need, and that's what I'd like to provide.

—*Benefits Specialist A. J. Anderson*

Part of a manager's job, whether you're managing people, projects, or specific kinds of work, is being able to get things done through others. Understanding "where they're coming from" in terms of their thinking preferences can be tremendously valuable because it gives you clues about what type of work they do best, how to structure tasks and assignments for optimum productivity, and even where someone else's strengths might fill in the gaps in your own thinking. But all too often, in most settings, we managers ignore the mental aspects of work, and as a result, we pay the price in both lost productivity and painful consequences.

Mary's case is a fairly common one. Managers tend to hire and choose to work with people who reflect their own mental preferences, partly because they "get" each other quickly, and partly because of the nature of the work itself. But what about the outliers? It's up to managers to learn how to encourage and cooperate with their employees' and others' efforts to adjust their job assignments and processes in a way that is consistent with getting the job done most efficiently and effectively for all concerned.

In this situation, Mary had an opportunity to explore ways in which she could use the preferences and skills of those team members who did not fit the group norm, finding tasks that required interpersonal skills and idea generation to improve department issues. In addition, once they understood the needed baseline, the outliers were able to beef up their skills somewhat and improve their performance with some targeted training. They were motivated by the focus on their new roles, but they still needed the attention to detail and administrative skills to perform effectively.

The Manager's Role in Employee Motivation

Motivation of employees is a key issue at all levels of supervision, management, and leadership. Throughout my travels working with and talking to people who are in charge of other people, I continue to find them making a fundamental mistake. They continue to believe and behave as if they are responsible for an employee's *motivation*. Although the relationship between the manager and employee does affect job satisfaction, countless books, articles, and programs have provided

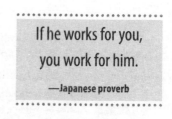

If he works for you, you work for him.

—Japanese proverb

evidence to generations of leaders that *the motivation of workers* does not come from the manager— it comes from within each individual employee. Why is this so hard to grasp? A possible answer is that we have established a cadre of leaders who think that visible action on their part is the primary way to lead—that you must *do* something or you will not be viewed as a leader by those who are led—and that motivating others also falls into this category.

The fact is, we all motivate ourselves. But managers can encourage self-motivation in a number of ways:

1. Provide employees with *work that they find stimulating.*
2. Provide a work *climate* that allows this stimulating work to be performed in ways that satisfy and fulfill the employee.
3. Provide incentives and rewards that supplement the self-actualization that the employee is already experiencing.

4. Provide the necessary tools, training, materials, and support to allow the employee to optimize quality performance, including in areas of lesser preference.
5. Stay the hell out of the way!

This surprisingly direct and simple process is founded on two human resources basics that are essential to effective management:

1. Know the employees. Understand their preferences, their skills, their expectations, and their job needs.
2. Understand the mental requirements of the work that is being done. This requires an investment of time, energy, and skill to diagnose the work elements of the tasks to be performed and then create a profile of the mental preferences required for that job.

The next step in this process is exceedingly elementary in concept, but impossible to carry out if the preceding steps have not been rigorously performed: bringing the employee into alignment with the work. Alignment is a critical issue that I explore in depth in Chapter 10. For specific tips on designing jobs with thinking preferences in mind, see the section "How to Turn Misalignment Around."

The motivation model that Daniel Pink proposes in his book *Drive*[1] dovetails well with Whole Brain Thinking. The three principles are:

• *Autonomy.* Provide employees with autonomy over some (or all) of the main aspects of their work.
• *Mastery.* Allow employees to become better at something that matters to them.
• *Purpose.* Take steps to fulfill employees' natural desire to contribute to a cause other than themselves.

Put It to Work

Take a moment to revisit your answers to the Zones of Preference exercise in Chapter 3, particularly the activities you underlined indicating the work you currently perform in your job that you don't enjoy.

• How does it feel for you to engage in that work?
• Do you procrastinate on it?
• If you had the autonomy to adjust those aspects of the work, what might you change and how?
• What learning and professional development activities might help?

- Applying what you learned about Whole Brain communication in Chapter 8, what key points would you need to cover in discussing the adjustments with your manager to get the results you want?

    Now try this exercise, thinking about the work performed by a direct report whom you know well.

- In what ways might you give this person more autonomy in terms of how the job is performed?
- Are there other tasks or learning and development opportunities you could suggest to help the person build his or her mastery?
- Applying what you learned about Whole Brain communication in Chapter 8, what would you need to cover to make sure that the person understands you and has the tools to succeed?
- What insights about his or her preferences and expectations can you apply to help this person find greater purpose in the job?

Delegating in all Directions

I do not believe that the effectiveness of the delegation process is dependent on the manager's having the authority to reprimand or fire a nonresponsive direct report. Any manager worthy of the name should be able to delegate successfully on the basis of the shared understanding of the task and its priorities and of the shared goals of the organization.

Consider for a moment a team leader who has no organizational power other than the team leader role, but who needs members of the team to accept delegation of work tasks. Here we are not dealing with the tools of traditional authority-based management, but rather with the sophistication of getting work done when you are not really in charge. Geoff Bellman's book *Getting Things Done When You Are Not in Charge*[2] is an outstanding source of wisdom in this domain.

In this book, I have tried to provide as many examples as I can to illustrate the consequences of aligned, misaligned, and nonaligned business relationships. Even under the best of circumstances, with two individuals who are clearly on the same mental wavelength, there is a need for testing understanding and clarifying any discovered misunderstanding, because there is always the possibility of a competitive outcome from two people who are strongly aligned in the same quadrant. Even under the best of circumstances, the person in charge—whether a manager or a team leader—will be at risk unless they ensure the person to whom he or she is delegating to really understands:

1. The "why" behind the task to be performed
2. The goal of the task

3. The specifics of the task to be performed
4. Who needs to be involved
5. The priority determined by the situation and the person in charge
6. The precise due date when action is required

The many references in this book to the consequences of mental preference all lead to the high probability that clear communication and alignment between a manager and an employee will result in effective understanding concerning the delegated task to be performed. In contrast, the various degrees of misalignment or nonalignment and subsequent unclear communication create a low probability that effective understanding and performance will take place. It stands to reason that if the employee does not completely understand the delegated context, goal, and task; does not accurately assess the priority; does not understand who is involved; does not capture the delivery date; and does not comprehend the consequences of failure, there is a high probability of disaster.

Complicating the delegating process are the typical dynamics of a manager/leader-direct report relationship. The manager feels that the work that needs to be done is simple and straightforward, and the employee doesn't want to appear stupid, so the delegation communication from the manager is often inadequate and the feedback from the employee is frequently misleading. The inadequacy of the communication is compounded by the likelihood that both verbal and nonverbal aspects of the manager's communication are, to some extent, misunderstood or misinterpreted by reason of the two people's mental differences.

The Whole Brain Delegation Walk-Around in Figure 9-2 is a tool you can use to substantially increase the probability of successful delegation. It offers a method of testing for understanding and clarifying misunderstanding that can be easily adapted for use by either the manager *or* the employee, since the objective is mutual understanding.

One way to use it is to diagnose each of the manager-direct report delegation outcomes in the model on a scale of 1 to 10, with 10 being the most successful, to determine the degree of delegation success.

Delegation is often taught "by the numbers" and encouraged as a characteristic of good management. That is, you do it in a certain series of known steps, and you get it off your personal agenda because, after all, managers are supposed to get work done through others, not do it themselves. Here's how Whole Brain Thinking brings a different level of sophistication and comprehension to the delegating process because it offers:

1. An early warning system through the diagnostic tools
2. Techniques and communication tools to improve the written and verbal aspects of the process

3. An effective method of testing for understanding and a road map (the Whole Brain Delegation Walk-Around tool) for achieving the understanding needed for effective delegation to take place

Whole Brain Delegation Walk-Around

A	D
• Are the facts understood? • Have money matters been resolved? • Have technical needs been met? • Is the proposed delegation logical? Rational?	• Are future consequences known? • Is the big picture understood? • What subtleties are involved? • What does your intuition tell you? • Are there creative opportunities?
• Are there sequential steps that are critical? • Have dates and timing issues been considered? • What are the risks? • Will the organization be affected? **B**	• Have all those affected been involved? • Have all relationship issues been taken into account? • Are there team implications? • Are values in alignment? • Are there training needs? **C**

FIGURE 9-2 The Delegation Walk-Around Model. Put your delegation method to the test by asking these questions of yourself before taking action.

Managing Up

What do we expect our direct reports to do: take the initiative, toe the line, follow orders, or interpret our leadership situationally? As a direct report yourself, how would you define your role?

When I was asked that question many years ago, I surprised myself somewhat by answering this way: "One of my key objectives in this position is to generate enough cash flow to earn my salary as early in the year as I can. If I can pay for myself by June, that means that everything after June represents added value to the organization. If I can pay for myself by April, that's even better, and if I can pay for myself as early as March, I will beat my stretch goal for the yearly performance of my entire component." Over the years, I have found this personal goal to be much more motivational to me than achieving the budgeted performance that I negotiated with my boss. I was going to do *that* anyway, but by paying for myself or my whole operation as early in the year as possible, I rewarded myself for my performance. It was actually a higher standard than the one that my leader expected, so as a direct report, I set my own standards of performance at a higher level than my boss's expectations. I think that many, many employees set higher standards for themselves than their leaders set for them. In your relationship with your own manager, this can provide a foundation for "managing up" effectively—for making yourself heard, respected, and valued. And of course,

> Hold yourself responsible for a higher standard than anybody else expects from you.
>
> —Henry Ward Beecher

understanding your manager's preferences will help you communicate and position your objectives in such a way that you will get the greatest buy-in. See Chapters 8 and 13 for additional communication and influence tactics.

Another approach is to work with your manager to turn as much of your job as possible into the kind of work that you really love. In the early stages of your career, you might be more inclined to discover what is out there and take on an array of assignments and learning experiences. Once you know the kind of work that stimulates you the most, however, you need to take the initiative to identify the elements of those work activities that are available in your occupation and can be made a part of your job assignment. The greater the percentage of this kind of work there is in your job, the more interest and passion you will have for doing the work, and therefore the better your performance will be.

In those situations in which *you* are the manager, establish a climate that will encourage your direct reports to take the initiative to identify the work that *they* really love. This is the work they find most satisfying—not necessarily the easiest or that they are fully skilled for yet. As with the first approach, I believe that this is a win-win-win solution to improving productivity, engagement, and work satisfaction. It is a win for you, it is a win for your employees, and it is a win for your organization.

> There are no traffic jams on the extra mile.
>
> —Zig Ziglar

Numerous studies reinforce the point that satisfied employees are more productive and engaged, and that their companies benefit as a result. It would be a serious mistake to write this off as "touchy-feely" stuff. For me, this is plain common sense. Supervising, managing, and leading in the ways that I have suggested will unleash the latent productivity of workers, which is beneficial to the organization and to its objectives and goals.

In summary, followers need good leaders, and good leaders need good followers. The organization in which they work needs a climate that encourages both leaders and individual employees to flourish. There is not much in the domain of management that can be better than this combination.

SO WHAT?

> Motivation comes from within, and it is essential to match employees with work that stimulates them.

> By applying Whole Brain Thinking to better understand job fit and manager-employee conversations about alignment, managers can set the stage for improved motivation, and employees can take steps to unleash their own inner motivation.

> The Whole Brain approach offers useful diagnostic tools to managers and team leaders to help them improve their delegation effectiveness.

> You have the responsibility to "manage up" when it comes to your own motivation and engagement, and to encourage your direct reports to be accountable for theirs as well.

> One way to manage up is to learn how to maximize the percentage of stimulating work in your job assignment and ask for what you need.

© Randy Glasbergen
www.glasbergen.com

"You seem intelligent, capable, level-headed and mature. That's a shame because I was really hoping you'd fit in here."

CHAPTER 10

Productivity Through Fit: Individual, Job, and Assignment Alignment

CHAPTER HIGHLIGHTS

> High productivity is based on the combination of individuals being stimulated by particular work, being aligned with that work in their jobs, and addressing any remaining blind spots.

> Understanding the mental preferences of individuals and the mental requirements of the work they do is a critical management skill and priority in order to achieve maximum effectiveness on the job.

> In most roles, "fit" really means a combination of alignment with existing skills, challenges and skill building for continued growth, and having the tools and strategies to situationally address the areas that are required for the job but are outside the person's comfort zone.

> Thinking preferences also affect which workflow and productivity strategies will be most effective for the individual.

> Using a Whole Brain approach to align individuals with their work and providing productivity tools that are aligned with their thinking preferences results in significant increases in productivity.

For as long as he could remember, Sean had wanted to work in advertising. When he landed an account executive position at a top firm, he was thrilled. It wasn't long, however, before his outlook changed.

A creative thinker with a big imagination and an even bigger dislike of details and structure, Sean was struggling to find satisfaction in his new role. While he enjoyed talking to the clients and the creatives about plans and ideas, the majority of his time was spent researching information about clients and their products, preparing proposals and progress reports, and trying to keep track of budgets and timelines. His boss was constantly on him about his record keeping and invoicing, and overall, he was floundering. It seemed to take all of his energy and then some to get his work done.

Sean couldn't understand it. Here he was, finally in his dream job, but he was unhappy, frustrated, and bored, and probably on the verge of being fired.

His manager didn't get it either. Sean had drive, enthusiasm, and impressive credentials. When she'd brought him on board, she'd thought he had all the makings of a hotshot ad executive, but he was barely getting by. The human resources director suggested that Sean complete the HBDI assessment to see if it would reveal any clues as to what was going on.

Looking at his profile results, they discovered that Sean's preferences were strongly in the D quadrant. Not only that, but he had a low preference, actually an avoidance, for detail-oriented, B-quadrant work. No wonder he was struggling. When it came to the majority of the work he was expected to perform, it was a total mental mismatch.

The firm's managers didn't want to lose Sean. They saw his potential, and when they found the opportunity to move him into a position in Creative where he was not only more energized and satisfied with his work, he excelled. In fact, his very first campaign won the firm a national advertising award.

Did this shift mean that Sean no longer had to deal with details? Budgets? Follow-up? No! But he was able to find the motivation and energy to deal with those tasks now that it was all in service of work that he clearly loved. It made all the difference.

> In business, respect for the individual means acknowledging that every individual wants to do good work and to contribute to the success of the organization.
>
> —Kashavan Nair

Engagement, Productivity, and Job Fit

People gravitate toward occupations that allow them to exercise their preferred modes of knowing. That's why we can develop HBDI occupational categories that contain "typical" profiles for certain kinds of jobs. But once employees occupy jobs—specific positions in specific organizations—they often find themselves dealing with a workload that demands they spend large blocks of time, possibly even a majority, operating in areas of lesser preference or even avoidance.

Such mental mismatches, persisting over the years, sharply increase stress and anxiety, which can and do raise not only the incidence of flu, colds, and absenteeism, but also that of heart attacks, nervous breakdowns, alcoholism, and substance abuse. Even when their motivation to do a job well is high, people who are mentally mismatched find it difficult to keep up with the job's demands, and they must often work extra hours to accomplish what others can do in less time. It can become not just a work burden but a personal and family one as well.

Sound overdramatic? Consider the number of employees who leave their jobs or are actively looking for new ones every year, in both bad and good economic times. Engagement data from Gallup show that only 30 percent of employees are actively engaged, and disengagement rates are increasing at an alarming pace as the "do more with less" mentality has piled on more responsibilities and tasks, whether or not they have anything to do with what the person does best. The impact isn't just on the individual; the organization also loses out in multiple ways. The most obvious is the lost productivity and discretionary effort of those who are doing just what they have to do in order to get by. Actively disengaged employees can also have a negative influence on other employees and push customers away. Turnover, quality, safety, profitability ... the list of costs goes on and on.

> People do not get tired out from working where work is intelligently handled. Work, if it is interesting, is a stimulant. It's worry and a lack of interest in what one does that tire and discourage. Every one of us should have our pet interests—as many as we can handle efficiently and happily. Our interests should never be allowed to lag or get cold so that all enthusiasm is spent. Each day can be one of triumph if you keep up your interests—feeding them as they feed you.
>
> —George Matthew Adams

As I touched upon in Chapter 9, I believe that engagement, and thus individual and organizational productivity, starts with a combination of people being stimulated by a particular kind of work and being aligned with that work in their job. By stimulated, I mean having work that is so interesting to them that if they had the opportunity to choose, they would select it for its inspiration and pleasure because the performance of it is rewarding in itself. This work is not necessarily the easiest—it is often the most challenging, but in a way that the individual finds inherently satisfying. Desire for this type of work is at the top of Maslow's hierarchy of needs;[1] it's called self-actualization. The opportunity to perform stimulating work is a major ingredient of motivation, since motivation always comes from within a person. Allowing people access to work that stimulates them pulls them into performing at their highest level of work performance. Just think of the kind of productivity, satisfaction, and fulfillment that both the individuals and their managers will enjoy as a result.

Making a Match

One of the advantages of the Whole Brain System is the capability of diagnosing the mental requirements for work. Using the Whole Brain Model as a diagnostic tool provides management with a way of diagnosing the mentality of the work elements that make up a job assignment. A job can be thought of as an aggregate of tasks composed of work elements. Each work element can be diagnosed in terms of the mentality required to perform it. This means that it is possible to profile and even design the total job on the basis of the distribution of mental requirements needed to perform that job at an optimum level. For example, analytic work elements, such as analyzing the information in a financial report, are A-quadrant in their mentality. Detailed administrative work elements, such as filling out and processing applications and forms, are B-quadrant in their mentality. Interpersonal-type work elements, such as contacting a customer, are C-quadrant in their mentality. And work elements that require strategic thinking, such as brainstorming on a more effective way to beat the competition or innovating products, are D-quadrant in their mentality. Once a pro forma profile of the job is complete, it can be compared to the individual's mental preferences, and the degree of alignment can easily be determined.

Let's take a look at an example of an employee's HBDI Profile compared to pro forma profiles of a range of jobs, from fully aligned to totally nonaligned (see Figure 10-1).

It is easy to come to the conclusion that when the employee's mental preferences are in alignment with the job's mental requirements, everybody wins. The better the alignment, the higher the productivity potential. When the managerial climate is supportive of the alignment initiative, higher productivity is more likely.

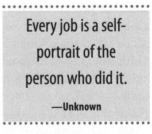

Every job is a self-portrait of the person who did it.

—Unknown

When working with business audiences, I sometimes ask them to pick a percentage figure describing their own productivity, then write down this private information on a piece of paper and stick it in a pocket. Later on, after talking about the business applications of my work and the opportunity to design jobs and assign people to those jobs, I ask them to write on another piece of paper what their productivity could be if their work offered them the opportunity to be inspired and stimulated, and to put this piece of paper in another pocket. At the end of the day, just before

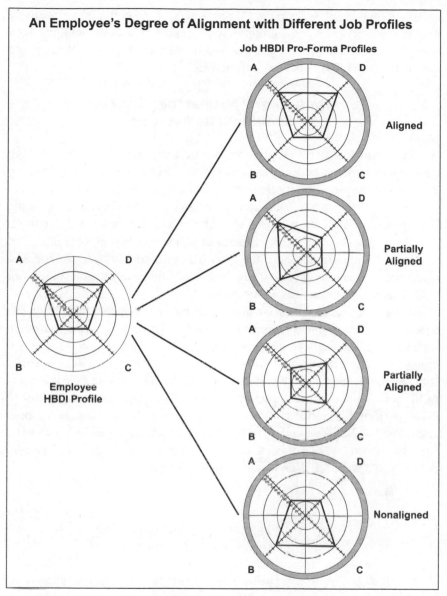

FIGURE 10-1 An employee's HBDI Profile compared with HBDI pro-forma profiles of jobs ranging from aligned to nonaligned with the employee's preferences.

the session ends, I'll say, "Oh, incidentally, what are you going to do about those two pieces of paper in your pocket?" People volunteer that the difference between the two numbers ranges from 10 to 50 percent—with the higher number always being on that second piece of paper.

Based on this and other observations, I believe the potential productivity gain in the average business group is 30 percent. To check this out, just look inward. What would a perfect job match do to your productivity? What would stimulating work do to your job satisfaction?

When Mental Mismatches Can't (or Shouldn't) Be Avoided

As Sean's story and my experience with business audiences show, a high degree of alignment between the individual's preferences and the thinking demands of the job is the ideal situation. But it's not always possible or practical to reassign people or completely redesign jobs. The key is understanding how the person's preferences line up with the job, then helping the individual find ways to be as effective as possible regardless. While some degree of alignment is important, the reality is that all of us work outside our zones of preference to some extent every day. But we can find ways to adjust the work to fit our mental preferences and competencies.

From a managerial standpoint, the first step is realizing that this person has a potential blind spot and taking steps to help him or her address it through such support as job aids, training, or coaching. The manager also needs to recognize the degree of energy, self-motivation, and passion that will be required if the employee has a lack of preference or an avoidance for particular aspects of the job. Quite often, the employees themselves have ideas about how to better perform the work based on how they prefer to think. Managers should encourage employees to take the initiative to make changes in the way the work is performed as long as the necessary outcomes are achieved. The productivity and work satisfaction gains can be enormous.

Thinking Preferences and How You Manage Your Productivity

In today's business world, where the large majority of work is knowledge work, each day can be different and challenging in its own way. Constant change means that most of us are dealing with simultaneous projects, shifting priorities, complex new problems, demands from people both inside and outside the organization, and a never-ending stream of interruptions. Managing your time effectively and staying productive is essential to getting the job done, but it can also feel like a constant battle.

Even though there are more productivity apps and tools available now than ever before, you may still be struggling. In fact, they could be making you feel more overwhelmed. That's because your thinking preferences affect the way you manage deadlines, tasks, projects, and even how you view time. As a result, the time and project management tools and techniques that work so well for someone else could be frustrating and distracting for you. The key is to understand how your thinking preferences affect your approach to work. Then you can find tools that align with your thinking instead of adding to your mental burden.

Your preferences will create both challenges and opportunities when it comes to your productivity. Once you have a better understanding of these, you can take advantage of the benefits of your preferences and avoid getting tripped up by the downsides. It's about managing your thinking rather than letting it manage you.

Here are some of the advantages, challenges, and opportunities of each quadrant when it comes to managing productivity, time, tasks, and projects:

A Quadrant

Advantage: Goal orientation. Focused on achieving results. Often skilled at using technology tools and systems to manage time effectively.

Challenge: Analysis overkill. May be so focused on the need for data or facts that analysis can take time and get off track. Focus on the bottom line may mean overlooking the big picture and other people's feelings and needs for coordination.

Opportunity: Technology. Use technology to set up a system that is efficient and effective and also makes it easy for others to schedule and know what's going on without requiring a lot of interaction.

B Quadrant

Advantage: Task orientation. Organized and focused on getting things done. May naturally put processes in place to manage time well.

Challenge: Getting bogged down. May like to do things the way they have been done before and resist change. Desire for closure may create stress. Also may get caught up in details and miss the big picture.

Opportunity: Tactical planning. Use a linear, practical system to create a structure that they can maintain, aiding in future planning as well as today's needs. Plan in buffer time for changes so that they create less stress.

C Quadrant

Advantage: People orientation. Sensitivity to others' needs allows for coordination and thoughtful planning. Good communication. Motivated to stay on track so that others' needs are met.

Challenge: Overcommitment. May say "yes" to too many commitments due to unrealistic view of timing and wanting to avoid conflict, creating stress and planning challenges.

Opportunity: Communication. Use people skills to graciously defer, delegate, or decline. Ask others for realistic time perspective. Find a system that is comfortable, engaging, and colorful to check on availability and stay on track.

D Quadrant

Advantage: Big-picture orientation. Often sees ways to be creative at getting things done in spite of challenges, adapting to the changing situation to make it work.

Challenge: Focus. May suffer from a lack of detail orientation combined with a desire to do it all, leading to overbooking and many delays in previously scheduled items due to time running over and unrealistic timeframes.

Opportunity: Getting creative. Find a new, visual system and/or device that makes time, task, and project management more fun and accessible and makes detail capture and follow-up easier.

And what about those times when you *want* to put someone in a stretch mode? Many new leader and high-potential development programs include job rotation assignments that intentionally move people around so they can benefit from the exposure to work that specifically isn't in their sweet spots. The idea is to broaden the person's thinking so that he or she can become a more well-rounded leader, but the key here is stretch, not flip-flop. If the assignment requires the person to stretch while still honoring enough of his or her preferences, there is opportunity for growth. If it's entirely within an area of very low preference or avoidance, there is a good chance for frustration and discouragement, which will be easier to bear only if the individual is highly motivated to learn and knows that this is only temporary.

When the goal is to stretch, first ask, is the person motivated? It will take a good amount of motivation and energy to be successful. Second, take the person's strengths and blind spots into account as you coach him or her to handle the responsibilities.

Put It to Work

Think about an opportunity or career progression you're interested in that will require you to stretch:

- What specific mental demands will be misaligned with your preferences?
- What is your usual reaction to this kind of work?
- How can you use your areas of stronger preference to build your inner self-motivation?
- What else should you watch out for?
- Who could you go to for help to widen your perspective and see past your mental "blind spots"?

Now try this exercise thinking about a colleague you know well or a direct report who needs to stretch in order to grow. How could you be a resource to that person in the process?

> I think it is an immutable law in business that words are words, explanations are explanations, promises are promises—but only performance is reality.
>
> —Harold Geneen

How to Turn Misalignment Around

My advice is to try assessing the work and those doing it in a small work group where job design issues and job assignment practices are sufficiently flexible to accommodate such a demonstration. In our company, we often pull in employees from different departments to get a good mix of mental preferences for a project. Sometimes a finite project will reveal preferences for work and competencies much more visibly, especially if the team leader is there to witness this in action. The following tips can help you get started. If you aren't in a managerial position, talk to your manager or supervisor and team up with the human resources department to problem-solve your misalignment issues.

> Every calling is great when greatly pursued.
>
> —Oliver Wendell Holmes, Jr.

Design tasks, projects, and jobs with mental preferences in mind:
- Analyze the work elements of tasks, projects, and jobs according to the quadrant they call for.
- Set priorities to identify the most important, primary elements required and the percentage time allocation for each, so you can make sure that the bulk of the time the person spends involves activities that call on the same mental modes as the most important work.
- Refrain from casually or inadvertently adding responsibilities to that position—even for administrative convenience—for any significant or undefined period of time if they unbalance the mental shift of the job, that is, shift it away from the quadrant required to achieve the purpose at hand, unless you have no other choice or the individual seeks to develop and is highly motivated to do so.

Encourage work and preference matching on an ongoing basis:

- Educate employees at all levels about how their thinking preferences relate to their productivity, effectiveness, and satisfaction.
- Cooperate with employees' efforts to adjust job tasks (consistent, of course, with getting done the job that has to get done). As discussed in Chapter 9, this is one of the key ways you can help unleash employee motivation.
- Provide productivity tools that align with the person's thinking preferences, or give the person freedom to select the tools that work best for him or her.
- Address any blind spots that come from areas of low preference by providing training, support, and other tools and, wherever possible, ensuring that the employee sees these activities as necessary to pursue in the service of successfully achieving his or her preferred work.
- Measure the resulting productivity gains.

> There is a time when misalignment might actually be a good thing. Early in one's career, misalignment can be a gift that helps a growing employee get clear about what their fit really is, as long as it does not derail their career in the process and they have other options to pursue.
>
> —Ann Herrmann-Nehdi

Most work—even physical labor—is largely mental. It stands to reason, then, that we will be most productive if we are doing work that calls for the mental modes we most strongly prefer. But there will also be some degree of stretch in any job; this is never an excuse for poor performance. It's up to managers to help people use their preferences in the service of the work that needs to be done, and it's up to the individual to take the initiative on his or her own behalf. When there is enough alignment in place, and the individual is motivated to develop enough skills to address the inevitable stretch requirements, the possibilities for productivity improvement are significant, providing the organization with an important competitive advantage.

SO WHAT?

> All too frequently, jobs are assembled without regard for the mental requirements it takes to perform them, and employees are placed in those jobs without regard for their mental preferences and the need for alignment.

> Nonalignment of employees with their work leads to poor performance, low productivity, and low job satisfaction.

> Every job requires some degree of stretch; it's up to the manager to recognize and coach employees who are in stretch mode, and it's up to the employees to take the initiative to use their preferences in service of the work that needs to be done and seek the necessary development to adequately address those areas of lesser preference.

© Randy Glasbergen
glasbergen.com

GLASBERGEN

"But how do we motivate them to
attend the motivation seminar?"

CHAPTER 11

Growing Yourself and Others: Developing, Coaching, and Mentoring with Thinking and Learning in Mind

CHAPTER HIGHLIGHTS

> Understanding how you prefer to learn and think allows you to take control of your own growth and development.

> Managers need to understand how their employees learn and think to support their development effectively.

> Groups of almost any size represent an array of different thinking and subsequent learning preferences—difference is the norm.

> Learning preferences and learning avoidances are both of key importance in development.

It was an interesting group—all headmasters of private schools from a region in the Southeast, gathered together to talk about improving overall student performance. But I could tell that one of the headmasters was distracted; his facial expressions and fidgeting were becoming harder and harder to ignore. So I decided I would take a moment to confer with him at the next break.

In the meantime, I introduced the next activity, one that involved using a metaphor. Suddenly this headmaster stood up and declared emphatically to the group: "Excuse me, excuse me. I don't 'do' metaphors." His intolerance for this activity that he clearly disliked—metaphors—was so strong that, even before experiencing it, he felt it necessary to stop the program!

Have you ever been to or participated in a training program, online learning, or any other sort of educational event that you absolutely hated? Maybe you were bored because to you, it felt like a one-way lecture, or you thought the activities were too touchy-feely or boringly predictable. Or perhaps you were annoyed by the lack of structure and no clear agenda because it was so hard to follow the instructor's train of thought. But then after the program was over, you discovered that some of your fellow participants had absolutely loved it. They felt it was one of the best learning programs they'd ever been to. You couldn't believe it. How could they possibly have learned anything from that terrible program?

> The only safe assumption is that every group represents a composite Whole Brain of thinkers and learners.
>
> —Ned Herrmann

In the same way that we have built patterns of preference over the course of our lives as thinkers, each one of us as a learner is a unique human being with a unique learning preference. As a student, you probably did much better in some subjects than in others and responded much more favorably to some teachers and teaching methods than to others. Think of the teachers and content that you can still remember today—years later—and then try to recall those that were lost almost immediately after the learning. Our research has shown that you probably retained some material more accurately and for a longer period of time than other material that was *delivered in a different way*. Our unique learning preferences are the result of the brains we were born with, combined with the years of experience that have developed into our own distinctive learning approaches over the course of our lives.

The first application of my study of the brain and the evolving theory of Whole Brain Thinking was in the domain of management education at GE's management education complex at Crotonville. The more I learned about the role of the brain in the learning process, the more curious and skeptical I became about the effectiveness of the programs I was involved with. To satisfy my curiosity, I began to evaluate the programs I was responsible for on the basis of what the participants actually learned and whether they learned what they were intended to learn. The study revealed that what the participants actually learned covered a wide spectrum within a course, even with a participant group of only 20 people. The study further revealed that less than half of that learning was the learning that was actually intended by the training program. This information was so shocking that I decided I could not report it to upper management without offering specific ways to correct the situation.

Further inquiry into the participants' learning preferences revealed a wide range, with several significant subgroups showing similar learning preferences.

Next, I diagnosed the faculty members and discovered that they too had strong personal learning preferences. My curiosity then led me to examine the design of the various courses that were being taught. I discovered that these were rather narrow in terms of the design methods used, and that they also seemed to match the learning preferences of the course leaders. No wonder we were having problems! The course design and the course leaders seemed to be in good alignment, but this was, in turn, in good alignment with only part of the class, perhaps as few as half. This meant that as many as half of the participants were so out of alignment with the course material and the course leaders that they were missing much of what they were intended to take back to their jobs.

In today's world, learning is no longer relegated exclusively to the training department. The advent of coaching and mentoring, "leader as teacher," and other initiatives have put managers and leaders squarely in the role of not just manager or leader, but also developer. The implications of these differences in learning preferences thus affect everyone—for each person's own development and the development of others.

My research has not only shown that the business world, or any large organization taken as a whole, represents a composite array of thinking preferences that are equally distributed across the Whole Brain Model, but that the same is true for learning. In other words, there is a balanced distribution of learning preferences, with each quadrant and each mode being equally represented and seeking a particular learning approach. But that's not all. There is also an equal distribution of learning *avoidances* across the four quadrants. And learning avoidances are even more significant than learning preferences because they cause people to tune out, just as the headmaster did with metaphors. Whether it is a learning, coaching, or mentoring program, a tuned-out learner is a waste of educational time and effort as well as corporate time and money.

The Impact of Design and Delivery on the Learning Outcome

Training and development budgets range from thousands to millions or even billions of dollars annually. Coaching and mentoring programs are now standard in most organizations. Much of this time, effort, and money may be wasted because people are expected to participate and learn in programs that are out of alignment with their learning preferences, out of alignment with their job needs, and out of alignment with their career paths. The degree of match between the learner and the development content, the way the learner learns best, and the mode of delivery are all critical considerations for achieving desired learning outcomes. If we fail to take them into account, the learner's engagement and attention can be affected, and he or she will fail to build the expected skills or competencies. At best, the outcomes will be temporary. My experience tells me that at least half of those attending in-house training programs or participating in coaching or mentoring programs are seriously out of alignment in one or more of these specific measures (see Figure 11-1).

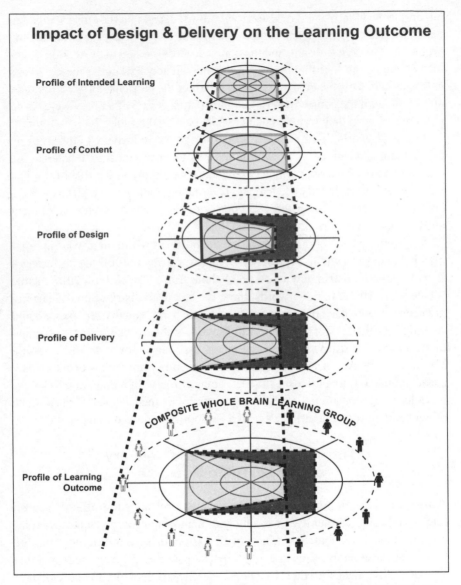

FIGURE 11-1 A Whole Brain group receiving intended learning through a Whole Brain design, compared with a delivery that addresses only left-mode preferences.

The alignment issue exists in programs in schools and universities as well. How many classes did you tune out of when you were in school? Our partner, Ann Louise de Boer, has conducted extensive research at the University of Pretoria that demonstrates how a Whole Brain Learning redesign improves learning outcomes in higher education. The research has looked at a range of learning challenges, documenting successful application of the approach in a variety of areas. In one example, grades in the School of Dentistry improved by 30 percent after the tooth morphology class was transformed. Ann and her team have qualitative and quantitative research showing how results will improve once alignment has been established. Other programs and results highlighted in their book, *Whole Brain Learning in Higher Education: Evidence-Based Practices*,[1] include engineering, information literacy, library leadership, management, and many others. Alignment clearly matters, and the team's ongoing research continues to substantiate this.

Learning Preferences Matter

In recent years, there has been some debate over the veracity of learning-styles research. A study conducted by the Learning and Skills Centre examined 13 models of learning styles, including the Whole Brain Teaching and Learning Model, and concluded that style matters when it comes to delivering effective learning and that the Whole Brain Model was a valid approach. The Centre's report, *Should We Be Using Learning Styles?*,[2] makes recommendations for students, teachers, trainers, managers, researchers, and others.

The implications for those of us who are managers, coaches, and mentors are significant. I believe that an understanding of thinking and learning styles matters both on a personal development level and in our responsibilities to grow those employees who report to us. Learning happens every day on the job, and understanding the way people learn is just as important as understanding how they think.

> Education, learning, and changing are so closely related to problem solving that they may all be names for the same thing.
>
> —George Prince

Growing Yourself: Own Your Learning

Think back to the last time you were fully engaged by a learning experience. Did it involve uncovering the facts, analyzing issues, and forming theories? Or maybe you had the opportunity to do hands-on practice: testing things out, following a clear, structured process. Perhaps you were working in a group, either face to face or online, listening and sharing ideas. Or were you experimenting with new concepts and ideas and growing through self-discovery? Once you understand how you prefer to learn, you can begin to take better control of your own growth and development.

Put It to Work

Refer to the model in Figure 11-2 as you consider how your preferences affect your learning and your best learning experiences. Next, take a moment to reflect on the best learning experiences you have had over the course of your life.

- *Which quadrants tend to be your preferred learning approaches, those that engage you and incite greater learning?*

 Now think about examples of learning that you did not enjoy at all, the ones where you most tuned out of learning. What types of experiences triggered your tuning out?

- *What are the consequences, and how many learning outcomes do you think you missed by tuning out?*

Whole Brain Learning Preferences: Where Are You?

A **Analyzer: Give me facts**
When learning, I enjoy:
- Acquiring & quantifying facts
- Clear objectives
- Applying analysis and logic
- Learning and forming theories
- Thinking through and critiquing ideas
- Understanding how things work
- Analyzing data or numbers

Explorer: Give me options **D**
When learning, I enjoy:
- Self-discovery and ahas
- Intuitive insights
- Using imagination
- Synthesizing content
- Seeing the big picture
- Constructing concepts
- Learning through visuals and metaphors

Organizer: Give me structure
When learning, I enjoy:
- Evaluating and testing theories
- Organized and structured content
- Clear agenda and directions
- Step-by-step flow of information
- Acquiring skills through practice
- Verifying my learning
- Concrete examples

B

Sensor: Give me interaction
When learning, I enjoy:
- Listening and sharing ideas
- Group and team interaction
- Valuing intuitive feelings
- Internalizing the content
- Hands-on experiences
- Movement
- Human interest stories

C

FIGURE 11-2 Whole Brain learning preference model summarizes learning styles by quadrant.

How Our Preferences Affect Learning

Remember the headmaster who declared that he did not "do metaphors"? That comment affected the way I handled the metaphor activity. I explained the rationale and the process we would use, as well as the intended outcome, so that he would buy into it and participate, and he did. When you've felt like tuning out, have you provided feedback or asked for alternative ways to access the content? Next time, consider asking for what you need and selecting programs that best represent your preferred approach so that you can get the most out of the experience. When you do not have a choice or are intentionally seeking a challenge, approach the learning experience as you would a new adventure, well rested and with a stretch mindset, knowing that it will take a lot more energy—and consider finding a learning partner you can work with to help.

People tend to assume that what works for them will also work for others, unless they know otherwise, so if you are learning in a coaching or mentoring situation, don't be afraid to ask for what you need. Most coaches and mentors will be very happy to help. After all, they want to make sure that their time and effort are not wasted!

Now let me be clear: understanding your learning preferences isn't about getting a free pass to check out when learning isn't aligned with your preferences. It's about recognizing when you might become disengaged and stretching yourself so that you can get the learning you need. You have access to all of these modes—you just need to find ways to make them work for you.

How does your learning mindset affect the way you learn? Significantly! Carol Dweck's research at Stanford University found that people who believe that their brain and intelligence can be "built" like a muscle (a growth mindset) will learn more effectively; those who do *not believe* that their brain can be built, that

> If you are in education, you are in the business of brain development. If you are leading a modern corporation … you need to know how brains work.
>
> —Dr. John Medina

we are born with our intelligence "fixed" (a fixed mindset) will struggle. So we know that a growth mindset is critical in order to engage in the learning and to achieve learning outcomes.[3] The very premise of Whole Brain Thinking substantiates this idea of a growth mindset. This, combined with the effective application of learning preferences to the learning process, can help instill that growth mindset. As a learner, you must first understand and believe that you *can* stretch your personal preferences and not get boxed in by your preferred modes or use them as an excuse to disengage. You most likely have a long list of examples where that has occurred already in your lifetime. When you recognize and accept that you have the ability to think and learn beyond your preferences, you can "own" your learning, find the motivation, take responsibility for your success, and get support to better meet your needs.

Learning on the Football Field: Getting What You Need to Win

A group of university football players at a top midwestern U.S. school used the HBDI assessment to help them uncover their learning preferences, and they saw a direct connection with their individual success and winning games on the field. They used the knowledge of how they think and learn to help both themselves and their coaches give and receive information more effectively in those crucial split seconds during a game, the make-or-break, win-or-lose moments. Everyone now knows how to make sure that the player or coach he is communicating with in that split second "gets it" as intended.

The correlation with the workplace—where speed of communication, comprehension, and application of learning have never been more critical—is clear.

One reason that informal learning, social learning, and communities of practice continue to grow in popularity is that they allow learners to ask for what they need "on the field" and better tailor the experience to fit their unique learning preferences.

Growing Others

One of the roles we have as managers and leaders is to support our employees in their development. Even those who don't have people management responsibilities are often called upon, either by the organization or by an individual, to serve as a mentor to someone who is growing in his or her role. No matter what the circumstances, one thing is clear: when you understand how people think and learn, you can make faster connections and cut through the noise so that you can focus on what really matters.

Think about the most effective coaches and mentors you've had throughout your career. One of the first things you may have recognized is that they really seem to "get"you, to understand you and know what you care about. Lewis Lubin,[4] an executive coach who uses the HBDI in his practice, calls this a process of finding the "chemistry of compatibility." It's the homework he does before beginning a coaching engagement so that he can gain some insights into how the person prefers to think and learn. This gives him a starting point for connecting with the individual in an authentic way, drawing in thinking preferences to find a shared comfort zone of language. By speaking from the mindset that connects best, he's able to ensure that both he and the person he's coaching are really hearing each other.

Thinking and learning preferences can also become the springboard for discussions with employees about how they can use their preferences more deliberately, and stretch to other quadrants beyond their preferences to meet specific competency requirements. If their developmental goals require them to be more strategic and holistic in their perspective, for example, how might they use Whole Brain Thinking to move out of their comfort zones and see beyond their blind spots?

Regardless of your thinking and learning preferences, all approaches across the Whole Brain Model are important and valid, which is why the most successful coaches have the thinking agility to move beyond their own comfort zones and filters. As Lewis says, it's not about being a chameleon or changing who you are; it's about adapting and being flexible to meet those you coach or your employees where they think (see Figure 11-3).

Coaching The Whole Brain Way

A	D
• Be precise and logical • Use facts and numbers • Pay attention to goals and data	• Be imaginative and holistic • Use metaphors • Pay attention to longer-term outcomes
• Be organized and structured • Use a step-by-step approach • Pay attention to process and details	• Be empathetic and caring • Use eye contact • Pay attention to feelings/relationships
B	C

FIGURE 11-3 Coaching the Whole Brain way: For best results, coaches must spend time in each of the four thinking quadrants. Here's a Whole Brain checklist to get you started.

The Mentoring Match

Lynne Krause of BBTD Services[5] has a long track record of using the HBDI and thinking preferences as the foundation for matching mentors and mentees. She says that matching people with similar thinking preferences leads to better communication, faster bonding, and increased trust, and the result is longer-lasting and more mutually beneficial mentoring relationships. In one example from the U.S. Naval Command, matching mentors and mentees based on their thinking preferences led to a 99 percent success rate in terms of the pair "sticking" and lasting over time instead of dropping off soon after the first meeting or two, a huge improvement over the previous success rate of just 50 percent.

Franklin University used the HBDI to accelerate the ramp-up time for its MBA students with their community business leader mentors. Discussing thinking and learning preferences right off the bat allowed them to set the stage so that each party could easily talk about what he or she was seeking and what that person needed most for success. The conversation made it easier and faster for the pairs to get to know each other, which accelerated their ability to use their time most effectively.

The take-away: if you are seeking out a mentor or coach, or are looking for the opportunity to grow your own skills by becoming a mentor, don't overlook the importance of thinking and learning preferences.

Everyday Learning with Thinking in Mind

For everyone, especially adults, learning takes energy, focus, and motivation. The way our society works today, there is a general avoidance of discomfort, with a strong desire to make things easier and more convenient. The discomfort created by the need to process new information or change the way you think is often a deterrent. Yet as my friend and HBDI practitioner Manny Elkind,[6] president and owner of Mindtech, Inc., once pointed out, "In many cases, if you are not somewhat uncomfortable, then you are probably not learning!"

In spite of 100 years of dogma saying otherwise, we now know that new neuronal connections can be created, even in the adult brain. Whether you are the learner or you need to help others learn and grow, the research has shown that context, emotional engagement, novelty, meaty challenges, sleep, planning for processing over time, and practice are all essential to making sure that the learning gets through and sticks. When you prepare your brain for learning, you will be more mentally prepared for the challenge. You may still not "like" the discomfort that a stretch may require, but you can own the challenge and view learning as a victory.

And that's important, because in today's world, learning isn't a choice; it's a necessity if you want to keep up with the pace of change around you. One of the ways you can grow and adapt is to practice accessing and developing your less-preferred modes. The following chart provides a sampling of four types of everyday activities that, through regular practice, will help establish and reinforce a more whole-brained, personal approach to work and life in general. It's your brain; for best results, use it daily!

A Program for Exercising All Four Quadrants

Building situational capability in each quadrant is like building a muscle; it requires regular practice doing quadrant-specific activities on a consistent basis. In this section, you will find a sampling of everyday activities that, if practiced regularly, will help you establish and reinforce a more whole-brained, personal approach to work and life in general. Modify, adapt, or change the activities as required.

Select a quadrant that you want to be more proficient in, and either pick one activity a day or repeat one until you feel that you've "got it," then move to another. Overachievers might try to do one from each quadrant every day!

Do you want to exercise your logical thinking? Your process orientation? How about your kinesthetic or risk-taking abilities? Go to www.whole brainbusinessbook.com to download the full seven-day program with plenty of quadrant-specific activities to choose from to build your Whole Brain Thinking muscles.

A Quadrant

Finance:
- Review your financial status for the current week, the past month, and the year to date.
- Download a financial planning app and set it up, then review it weekly.
- Calculate how much money you will need in 10 years, and develop a plan to get there.

Goal Focus:
- Take a moment to establish or review your personal goals for the month, quarter, and year (a minimum of one, but no more than three). Note these so that you can monitor your progress.

- Find a goal-setting app that you will actually use, and stay at it for at least a month.
- Compare the results of last week's activities with your objectives for the week. What can you do to be more realistic in your goal setting this week?

B Quadrant

Planning:
- Plan this week's priority activities, and schedule them on your calendar with reminders.
- Download a new planning app and/or calendar that will work best for you, given your preferences.
- Pick a project that you are working on and develop a plan, either starting at the beginning or starting with the end in mind and working backward. Note deadlines, outcomes, and key players.

Timing:
- Experience a perfect day of being there on time for every planned activity.
- Find a productivity app or use your phone alarm to improve your use of time throughout the day.
- For one full week, track how much time it actually takes for you to accomplish tasks, and compare this to your assumptions. Readjust your planning based on realistic time frames.

C Quadrant

Empathy:
- Show someone who needs empathy that you care by taking the initiative and verbally expressing it in a way that the person will appreciate (for example, send a note, a phone call, an e-mail, a card with a personal message, an invitation to coffee or lunch, or something similar).
- Use social media with a focus on listening to better understand others rather than as a forum for posting your own ideas. Pick someone whom you do not know well and read all of his or her posts. What do they say about the person, and what can you learn?
- Focus on being intentionally curious about other people all day, asking questions about them, avoiding "I" statements and talking about yourself, and reducing your airtime to well below 40 percent.

Spirituality:

- Discover something about your spiritual self by devoting 15 minutes every day to spiritual reflection.
- Try an app or subscribe to a news feed to help you meditate, focus, see daily inspiring quotes, or engage in other activities to help you keep spirituality top of mind.
- Spend time exploring spiritual practice by asking a friend about how he or she practices spirituality or reading a book on the topic.

D Quadrant

Creative Thinking:

- Draw a metaphor of your last vacation or activities you engaged in last week, and have someone else look at it and interpret the meaning.
- Search for and download one of the many creativity apps, and use it every time you need to solve a problem.
- Take a "theta break" for 20 minutes (take a walk, listen to music, or do something similar), and see what ideas emerge. Be sure to capture them!

Intuitive Ahas:

- Make an important decision based entirely on your intuition.
- Use a program, recorder, app, or paper notebook to help you capture your intuitive insights easily throughout the day, when exercising, and when you wake up. Make sure to stop and capture them.
- Try solving a problem by thinking about it before going to sleep and capturing any intuitive ideas that emerge while you are sleeping or upon waking, even if they are not 100 percent clear yet. Next look for ways you can use that insight to solve the problem.

SO WHAT?

> You need to understand how you think and learn so that you can "own" your growth and development.
> It is critical to rethink many of the traditional approaches to the design and delivery of intended business learning; they are often ineffective and thus extremely costly because much of the investment of time and money is wasted.
> By aligning their programs using a Whole Brain Learning approach that designs learning with the learner in mind, schools and universities can significantly improve learner outcomes.

> The best coaching and mentoring results start with an understanding of and ability to adapt to the person's thinking and learning preferences so that you can quickly connect and both parties will be heard.
> Whole Brain Thinking helps you, and those you are responsible for developing, break out of mental comfort zones to reach new competency levels.
> To keep growing and learning, exercise all four quadrants regularly—ideally, every day.

T.E.A.M.

TOGETHER
EVERYONE
ANNOYS
ME

GLASBERGEN

"Before I begin, I'd just like to make it known that I didn't volunteer to do this presentation."

CHAPTER 12

Teams that Work: Getting Advantage from Difference

CHAPTER HIGHLIGHTS

> Similar-thinking, homogeneous teams can achieve a consensus of opinion quickly and will typically respond in ways that are predictably consistent with their quadrant preference, which is an advantage if speed is the primary goal.

> Diverse, heterogeneous teams behave in entirely different ways. They experience difficulty in reaching consensus, but because of their diversity, they can be synergistic and therefore ideal for creative and complex assignments.

> Once team members learn to function well in heterogeneous combinations, team membership can change with minimum effect on performance.

> Managers and team leaders play a key role in making sure that diverse, heterogeneous teams get the full benefit of their differences.

> Organizations of more than 100 members are likely to have enough diversity of thinking available to provide an ideal pool from which to build homogeneous and heterogeneous teams.

> High-performing teams share common characteristics, and each of these correlates with different thinking preferences.

A number of years ago, Shell Oil was working on a billion-dollar proposal to design a superior offshore rig and drilling method to optimize the deepwater oil exploration process. The company had brought together a team of world-class experts in each of the technical phases of offshore drilling, from drilling experts to offshore platform experts. The plan was to combine the team members' expertise in a synergistic way so that they could create the optimum drilling process.

For all their impressive credentials and expertise, however, the team members were getting nowhere. The experts were so skilled in their own specific areas, and their expertise was so deep and narrow, that impenetrable silos had developed. No one could get through to anyone else. This group of world-class experts was as ineffective at this task as a classroom team of kindergarten students would have been.

No one can whistle a symphony. It takes an orchestra to play it.

—H. E. Luccock

What we and the team members themselves discovered as we worked with them was that there were major technical barriers between the individual areas of expertise. Different team members saw the problem very differently and were unable to relate to solutions based on technologies other than their own. They were bringing widely varying thought processes and perspectives to the table, all of which were important for developing this complex proposal, and all of which would be essential to implementing the project successfully, but if the team members couldn't communicate with one another or see outside their silos, they would never get the technical synergy they were looking for.

Ultimately, after working through an understanding of their different perspectives using the HBDI Team Profile, and then applying several different creative processes, they jelled and were able to get the breakthroughs they hoped for. How many teams never really get there, or end up with suboptimal results?

Teams are the engine of the workplace today, and we need synergy to get results, whether the group is very different—heterogeneous—in makeup, like the team at Shell, or whether its members are more similar and homogeneous in background, skills, and perspectives. When it comes to thinking, there are advantages and disadvantages to both kinds of teams, and whether you're assembling a team, leading one, or just participating on one, it's important to know how to get the advantages of all that collected intelligence.

I Like the Way You Think: Consequences of Similar Thinking in Homogeneous Teams

Each individual in an organization has a distribution of mental preferences that can be displayed in the form of an HBDI Profile. As you learned earlier, an organization with more than 100 members is likely to have a well-balanced distribution of individual profiles in all four quadrants and all four modes. The composite average of all individuals approximates a balanced Whole Brain HBDI Profile. Because of the broad and relatively equal distribution of the employee pool across the Whole Brain Model, combined with the functional similarity that is often present, it is easy to form teams of five or six individuals who have approximately the same profile—that is, their mental preferences are quite homogeneous, so they're more similar than different in their thinking (see Figure 12-1).

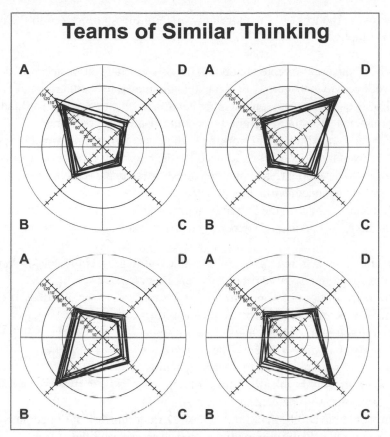

FIGURE 12-1 Examples of composite HBDI Profiles for quadrant-specific homogeneous teams.

Homogeneous Teams: How Each Quadrant Shows Up

Chances are you have been on such a similar-thinking team before. Functional teams, for example, are frequently similar in their thinking. The impact of forming teams this way can be fascinating to explore. It's something that has been demonstrated many times in programs we have run (both public and inside organizations) with about 100 business managers in attendance. Here's an example of what occurs: we'll create four homogeneous teams, each with a strong lead characteristic in one of the four quadrants—that is, a five-person A-quadrant team, a five-person B-quadrant team, a five-person C-quadrant team, and a five-person D-quadrant team. In each case, the strongest preference in each of the teams will be in a particular quadrant.

I then simultaneously ask the members of all four teams to describe the work that they find most satisfying and that they're most attracted to. There will be highly consistent responses within each five-member team, but these responses will be extremely different from one team to the next. For example:

- The A-quadrant-oriented team will quickly reach a consensus around work activities that are logical, analytical, quantitative, and rational.
- The B-quadrant team, on the other hand, will quickly coalesce around organized, structured, detailed, and administrative-type work.
- For the C-quadrant team, working with people will be an absolute must. The team members will cite a need for their work to give them an opportunity to develop interpersonal relationships, to express their feelings, and to work in tandem with other people.
- In contrast, those in the D-quadrant group will describe themselves as creative, conceptual, and experimental risk takers.

If this same task were given to the same four teams, but instead of having them respond in one large room, you sent them to four separate conference rooms and gave them 15 minutes to reach a consensus and return prepared to report, the behaviors of each team would also be quite different. The first groups back would predictably be the A and B teams. The C team would typically return a few minutes late. But in 90 percent of the cases, the D team would have to be sent for, because D-quadrant-oriented people would have the most difficulty complying with the time rules of the exercise.

> Where all think alike, no one thinks very much.
>
> —Walter Lippman

A general characteristic of homogeneous teams is the ability to reach a consensus quickly. People who think alike tend to come to an agreement quite rapidly. Since they are on the same wavelength, they have similar interests. Words mean about the same thing to them, and their approach to a given situation is likely to be quite similar.

You can imagine how comfortable it is to be on a team in which everyone "gets" you and has a similar perspective on the problem or issue and how to go about solving it. Morale is generally high, and conflict is low. People will enjoy themselves and feel that they are both heard and validated. There are times when this is a huge advantage. If a quick consensus is what you need, and speed is your ultimate goal, a homogeneous team is the way to go.

But there are pitfalls. "Groupthink" is a term we have all heard and most likely experienced for groups that think similarly and get stuck when they need breadth of thinking. These are circumstances in which a diverse, heterogeneous group can really have a differentiating impact.

What's the Difference? Diverse, Heterogeneous Teams

What would happen if you reconfigured the four teams into four new teams, each representing a fairly equal distribution of preferences across the four quadrants (see Figure 12-2)? Each team would be a little composite "whole brain." Now, if you gave the teams the same assignment to identify the work they are most attracted to, it would be extremely difficult for each team to reach a consensus. And if they were assigned to four different rooms and given 15 minutes to reach agreement, none of the teams would be back on time; all of them would have been delayed by the different perspectives at the table. A characteristic of heterogeneous teams is the difficulty of reaching swift consensus.

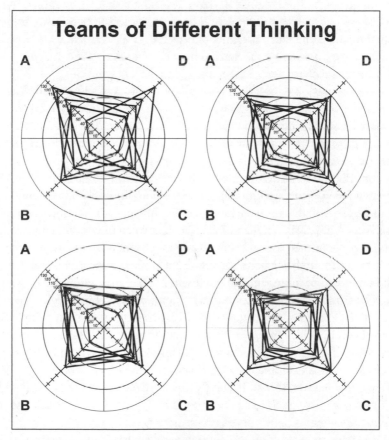

FIGURE 12-2 Examples of reorganizing a population of homogeneous teams into heterogeneous Whole Brain teams.

Another example of the differences in team behavior and outcomes occurs in problem-solving situations. In our first example, we form four homogeneous teams, give them an identical problem situation, assign them to separate team rooms, and give them four hours to come up with a solution. Typically, all four teams of this type will report back in approximately half the time allocated with a range of reasonably adequate solutions. The A and D teams will have the most technically astute and unique solutions, respectively. The B team will usually have a safer solution, but will have thought through all of the execution and logistics details and will already have a plan in place. And the C team will often have had a great discussion and listened to all of the ideas at the table, but the desire for consensus will have slowed them down a bit. If the exercise is repeated with the heterogeneous teams, all the teams are likely to take the full amount of time, and several of them will ask for more time. Instead of a single solution, each of the teams will have several alternative solutions. In most cases, these alternative solutions will be superior to the consensus solutions reached by the homogeneous teams. Words like *comprehensive, creative*, and *innovative* would describe the heterogeneous solutions. Words like *obvious* or *adequate* would characterize the homogeneous team solutions.

These conclusions are based not on one or two samples, but on literally hundreds of workshop and real-world consulting experiences working with real teams and critical business challenges. A six-year study at the U.S. Forest Service[1] also confirmed what we've seen in these individual experiences: teams that are balanced in terms of thinking preferences are more effective; they consider more options and make better decisions. The study also found that when faced with a complex challenge, whole-brained teams were 66 percent more efficient than homogeneous teams. In fact, 70 percent or more of the teams were "successful" at the assigned project when they were whole-brained in makeup, versus 30 percent or less when they were not.

What are the implications for you, as a leader, manager, or team member? The more complex the challenge you have to deal with, the greater the need for breadth of thinking, with team members who have preferences that are well distributed across analytical A-quadrant thinking, more structured B-quadrant thinking, interpersonal C-quadrant thinking, and risk-taking D-quadrant thinking. In other words, difference gives you the advantage.

But as the Shell example showed, it's not as simple as just bringing together a group of people who think differently and have unique viewpoints. There are some key issues that need to be understood and resolved before the benefits of these different teams' concepts can be realized.

While in many instances, competition between like-minded team members can occur, the power of the homogeneous approach to team formation typically lies in rapid consensus building. This can be an advantage when time is of the essence, but it can also produce less than optimum results, since the rapidly formed consensus excludes alternative approaches that may be essential to the situation at hand. Another likely outcome of homogeneous groups is that they tend to rapidly establish group norms and an overall group culture. In the nonbusiness world, gangs and tribes exhibit some of these same characteristics.

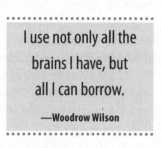

I use not only all the brains I have, but all I can borrow.

—Woodrow Wilson

The heterogeneous teams face an entirely different group issue—dealing with differences among the members. In the ideal heterogeneous group, the differences are significant. One person may have extremely strong preferences for logical, analytical, quantitative processes and a distaste for anything dealing with feelings and emotions, while another team member may have the exact opposite set of preferences. Another pair might be made up of a highly experimental, risk-oriented, adventurous spirit who abhors the status quo, and a highly traditional and security-minded individual. These differences can be synergistic and positive, or they can be hostile and disruptive.

A board member at a nonprofit described a situation that became so difficult that during their monthly meetings, she could hardly stand sitting next to the person who was most different from her. Each meeting became more and more uncomfortable. Results began to wane, and the rest of the team tired of the internal "noise" it was creating. Finally, one of the two resigned from the board.

Have you had an experience with a diverse team where one or two members (perhaps even you) had differences that became toxic to the whole team experience? The good news is, it does not have to be that way.

Getting the Benefits of Cognitive Differences

To optimize team performance, it is essential for the heterogeneous team to build a climate that not only tolerates differences but embraces them. Crucially, this means that everyone needs to recognize how and why different thinking preferences contribute to overall objectives, and team members have to be able to communicate effectively across quadrants, regardless of their own preferences; they have to speak and listen in a way that respects others' thinking preferences. This often takes more time up front, but it is clearly worth the investment.

Managers and team leads play a pivotal role in ensuring that the team gets the benefits of differences rather than devolving into conflict and chaos. The more diverse a team is, the more important it is to have a skilled leader in place who can manage, facilitate, and incorporate Whole Brain Thinking practices within the team. If you are assembling or leading teams, you have to set them up for success by creating an environment in which diverse thinking is respected, managed, heard, and applied. In my experience, the earlier this happens, the better. By giving the team members a clear picture of their thinking, the leader will have the tools and language to accelerate that process.

HBDI practitioner Bob McKown describes how, as he used the HBDI Team Profile with the health and wellness department of a large university and medical center, the team immediately began to see and easily discuss the differences they had. This management team comprised physicians, researchers, psychologists, counselors, occupational health professionals, and nurses, making for an extremely diverse team profile, with strong preferences occurring in every quadrant.

As they explored the HBDI Preference Map in the team report, it became clear that the director of the department had a strong upper A/D preference, while, in contrast, many of the team members had strong B-, C-, and B/C-quadrant preferences (see Figure 12-3). As a result, they frequently struggled with communicating and interacting with the director. She often asked questions that they either had never thought of or, if they had, were not prepared to answer. Likewise, the director was frustrated that so many of the people on her team trudged through strategic and budget conversations with great difficulty. The good news was that the team *had* breadth of thinking; the challenge was making sure that it didn't get in the way.

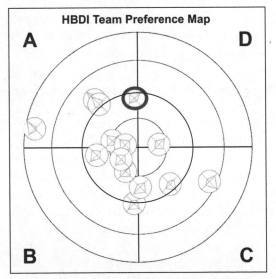

FIGURE 12-3 HBDI Preference Map showing the director's preferences related to the rest of the team's.

With the insights from the HBDI Preference Map, everyone was able to come together and develop intentional strategies to use the Whole Brain Model to improve communication by purposefully recognizing the unique differences in thinking within the team. Then, as Bob tells it, "An amazing thing happened." As they discussed the different thinking preferences, team members with a particular strength in a given quadrant began to volunteer to help others who had lesser preferences in that quadrant in their communication efforts. In effect, they began to identify "thought leaders" within each of the four quadrants.

The team members then began to plan how they could better apply the specific quadrant strengths of the staff members and discussed how they needed to ensure heterogeneous makeup of all their project teams. Ultimately, the Whole Brain Model has created a common language within this diverse team. Many staff members now display their mini HBDI Profile cards at their desks, and the director has a list of the preferences of each member of her staff on the board next to her desk for easy reference so that she can continuously look for ways to leverage the cognitive diversity available to her.

The advantages of cognitive diversity in teams can be applied to creativity, problem solving, strategy formation, and other critical business activities. However, there has to be a willingness to make an investment up front in ensuring that team members understand how each person's preferences contribute to the task at hand and how all the members can work together effectively to fully leverage the diversity of thinking available to the group. Teams are often so focused on getting to the task that they bypass this essential step. This is even more critical when the team is virtual, as this creates more opportunities for miscommunication. No matter what the objective or function of the team, human assets are too precious and costly to waste by putting people together on a haphazard basis without understanding the consequences.

In the case of heterogeneous team formation, some theorists might say, "Oh, this is just about applying constructive dissonance." My answer is, "Absolutely not!" In constructive dissonance, the objective would be to sustain the dissonance in the hope that something positive would result from time to time. The dissonances are constant. The heterogeneous diversity that I'm talking about is based on synergy, which resolves the diversity with a high-value outcome

> The way a team plays as a whole determines its success. You may have the greatest bunch of individual stars in the world, but if they don't play together, the club won't be worth a dime.
>
> —Babe Ruth

that everyone sees the benefit from. When this occurs, it doesn't take long for diverse individuals to begin to respect and honor the differences that brought about the synergy. In my experience, this is a much more positive way to take advantage of the reality of differences in the workplace.

When team members understand the importance of having a breadth of thinking and how each person's thinking adds value, differences are viewed in a nonjudgmental way, and the team has a new context in which to tackle the inevitable challenges that come up.

A professor who uses this approach in MBA team programs explains it this way:

> Once they get the concept that we all have brains, we just use them differently, and that we need all of those differences to get the job done, they get over the typical quibbling that takes up so much team energy and drags down the team's effectiveness.

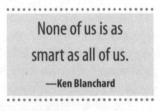

None of us is as smart as all of us.

—**Ken Blanchard**

Too often, the time spent up front is written off because it's considered yet another one of those typical "feel-good" team-building activities with no concrete outcomes. Not at all! This is about setting the stage and developing the processes to harness the diversity of thought necessary to tackle the tough issues that we, as managers, and our organizations are facing today. This is an investment that pays off indefinitely: experience has shown that once people have felt the stimulation, excitement, and improved outcomes of being on a well-managed, high-performing heterogeneous team, they can participate in other diverse teams without going through an elaborate learning curve. In other words, heterogeneous team skills, once acquired, are transferable to other heterogeneous group situations. Given the 100-member organization described earlier, these people could, through a series of team engagements, become a highly flexible candidate pool for almost limitless combinations of heterogeneous teams. Such an organization would be well on its way toward being a critical mass with great high-performing, creative potential, ready to unleash that potential at any given time. As the March 2014 *Harvard Business Review* article "The Case for Team Diversity Gets Even Better" put it: "When teams are diverse, meaningful innovation is more likely to happen."

High-Performance Teams

The ability to profile employees' mental preferences provides an opportunity to assemble teams that can perform at quantum levels higher than the norm. Not only can the profile data provide the basis for building a heterogeneous team that has a greater potential for effective problem solving and innovation, but profile data can also reveal the presence of a critical mental skill—that is, a particular mental preference of the team members that allows the team to have a common capability and still be heterogeneous.

For example, research by our partners in Germany has shown that one of the specialized mental capabilities that all high-performing teams of software engineers have in common is the ability to mentally visualize the objective of their software design. Having a unified view of the design objective greatly facilitates the team's creative interaction around the proposed design. Imagine for a moment the difference between a diverse team that has a common design objective and one that doesn't have this common point of view. In the first case, you have the analogy of a jigsaw puzzle with five or six people pooling their resources and finding and inserting the right pieces. In the second case, you have the five or six people working on separate puzzles that have nothing in common other than that they are jigsaw puzzles.

As in this case, this common characteristic of visual capability can be identified by applying the HBDI and a supplemental questionnaire that is relevant to the team task. This combined input will greatly facilitate the building of a team whose high-performance potential has a greater chance of being achieved.

Another characteristic of high-performance teams is the ability to bring more than one creative process to bear on a particular problem situation. The array of problem-solving processes that exists is impressive—just Google "problem-solving tools and processes" to see. (See Figure 22-1 in Chapter 22 for a Whole Brain array of creative processes.) Yet all too often, teams fall back on only one, namely, brainstorming or some variation on it. Imagine that, in this case, we are not using a single process to develop ideas, but are applying multiple processes in a manner that could be called "process storming." The number and quality of ideas generated by this creative problem-solving strategy are significantly greater than what would come from a single process. Good teams that apply process-storming techniques *can become* high-performing teams.

An important characteristic of high-performing teams that is confirmed by much of the research on team performance by Jon Katzenbach[2] and others is clarity of purpose and goals. Teams that share that results orientation—a more A-quadrant characteristic—will more easily endure the natural ups and downs of the team dynamic and push through to performance because they're keeping their eye on the goal.

Accountability is another characteristic that is typical of teams with top performance. This

> **Problems can become opportunities when the right people come together.**
>
> **—Robert South**

more B-quadrant characteristic helps drive a sense of both individual and group commitment and reduces the friction often created by team members who may not always pull their weight.

"Diverse by Design" a Sure Bet at Caesars

The experience of the gaming-entertainment company Caesars Entertainment is a good example of how cognitive differences in teams, when managed well, can lead to higher levels of innovation and better business outcomes. The company deliberately assembles teams with the diversity to tackle tough business problems, come up with fresh ideas, and take advantage of its most complex opportunities. Based on employees' thinking preferences and predispositions, along with other relevant dimensions of diversity, "Diverse-by-Design" (DbyD) teams are formed and assigned specific projects. While the fundamental team objective is clear, Fred Keeton, Caesars' vice president of external affairs and chief diversity officer,[3] says that the team's instrumental approach to driving enhanced outcomes is produced through the team's overall diversity. And this approach, he adds, "is universal and can be applied across all business functions."

Keeton describes this as a process of yield-managing cognitive diversity, which he defines as "leveraging cognitive abilities and predispositions based on individual backgrounds, experiences, and genetic wiring to generate and obtain specifically desired business outcomes." While diversity is sometimes viewed in terms of compliance or HR metrics, Caesars' experience demonstrates how diverse teams can be created and leveraged to drive the business forward and solve the most complex problems organizations face.

Other characteristics of high-performance teams include passionate intensity, commitment, and focus. The team members' level of interest in the task at hand is usually very high, so there is also a high level of inner motivation to apply to the team task. This strong motivation contributes to *focus* on the team task and *commitment* to achieve its goal. It is frequently the case that the strength of an individual's preference is predictive of the passionate intensity of his or her team interaction. HBDI Profiles that are particularly "spiky" provide advanced evidence of the likelihood of this passionately intense team interaction occurring.

Again, this level of passion and intensity requires experienced team leadership to deal with the potential interpersonal dynamics. In other words, just assembling a diverse team isn't enough. Managers or team leaders have to make sure that the diverse team members take the time not only to acknowledge their differences, but also to determine how their varied cognitive preferences will contribute to achieving the outcomes they've been tasked with. They also serve an important function as facilitators to ensure that the team hears and takes advantage of the full breadth of thinking available to it. In the *Harvard Business Review* article "Putting Your Company's Whole Brain to Work,"[4] Dorothy Leonard and Susaan Straus emphasize that without an effective leader, the team can devolve into unproductive conflict or conflict avoidance, in which case one approach dominates to the point that other perspectives remain unheard. Either way, the value of all that diversity is lost.

> Diversity and inclusion are most potent when channeled toward a company's hardest problems, or most complex opportunities. If managed appropriately, they can drive profoundly enhanced outcomes.
>
> —**Fred Keeton**

High-performance teams made up of diverse members who have the common characteristic of *imagination* are also likely to be very creatively productive. Teams with diverse preferences but with the common quality of imagination are usually capable of higher forms of synergy than teams without these characteristics. Imagination helps them make effective use of diverse capabilities such as logic, analysis, and intuition, as well as organizational and interpersonal skills.

> If people even partially internalize the inherent value of different perspectives ... they will be better equipped to listen for the "a-ha" that occurs at the intersection of different planes of thought.
>
> —**Dorothy Leonard and Susaan Straus**

Even with all of these characteristics in place, however, an essential ingredient in the recipe for team performance is the climate in which the team functions. The extent to which that climate is supportive, nonbureaucratic, flexible in meeting team needs, and rewarding of team performance represents the degree to which the team can take advantage of its own inner resources to achieve its goals without counterproductive interference from outside the team. Taken together, these ingredients contribute to high team performance. When there is a champion in the team or a management champion who is supportive of its work, the likelihood of team success is further optimized.

> Progress is 95 percent routine teamwork. The other 5 percent relies on restless, inner-directed people who are willing to upset our applecart with new and better ideas.
>
> —Michael LeBoeuf

Put It to Work

Think of a team you are currently on or recently have had experience with.

- How well does that team leverage the breadth of thinking available to it?
- What percentage of the meeting time is value added?
- How much time is wasted on nonessential items, quibbling between members, miscommunication, and other issues? Take a moment to calculate the amount of time that represents in a month.
- Now take a guess at the costs represented by those in the team who are taking that time.
- Do the math to come up with the monthly cost, and then multiply that by 12.
- What is one thing that the team could do to reduce that waste, not to mention the opportunities lost?
- How might you help in this process?

SO WHAT?

> Organizations can become a dynamic pool of diverse, synergistic team members who work together productively to drive business outcomes.
> Mentally balanced teams consider more options, make better decisions, and exceed expectations more often than homogeneous teams.
> The more heterogeneous (mentally diverse) a group is, the more it needs a multidominant facilitator/leader.

> Heterogeneous groups can be extremely creative and successful, *or* they can "crash" if they do not take the steps and the time necessary to find synergy.
> The first step to increased team performance is providing the team members with data on how they are similar or diverse in their thinking, and the implications for the task at hand. Too often, this step is skipped.
> A supportive, noninterfering team climate is essential to sustained high performance.
> Virtual teams need a common language even more than colocated teams to increase the speed of relationship building and decrease miscommunication.

© Randy Glasbergen. www.glasbergen.com

GLASBERGEN

"Your presentation was thought-provoking.
I thought you'd never shut up. I thought
I might die of boredom. I thought about
smashing your projector with my shoe…"

CHAPTER 13

Influencing, Getting Buy-In, and Connecting with Your Customers: Thinking Behind the Pitch

CHAPTER HIGHLIGHTS

> Understanding how someone thinks provides clues about how that person will engage, influence, and drive his or her decision-making process.
> Whether your customers are external or internal, everyone in business today is involved in selling.
> Marketing, advertising, selling approaches, and products can all be analyzed in terms of thinking preferences.
> People respond more positively when ideas, solutions, or products are presented in a way that aligns with their thinking preferences.

Susan had been calling on Dr. Wilburn for seven years now. Although he had always been polite, he wasn't what you would call warm. Their conversations were strictly business and consistently brief. She knew that many physicians had grown weary of all the calls and visits by pharmaceutical sales reps, but she also knew that her specific drug line would be extremely beneficial for a specific segment of his patient population— if only he would give her the attention and time to understand why. She'd shown him the clinical trial reports, the specifications, and the statistics, but she couldn't seem to break through.

One day, as she began to pull up some recent data for him to look at on her new tablet computer, Dr. Wilburn commented on the photo on her screen—a picture of her family on a sailboat.

"Oh, you like boating? You have to see this, then."

He pulled out a state-of-the-art gadget and scrolled through recent vacation photos of himself and his family out on their boat.

"Can you believe how crisp the detail is?" he marveled. "It's as close as you can get to being there!"

He confided that new, innovative technology was his secret obsession. He was always upgrading to the latest and greatest "toys," and he loved experimenting with the new features to see what possibilities there might be for using technology in his practice or for helping him stay connected to his family who lived far away.

The conversation had finally moved beyond the businesslike formality of the past seven years, but for Susan, there was something even more significant about this exchange. She realized something about Dr. Wilburn's thinking, and also saw why she'd never been able to break through in all that time.

> Most people think "selling" is the same as "talking." But the most effective salespeople know that listening is the most important part of their job.
>
> —Roy Bartell

"I'd always assumed that because he's a doctor, his thinking would be very clinical, analytical, and by the book," she recalled to her manager. "But it turns out, he's much more conceptual and people-oriented in his thinking. I was talking about cold, hard facts when I should have been talking about possibilities and patient benefits. No wonder he'd been tuning me out."

Tiffany McMacken[1] of Purdue Pharma says that picking up on these kinds of clues makes all the difference in today's pharmaceutical sales environment, where it's not uncommon to get only two or three minutes to spend with a physician, or where there are numerous gatekeepers to get through just to see the decision maker. Understanding how people think helps you not only understand how to "speak their language," but also determine what will engage their attention, drive their decision-making processes, and influence them—especially when you only have two or three minutes with them!

At this point, you might be thinking, that's all very interesting, but I don't work in sales. I would challenge you to take a closer look at what you do and see if that's really true. As Dan Pink suggests in his book *To Sell Is Human*,[2] and as numerous others have pointed out as well, no matter what your specific role is, all of our jobs involve selling in one way or another, whether you're making a pitch, influencing a decision, getting buy-in, selling your ideas, or selling yourself. Building your

> "The key to successful leadership is influence, not authority.
>
> —Ken Blanchard

influence, which is so crucial in today's environment, often means being able to "sell" up, down, across, and outside the organization. There's a great deal we can learn about connecting and influencing from the best in the sales profession that we can then apply in our own way to be more successful in our own specific responsibilities.

Not only has influence become more critical in business, when you consider all the people who may have to weigh in on a decision or be convinced of your idea or its value, but your "customer" base has gotten larger, more diverse, and more distracted. Forget the Golden Rule. To get to the "yes" quickly, you have to apply what Dr. Tony Alessandra calls the *Platinum Rule*[3]: treating others the way *they* want to be treated. Thinking preferences provide the clues to get you there faster and on point.

Overcoming Resistance and Skepticism

Do you remember the last time you were being pitched by someone who really didn't "get you"? Our tolerance for such a mismatch as receivers is very low, yet it happens more often than not when *we ourselves* are trying to influence *others*. It might happen when you're trying to influence your boss or spouse to take action, or when you're working with a colleague who just doesn't see things your way. Maybe you're attempting to teach your child a new skill or are in the middle of a presentation to a tough audience. Progress is slowed or even stopped completely simply because your audience is hearing or viewing the messages through a thinking lens that's very different from the one you're presenting through.

HBDI master facilitator Chuck McVinney[4] delivers a program called "Faculty Leadership for Scientists and Engineers" with Charles Leiserson, a professor of computer science and artificial intelligence at MIT. They've conducted this program, which incorporates Whole Brain Thinking into leadership development, with faculty members at numerous major universities, including the MIT School of Engineering, Carnegie Mellon University School of Engineering and Computer Science, UC Berkeley School of Science and Engineering, Harvard University Division of Computer Sciences, and the National University of Singapore.

As with many presentations delivered before a group, the kickoff is very important because it's all about getting buy-in. If you don't have that to begin with, you've lost your audience for the rest of the program. So that first introduction of the Whole Brain Model in this program is, at its core, like a sales pitch; whether or not the faculty members "buy it" depends on how aligned their thinking is with the mentality behind how it's presented.

Figure 13-1 shows a highly visual representation of the model as a metaphor for how the brain works. For many people, this message resonates instantly. The colorful, image-filled depiction of the different thinking styles makes the concepts clear to them. They get it, they accept it, and they're ready to move on.

For the strong A-quadrant thinkers who make up the science and engineering faculty in Chuck's leadership sessions, however, it's a different story. He found that they would see this image and start analyzing and interpreting it in a completely different way. Even though the model is a metaphor, they

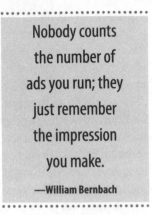

Nobody counts the number of ads you run; they just remember the impression you make.

—**William Bernbach**

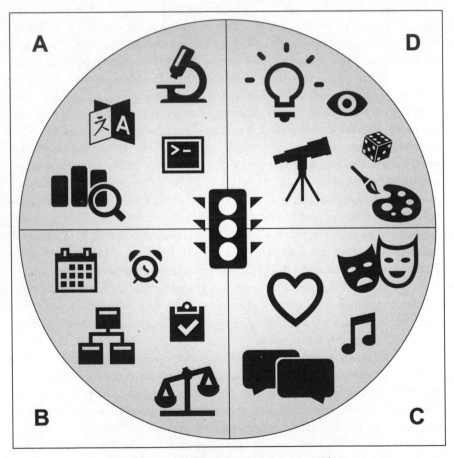

FIGURE 13-1 The Whole Brain Model: A metaphor.

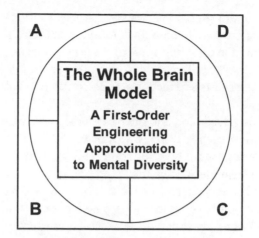

FIGURE 13-2 The Whole Brain Model: A first-order engineering approximation to mental diversity.

were viewing it from their own literal, analytical perspective, and the walls went up. They simply weren't going to accept this conceptual framework on its face.

Chuck and Charles realized that they needed to essentially "sell" the model in the way this audience would best understand it and buy into it. That's when they came up with a new visual to introduce it (see Figure 13-2). Note the description: the A-quadrant nature of it matches the thinking preferences of their audience. Since they changed the presentation, the difference in response and buy-in has been dramatic. The faculty members accept it and move on.

Marketing, Advertising, and Thinking Preferences

Studies of magazine ads that I have conducted reveal that those ads run the gamut of mental options for each quadrant and each mode of the Whole Brain Model. The studies also show that ads tend to cluster in terms of style, format, and location based on the product or service being advertised. For example, ads dealing with financial investments are almost always black and white, very straightforward, crowded with numbers and percentages, and generally located in the first few pages of a magazine like *Forbes* or *Bloomberg Businessweek,* or clearly depicted on websites. Ads and sites for vacations are dramatically different. These are almost always four-color, with exotic scenes provocatively displayed, or with hot-air balloons or sunsets in the background. Family healthcare ads and websites are often soft-focus photos of caring parents and smiling children, designed to pull at our heartstrings. Automobile ads, particularly those in automobile magazines, are often multiple-page foldouts in full color, ranging across all four quadrants in order to appeal to every potential facet of a prospective buyer's fantasies. Automobile websites frequently feature videos, clickable feature charts and technical specs, testimonials, and gorgeous photography.

In television advertising and online videos, there are numerous examples as well, such as the classic "Mac vs. PC" commercials. In one ad, the Mac explains that he's "into doing fun stuff, like movies, music, podcasts, stuff like that," while the PC responds that he, too, likes fun stuff, "like timesheets, spreadsheets, and pie charts." The PC is described as a "wizard at numbers," who wants to help people "balance their checkbooks," while the Mac is good at "creating stuff" and "stimulating imagination."

These ads are prepared by professionals who have diagnosed the market with costly research, including special interviews and focus groups. The objective is to align the product with the market segment that is likely to purchase it. On the average, this seems to work. But my feeling is that advertising agencies frequently fall far short of their goal because they do not take the rather predictable mental preferences of the target population into account. I believe the same is true of marketing and sales departments, of manufacturers, and of service deliverers. While the entirely new field of neuromarketing has arisen to attempt to capture and study consumers' sensorimotor, cognitive, and affective response to marketing stimuli, the solution doesn't have to be that complex. Whole Brain Thinking provides a much more straightforward approach for understanding the mentality of the product, then matching it with that of the target audience we're trying to reach—and then aligning the marketing, advertising, and sales approach to seal the deal.

Connecting with Your Customer

Developing products with customers in mind takes the idea of Whole Brain design to a new level. A lot of organizations talk about being customer-focused and customer-centric, but Microsoft,[5] with the launch of its Kinect peripheral for Xbox 360, did a fantastic job of really looking at who its customer was, and in the process was able to actually improve its design and development approach.

To showcase Kinect's features, the development team at Microsoft Game Studios' Good Science Studio was given the task of making sure that the series of games that shipped with the new peripheral would appeal to the whole family, not just the typical "gamer." Recognizing from our data that the world is a composite Whole Brain, the team members used the Whole Brain Model as a foundational design principle and designed games that appealed to all of the different thinking preferences. Thinking preferences were factored into the game features, the user testing phases, and even as they looked at the makeup of their own team. According to the design team, the benchmark testing they conducted after the game's release confirmed that the Whole Brain design approach had paid off: the most whole-brained game proved to be the most popular.

> It is not your customer's job to remember you. It is your obligation and responsibility to make sure they don't have the chance to forget you.
>
> —Patricia Fripp

Another company that puts thinking at the heart of its customer approach is Telecom New Zealand.[6] How often have you called a customer service number and been totally frustrated by the response and attention you received? Maybe you had to call back again and again to get a satisfactory resolution to your problem. This isn't just annoying for you; it's wasting time and money for the company—and probably damaging its reputation. Telecom New Zealand wanted to get out in front of this issue. To reduce repeat calls to its call centers and increase customer satisfaction rates, the company implemented Whole Brain Thinking training for its call center representatives to help them pick up clues about their customers' thinking preferences so that they could tailor their responses in the most effective way for that person. This meant moving away from a canned script to a more adaptive style, but as the company has discovered, it has ultimately made the call center representatives more efficient. Whereas some customers may have felt rushed and others shortchanged in the past, now all customers spend the "right" amount of time with a representative.

The results have been quantifiable in a number of different ways: the company has experienced a dramatic improvement in postcall surveys, including team customer satisfaction ratings of 4 out of 4, increased dials-to-calls-completed, and improved sales results. In fact, it saw satisfaction scores increase within weeks of undertaking the program, and according to the company's independent auditors, for every $1 it invested in the Whole Brain Thinking program during the first year of the initiative, it made $12 in return. That's what

I would call a significant Return on Intelligence (ROI®)!

Depending on your role, your customer might be a broad consumer audience, like Microsoft's, or an individual on the other end of the phone, like Telecom New Zealand's. It could be a client that you've been trying to make headway with or a colleague in another department. Maybe you need to get buy-in from your boss or rally the team behind your vision. No matter whom you are trying to influence, when you're able to "meet them where they think," you'll be more efficient, and you'll have a better chance of getting the response you're looking for.

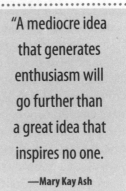

"A mediocre idea that generates enthusiasm will go further than a great idea that inspires no one.

—Mary Kay Ash

Put It to Work

Whether you're designing a product, a presentation, a website, or an advertisement, or simply preparing for a one-on-one conversation, stop for a minute and think about your customer.

Consider an idea that you have or have had in the past and how you might best pitch it based on who the customer or audience is:

- What information does that person need in order to make the decision or resolve the problem?
- How can you present the information in a way that will satisfy his or her needs?
- What strategy should you use to influence or shift his or her thinking?

Here are four examples of customers you might encounter. How would you prepare for each?

A. "Just Give Me the Facts"

Customers with a strong A-quadrant preference are looking for the facts, not the fluff. They prefer:

- Technical accuracy
- Well-articulated ideas
- Data and fact-based charts
- Brief, clear, precise information

They often use a more formal approach and may have already done some research, so they're expecting you to know your stuff. Look for clues to that formality, and be prepared to respond with data to back up your statements.

Be succinct and precise, to the point and brief. The bottom line: don't waste their time. *How would you position your idea for this audience?*

B. "What's the Plan?"

Then there are those with a preference for B-quadrant thinking who want plenty of detail. They prefer things like:

- Thorough information with references
- Timelines and procedures
- Concise, step-by-step approaches
- Reliability and follow-through

They are usually looking for a clear, linear walkthrough of the information. And because they're typically very organized, you need to present yourself that way, too. These customers want to know: What happens next? How will that happen? What are the timelines? Reliability is important. Make sure your response is timely, thorough, and accurate. *How would you position your idea for this audience?*

C. "Show Me You Care About Me"

People who have strong C-quadrant preferences really want to engage with you. They prefer:

- Open, informal discussion
- Expressive body and voice
- Introductions and conversation
- Authenticity—no hidden agendas

They're looking for genuine interest. Because they're usually very expressive, you can pick up from their gestures and their animated expressions that they are looking to connect with you. Canned questions and generic, scripted interactions won't cut it. Make eye contact, engage them with people-centered examples, and look for ways to make a personal connection. *How would you position your idea for this audience?*

D. "What Are the Possibilities?"

The D-quadrant thinkers want the big picture. They prefer:

- Minimal details
- Metaphors and visuals
- Conceptual frameworks
- Freedom to explore

Unlike B-quadrant thinkers, these customers don't want to get bogged down in the details. Be sure to include the big picture and the "why" behind your idea. They're often looking for creative options, so find opportunities to be flexible where you can, and have possible alternatives to the standard approach ready. Because they tend to use picture words in their interactions, one effective way to get your point across is to use metaphors that artfully describe what you're talking about. *How would you position your idea for this audience?*

When preparing for any important discussion or presentation, follow these Whole Brain steps to cover each quadrant for best results:

1. First, give context to clarify very early on why you are there: What it is that you want to get across and why? What's the big picture? Why does this matter? Without context, your messages can be misunderstood or even ignored. (D)
2. Have an agenda or outline in mind, even if it's brief, to let the person or people know where you're going and what to expect—and then stick to it. In addition to helping you stay on point and demonstrate a clear purpose, this step will ensure that you hit on everything you set out to address. (B)
3. Present the key data and facts that back up your intention. Now that you've set up the context and the agenda, you can dive into the content. Your "customer" will have the clarity and perspective to view it through the appropriate lens and hear it the way you meant it. Be prepared with the necessary knowledge to ensure credibility. (A)
4. Engage with interactions and relevant stories, make great eye contact, and listen. Our brains are always looking for connections. By facilitating this process and helping your customer make the connections throughout, you'll have better impact, and the messages will "stick." (C)

SO WHAT?

> No matter what your role is, an essential part of your job is to sell, influence, or gain buy-in in some form or fashion.
> By understanding how those you seek to influence think, whether they are your customers, colleagues, boss, or family members, you can get to the root of how they make decisions and, as a result, influence them in a faster, more positive way.
> The Whole Brain approach, through its diagnostic power and design direction, offers a practical framework for improving presentation, product, and service design as well as other customer-facing activities.
> When in doubt, use a Whole Brain approach to ensure that all audience members have their needs met.

PART 3

Leading the Way Through Business Complexities

© Randy Glasbergen / glasbergen.com

"I'm not lacking leadership skills.
Everyone else is lacking followship skills!"

CHAPTER 14

Whole Brain Leadership: The Secret to Thriving in Today's World

CHAPTER HIGHLIGHTS

> Understanding and accepting the consequences of your thinking prefer-
  ences is the first step toward becoming a better leader.
> Being an effective leader requires using a Whole Brain approach with
  everyone you work with.
> Every stage of leadership requires Whole Brain Thinking, but in different
  degrees based on the work required. The model in Drotter, Charan, and
  Noel's book *The Leadership Pipeline*[1] can be mapped against the Whole
  Brain Model to reveal the thinking required at each stage and how the
  thinking shifts as the person progresses as a leader.
> To become a Whole Brain leader, you also have to recognize where your
  mental blind spots are.

Meeting the rapidly escalating demands for energy in India, the second
most populous nation in the world, is no easy task. For the leaders at
power company CLP India,[2] it was both a huge opportunity and a huge challenge. It wasn't that they lacked experience or technical skill. They were
all highly talented people with deep industry knowledge. But would that be
enough to meet the growing capacity needs? To take advantage of innovative
renewable fuel options? To attract the best and the brightest to work in remote
locations in a not-so-glamorous job?

At a start-up, a creative agency, or a hospitality company, it's usually pretty
well accepted that the leaders need to be comfortable with risk taking, imagination, relationship building, and other right-mode, C/D thinking skills. But

203

what about an accounting firm, a manufacturing facility, or a utility like CLP?

Rich DeSerio,[3] former manager of IBM's award-winning Leadership Development Program's Global Design Team, once said that good leaders move *in anticipation of an event*, rather than in reaction to it. This is particularly true when the world is constantly changing all around us and growing more complex. Leaders often cannot look to the past for guidance on how to handle today's issues because they're dealing with challenges that have

If you seek to lead, invest at least 50 percent of your time in leading yourself.

—Dee Hock, founder and CEO emeritus, Visa

very little precedent. This isn't an isolated phenomenon, affecting leaders only in certain industries; it's universal. Every business has to be more agile and anticipatory to stay ahead.

Rich puts it this way:

> The most important factor IBM looks for in leaders, aside from all the common things, is the ability to lead in a very uncertain world. Markets, economies, these all used to be very predictable. There used to be a very prescribed path. Today, the theme is charting your own course through new waters. There is no one to go to because there are no people who have done what you have to do. You no longer have access to that advice. It's up to you.

People often want to know what the most effective leadership style is. The fact is, there is no "one size fits all" effective leadership style. Leadership is personal; it's individual. The best leaders aren't trying to be someone they're not or to force-fit themselves into a prescribed mold. They understand their *own* style—who they are—and have learned how to leverage it.

So if there is no one type of leader you have to be, what's the key to being an effective leader? Our colleague Michael Morgan[4] in Australia often points out that it doesn't matter what kind of business you're in; *being successful in business requires Whole Brain Thinking*. I would add that no matter what your personal leadership style is, being a successful leader requires Whole Brain Thinking. This means that you understand both your preferences and your blind spots so that you can fully leverage your mental strengths and stretch outside them when necessary.

In fact, the role of CEO actually requires Whole Brain Thinking by design because it necessitates working with and leading a wide range of functions, from finance to strategy to people issues to execution. Our research on CEO HBDI thinking styles (see Chapter 20) data has demonstrated that CEOs have a high percentage of the rare (less than 3 percent of all profiles) Whole Brain profile that has preferences equally distributed across all four quadrants. But the demand for Whole Brain Thinking is no longer limited to the CEO ranks. Our world now requires adaptive and integrative thinking that spans all four quadrants. We no longer have the luxury of relegating ourselves to limited brain bandwidth.

Today's effective leaders are "thought" leaders, highly skilled thinkers who are able to situationally access the different thinking styles across the Whole Brain Model that a given challenge requires, irrespective of their natural preferences.

Leaders at CLP India were able to push the company to lead the way in renewable energy because they learned that their highly technical, analytical style of thinking wouldn't be enough to meet the demands of the market. They "built up the red C quadrant, emphasizing a core CLP value: respect for people, as well as collaboration and communication, and the yellow D quadrant for special projects requiring innovation," as our colleague Prasad Deshpande puts it. He worked with the leaders, using Whole Brain Thinking as the catalyst to change their mindsets about growth, social responsibility, sustainability, and what it takes to build a brand that can attract the best talent available, and in so doing helped the leaders change the culture of the company as well. (To learn more about the CLP program, you can read the full case study at www.wholebrainbusinessbook.com.)

The leadership mentality is the driving force in a company, and the ability to shift one's thinking to match the needs of a given situation is essential. But for the great majority of us who do not have multidominant profiles, this requires learning how to expand our mental bandwidth and unleash our full thinking capacity as we lead.

Growing into Whole Brain Leadership

Ram Charan, Stephen Drotter, and James Noel developed the Leadership Pipeline model, based on 30 years of consulting work with Fortune 500 companies. In their book *The Leadership Pipeline*, they argue that one of the major problems newly promoted leaders have is a difficulty in letting go of the habits that made them successful in the past. Managers accept a promotion to a higher level in the organization without accepting or being prepared for the thinking requirements, behaviors, attitudes, and skills of the new position. In most cases, leaders are not even made aware that the role requires new thinking skills.

This concept of a Leadership Pipeline begins with a basic level of ability and self-knowledge, followed by six higher levels of leadership functions, each of which requires new responsibilities, competencies, and thinking requirements. In mapping the pipeline (see Figure 14-1) against the Whole Brain Leadership Model (see Figure 14-2), we've found that all four quadrants of thinking are involved at each level, but the degree changes in a very specific way.

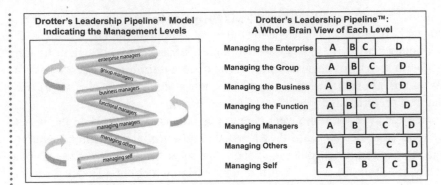

Managing the Enterprise	A	B	C		D			
Managing the Group	A	B	C		D			
Managing the Business	A	B	C		D			
Managing the Function	A	B	C		D			
Managing Managers	A		B		C		D	
Managing Others	A		B		C		D	
Managing Self	A			B		C		D

FIGURE 14-1 Drotter's Leadership Pipeline: A Whole Brain view.

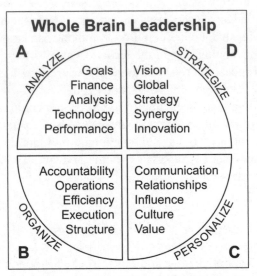

FIGURE 14-2 The Whole Brain Leadership Model.

As you can see in Figure 14-1 (with the relative size of each quadrant at each stage representing the degree of influence for that quadrant), more tactical, B-quadrant thinking dominates the lower levels; interpersonal, C-quadrant thinking grows in the middle stages; the strategic, "big-picture" D-quadrant thinking requirements begin to emerge more strongly at the higher levels of the pipeline; while the analytical A-quadrant thinking stays fairly consistent.

Understanding where you are coming from in terms of your thinking baseline and mental habits is essential in preparing for the different mental demands that your growth and development will require, as well as the mental habits you will need to move away from if you are to be most successful.

Breaking Existing Patterns

Ultimately, becoming a Whole Brain leader is about building your thinking agility, and that can be uncomfortable. You've developed your mental habits—those routines that have always worked for you—and they feel safe. But when leaders approach a new situation with their habitual thinking, they severely limit their ability to generate new ideas or solutions. If your brain continues to process your thought patterns using the same neural pathways that it used in the past, your ability to lead in different ways will not evolve to meet the new demands of the situation. Leading in new ways requires new connections and processes in the brain, breaking your existing patterns.

We know that when you actively engage the brain's capacities, drawing from all four quadrants, you have a larger "playing field" from which to draw your thinking—there is more cross-fertilization between neural synapses, providing the opportunity for new connections to form.

A leader of a large multinational firm once approached me after discovering his HBDI Profile as part of a company coaching initiative and said, "This explains it all." After some discussion, it became clear that he had become so used to living in the A quadrant—thinking analytically, driving performance, and living with the numbers—that he had totally neglected his more C-quadrant relationship skills. Up to that point, his roles had not required the level of social savvy that his current role demanded, and now he was in the hot seat; in fact, that was why he had been encouraged to pursue this coaching. He had found himself making excuses to himself and others, saying, "That's not the kind of leader I am. I don't do the soft stuff—I do the hard stuff," and the like. When he discovered through his profile that he had access to all four quadrants and that he could learn to shift his thinking, he realized that it was time for him to do so—time for him to make it his personal objective to grow and develop in his less-preferred modes. It was up to him, he was motivated, and he had the resources provided to do the work.

Put It to Work

Review the Whole Brain Leadership Model (see Figure 14-2).

Where do *you* begin? The best way to start on this journey is to break down the walls that may have accumulated over the years. These walls insulate you, to a degree, from others: your direct reports, colleagues, the layers below, even your family.

Answer the following questions to get started:

- What do you consider to be the characteristics of an ideal leader?
- What do those characteristics really look like? How do they show up at work?

- Using the Whole Brain Model, how would you describe your leadership style? Your ideal leader?
- How do you feel about your role as a leader or prospective leader?
- What are your greatest leadership strengths? Your greatest challenges?
- What mental habits have you formed?
- If you have completed your HBDI assessment or other assessments, what impact has that had on your approach and your effectiveness as a leader?
- Think about the feedback you have received from others. How might a direct report or colleague who is quite different from you describe your leadership style? What might such a person see as blind spots?
- How can you best address your blind spots by shifting modes in your thinking?

Once you have a better understanding of yourself through the lens of Whole Brain Thinking, you can begin to see opportunities for optimizing your approach to decision making, team development, and dealing with key leadership issues. As a leader, you will get the greatest value from Whole Brain Thinking by being *situational* in your daily activities. The idea is not to attempt to change the unchangeable but to take advantage of the flexibility we all have to become situationally more effective across a broad range of key leadership issues.

An example that comes up frequently for many leaders today is strategic thinking—not the rigors of strategic planning, but the kind of thinking that should precede strategic planning (see Chapter 16). Experience has demonstrated that it's quite possible to open up senior leaders to their strategic thinking potential in as short a time as three days. Once it is experienced, this mode of thinking almost instantly becomes more available on a daily basis.

Focus your leadership training and development priorities on ways to unleash your thinking capability across the mental aspects of the key leadership issues that you are faced with. Over the course of your career, you've probably already demonstrated an enormous capacity to deliver the functional system requirements. To optimize business results in today's world, however, you must now go beyond your day-to-day mental boundaries. For this reason, you must be able to access and develop those mental processes that are still at the lower levels of your learning curve. In addition to strategic thinking, modes that are in high demand today include critical thinking, mindful focus, collaboration, empathy, problem/dilemma solving, intuitive thinking, conceptualizing, dealing with ambiguity, visualizing, and creative processing. (For more on critical twenty-first-century leadership competencies, see Chapter 20.) All of these are like ripples in a pond: they generate additional ripples. To see what I mean, let's look at a specific example of such a "ripple effect."

Learning to Be Situationally Whole

Years ago, I asked participants in a class in advanced management whether they could draw. About 8 hands out of 100 slowly raised. When I asked them if they would like to be able to draw, 80 hands shot up without hesitation. Aha! What would happen if I taught the 80 how to draw? What if I affirmed them in their desire? What would that lead to? What would be the consequences? After the response I got from that group of 80, I decided to help many hundreds more leaders learn how to draw. The objective was not to have them become artists, although some did. The objective was to help them to do something they had always aspired to but could not do because they had no good way to access their latent capability. Once that capability was accessed, the affirmation was enormous. Suddenly they could "see," not for the purpose of drawing, which of course they now could do, but for the purpose of *understanding* more of the world around them. They were very good at thinking analytically, but "seeing" previously unseen possibilities opened up a whole new domain of thinking for them. New creative thinking skills became less intimidating. The notion of strategic thinking began to make sense.

Seeing is a great example of the kind of stuff leaders need to be able to do. You can hire experts in finance and lean and technology. What you can't hire is your own ability to think critically, creatively, and strategically, to think visually, intuitively, and globally—to be able to project your leadership out into the future.

> The moment you stop learning, you stop leading.
>
> —Rick Warren

The human brain is still quite malleable when we are in our thirties and forties, and even in our fifties and sixties—much more so than we used to think. Significant learning can still take place well beyond our traditional school years. The benefits to a business of having a business leader who is able to think more effectively are beyond calculation. No matter what your thinking preferences may be, the degree of wholeness of your mental process is the degree to which you are situational. I have discovered that even in our secondary areas of mental preference, we can become quite knowledgeable and even expert level if we are motivated to use these modes situationally. So no, we do not have to have a perfectly balanced profile in order to be whole. That, to me, is a message of hope!

I'm not suggesting that you abandon your natural preferences. Rather, this is about using your strengths more effectively in service of the business's needs and, just as important, learning to see beyond the mental blind spots that may have resulted from your having applied and reinforced your preferences over the course of your life, education, and career. Embracing complexity requires constant learning and exposure to diverse points of view. You will have to break through your existing mindsets and "mental defaults" to be able to appreciate and take advantage of new perspectives and approaches. Believe me, it is worth the effort.

Tips for Exercising Whole Brain Leadership

1. **Understand all the brainpower that's available—your own as well as others'.** Ask yourself, "How much brainpower do I really use—both of my own, and of my people?" What has been called "management by walking around" (MBWA),[5] I call "leveraging the mental landscape." If you're not spending at least half your time visiting the offices or connecting virtually to engage the thinking and array of quadrants of your direct reports, the field, and your customers, you're insulating yourself from reality and missing out on the full breadth of thinking resources that you have available.

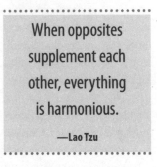

When opposites supplement each other, everything is harmonious.

—Lao Tzu

2. **Ask yourself, "How can I apply this new understanding of thinking to an issue we are facing right now?"** We need to figure out how to listen for, and leverage, the differences in thinking on our teams, especially when we are facing tough new challenges. Who brings fresh thinking to the mix, for you and the issues you are facing? Are some of those ideas even a little uncomfortable? If they're not, maybe you need to hire someone who makes you uncomfortable and challenges you— and once you do, *listen to that person's ideas.* Consciously look for, encourage, and cultivate all styles of thinking, because your organization's health and survival depend on it.

   As Rich DeSerio points out, IBM views diversity as a competitive advantage—the broad definition of diversity, including diversity of thought. "We strongly believe and emphasize: the more perspectives and viewpoints you can get, the better."

3. **Get out of your own "thinking confines."** Managers look. Leaders see. It's very easy to get contaminated by your own industry mindset or by your own internal culture mindset. The constancy of complexity and change means that it's probable current ways of doing business will be altered dramatically by a new technology or trend in the future. Adopt an approach that allows you to regularly escape your thinking confines to improve your strategic and innovative thinking about

these possibilities. Learn to scan the horizon for new ideas and trends. Think beyond the boundaries of your world: strategically scan the web, read books and magazines, attend different conferences, and network widely to learn about industries that have nothing to do with yours today, but that might affect you tomorrow. Look outside your current worldview, or risk being caught off-guard.

4. **Play to people's strengths.** Whenever possible, assign with thinking in mind and look for fit (see Chapters 9 and 10). Having people disengaged and burning out because their jobs don't match their individual thinking preferences can cost your company millions of dollars. Use the HBDI and other Whole Brain tools to understand how you and your people think and how to best utilize their diverse talents.

5. **Manage your blind spots.** Most leaders have tasks and responsibilities that include areas of lower preference and skill. Seek out and leverage feedback from others to ensure that you are fully aware of your blind spots. Take action to address them by beefing up your skill set and/or leveraging the complementary skills on your team to get the work done. You will help those you lead better understand how to develop in areas of lesser preference by modeling this yourself.

6. **Remember that thinking is a form of doing.** As leaders, many of us know but forget that our primary job is to think. We need to optimize what we're doing with our thinking time. Our culture is focused on "do, do, do," to the point where thinking has been devalued. Many leaders have begun to view thinking time as a luxury, even as nonproductive time. The notion of a leader saying, "My primary job is to think," induces guilt, or makes us anxious that it might look as if we're not doing anything at all. But thinking should be the primary focus of every leader. It's your responsibility to own, schedule, and protect your thinking time, as well as the thinking time for those you lead.

SO WHAT?

> All leaders have access to all four Whole Brain quadrants; however, only when we decide we can be situational in our thinking do we optimize and leverage our own brainpower.

> Breaking existing patterns and leadership reflexes is the first step in becoming more situational.

> Leaders will see a significant improvement in their ability to lead others when they invest the time and energy in understanding and speaking the language of those they lead.

> Being a situational Whole Brain leader does not require that you abandon your natural preferences; it does require that you break out of your thinking confines. Recognize your blind spots, learn how to grow beyond your mental defaults to get the results you need, and take advantage of all the thinking resources available to you.
> This is no longer just the realm of the CEO; leaders at all levels require adaptive and integrative thinking that spans all four quadrants in order to lead successfully in an increasingly complex world.

Copyright 2004 by Randy Glasbergen.
www.glasbergen.com

WHY ARE WE
DOING THIS?

"It's not a great mission statement,
but we'll revise it if things get better."

Making Vision and Values Actionable: How to Align Any Business for Optimum Performance

CHAPTER HIGHLIGHTS

> Most organizations today have statements that articulate their vision, mission, and values as a way to create cohesion across the culture. Leaders need to be involved in the development of these statements to ensure buy-in and alignment with them.

> These statements, which often draw on different mental preferences, are typically developed separately from one another, exacerbating the potential for misalignment.

> The Whole Brain approach provides a method of diagnosing the mentality behind these statements and providing context so that everyone in the organization can better understand them and the behaviors that are required for alignment.

> Once they have been fully analyzed through a Whole Brain diagnostic lens, the vision, mission, and values become much easier to understand, communicate, and make actionable.

I was sitting in the waiting room, having been invited to present my Whole Brain Thinking approach to the board of a billion-dollar communications company that was interested in applying it. While waiting, I looked around the well-appointed room and noted a portrait of a distinguished-looking gentleman who was apparently the company's founder. On either side were framed parchment documents describing the mission of the organization and its core values. The mission statement was a very impressive, well-crafted document, impeccably hand-lettered on fine-grain parchment and handsomely framed. I read each document carefully, as it gave me insight into the company's culture. As was my habit at the time, I decrypted the language by diagnosing the

213

mentality of certain words so that I could create a thinking preference "profile" of the documents—a way to get even greater clarity about the culture. We've since automated this process, and the resulting profile is called the HBDI Text Profile. The HBDI Text Profile of this company's mission statement is shown on the left side of Figure 15-1.

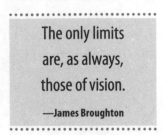

The only limits are, as always, those of vision.

—James Broughton

I had just finished preparing this profile when a staff member let me know that it would be another 10 to 15 minutes before I could come into the boardroom, so I decided to do an HBDI Text Profile of the company's corporate values statement, the similarly framed document on the other side of the founder's picture. I diagnosed each word in terms of its preference characteristics and aggregated the individual elements into an overall profile (see the profile on the right in Figure 15-1).

I was then invited into the boardroom and offered a seat next to the president. After a brief introduction, I was given 45 minutes to present my material, during which time there were numerous questions and nonverbal reactions to what I was saying. This segment was followed by an open discussion of the possibilities for applying my work within this organization.

At the end of the allotted time, the president said, "Ned, I would like to give you a parting gift. Here is a card containing the mission and corporate value statements upon which our business is based. This card is carried by thousands of our employees, who are proud to work for this great company."

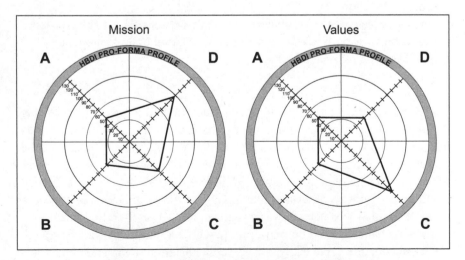

FIGURE 15-1 The HBDI Text Profile of a communications company's mission statement and corporate values.

I accepted the card and noticed that it contained the two statements I had just diagnosed before entering the meeting. When I got back to the hotel, I took half an hour to document my experience in the boardroom, including capturing a generous sampling of statements that I could quote verbatim. Seeing the possibility of a small case history, I then developed an HBDI Text Profile of my experience with the board. Figure 15-2 shows all three profiles plotted together.

My wife, Margy, who always accompanied me on these trips, expressed an interest in a Japanese dinner that night, so we found a nearby restaurant that featured open seating around individual grills. We were seated next to a young couple, and the four of us were the only patrons at that particular grill, so we had a chance to talk. When I asked them what they did and where they worked, they told me that they were both professional employees working for the company that I had just visited. It didn't take much probing for them to reveal

> The reality is that we lose respect for our leaders if we do not approve of their conduct—public or private. Leaders who do not command our respect reduce the legitimacy of their leadership and lose our trust.
>
> —Keshavan Nair

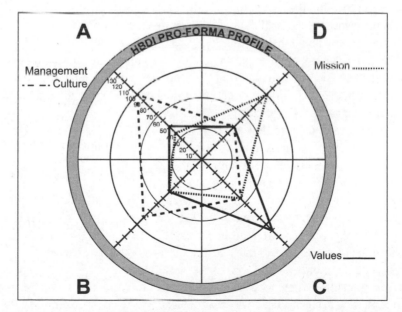

FIGURE 15-2 Composite HBDI Text Profiles of mission, values, and management culture.

their lack of satisfaction with their work for that company. In their own words, they described a pious, crass, self-serving management that did not live up to its stated objectives. When I took the president's plastic card out of my pocket, they burst into laughter. After a minute, they said that not only did they not carry those cards in their wallets, but they had trashed them as soon as they discovered that the company was not living up to the values as they were stated. They added that they were both actively looking for a better place to work and would leave in a heartbeat if the opportunity presented itself.

I seldom have the opportunity to so quickly verify the consequences of a gross misalignment like the one these HBDI Text Profiles revealed. If the leaders are to have credibility, the words describing key leadership issues must be matched by the leaders' behavior. No matter who puts the words together, it is the responsibility of the leaders to make certain that the intent of those words is translated into leadership action. Prior to having a text profiler based on Whole Brain Thinking, there was no easy way to diagnose these kinds of leadership statements, and therefore they have been promulgated without regard for the leadership mentality that they reveal and the consequences of their misalignment with management behavior. Now that there is a way to diagnose the mentality of these statements, making certain that they are strongly aligned should be a New Year's resolution of leadership teams—unless of course, they don't give a damn about their credibility.

> When CEOs are asked how much of the knowledge in their companies is used, they typically answer, "About 20 percent."
>
> —Charles Handy

The vision statement, mission statement, core values, and annual report are among the key documented materials that come out of the leadership team. As they establish the purpose and direction of the business, these documents represent the thinking of the leadership.

In most cases, however, they are developed by committees, separately and at different times during the team's tenure. Therefore, they reflect thinking that may be appropriate to different people, situations, and time frames. Even when they are written by the same group at the same time, they are often different! In any case, I believe the business leaders must ensure that these written statements are consistent, and

> Imagine the implications for a company if it could get that number up to 30 percent.
>
> —Betty Zucker

that, taken together, they document the purpose and direction of the business on an everyday basis in such a way that the leaders' behaviors exemplify them. We can't have this year's vision and last year's values if they no longer apply.

We shouldn't have an annual report that conveys a different message from the current mission statement on which daily decisions are being based.

The Whole Brain approach provides a consistent method for diagnosing the mentality of each of these documents or statements, allowing for a clear comparative analysis. For example, Figure 15-3 shows an array of what I refer to as the key leadership issues of a large U.S. corporation.

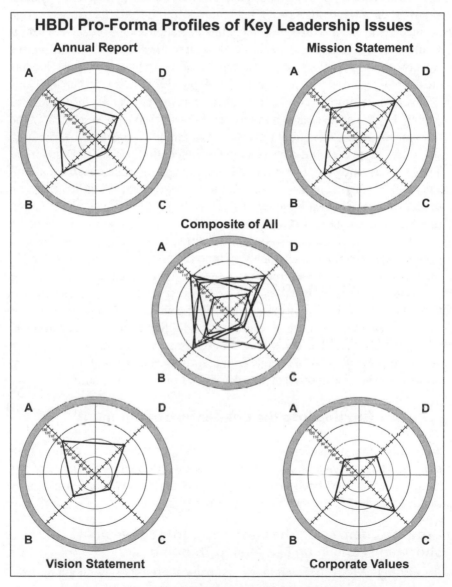

FIGURE 15-3 Key leadership HBDI Text Profiles for a U.S. corporation. Pro-forma profiles of key leadership issues.

These HBDI pro-forma profiles were developed by creating an HBDI Text Profile of each descriptive word, sentence, paragraph, or page of a particular document. Also included in the analysis were any charts, graphs, financial data, or illustrations. For example, a page of financial data would be diagnosed as an exclusively A-quadrant element of the complete document. An illustration of a family enjoying a picnic, in which the company's products were displayed, would be considered primarily a C-quadrant element, with perhaps a D-quadrant contribution if the products were being newly introduced. In contrast, a page devoted to the manufacturing assembly line operation and its production results would contribute a strong B-quadrant element to the overall diagnosis. In this way, the thinking preference characteristics of the statements and documents are diagnosed and aggregated into an overall profile of that key leadership issue.

Even to the untutored eye, it is clear that the key leadership issues as depicted by the profiles shown in Figure 15-3 are reasonably consistent in the rational and analytic A quadrant, less consistent in the organized, structured B quadrant, and even less consistent in the conceptual, visionary D quadrant. They are flagrantly inconsistent in the humanistic, interpersonal C quadrant. This lack of alignment lessens the credibility of the leaders unless they can model what is being expressed. In this case the profiles validated a situation in which management was proclaiming values that were not actually being carried out. It described things to the investing public that were not experienced by the customers and employees, and the good intentions embedded in the vision statement were more of a pipe dream than a reality.

I find it extremely revealing that, in the vast majority of cases, it is the C or D quadrant that is consistently out of alignment with actual behaviors. This is where the rubber tire of leadership credibility meets the hard pavement of employee reality. The documents and statements that leaders create invite people to compare their intentions with their performance, and there are consequences when the described behaviors aren't in sync with reality.

Digging into the Challenge of Alignment

So what's going on in these organizations? Why is this such a common phenomenon among leaders, even in companies with strong roots in visionary, inclusive leadership? I believe there are several reasons. We can learn a lot by looking at what happens with vision as companies grow.

Growing Companies: The Classic Struggle Between Short- and Long-Term Leadership Thinking

It's instructive to realize that many companies, even those with a long-term vision and a solid business plan, fail to survive infancy. The actuarial statistics are ominous. For every 100 new businesses, fewer than 50 survive the first five years, and fewer than 33 survive the first decade.[1]

Very early in the life cycle of any new business, it becomes apparent that too much attention is being paid to the future dream and not enough to the realization that you have to deliver the product or service and invoice it in order to generate cash, and cash is always in critically short supply. If there is a D-quadrant dreamer involved in this infant stage, the wake-up call comes early, even if it's filtered out.

Whatever action the company takes, it must happen, and it must happen fast. Entrepreneurial thinking must be curbed in favor of operational action. Long-term vision must take a back seat to immediate implementation of short-term plans.

It doesn't take long to discover who is needed to build the product, deliver it, render service, and collect for it—in general, the employees and teams that can produce short-term results. Those who cannot contribute to this process are often reassigned or laid off. Since what little capital was raised to start the business has often already been consumed, the critical issue now is cash flow. Survival depends on cash generation, and an accelerated planning cycle, if there is one, is in terms of weeks and months rather than years.

Under these conditions, while the organization's vision needs to be clearly established to keep the organization on track, the leadership mentality must shift to be much more strongly oriented toward the A/B quadrants: infrastructure, processes, results, and execution. It's a ten-hours-a-day, six-days-a-week focus on short-term results. The people in charge can't be bothered with anything that does not produce immediate results, and when those results happen and people are recalled or newly hired to deliver the product or service or help run the business, the leaders in charge must reorient them to the short-term business plan in the context of the long-term vision—because that's what's producing results. While the focus is heavily weighted toward the A and B quadrants, it's often the initial vision and passion of the C and D quadrants that will have helped attract talent, show devotion to customers, and provide the energy required for the culture to sustain these efforts.

Those businesses that survive infancy and move into the adolescent stage tend to perpetuate the leadership that has helped them survive. As a result, unless they work hard to keep the C-oriented cultural appeal to attract and retain talent, and provide the right service to their customers and the D-directed ongoing innovation and clarity of vision alive—as many companies in Silicon Valley do today—the typical established management culture will now have a solid A-quadrant/B-quadrant tilt in its DNA. These leadership genetics are pretty well established by this time, and as incremental success is achieved, the mode of leadership is cloned. If the long-term vision was put on hold to manage short-term needs, it may have been forgotten by this point or it may simply be paid lip service, leading to misaligned messages both internally and externally.

As the company moves through adolescence and begins to mature, it's often relatively easy for outside observers to notice that the company is beginning to run out of steam, even though insiders may not see it. The warning signs that this is happening can usually be found in a variety of areas: no new products are being developed, services are becoming obsolete, credibility within the marketplace is dwindling, competitors are now delivering better stuff at lower prices, and missed opportunities abound. The sad truth is that the short-term mentality that avoided early death set the pattern for death to occur in late adolescence.

To be in the 33 percent of companies that survive the first 10 years, the leadership must move from being focused on survival to being balanced and whole-brained: honoring the technical and financial aspects; the processes, execution, and quality; the devotion to talent and customers; and the ongoing innovation, vision, and strategy. Just having the right direction of leadership mentality is not enough—you need the competencies that go along with a more opportunistic, whole-brained leadership to move the organization to the next level.

This is often challenging at the individual leader level as well, not just a problem with the management culture. The path to leadership is a progression built on proven ability and success in roles that have often been more tactical and functional. That's what you have been measured against up until this point. Suddenly, as you progress up to new leadership levels, a mind shift is required, one that necessitates moving away from a primary focus on A- and B-quadrant thinking to building up the interpersonal C- and strategic D-quadrant thinking styles. (For more specific insights on what is required at each level, see "Growing into Whole Brain Leadership" in Chapter 14.) The bottom line: the company can't make the shift if its leaders don't.

This level of leadership includes having an updated vision of the company that will take it to its next phase of maturity: a long-range strategic business plan that is focused on providing the human resource assets capable of innovative new product development, financial and funding know-how, technology and IT, marketing and sales savvy, and the risk taking needed to grow. The pendulum that swung from the founding dream to the hard-nosed survivor must now swing back to a multidominant center position that can conceive and deliver mature business results.

The more A/B-quadrant leadership DNA will treat the swing to the right as a virus, and the organization's immune system will try to throw it off because it feels like a threat and appears too risky. Early diagnosis of this illness is very elusive. The first medication is instant rationalization. The thinking trap is believing, "The leadership style that took us through infancy and near bankruptcy to today's success is good enough to now take us to our corporate destiny. Why take unnecessary risks?"

Shifting the mentality of previously successful leadership to what is required for future growth is extremely difficult. If the company wants to be among the businesses that achieve "prime," then it must find leaders who can accomplish the mental shift to situational wholeness, either from the inside or from without. The entrepreneurial founder who stepped aside for survival may return at this point, if a balanced team and the right conditions are in place—as Steve Jobs did at Apple in 1997 after having been fired by the board in 1985. Having evolved as a leader, he brought on Tim Cook in 1998 to provide the necessary balance required to take Apple to the next level.

Ultimately, for a company to achieve optimal long-term business results, it must have situational Whole Brain leadership. This is not a theory. This is hard reality.

A Case Example of Aligning for Sweet Success

Cookie Time,[2] an iconic New Zealand snack company, had experienced impressive growth since its inception, being transformed from a single-person entrepreneurial business into an organization with multiple product lines and 42 franchises. However, the company had reached the point where realignment was necessary to ensure that it would be able to sustain its growth over the long term. The challenge would be to restructure for continued innovation and the introduction of new, specialized functions without losing the qualities and characteristics that the company valued and that had been integral to its success thus far.

Cookie Time's goal was to manage change successfully in order to transform the entire business, with a vision of becoming New Zealand's most-loved snack foods brand by winning the hearts and minds of consumers. To achieve the vision, it would not be enough to simply introduce a new structure and explain what people's roles would be. Because true organizational transformation depends on every employee's being able to see the bigger picture of change, the company determined that Whole Brain Thinking could provide a common language and foundation to communicate what it wanted to achieve and get buy-in from everyone involved. By first using the HBDI to identify thinking preferences, and then using the Whole Brain Model as the basis for communicating the vision, values, and guiding principles, the leaders were able to effectively explore and elaborate on different elements of the culture. This process allowed them to articulate the vision in a way that resonated with the employees.

With a common language and support for the vision, more well-rounded programs for employees, and more appropriately balanced teams, Cookie Time has improved its financial position and enjoyed outstanding growth since the initiative began. The CEO attributes these successes to the cultural foundation and clarity provided by the HBDI and Whole Brain Thinking. The company was able to adopt a new strategic approach and develop the structure to support it without losing the core characteristics that it has always valued.

Enterprise Alignment: It Starts with the Individual

From smaller growing companies to huge, established corporations, the concept of thinking preferences and Whole Brain leadership clarifies a wide array of alignment issues. Alignment starts at the individual level. Whether it's the alignment of our mental preferences and our educational choices, the alignment of how we prefer to think and our occupational choices, or the alignment of those things that we are most energized by and our actual work assignment, I believe that most of the business world is out of alignment rather than in alignment. Too often, it is relatively rare for people to be truly aligned with the activity they are involved with, whether it is going to school, pursuing a career, or performing a job.

As I explored in Chapter 10, I anticipate that Maslow's notion of self-actualization[3] would occur more frequently if there were a strong alignment between how we think and what we are doing, and that if this were the case, the level of effort required to engage in that activity would be more relaxed, free-flowing, and therefore more efficient in the use of our mental faculties. When we are too far out of alignment, we have to struggle to perform, because what we are doing is not really what we are interested in doing.

In today's competitive talent market, alignment is the path to competitive advantage. Just imagine what it would be like if your organization had made a concerted effort to understand the mental preferences of its people, to diagnose and understand the mental requirements of the work to be done, and then to sort out the work and divide it up into packages of activities that could be matched as closely as possible to the mental preferences of the people in the organization—with growth and learning support provided for those areas that were not aligned. This would create individual alignment between people and their work not only at the micro level, but also at the macro level, leading to alignment across the organization. Can you imagine what a positive impact that would make on your productivity and the performance of the organization? Wouldn't that be an organization that you and others would want to work for?

I see an opportunity for each individual, from leaders to the front lines, as well as the whole enterprise, to seek alignment of the various segments of personal and business life by making adjustments, not only in the mental approach we take to those elements, but also in those elements themselves. Success, satisfaction, fulfillment, and the simple pleasure of our daily existence can improve when personal alignment is achieved. And once individual misalignment has been addressed, enterprise alignment must be tackled. Such clarity of understanding across the enterprise can only serve to improve business results, as more engaged employees better satisfy customers and ultimately drive shareholder value.

Sound too good to be true? Our experience has demonstrated that those organizations that proactively address these inevitable alignment issues improve engagement, better understand and connect with customers, unleash innovative thinking at all levels, and consistently win the war for talent. They build a culture in which the leadership "walks the talk" and people feel valued because leaders understand how to best leverage the thinking that is available to them—the only path to business results. This is no longer a "nice to have," but rather a must-do for any business to compete successfully and thrive in today's environment. So where do you start?

The Key Roles of the CEO and the Leadership Team: Diagnose and Take Action

Let's go back to that billion-dollar communications company, with its carefully crafted mission and values statements that no one believed the leaders were truly embodying. The most effective approach to the enterprise alignment issue is to develop a vision, a mission, a set of goals and objectives, and a definition of the organization's values, then compare the alignment between the mentalities of those issues, the alignment between them and the leadership action, and the total array considered from the standpoint of the organization as a whole. Experience tells us that it would be rare indeed for all these significant business issues to be in alignment without conscious preparation. Once their degree of

> The standard of leadership depends not only on the qualities and beliefs of our leaders, but also on the expectations we have of them.
>
> —Keshavan Nair

alignment is determined through the visualization of an HBDI pro-forma and Text Profiles, however, it becomes much easier to recognize, communicate, explain, and address the gaps.

In my experience, it is likely that different functions of the business within a given organization will be at different levels or degrees of alignment. For example, the engineering function may be in stronger alignment than the manufacturing function, and the marketing and sales organization at a different level of alignment from engineering and manufacturing. Under these conditions, it is less likely that the integrated business can be successful. To overcome this, the leaders of those functions need to work closely with the CEO to understand these issues and the roles they play in causing cross-enterprise misalignment, irrespective of people's natural preferences.

Thus, one of the roles of the CEO and key leaders is to do their own internal alignment work, understanding how they think so that they can function as an aligned "first team," loyal to the needs of the team they report to and honoring the needs of the enterprise more than the needs of the individual function they lead. The next step is to diagnose the cross-enterprise alignment issues and put together a plan to do something about them. There are, of course, two sides of the equation: the vision, mission, values, and goals of the organization, on the one hand, and the orientation of the culture and the human assets, on the other. The top leaders need to be crystal clear about what they want and be prepared to address and align both. They can change the vision, change the mission, or change the objectives of the organization (values are rarely changed, however) to better meet the reality of its culture and its human assets. Leaders can also change the nature, the mix, the capability of the human assets, and the culture to better meet the vision, objectives, and goals of the organization. One of the significant ingredients of the decision process is the ability to diagnose, to measure, to understand, and to easily compare.

Here is how this works: once the leadership team fully understands the dynamics of its thinking, its process flow, and its internal alignment issues using a tool like the HBDI Team Profile, it can then explore and quantify the aggregate brainpower, in terms of the HBDI averages, of each function of the organization. Next, by developing HBDI Text Profiles of the key leadership issues, such as the vision, values, mission, goals, and objectives, the leadership team begins to understand the relationship between those issues and aspirations and how the organization as a whole and its functions

> Then the LORD said to me, "Write my answer plainly on tablets, so that a runner can carry the correct message to others."
>
> —Habakkuk 2:2

are or are not aligned. Finally, adjustments may need to be made and plans designed to address the gaps. This may include coaching or specific development for key leaders who are "not there yet." For many businesses, the availability of this tool represents the first time the CEO and the leadership team have had a way of assessing the degree of alignment between these major aspects of the business. One CEO we work with pulls this data up every time his team members get together to address critical leadership issues so that they never lose sight of how important alignment is to their ability to lead the enterprise effectively.

What Story Does Your Annual Report *Really* Tell?

Annual reports serve an important purpose—they tell a very public story about the business to the investing public, the employees, and ultimately the world at large. But too often, the story that is being told by the annual report is not the story that the company intends to tell, because the mentality of the document and the communication approach are often not fully understood. The HBDI Text Profile and pro-forma diagnosis can be very useful in uncovering and addressing this issue.

Here's a real-life example of just such an experience. At a meeting for DuPont's top 200 high potentials some years ago, I established the premise of the Whole Brain Model, presented the group's data (averages and composites), and shared with the group a diagnostic HBDI pro-forma profile of that year's annual report, titled "A Global Entrepreneur." The HBDI pro-forma was met with a gasp, laughter, then applause. The reason for this reaction was the contrast between the group's HBDI data, the report's title, and the HBDI pro forma of the report. The organization, like all large organizations in every industry, was a "whole brain." However, the content and layout of the annual report, while it was titled "A Global Entrepreneur," implying a big-picture, strategic, futuristic, risk-taking organization, was actually strongly tilted to the A quadrant: a financial, bottom-line, technical, analytical mentality. The CEO, Ed Woolard, stood and thanked me personally for this enlightening revelation.

In the years that followed, I tracked the DuPont annual report. The HBDI pro formas changed gradually but consistently to reflect DuPont's vision. A few years later, DuPont's annual report won the prestigious Mead Award for Best Annual Report. The company attributed this success in part to the understanding brought to it through Whole Brain Thinking analysis and the presentation of the HBDI pro-forma profile in that high-potential meeting.

Put It to Work

Organizational Alignment

Take a moment to review your organization's key statements (or those of an organization you know well if your organization doesn't have them), such as the vision, mission, values, and goals, and consider the degree to which the culture is aligned or not.

- What is out of alignment? Does the behavior of the leaders align with what is stated?
- What are the implications, both internally and externally? Is this something customers might notice?
- How do employees respond? Do you or they understand, pay attention to, or aspire to align with these statements? Some more than others?
- What might the organization do about this?
- What can you, your leader, or your team do to improve the alignment?

Personal Alignment

Close your eyes for a moment and think about where you would like to be in 10 years. Perhaps you want to reach new career heights, run your own company, give back, become an artist, go back to school, or organize and plan your life so that you can be ready for your next phase.

- Write down your vision based on your reflection. Capture the key ideas, images, and outcomes you want to achieve.

Think about the implications, using the Whole Brain Model to get a thorough understanding of all the issues and consequences.

- How will your preferences help or hinder your progress?
- How well does this fit your dream?
- What needs to happen first, then next?
- What are your key milestones? What is your timeline?
- Now ask others in your family (for example, your spouse or partner and/or your kids) to develop their own visions, capture them, and share them.
- How do your preferences affect your reaction to their vision? Their reaction to yours?
- Is there alignment between each of your visions? If not, how do your preferences help explain that? What might you do to get greater alignment?

Fascinating and important conversations can take place after this exercise to get greater alignment and/or to find a way to ensure that all visions are accomplished.

SO WHAT?

> When an organization's key leadership issues, statements, and documents are in alignment, the message becomes clearer, the leadership's credibility improves, and employee engagement and retention increase.
> Shifting from a short-term focus to situational Whole Brain leadership is essential for long-term organizational growth and survival.
> Individual alignment and enterprise-level alignment are both critical to business success.
> Using the Whole Brain approach allows leaders to diagnose and bring into alignment the mentality of key leadership documents, behaviors, and the culture for improved cohesion and success.
> The CEO and the top leadership team can get started by first diagnosing and addressing their alignment as a team and then tackling alignment between functions and across the enterprise.

"To survive in the new global economy will require massive consistent effort and immediate bold action! Without further delay, I am putting together a 10 year plan to study the problem further."

CHAPTER 16

The Essential Shift to Strategic Thinking: Making Strategic Planning Pay Off

CHAPTER HIGHLIGHTS

> In most organizations, more emphasis is placed on strategic planning, while the importance of strategic *thinking* is overlooked.

> Effective strategic planning requires an ability to *think* strategically.

> Strategic thinking draws primarily on D-quadrant mental processes, while strategy and strategic planning are Whole Brain processes.

> Creative thinking and strategic thinking are mental cousins. Since there are proven ways of tapping into and unleashing an individual's creative potential, there are also steps you can take to build your strategic thinking potential.

G E's corporate executive office had commissioned me to develop a strategic planning program as part of the effort to get GE's culture to approach business more strategically. In response, my executive education colleagues had developed a weeklong workshop directed at the company's top 200 general managers and planning executives. A short time later, the CEO requested a shorter program for the 10,000 downline managers in the company who needed to understand strategic planning in order to further this planned cultural change. While the program I developed was judged very successful, my sense that I had somehow missed the mark persisted. I didn't feel that the program fully conveyed what the strategic thinking part of strategic planning really means, but I couldn't figure out what I should have done instead. It took Henry Mintzberg's article[1] on how people could be smart and dull at the same time to provide the first clue.

First, it is useful to understand that strategic planning differs mentally from operational planning. Operational planning requires more structure and deals with facts, logic, analysis, sequence, detail, time, history, process, and procedure. In strategic planning, which is more experimental, we need strategic thinking, which deals with vision, insight, inference, intuition, trends, patterns, integration, synthesis, projections, risk, and global thinking.

Since none of us had thought about the mental differences between operational planning and strategic planning, neither the content nor the delivery of the workshop took into account the critical shift required from the more risk-averse, safekeeping, lower-left B-quadrant modes called for in operational planning to the riskier, experimental, upper-right D-quadrant modes that were crucial to strategic planning. Unwittingly, we had largely ignored the right-mode quadrants. From beginning to end, the strategic planning workshops and programs emphasized A- and B-quadrant processes and techniques while overlooking major aspects of the C- and D-quadrant thinking modalities that were required to build a truly *strategic* plan.

> To stay ahead, you must have your next idea waiting in the wings.
> —Rosabeth Moss Kanter

> Almost all men are intelligent. It is method that they lack.
> —F. W. Nichol

Even more crucially, we had greatly underestimated the learning challenge that was inherent not only in this short program, but also in the entire cultural shift required for success. Any move away from a preferred or primary thinking mode to an area of secondary (mid-level) or even tertiary (low) preference sharply heightens the demand on a person's mental energies, especially if the person's normal operating mode happens to be diagonally opposite to the material being taught. Since the vast majority of the people participating in these programs had strong preferences for the logical, analytical, rational, and operational planning modes, it was an enormous leap for them to comprehend strategic thinking and planning, let alone learn how to implement it.

Chuck McVinney,[2] who often conducts Whole Brain Strategic Thinking workshops with our clients, suggests that it's particularly difficult to think strategically when you're "mired in the swamp" of today's issues and short-term goals. He notes that there is a seemingly universal resistance to long-term thinking because today's problems are so complex and all-consuming. Leaders and managers can get away with staying focused on the short term because the organizational culture—and the stock market—are so fixated on the immediate numbers and priorities,

> A man to carry on a successful business must have imagination. He must see things in a vision, a dream of the whole thing.
> —Charles M. Schwab

that the tendency is to become more reactive than proactive. They stay in the safekeeping mode because it fits today's needs and, often, because it's a mental comfort zone for management. The business's long-term success suffers as a result.

Strategic Thinking Must Precede Strategic Planning

Strategic planning, when well done, is a Whole Brain process and is not a walk in the park. It's actually a pretty difficult process that requires a great deal of homework, scanning of the environment and competitors, attempting to "see around corners," and analysis of and research into customers' needs—not only those needs that are already articulated and served, but also those needs that are unarticulated and as yet unserved. In the typical situation, senior executives plunge into strategic planning because "it's the thing to do," without ever really stopping to define it or ask themselves what it is or how to do it, let alone what the thinking requirements should be or how to shift their thinking to best engage that thinking. As a matter of fact, there aren't too many senior executives who actually know what an effective and truly *strategic* plan is and how to best differentiate it from an operating plan. Strategic plans deal with the future, with products, with markets, with customers, and with the business environment in which those markets and customers are served. There are a number of outstanding experts on strategic planning. In contrast, there are very few on *strategic thinking*.

Imagination is the beginning of creation. We imagine what we desire; we will what we imagine; and at last we create what we will.

—George Bernard Shaw

This isn't just about semantics. The two are very different, and strategic thinking must precede any attempt to create a strategic plan. Strategic thinking is a mindset that allows you to:

- Anticipate, invent, and understand potential future events and issues.
- Imagine and create alternative scenarios.
- Destroy your preassumptions to free up new perspectives on your business.

Then, and only then, can you:

- Assess and understand your options.
- Decide on your objectives.
- Determine the direction to take to achieve those objectives on a *winning basis*.

Beyond the strategic plan, strategic thinking as a competency has become an even more critical part of day-to-day decision making. The continual shifts and changes in the environment—external and internal, those that we can control and those that we can't—mean that the skill of strategic thinking is essential for staying fast, flexible, and ahead of the curve. It's a skill that we need to be developing in ourselves and in our leaders and employees at all levels, even if they are not part of the formal strategic planning process, since the pace of change is affecting everyone and decisions are being made much closer to the customer.

While successful long-term organizational strategy requires all four quadrants, strategic thinking is largely a D-quadrant process (see Figure 16-1). Strategic thinking deals in futures, in patterns, in trends, and in nuances

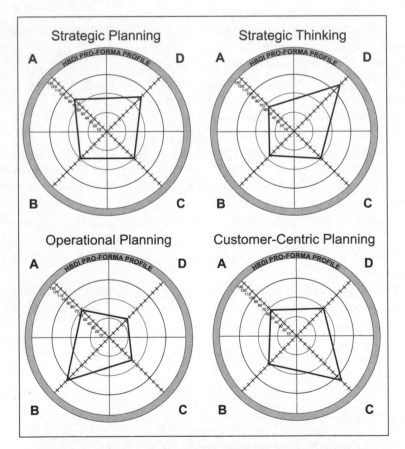

FIGURE 16-1 Understanding the differences between strategic thinking and strategic planning. HBDI pro-forma profiles for operational planning, strategic planning, strategic thinking, and customer-centric planning.

that require an ability to sense emerging strategies in the middle of daily business chaos. It deals more in fuzzy logic than in the kind of logic that we use to analyze and diagnose. Whereas key segments of a strategic plan can be described in facts and quantified in numbers, strategic thinking is best revealed in concepts, visuals, and metaphors, and through creative thinking and intuitive flashes. This requires tapping into our highly perceptive nonverbal brain, using mind hacks and other techniques like visualization, creative model building, doodling, and sketching. Most strategic plans have a visible structure and sequence; strategic thinking is largely conceptual and starts with the end in mind.

How, then, do executives and managers who are trained in the reality of the here and now, who quantify with facts and numbers and live in analytics, make sense out of something that feels like a cloud of smoke or a handful of air? Well, it takes a totally different mindset, and you don't acquire it just by reading about it. In my experience, most managers and leaders need to go through a transition stage. They need to metamorphose into a mental state in which they place the same value on the insights emerging from a nontraditional conceptual, metaphorical model as they would on a spreadsheet of production numbers or on the diagnosis of a customer's annual report.

Once there is buy-in to the process and the transition takes place, a wealth of untapped new thinking suddenly starts to emerge, and breakthroughs occur. A senior team from a global semiconductor company worked through a metaphorical process in which it used animals to describe the company's various stakeholders. When the distributors were described as snakes, sloths, and similar animals, the group suddenly realized that the company was overlooking a great opportunity and that the best strategic option for increasing its market share was readily available: tapping

> Strategic leadership requires one other skill. It is a readiness to look personally foolish; a readiness to discuss half-baked ideas, since most fully baked ideas start out in that form; a total honesty, a readiness to admit you got it wrong.
>
> —Sir John Hoskyns

into the distributor base, which the company had been treating as substandard, "backup" customers. As the group looked at the future market opportunities, this approach was forward thinking and a competitive advantage for the firm. Had they not been open to the notion of using metaphors, they would never have uncovered that option.

Eight Processes for Transitioning to Strategic Thinking

From my experience working with a large number of managers and senior executives who have been in the midst of making this metamorphosis, I've noted the following processes as essential steps on the path of transition:

1. **Know your preferences.** Strategic thinkers must understand their own mentality. That is, they need to know the reality of their own thinking preferences, which lead to their everyday business behaviors. Managers and leaders are often capable of doing certain things very successfully, and at the same time totally incapable of doing other things. For example, there are some very successful business managers who cannot fathom an annual report or, for that matter, a financial statement. Others do not have the ability to develop a strategy, or even to understand what a strategy is. To understand strategic thinking, you need to first know what your thinking baseline is.

2. **Define strategic thinking.** A clear definition of strategic thinking must be understood and accepted in order to help leaders access it. Most organizations have a process in place for strategic planning. Revisiting this process to clarify the strategic thinking components needed is a critical step. For those managers who are looking to build their strategic thinking muscle, it is important to set the context for the what, the how, and the why of strategic thinking as a competency and its implications for their role and their decision-making approaches.

3. **Stretch to and leverage D-quadrant thinking.** Whatever their profile of mental preferences, strategic thinkers must be able to make use of their D-quadrant mental capabilities, at least situationally. They must have a sense of the future. They must be able to take a risk. They must be able to perceive patterns. They must be able to deal with ambiguities. They must be able to think in metaphors. They must be able to visualize. And, of course, they must be able to think holistically—that is, see the big picture and scan the environment. And they must be able to access, respect, be aware of, and trust the validity of their own intuition.

   All these capabilities are available to each of us in our existing array of mental options, but usually in different degrees. It's likely that we used these mental processes as children, but we began to be talked out of their validity by our parents and teachers, and then by all the other influential people throughout our life. These forms of mental processing are not typically strongly advocated in the business environment, but many successful CEOs use them frequently, whether they are aware of it or not.

For example, on a major transaction such as an acquisition, when the time for a final decision arrives and all the facts are in, all the spreadsheets have been diagnosed and analyzed, and all the staff work has been done, the CEO often leaves the cluttered boardroom and takes a short break outside the room, say on the balcony or someplace else where he or she can get some perspective. After a few minutes, the CEO comes back and says, "We're gonna go!" There are no new facts. There is no brilliant new financial diagnosis. That decision is based on an instant holistic review of all the factors involved, and an intuitive conclusion to take action.

4. **Get uncomfortable.** Strategic thinkers need to be open to new ways of thinking and learning that at first may feel silly or uncomfortable. Doing so allows them to get smart in areas where they are currently somewhat dumb, even if what they are doing does not look or feel "smart" to them at the time. There are proven ways of tapping into and unleashing creative and strategic potential, for accessing previously self-censored intuition, and for seeing patterns to gain clarity of vision.

5. **Use metaphors.** A critically important thinking process that might seem ridiculous to a bright MBA is to think metaphorically. Metaphors are a terrific way to tap into the brain's insights that are most difficult to express in words. One of my valued colleagues, Ayn Fox,[3] developed a process years ago in which participants in a learning session select a toy or creative item as an object that has attributes that describe themselves. For example, "*I am like this* kaleidoscope *because* I have many facets of interest that constantly change." Or, "I am like this electronic plasma sculpture because I, too, radiate energy in all directions, and when I come in contact with others, this energy is often transferred to them." The metaphors would inevitably provide *aha* moments that would surprise the individual as he or she described it, in terms of both the accuracy and the degree of insight that they provided.

I adapted an idea from the Wharton School to use "car metaphors" to reveal a person's attitude about a company, a customer, or a situation (see Figure 16-2). This powerful exercise is done by drawing little basic sketches (even stick figures are fine) of imaginary cars or other vehicles that reveal the type and/or model (for example, sports car, sedan, Toyota Prius, Dodge Minivan, BMW, school bus, tank, or spaceship), how it is accessorized, and the environment it's in. In ways that words often can't express, these sketches clearly bring to bear a person's point of view with respect to his or her own company and a competitor, or to the company today and 10 years in the future. They reveal unarticulated thoughts that are otherwise very difficult to access and are extremely useful when thinking strategically.

FIGURE16-2 Two examples of vehicle metaphor drawings revealing different views from differing perspectives—the company in the future (left) and the company today (right).

Another technique is to select an animal for its characteristics as a representation of the company, a customer, or a competitor (for example, an eagle, a tiger, or a snake), as the semiconductor company did. A variation is to write a story about being that animal as it relates to the world in general, or as it relates specifically to your competitor or customer. Important insights and nuances are revealed as the choice of animal and story are shared with others.

These few examples of the use of metaphors demonstrate that it is extremely powerful and extraordinarily successful. Through practice, metaphorical thinking can become an important pathway to hitherto unused mental insights and skills.

6. **Build models to tap into your innate creativity and gain strategic insight.** One of the most effective techniques for accessing strategic thinking is what I call "creative modeling." This is the use of creative materials to build a model of an organization or an entire company that portrays the most significant attributes of that organization. This is not a literal model that looks like the headquarters building, but rather a metaphorical construction that reveals attributes that have not been previously articulated.

Imagine for a moment building a creative metaphorical model of your company, and alongside it building a model of your key customer. In between the two models are the connections (or absence of connections) that represent the relationships you have with your key customer. In the many hundreds of times that I have used this technique, I cannot recall a single instance in which the model maker did not discover something new and important—most often of strategic importance—about either the company or the key customer. The process is so engaging and so much fun that before you know it, you have selected a piece of creative material and assembled it in such a way that it reveals something important that you never thought of before. That is only one aspect of the power of this technique, which allows you to think three-dimensionally about any given situation.

7. **Understand the mentality of your culture.** As discussed in detail in Chapter 15, another insightful process that we have used is diagnosing and developing the HBDI pro-forma profile of a company's culture, annual report, vision statement, mission statement, and statement of core values. The profiles are then analyzed in terms of their alignment with one another and with the corporate culture as well as with the HBDI Profiles of key leaders and functions. This process often triggers insights about your current state. You can then use the profile to describe the desired future state, providing another way to articulate perspectives that are often hard to verbalize.

8. **Step out into the future.** This involves bringing your team together and having them try to visualize (using a guided visualization or other techniques) themselves as individuals and as the business as a whole, 5 to 10 years into the future. They then reflect and capture their thoughts on the company's vision, mission, products, markets, and customer expectations, and discuss each person's perspectives and the implications and consequences of building out into the future.

   If even the idea of a visualization or guided fantasy makes you uncomfortable, here's an approach that Chuck McVinney uses with research leaders and others who work in technical, scientific, or highly structured fields and have trouble being visionary or tapping into their imagination: instead of having someone imagine the future—an exercise that might come easily to an individual with a strong D-quadrant preference, but could be mentally draining for someone who prefers highly analytical and logical thinking—he asks the person to step into that point in the future and then analyze the history that led him or her to it. Rather than feeling blocked by the struggle to imagine the future, the person can focus on solving an analytical problem: How did we get here? What steps were involved? What made this successful? Once a person's own mental barriers are down, strategic thinking becomes much easier and more enjoyable to do.

As you can see, these are not the usual types of management activities, such as gathering and analyzing data. The techniques are so indirect that they seem like a back road, but in reality they represent a shortcut to attaining the perceptions needed to think strategically and subsequently build a strategic plan.

What look like clouds of smoke that you can't grab are actually elements of solid understanding that defy rational processing. Among the people who have experienced these techniques for themselves, successful results—and conversion to believers—is close to 100 percent.

A whole spectrum of similar activities makes up a universe of techniques that facilitate strategic thinking processes. Mixing, matching, and sequencing them to apply to different business situations can make the transition of traditional thinkers to strategic thinkers a more likely outcome. The fresh perspectives that are gained through this transformation greatly benefit the more formal strategic planning processes that follow. The individuals involved are now much more sensitive to patterns, trends, nuances, and unarticulated needs and opportunities. They are able to better conceptualize and visualize existing relationships and future projections. They are, in a word, smarter about the process of strategic thinking and its follow-on action step, strategic planning.

> A moment's insight is sometimes worth a life's experience.
>
> —Oliver Wendell Holmes, Sr.

Put It to Work

Metaphor is one of the easiest tools to learn. Practice by trying the car/vehicle metaphor described earlier:

- On a blank sheet of paper, draw a car or some other vehicle that represents your company as you see it today. (You don't need any skill in drawing to do this—stick figures are fine.) Have fun with it! This does not have to be a realistic car; for example, you can have as many steering wheels as you want.
- Sketch in the environment. Is the road bumpy? Is there a dead end? A long road ahead? What does the terrain look like?
- Next, draw another vehicle (it does not have to be the same type of vehicle) that represents how your company should be in the future, say in 8 to 10 years, if you are successful.
- Now compare the two. What is different? What can you learn about what might need to change in order to get you to that successful point in the future?

You can use this exercise for individual, team, or organizational applications. Try it! It works!

SO WHAT?

> Strategic planning is a difficult process that often doesn't work because the strategic thinking mentality needed to conduct it is not understood and therefore not practiced.

> Many very capable executives are not very smart in the strategic domain, but they can develop skills through an application of Whole Brain Thinking.

> Experts in strategic thinking have special techniques that provide effective D-quadrant training to help executives who are not familiar with this mode to stretch and develop strategic thinking skills.

> The level of success using these techniques with executives is very high when positioned in a way that executives understand.

> While strategic planning is a Whole Brain process, awareness, familiarity, and particularly skill in D-quadrant strategic thinking are important ingredients in effective strategic planning.

"At one point, I had seventeen vice presidents. That's when I realized it was time to restructure the company and get back to basics."

CHAPTER 17

Reorganization That Really Works: Energizing for Breakthrough Business Outcomes

CHAPTER HIGHLIGHTS

> Too often, reorganization focuses on cost reduction instead of growth-driven strategic reinvention, resulting in lackluster outcomes that can be avoided.

> Reorganization is a Whole Brain process, yet all too frequently management implements it with a sole focus on ROI (return on investment) and execution (A and B quadrants), which can be counterproductive because it overlooks essential elements in the C and D quadrants (for example, culture, morale, and vision) that can make or break the success of the initiative.

> Most organizations are sufficiently diverse to provide Whole Brain reorganization project leadership and Whole Brain implementation teams.

> Reorganization is an opportunity for the whole organization to get energized by "going creative."

It was another classic M&A challenge: a big national bank was acquiring a regional bank. After the merger, the bank would require 900 fewer employees, and 40 branches would be closed—in short, the merger would create one community from a national bank of 38,000 people and a regional bank of 640 people. The challenges were tough. Was there a way to reorganize without the risk of losing a significant number of key staff members, and without the expense and morale problems associated with forced transfers and retrenchments—not to mention the possible loss of new and existing customers?

Whether you call it reorganization, realignment, restructuring, reinvention, or reengineering, most of these interventions are costly and painful—and, in the end, don't work. This is freely admitted by the gurus who invented reengineering. My belief is that if the interventions had been properly conceptualized, managed, and carried out, the vast majority of these "re" efforts would have been wonderfully successful.

Ann McGee-Cooper and Duane Trammel,[1] longtime HBDI practitioners and consultants, share the story of an engineering company that was facing the reorganization process with trepidation. The last effort had not been well received by the staff, and the leaders were concerned about running into the same challenges again. Ann and Duane's first step was to look at the process from an HBDI thinking preference perspective. Since this was an engineering company, they weren't surprised to find that its preferred process work flow as a team, as revealed in the HBDI Team Profile, started in the left-mode quadrants: B, then A, then D, then C.

> Everyone's role perception tells you their assumptions about how things are supposed to operate around here. To re-engineer a company, those perceptions have to be aligned with today's realities, not wistful memories of yesterday.
>
> —Charles Geschke

Ann goes on to describe the "aha moment" that occurred when they engaged in an activity to elucidate the process from a thinking perspective. When they saw the HBDI Team Profile analysis, it showed that the team had a preferred thinking and process flow that went from B to A to D and then to C (organize, analyze, strategize, personalize; see Figure 17-1). Suddenly the challenge the company had faced with the reorganization in the past made sense!

What I could see clearly and what the whole team could see once we stepped back to look at it is this: If you start with B and do a whole lot of detailed work and then do A, you're so invested in that plan that when you get to D, there's no way you're going to scrap it and start over with a new paradigm. That means the person in the group with a strong D-quadrant preference was seen as not a team player and not on board because he was just waiting to get to the place where he could get out of the current paradigm that he thought wasn't working and come at it with some creativity. Then when we got to C ... well, at that point they were out of time, energy, and resources. They could suddenly see their resistance to a totally new approach from the D quadrant, much less working on C-quadrant concerns. By the time they got to the C quadrant, they were wiped out.

While technically, this company *had* a Whole Brain process, the reality was that its management tilt to the preferred B and A quadrants was taking over. As the process flows indicated, often no energy or time was spent on right-mode imaginative and people-oriented thinking, which are essential

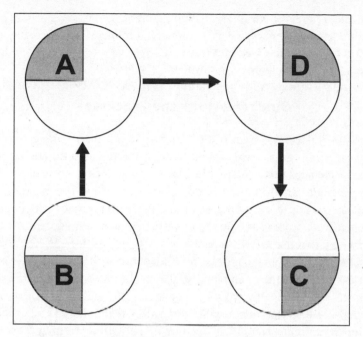

FIGURE 17-1 Sample HBDI Team Profile process flow of preferences.

components—the company never really got to the C and D quadrants. With this in mind, they decided to design future meetings *reversing* the team's default flow and starting with the overlooked quadrants: C to D to A and then B (personalize, strategize, analyze, organize). By reengineering their process, they were able to address the critical areas of people, communication, vision, and change more effectively, and they finally had a successful reorganization!

While we often call it reorganization, from a thinking perspective, the word *reinvention* is a better word for what should take place when major change occurs, and *Whole Brain reinvention* is the best descriptor. The process of invention is very clearly a double-dominant A/D-quadrant activity. As we saw in Chapter 7, data from the National Inventors Hall of Fame and the Lawrence Livermore National Laboratory demonstrate that the A/D 1-2-2-1 profile is the norm for the inventive mind. (For more information on the HBDI preference codes, see the HBDI Profile Interpretation Guide in the Appendix.) The A quadrant contributes logical, analytical, rational, quantitative, financial, and technical mental processes. When the imaginative, conceptual, holistic, experimental D quadrant is included, this synergistic combination makes all the difference in the thinking process. When you then add the necessary qualities of the B quadrant, with its specialization in form, sequence, chronology, and implementation, and the required qualities of the C quadrant, with its specialized preferences for interpersonal relationships, work, spirit, and communication expressiveness, we have a much more mentally complete process to support the outcomes we want from an effective reorganization, which so often requires a reinvention of the culture.

Don't Overlook the Processes

Reinvention is part of reorganization, and too often these projects are painful because things get moved around without enough attention being paid to the process changes that need to take place as well. Reinvention of a business needs to include targeting the key processes involved in that business. This could mean the entire sales process or just the billing process. It could be as comprehensive a process as new product development or manufacturing automation, or as specific a process as the training of production line workers. A key factor in identifying a process for reinvention is that it must be critical to the success of the business, and it must also involve a change of state.

The best way to understand a state change is through an example. As the cofounder of a firm that mentors Silicon Valley technology start-ups, HBDI practitioner Paul Gustavson[2] has been involved with more than 50 start-ups and many other fast-growth companies during his career. An organizational design expert, he uses this simple example of a bakery business with three critical state-change processes to explain what kind of processes are candidates for reinvention:

1. The first bakery process involves taking raw materials and mixing them together to create batter: *change from raw ingredients to batter.*
2. The second process involves shaping the batter into the form of a cake and baking it: *change from batter to cake.*
3. The third process involves icing and decorating the basic cake to create an attractive birthday or wedding cake: *change from basic cake to decorated cake.*

Each of these processes is discrete, and each causes a change of state: from raw materials to batter, from batter to cake, and from cake to decorated cake. The reinvention or reorganization challenge is to creatively change one, two, or all three of these bakery processes in order to reduce the cost, decrease the time required, improve the taste, enhance the appearance, or achieve all four simultaneously. Add to the results already described a reduction in the number of people required, and you now have a mini-example of reorganization at its simplest.

An operative word in this discussion is *creatively*. Without creativity, reorganization efforts are often "awkward examples of management muscle," which may get good marks for intent, but very bad marks for results.

If you trace the motivating force behind the typical reorganization project, you will often find a management decision that was based solely on A- and B-quadrant thinking outcomes, as was the case with the engineering firm in the previous example. The objective of the reorganization intervention becomes so narrowly focused on cost reduction, for example, that creative possibilities are not even considered. The strong A/B thinking preferences become the basis for the decision-making style, which in turn becomes the basis for the operational style of dealing with the problem situation. These styles reinforce each other to such an extent that a fragile creative idea doesn't have a chance. In addition to smothering creativity, the strong A/B management decision process also influences the makeup of the teams or project groups that are assigned to carry out the intervention. It is all too easy for A/B-mode managers to select A/B-mode teams to carry out their mandate. After all, they are selecting people in their own image to implement their perception of the needed action, when in fact a Whole Brain approach is what's really needed.

Redesigning for Accelerated Performance: Appreciating and Applying Difference

In working with start-ups and fast-growth companies, Paul points out, the ideas for gaining greater competitive advantage are in people's heads regardless of the industry, and we need to tap into their full capacity. Start-ups, whether they're an entire organization or a new team, require an enormous amount of knowledge, and that means that we need people to learn quickly. Understanding their thinking and learning preferences is a critical step.

For example, when Hallmark Cards was pursuing an aggressive growth target, the IT division needed to redesign itself and generate new, more robust ideas to support this goal. Paul helped by using Whole Brain Thinking as the start-up tool for all of the IT design teams. The first step was using the HBDI profiles to increase awareness of the differences in people's mental processing so that the division could develop an appreciation of that diversity and the benefits of having members who approach issues differently—especially when it comes to generating more *robust ideas*. By using this approach, the IT design teams came to have more tolerance, move to acceptance, and, as time passed, become better able to understand and use the learnings and applications of Whole Brain Thinking. The appreciation of differences allowed the team members to intentionally seek one another out, think in a more holistic way, and come up with better ideas and solutions for growth. From there, they hammered out the "how" of the implementation and the processes that would be required for ongoing learning, growth, and sustainability, increasing the number of robust ideas, as they had set out to do.

What was very significant about this Whole Brain application to the redesign process, Paul says, is that it was strategy-driven. Based on performance goals that IT outlined through its strategy, the design was created to achieve that performance. Whole Brain Thinking was built into an overall IT framework that was interconnected and linked to other systems.

In many situations—for example, when a major restructuring entails establishing project teams to review which roles (and people) should stay and which should go—these critical steps are overlooked. In the language of the Whole Brain Model, that type of experience will then typically play out as follows:

- Those with more A-quadrant thinking preferences may believe that the restructuring is a good idea because it can save money, but they may be concerned about the accuracy (veracity) of the economic analysis.
- Those with more B-quadrant thinking preferences may believe that the restructuring will make the organization more efficient, but they may also worry that the confusion and process changeover will create risk, chaos and inefficiencies in the short term.
- Those with more C-quadrant thinking preferences may be troubled about a potential loss of people's livelihoods, but they can also think positively about how the new merged culture might provide new growth opportunities and benefits for associates.
- Those with more D-quadrant thinking preferences may be excited about the possibilities the new entity will provide, but they may worry about how well the vision of the future of the organization has been thought through.

While all these perspectives should be taken into account as the major decisions are being made, without the tools to work together and value the thinking of all four quadrants of the Whole Brain Model, there is no shared purpose and common ground. Instead, there is stress, conflict, insular decision making, and, ultimately, less-than-optimum outcomes. Most of that can be avoided!

One of Paul's favorite statements is, "Organizations are perfectly designed for the results they achieve." This is a devastatingly accurate prediction of the bottom-line results of each business organization. If success is to be the final result, then we must design the organization to be capable of producing that result. I would add to Paul's quote that it is the leadership of the organization that determines the outcome. Organizations, taken as a whole, represent a composite whole brain. This means that the mental diversity is already in place to assemble the teams to implement a successful reinvention, redesign, or reengineering project. Too often, the missing element is Whole Brain management.

Put It to Work

Think of a time when you were part of a reorganization or reengineering effort (or when you observed a friend, colleague, or family member who was involved with one). Use the Whole Brain Model to diagnose what could have been improved:

A. Were the desired financial and business objectives actually achieved within budget and as planned? If not, perhaps the analysis overlooked key elements from other quadrants that affected the process. What might those have been?

B. Were timelines and schedules well planned, communicated, and respected? If not, then the planning process was not thorough enough and overlooked key elements from other quadrants that affected the process. What might those have been?

C. How did the culture, the workforce, and customers respond? Were there any losses? If so, then most likely key people-related elements were overlooked from the C and other quadrants that affected the process. What might those have been?

D. Was this a good strategic decision? Were there any innovations or creative solutions that emerged? If not, then key elements were overlooked from the D and other quadrants that affected the process. What might those have been?

Mindful Merging: Restructuring That Doesn't Fall Apart

So what happened with the bank merger I told you about at the beginning of this chapter? Knowing the history of how mergers and restructurings typically happen—and often fail to deliver—the banks recognized that they had to find a better approach. Working with HBDI practitioners Robert Webber, Colin Pidd, and David Clancy,[3] they realized that integrating the Whole Brain Model and Whole Brain Thinking at the organizational level would provide a common language and a more holistic way of looking at all of the strategic initiatives and planning.

A Whole Brain project team was assembled to ensure that the appropriate decisions would be made and that a strong culture and community would emerge from the process.

In addition, to complement the more A/B-oriented thinking of the bank's executive team, a "Merger Management Team" (MMT) was also established. This team had an entirely different profile, with stronger preferences in the C and D quadrants. The MMT members required training in the business aspects of the merger, but their preferences for conceptual, "big-picture" thinking allowed them to enthusiastically embrace the challenge of developing an innovative approach to the merger. They were also very committed to preserving the jobs of their colleagues and fostering a strong sense of organizational community.

The end result was that the two banks successfully merged. They closed 40 co-located branches, but there were no retrenchments (no one was paid to go) and no forced transfers, and there was 86 percent support for the industrial relations agreement. In addition, staff turnover was reduced from 14 percent to 6 percent. A trade-off was that the management of the integration took longer, as natural attrition was the strategy for avoiding forced retrenchments. A bonus for customers was increased opening hours: the staff members agreed that, to make the merger successful, and taking into consideration the commitment to retain jobs, they would open key branches on Saturday.

To top it all off, as a result of all these benefits, the $10 million that had been set aside for redundancies was no longer needed! (For more complete details on this case study, please visit www.herrmannsolutions.com.)[4]

Reorganizations and reinventions will continue to dominate the business landscape. Lessons learned for successful outcomes include:

Step 1. Install a Whole Brain management team in the leadership roles of a reorganization project.

Step 2. Create Whole Brain implementation teams.

Step 3. Apply appropriate creative processes in all the activities of the leadership and implementation teams to bring needed innovation to the inevitable process changes and other issues that will emerge.

To optimize reorganization interventions and help guarantee their success, organizations need to balance the typical A/B management tendencies with a deliberate focus on and injection of more C/D thinking. By so doing, not only will they successfully reorganize, but they will reinvent and reenergize the entire business.

SO WHAT?

> Reorganization interventions frequently and unnecessarily fail to produce the intended results.

> Reorganization projects are habitually led by A/B management that is incapable of conceptualizing the intervention in Whole Brain terms.

> Organizations are perfectly designed for the results they achieve.

> A Whole Brain approach, including the involvement of a Whole Brain reorganization team, can help companies overcome the common pitfalls of complex mergers and restructuring initiatives.

> Economic crises require tough, savvy, future-oriented management decisions. A Whole Brain approach provides the foundation to make sure that such decisions can happen.

"It has come to my attention that the building is on fire. Let's set up a meeting for next week to decide what sort of action we might take to deal with this crisis."

CHAPTER 18

Dealing with Disruption: When Business Adversity, Risk, or Crisis Strikes

CHAPTER HIGHLIGHTS

> Economic crises often stimulate inappropriate, counterproductive management behavior.
> Leaders' traditional ways of taking action in a visible crisis, such as micro-management and cost cutting, are often detrimental. Thinking preferences have a critical impact on all actions when dealing with a business disruption situation.
> Windows of opportunity are usually overlooked because legitimate safe-keeping management thinking runs amok.
> The complexity involved in the wake of disaster situations and other large-scale business disruptions requires a Whole Brain approach to decision making.

Another economic downturn was looming—the second in a decade, and one that by all appearances seemed likely to dwarf the previous crisis. The CEO of a small but growing business wanted to make sure that his company didn't suffer the same problems it had before. When the economy had dipped eight years earlier, clients had cut back on services, product shipments were canceled, and sales and profits had plummeted. This CEO had a strong A-quadrant thinking preference, which he immediately began putting into action when he saw signs that the economy was receding. He put a very linear process in place to make preemptive budget cuts across the board. A new product launch was put on indefinite hold. Travel was allowed only in rare circumstances. "Nonessential" activities like a planned sales retreat were canceled, and the marketing team was trimmed back to a single administrative staff member. It was all straightforward, direct, and firm—no exceptions.

Did all the cost-cutting activities help the company fare better during the crisis? In fact, as the CEO himself will tell you, it lost much *more* during this second downturn than it had in the first: The cuts were so deep and his focus on budgets and numbers was so narrow that he couldn't think about growth, and that kept him from making a critical strategic hire. Not only did he lose sight of the company's strategic purpose, but he lost years of momentum. This loss of a long-term perspective ultimately put his business at greater risk than it had been after the first economic crisis.

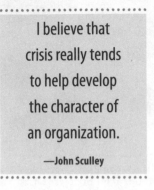

I believe that crisis really tends to help develop the character of an organization.

—John Sculley

During an economic downturn, when many companies feel the beginnings of a financial crisis in the form of falling revenues, management mentality often experiences an upper-left A-quadrant narrowing of focus to the numbers along with a lower-left B-quadrant safekeeping downshift. It is very tempting for managers who lean in those directions anyway to have an excuse for doing it on purpose. That is, they immediately begin to turn out the lights, lower the thermostat, cancel any discretionary spending, scrimp on needed purchases, and in general behave extremely conservatively with regard to any activity involving money, materials, or people. All that matters are numbers, and for those who have a high need for visible action, putting on the brakes is an obvious first option that observers of the managerial process can note and applaud.

When the question is asked, "What's management doing?," it's comfortable and easy to answer, "It's taking the lead in saving money." Travel is curtailed. Expense account rules are tightened. Trade shows are canceled. Purchasing ground rules are severely tightened. Building for inventory stops. Advertising is pulled. Hiring ceases and layoffs begin. This is crisis mentality, which responds in the only way it knows—a knee-jerk retreat to safekeeping supervision of all identifiable processes and costs in the business. And it feels good because people are *doing* something.

The thought that this might be a window of opportunity for a particular product line never survives its initial introduction as a creative idea. The suggestion that this is the time to advertise, and to do so more creatively than before, is not given serious consideration. The idea of investing in retaining the trained workforce is rejected out of hand. The even more outrageous thought that this is an ideal time to further develop and hire key employees is shot down the moment it is verbalized. A senior vice president questions every possible expense: "Is this absolutely necessary?" "Isn't there a cheaper option?" "Do our customers really need this?" Micromanagement and downward, one-way communication prevail.

While some of these actions may be appropriate, these edicts frequently add up to overkill and can be severely counterproductive. This kind of thinking exemplifies a legitimate, much-needed B-quadrant mentality—but in this case, it has run amok. And whether they work or not, these behaviors tend to place great power in the hands of those people who perform the safekeeping functions (for example, financial, operational, and administrative management). Once it has been given away, that power is difficult to reclaim.

Ironically, for managers who were brought up under traditional, status quo, safekeeping, security-minded management, the situation represents a return to sanity. They welcome it and collaborate enthusiastically to make the management culture one of survival. In many situations, however, it is just the opposite. It is a return to past practices that may have taken a whole generation to overcome.

It takes a certain leadership strength to stick to the vision that brought the company this far, to reexamine current events with a view toward midcourse corrections rather than a 180-degree turnabout. It's not easy to keep an eye on the future when you're putting out today's fires. But there is one kind of business that is frequently more successful in maintaining the strategic view while dealing with an immediate crisis: those run by families. Family-owned businesses tend to avoid the knee-jerk lower-left shift because they are by their nature focused on future generations. They don't ignore reality—they take the crisis situation seriously--but their inherent long-term focus on the company's viability beyond the current generation of leaders is quite often a significant strategic advantage. There is plenty we can all learn from their example.

Whatever its nature, when a crisis appears, the appropriate leadership response should always include a four-quadrant walk-around of the decision process in each of the company's key functions (see Figure 18-1) as well as at the CEO level, applications of creativity rather than a crowbar to problems, and diagnosis of the economic facts of life with a simultaneous assessment of appropriate risks and respect for the leadership intuition that brought us this far. Whatever decisions you make to deal with an impending crisis, don't lose sight of the long view.

A difficult economic environment argues for the need to innovate more, not to pull back.

—Ken Chenault, CEO
American Express

In fact, if you're going to apply Whole Brain Thinking as a leader, there's no better time than during a period of business crisis. This is the time to develop multiple options rather than considering only those that are security-minded and safekeeping, to employ savvy leadership rather than micromanagement. This is a time for wide-angle binoculars and celestial telescopes rather than

Analyzing Decisions in a Business Crisis

A	D
Analyze the benefits as well as the costs/downsides of the decision.	Review the long-term strategy and the decision's place within that strategic framework.
Assess and evaluate execution options as you get organized, building in flexibility to adapt if necessary. **B**	Look at the people implications of the decision, including stress and morale. Communicate with transparency so employees and customers alike understand that the strategy is still on track and that this is a temporary bypass. **C**

FIGURE 18-1 Walk-Around: analyzing decisions in a business crisis.

microscopes. A lower-left downshift is the natural inclination, but in crisis after crisis, the companies that fare best are those that are both realistic about the situation and committed to the long-term vision. They are prudent, but not at the expense of ceasing to keep customers loyal and retain good people.

Under Pressure: Getting Priorities Straight

Disruption of all kinds is everywhere in today's world. In just one example, within a two-year time frame, organizations in New Zealand faced financial industry turmoil, earthquakes, an oil spill, and biosecurity threats. The challenge for leaders is to navigate through and out of this disruption, and the best way to do that is with Whole Brain Thinking, as our colleagues in New Zealand discovered.

In looking at how organizations can be more adaptive and resilient during the recovery phase of complex, disruptive events, Dean Myburgh, Chris Webb, and Dr. Erica Seville[1] focused on effective decision making and the key role it plays in helping to reduce vulnerabilities, especially in a disaster situation in which knowledge of and control over the environment are evolving and inadequate. Their research found that, because of the complexity involved, effective decision making in the wake of a disruptive event requires that leaders consider and balance their thinking with that of others, as well as engage new approaches.

In relative terms, decision making during a crisis-recovery situation is challenged more by the complexity involved than by the speed with which decisions must be made—even though speed is often the primary focus.

Reflection that facilitates holistic decision making to address the complexities and the varying nature of recovery situations is vital if organizations are to enhance effective and responsive decision making.

While there is a tendency to "go A/B" in a financial crisis, in a disaster-recovery situation, the leaders may feel that they don't have time to spend on the supporting data or processes and procedures. And this means that there's a potential to overlook important considerations for decision making, particularly when it comes to what gets priority attention. Taking a Whole Brain approach allows the decision makers to look at the nature of the decisions and what mental resources they will require as well as the extent to which they will contribute to the desired outcome.

An Example of Implementing a Whole Brain Approach

Since economic downturns are, unfortunately, fairly common these days, let's look at an example of how you might apply this in practice to a component of responding to a financial crisis.

Once you've clarified your initial decisions and completed the Whole Brain Walk-Around as shown in Figure 18-1, you'll have several specific initiatives to take on. One typical response is the *development of a cash management program*. In most organizations, cash management is the responsibility of the finance function only. But if you look at it more closely, you'll see that everybody in the organization plays a role in cash management. So instead of the usual negative actions involving misunderstood cuts and rash decisions, as described earlier in this chapter—the result of viewing the issue from a narrow functional and thinking preference standpoint—a very positive and effective approach is to make it an organization-wide effort and engage everyone's best thinking.

Organizations that launch effective Whole Brain enterprise cash management campaigns are universally surprised by the results. There is excess cash *everywhere*. The exact amount depends on the functions and size of the organization, but the total is always a pleasant surprise.

Every member of the organization should be involved, and every function should set up a cash management project team, with each of these teams being heterogeneous (that is, made up of people who together represent a full range of mental preferences). Each person broadens the scope of the team's constructive actions and recommendations.

> You must deodorize profits and make people understand that profit is not something offensive, but as important to a company as breathing.
>
> —Sir Peter Parker

The effective cash management program that I designed a number of years ago for General Electric generated more than $500 million in its first year of implementation. A major benefit of launching an effective cash management campaign is that the organization becomes trained in those techniques and attitudes that sustain the positive effect for several years after the launching of the initial effort. In fact, effective cash management changes the culture of the organization. Instead of feeling isolated from the organization's initial crisis and ongoing everyday problems, employees become part of the solution. It has been my experience that whether teams find $50 or $5,000 or $100,000, they are so fulfilled by the team results that they are motivated to continue their efforts.

The key outcomes from programs like effective cash management are positive, quantifiable, visible results. Compare these outcomes to those of the typical negative, demotivational activities that result from crisis management. Well-designed programs tap into all four quadrants and, as a matter of fact, can be so successful that the crisis is avoided altogether.

Whether the program is addressing cash management, new product ideas, customer retention issues, or any other crisis-related initiative, there are steps you can take to make sure it's successful. The following tips will help you design a program that hits all four quadrants.

Secrets of Success in Creating an Enterprise Program Designed to Overcome a Crisis (and the Primary Quadrants Involved)

1. Set up a Whole Brain team, clarify the program and the results that you want to achieve, and solicit C-level leadership support if possible. (A, B, C, D)
2. The results should be quantifiable, easy to measure, and reportable. (A, B)
3. Official scorekeeping should be the responsibility of the business function that is normally involved (for example, for cash management, usually finance). (A)
4. The program should be holistic and organization-wide, with the involvement of everyone. Reach out to the learning and communication teams for help as needed. (C, D)
5. Whole Brain teams of up to seven people should be formed in all functions and locations, all with the same specific assignment. For example, for cash management, the assignment should be to find all the cash in a specific segment of the business. (A, B, C, D)

6. The results of the program should be reported and communicated as soon as possible, widely, and regularly, on a specific schedule. (A, B, C, D)
7. The reporting process should focus on team results. (A, C)
8. Teams should be given recognition in the company (newsletter, intranet, etc.) and specific rewards. (A, C)
9. The rewards should be real and meaningful (for example, for cash management, proportional to the amount of cash found). (A, B)
10. The rewards should reflect the culture of the organization. (C, D)
11. Senior management should be involved in the recognition and reward process. (A, B, C, D)
12. Lessons learned should be captured using a postmortem evaluation process with consideration of making the program an ongoing effort.

Whatever the disruption may be, there's one thing we can expect: there are sure to be more on the horizon. We were surprised to see how many of the business leaders participating in a program on how to apply Whole Brain Thinking to risk management and disruption realized that they were really unprepared. They had not thought about the possible need for disaster recovery or how they might respond to a major crisis—unless, of course, they had recently been through one. But preparation is critical; without it, we just react. One of the take-aways for these leaders was an action plan using a Whole Brain Walk-Around to think through what they needed to pay attention to in each quadrant in order to be prepared.

The CEO of a midsize business in the automobile industry recently demonstrated just how critical it was to prepare in a Whole Brain way. Although his primary preferences are more oriented toward the D quadrant and, to a lesser degree, the C quadrant, he has always made sure to cover his bases in areas of lesser preference by surrounding himself with complementary thinking partners. Listening carefully to his advisors' suggestions, he closely evaluated the firm's needs and chose insurance that had both the necessary protection and appropriate financial coverage in case of an incident. When a fire destroyed 90 percent of his offices and facilities, he was well covered and had in place much of what he needed financially to minimize the unavoidable stress and disruption that such an incident creates. This is a great example of being a situational Whole Brain leader.

How prepared are you? The most effective way to avoid a knee-jerk reaction is to adopt a Whole Brain approach to managing risk and your reaction to disruption, and to do it now, before a crisis occurs. This allows you to see the situation more clearly and reframe it, ideally as an opportunity to creatively reenergize the organization. One of the reasons it is essential to bring together the kinds of heterogeneous Whole Brain teams that we discussed in Chapter 12 is that the process immediately becomes easier to address, as more of your bases are covered. But even if you don't have a Whole Brain team available, you can still apply Whole Brain Thinking to get the benefits of that thinking diversity by making sure that the team members understand their mode of thinking so that they can proactively address any gaps that may exist and reach out to others outside the team as needed.

What Pressure and Stress Do to Your Thinking

Disruption is a big stress producer, and this has consequences for how your brain processes information, typically interfering with your ability to think clearly at a physiological level. It creates a sort of "all circuits are busy" feeling. The HBDI Profile shows how your profile may shift under pressure from your normal day-to-day approach (see Figure 18-2 for an example). Our research has shown that many (but not all) people experience a shift toward the B or C quadrant in response to pressure.

How does your thinking shift under pressure? How might that impact your effectiveness in a crisis? It can sometimes help, but it can also create challenges. Keep that in mind as you do your Whole Brain business disruption planning.

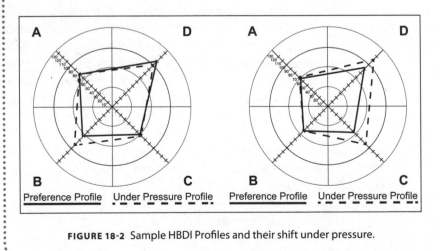

FIGURE 18-2 Sample HBDI Profiles and their shift under pressure.

Put It to Work

Think back to a situation, either personal or professional, that was a disruption to your world:

- How did you respond?
- Which quadrant(s) did you focus on most?
  A. Gathering facts and problem solving
  B. Getting organized, assessing the risk, and building a plan
  C. Checking out who else may be affected, engaging with others to respond, reacting emotionally, and communicating
  D. Scoping out the big picture and getting creative about options as you thought up out-of-the-box ideas
- What did you overlook?
- How did pressure affect your thinking?
- How was your response different from that of others involved?
- How could a Whole Brain approach have helped you respond even more effectively?

SO WHAT?

> The natural inclination to limit our thinking by downshifting to one or two quadrants in a financial crisis can often do more harm than good.

> The organizations that are most resilient in crisis situations or in the wake of business disruption are those that take a balanced approach to decision making while keeping the strategic, long-term view in sight.

> Leaders who fail to use Whole Brain Thinking may overlook important considerations that will have a significant impact on priorities, decisions, and actions.

> Positive programs that engage the thinking of all involved, such as the effective cash management example, can generate the needed cash or other results quickly, and therefore reduce the economic threat.

> Negative programs usually don't produce much cash, but usually do demotivate employees. At an individual level, you can use Whole Brain Thinking to better respond to both personal and professional disruptive events.

"We need to make some big changes around here.
The kind of changes where many decisions are
made but nothing actually happens."

CHAPTER 19

Making Change Work: How to Break Through the Mindset Barrier

CHAPTER HIGHLIGHTS

> We all have already formed mindsets or mental maps that become our point of reference as we look at the world.
> To facilitate organizational change successfully, you have to understand how mindsets create resistance to change.
> People with different thinking preferences react to change in different ways.
> Communication strategies concerning change need to accommodate the full range of thinking preferences.
> Change is a Whole Brain process.

Imagine that you are in recovery after a triple bypass. You are not feeling your best, but at least you are alive. You open your eyes, only to see your doctor leaning over you and checking your pulse. He smiles and says, "Welcome back." You try to smile back. He then says, "I hope you will learn from this. You need to take better care of yourself. You need to change your lifestyle." You nod your head and mumble, "Of course I will."

The reality is that if you are like most people, you will not! According to Dr. Edward Miller, dean of the medical school and CEO of the hospital at Johns Hopkins University, 90 percent of people who have bypass surgery do not change their lifestyles.[1] If 90 percent of people do not change when faced with a life-threatening situation, imagine how few people change for smaller, less important things. And if it is so hard to get one person to change, imagine how hard it can be to get a group to change. And it is even harder to change an entire organization, made up of people with different agendas, different mindsets, and different ideas.

Changing your own mind is hard enough. Changing someone else's is almost impossible. When he was a new CEO, Jack Welch of General Electric once complained that trying to bring about change "was like running into a brick wall. ... I give all these speeches, but nothing ever happens."

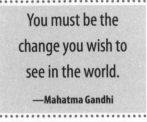

You must be the change you wish to see in the world.
—Mahatma Gandhi

Trying to make change happen isn't just a cause of frustration in the senior ranks. HBDI master facilitator Cynthia Radford[2] shares a story that's all too common in organizations: a manager was hired to help the company she was working with innovate its processes and approaches, to make some long overdue changes to "how we do things."

"He really started picking up the innovation bandwagon and was trying to push some long-held policies and get them moving," Cynthia says. "And then I got a note from the CEO saying, 'I just wanted you to know he is no longer with the organization.' Sometimes leaders at the top say they want a change agent, but then when they realize what that means—that at a personal level, they may need to go about doing things a little differently—their reaction is, 'Are you kidding? We really don't want to do things that way.'"

> The central issue for business is never strategy, structure, culture, or systems. The core of the matter is always about changing the behavior of people.
> —John Kotter

Mindsets and Change

Most of us have tried to change not only our own minds, but other people's minds as well. My guess is that more often than not, we have failed. To understand how to facilitate change, you first have to understand how our minds—and our thinking—react to change. Change is frequently viewed as disruptive and negative, even when the outcomes are known to be positive, as with bypass patients. It's uncomfortable to change the status quo. Even if change is inevitable and must happen if an organization is to survive, it is still often fiercely resisted because it can feel like a threat to the systems that are in place.

Positive, creative change requires a *mindset* for change. A mindset is the way we see things, the part of our "cognitive unconscious" where we have already formed mental maps that become our point of reference for how we look at the world. The dominant thinking preferences that we have as individuals, teams, or organizations contribute to our inherent mindsets, acting as filters for how we perceive change. The way we grow up also creates mindsets. Along with our values, they're embedded in our memory, and we naturally (and often unconsciously) maintain these mindsets for much of our lives unless we have a compelling reason to change them (For more on values, visit www.wholebrainbusinessbook.com to download the bonus chapter, "Your Hidden 'Owner's Manual': A Whole Brain Approach to Personal Values.") For example, you might have been brought up with a mindset that says that owing money to someone else is bad and should be avoided at all costs. Someone else might have grown up with the mindset that an employee's rights should be guaranteed in all circumstances. Both of these mindsets would be hard to change at the drop of a hat. Some mindsets are small and personal; others can be bigger and shared by an entire nation. In Australia, for instance, the national mindset is that sport is a very important part of life, whereas in Singapore, it's not as strong a part of the culture.

Teams, functions, organizations, and indeed entire industries can get locked into their mindsets. When everyone in a group or organization holds the same mindset, it becomes self-reinforcing. No one questions it, so it becomes reality. Any other view gets blocked out and ignored. This is why it is so hard to overcome "groupthink" and change organizations from the inside. Most radical changes come from outside an industry, or from those who bring a different mindset to an industry and dare to think differently.

Why Changing Minds Is Difficult

Although we know that the brain can change, there are a number of reasons why changing people's minds is so difficult:

1. **Mindsets are powerful.** Deeply held mindsets can be so intensely anchored in your memory that you may feel that no amount of persuasion would change your mind. This is why just giving someone a whole lot of facts about why he or she should change will do little to change the person's mind. The individual's current mindset will automatically reject the information, often before he or she has had any chance to give it full consideration.
2. **Our natural brain biases can get in the way.** As Nobel Prize winner Daniel Kahneman explains in *Thinking Fast and Slow*,[3] we think of ourselves as being in control of our minds, but in reality we have two systems that govern how the mind works: one that we control, and

another that we do not control. System 1 represents the conscious self that makes choices and decides what to do. System 2 represents the instinctual mental processes that allow us to make quick decisions with little mental energy. We could not survive without System 2, and yet it often causes us to make errors in specific situations because of the natural brain biases that exist. There is a plethora of new neuroscience research on mental biases that is advancing our ability to understand and better address the mindset challenge. (For more resources, visit www.wholebrainbusinesssbook.com.) When we understand how our mental maps are working, how they're subject to bias, and how they have created our mindsets, we are better prepared to adapt and respond to the change that is constantly occurring around us—as well as get buy-in to change from others.

3. **Although it is possible, forming new connections in the brain requires effort and motivation.** Change also frequently requires that we challenge our existing mental maps and form new connections in the brain. This is difficult because our mindsets are firmly ingrained in the brain. They're also reinforced by the structure and the very nature of the brain itself. As Dr. Michael Merzenich,[4] a professor emeritus neuroscientist at the University of California, San Francisco, and an expert on the brain's ability to change (known as plasticity), has pointed out, "The brain was constructed to change." However, our mental maps lead the brain to fill in gaps that we might initially see and then quickly move on, often with incomplete information. All of our experiences preprogram what we see and how we think or feel about a given topic or model. For example, when asked in a team-building workshop to share some specifics about his emotions and feelings with the whole group, one manager shut down and refused to engage, later explaining: "It's just too uncomfortable. I got burned once doing that—I won't do it again!" It was apparent that this person had shut down his mental process because of a previous experience, and that his willingness, energy, and motivation to overcome that and stretch, to form new connections, were not there.

4. **Thinking habits and mental maps change the brain**. Neuroscience tells us that our mindsets and mental habits, the long-term concepts that structure the way we think, are instantiated in the synapses of the brain. Dr. Merzenich found in his research that habits actually showed up on MRI scans. In studying flute players, he found that their brains had developed larger representational areas that control the fingers, tongue, and lips. He could see that flute playing had physically changed the brain. Businesspeople are like flute players. They have developed thinking habits or mindsets that have changed their brains.

The cumulative weight of knowledge and experience and the mental maps that have formed make it very hard for you to change your mind. For many of us, our thinking preferences have become mental habits that we have to change in order to tap into other available thinking. On the positive side, findings now show that while the formation of new synaptic connections (neurogenesis) is difficult, it is possible *through learning*. This is a message of hope, and it provides a pathway to overcome the mindset challenge.

When 90 percent of heart patients don't listen to their doctor, you know that something is wrong. But once you look at it from a brain-based standpoint, the answer becomes evident: our thinking relies on our mental maps and mindsets, not on facts. If a fact does not fit the mindset, it gets rejected instantly. Think of the times when this "curse of knowledge and experience" has prevented you, your team, and your organization from moving forward with needed change. To overcome this, you need awareness of your mental maps and habits as well as energy and motivation to break through the mindset barrier.

And if you're trying to change someone else's mind? You'll first have to discover what a person's mindset is on a specific issue, how he or she thinks about it, and why he or she has it. Once the person is open to a shift in thinking, it is also critical that *that person believes that he or she can change and grow*. As discussed in Chapter 11, Carol Dweck's[5] research at Stanford University has shown that people who have a *growth mindset* (who believe that their brains can be "built" like a muscle) will be able to learn and thus change more effectively than those with what she calls a *fixed mindset*. Based on her research, the good news is that we can change from a fixed to a growth mindset.

Breaking Through Mindsets, Fear, and Reaction to Change

If you cannot change someone's mind by providing the facts, then how can you engage the person's mind in such a way as to break through the mindset barrier? One proven "mind hack" that you can easily adopt is a Whole Brain approach.

Our associate Chuck McVinney[6] finds that the real issue in managing change is first managing the *fear* of change, which manifests itself in different ways, depending on the person's thinking preferences. Those with strong preferences in the A quadrant, for example, may be

> Every day the world turns upside down on someone who thought they were sitting on top of it.
>
> —Glen Tullman, CEO
> Livongo Health

uncomfortable with the ambiguity, emotions, and feelings created by change and the unknown. People with more B-quadrant preferences may feel a lack of security and be uncomfortable with the unpredictability that change may bring. Others who have a strong preference for the C quadrant may over-react emotionally and tune out before they understand the reality at hand, while those with D-quadrant preferences may feel confined and worry about the loss of freedom of choice, leading them to desire to "jump ship" quickly. Figure 19-1 demonstrates some of the specific questions that people in each of the quadrants will have about change.

To get people on board with change, you first have to understand the thinking lens that they will be reacting through and then be able to answer the questions and concerns that will matter most to them. Communication is critical during change, but if you communicate outside of someone's mode of preference, you can actually make things worse.

By taking a Whole Brain approach and walking around each of the quadrants, you can not only reduce the potential discomfort of change, but also provide both the context and the detail to keep people from "filling in

Getting People on Board with Change

A	D
• What is the bottom line? • What are the facts? • What are the financial consequences? • What's the logic behind the decision? • What's the goal or objective of the change?	• How is this going to affect my future? • How does this fit into the big picture? • What's the "why" behind the change? • Do I have freedom to influence how this gets rolled out? • How might this constrain me?
• Are there specific timelines? • What are the specifics of the change? • What's the track record for this type of change? • Are there references I can talk to? • How can I minimize surprises? • What are the risks to me? **B**	• What will the emotional impact be on my family, my team, and me? • What are the implications for my customers? • Who will be available to listen to my concerns? • Can you engage me personally before you get focused on all the facts? **C**

FIGURE 19-1 Walk-Around: getting people on board with change. Be prepared by answering the questions in each quadrant to help gain understanding and buy-in to the changes you're proposing.

the blanks" and making assumptions about what the change really means. Many mergers and acquisitions that propel enormous levels of change across an organization stumble or cause even more disruption than the change itself because the organization doesn't have a communication strategy that takes into account different thinking preferences, mindsets, and cultural expectations. While the C and D quadrants can understand the contextual framework, the A and B quadrants want data and detail, and if they don't get it, they start filling it in themselves, whether their assumptions are right or not, and often fueling their worst fears about change. It doesn't have to be this way! The experience of a global consumer packaged goods company shows how a Whole Brain approach can make the difference.

We worked with this company as it was in the midst of a huge change initiative resulting from a forthcoming acquisition, one that was sure to send shock waves across both organizations. The company wanted to be proactive about preparing both organizations for the change, so it started by training more than 60 change agents from around the globe in Whole Brain Thinking, the change process, and communication. This team was then deployed, program in hand, to provide context and process training across the globe.

As part of the communication and training program, the team used the HBDI Profile grid to invite participants to describe the culture of each organization. As it turned out, the response was consistent worldwide: each person "drew" the profile of the perceived culture of the two organizations, and nearly everyone drew a similar profile for each. One organization had a strong A/B culture, while the other—the one being acquired—was more C/D. The consistency of the perceptions across the globe was impressive, highlighting both the reality of the differences and the opportunity for balance from the two organizations coming together.

Using the Whole Brain Model as a translation device, the process gave participants the means by which they could describe the differences and then easily open up about how they felt about the impending changes, their fears, and other concerns—which in this type of situation are often left unsaid and then fester. Since the communications had been developed with Whole Brain Thinking in mind, the dialogue was easier than it would have been if the team hadn't been able to tailor the conversation based on preferences. This unique approach paved the way for a change that, although it was still difficult, was successful in the end. (For more on reorganizations, see Chapter 17.)

Of course, change doesn't have to be on the massive scale of a corporate M&A to benefit from Whole Brain Thinking. More often, changes are smaller and incremental, and are communicated at a one-on-one or team level. Sometimes you will be communicating the change, and sometimes you will be the recipient of that communication. Either way, Whole Brain Thinking can help you embrace and lead more effective change.

Making Change Happen

A number of years ago, an HBDI practitioner was working with a data mining company that was relocating employees from the West Coast of the United States across the country to a new location. Many of them were struggling, either with their own fears about the change or with getting buy-in from their partners and families to make the move. Part of the practitioner's coaching work involved helping the employees understand how people with different thinking preferences react to change and how to adapt their communication with their family members to help them deliver the messages most effectively.

Those with strong A-quadrant preferences learned that they needed to be more patient with their partners and avoid the tendency to want to "talk them out of their emotions." On the other hand, those with stronger C-quadrant preferences, both employees and partners, discovered that they would probably need to go through *many emotions* before they would be ready to accept change or listen to reason, and that they might have to go through a type of "mourning" period for this kind of big life change, particularly since it would require leaving and/or otherwise affecting folks who are important to them.

C-oriented employees who would be breaking the news to an A-quadrant partner learned that they would have to tone down their natural emotions and focus on the main points or their partner would get frustrated because he or she just wanted the "bottom line." Sharing the news with a more B-quadrant family member would typically require additional preparation, since this person would want to know the timing, details, and logistics of the change. Painting a picture of life in the new location and all the opportunities that it could provide would help when communicating with more D-oriented family members.

Here are some tips developed from this engagement that you may find helpful in your change efforts:

- If you are breaking the news:
  - Be sensitive to the needs of all four quadrants.
  - Practice beforehand so that you can be sure to overcome the impact of your own preferences.
  - Even if you know your audience, recognize that the needs of each quadrant are valid and that under pressure, people may respond differently from the way you expect them to.

- If you are receiving the news:
  - Know your thinking preferences and watch for pressure-related responses that may affect the way you "hear" the news.
  - Know your needs.
  - Take the initiative to ask questions and get the answers you need to avoid making assumptions that may or may not be correct.

If you are communicating change, the embracing change walk-around in Figure 19-2 provides tips for hitting all the quadrants with your messages to ensure that the change is fully understood and that potential fear and discomfort are alleviated.

> Nothing endures
> but change.
>
> —**Heraclitus**

Embracing Change Walk-Around

A	D
• Be realistic. Get the facts and the research behind the change. Look for any logic that can help you understand it. • Analyze ways you can use this to your advantage.	• Describe the change in as many ways as possible, using as many different mindsets to explore what it is about and its potential impact. Imagine how it can create new opportunities.
• Make sure you and your team have or seek out the resources to make the change. Develop a plan to find and sustain those resources and/or ways to do without them in the future. **B**	• Look for elements of the change that connect with your values. How can this affect you and others positively? • Articulate what you can do to build positive energy and who can help. **C**

FIGURE 19-2 Walk-Around: embracing change. Use this as a prompt to help you better embrace and help others embrace change.

Put It to Work

- Think of a change you would really like to make, one that requires you to get buy-in from another person—for example, a boss, partner, colleague, or friend.
- Start by thinking about what that person's preferences are. Refer to the Whole Brain Model in Chapter 2 if you need some prompts.

- Once you have established your best guess as to his or her preferences, write out what you think the person will want and need to hear. Go quadrant by quadrant, starting with what you think is his or her most-preferred quadrant, then going to the second-most-preferred quadrant, and so on.
- Now consider the person's reaction. Visualize what he or she will:
  - Ask.
  - Say.
  - Worry about.
- Take time to practice your "pitch." Take into account what the person will want to hear and how he or she is likely to react, and build those elements into your pitch. Then practice saying your pitch out loud.
- If possible, have your notes available to you during your conversation. Listen for clues about what this person needs most from each quadrant, and use your notes to respond.

Use this process whenever you are in a situation where you need to get someone on board with change, You will be surprised how much easier it will be for you with a little preparation!

Change Is a Whole Brain Process

Keep in mind that the change process in itself requires Whole Brain Thinking. Based on our years of experience applying the model to change efforts, it is important that you address each quadrant in your planning, organized in a slightly different sequence:

A. What is the rational or "business case" for change?
D. What are the "why" and the vision of the new future state?
C. Who will be affected? Who needs to be involved? What communication and partnerships need to be developed?
B. How will we mobilize energy, build a plan, and take steps to move forward and make it happen?

Using Change to Move from Loss to Creative Thinking

Although we don't always recognize it, change in an organization requires letting go, and in that way, it can be like losing someone in our lives. We grieve. So we can learn a lot about change from Elisabeth Kübler-Ross,[7] who was a renowned expert on death and dying. She described grieving as a process that starts with denial, something that often occurs with change efforts. Next, there is anger—why me, why this change, and why now? Once we are past anger, we enter a stage of acceptance: "Okay, it's going to happen, so how can I allow it to happen with grace, humor, and dignity?" In terms of the change issue, it's at the acceptance stage that creativity can offer a new perspective. Now that we've accepted the fact that it's *going* to happen and *must* happen, let's make the best of it, which means not just tolerating change, but, through creativity, making it a positive, constructive process that reaches a conclusion that is better for everybody than the prior condition (see Figure 19-3).

We are really dealing here with two processes. One is the change process, and the other is the creative process (covered in more detail in Part 4), which provides solutions to problems and ideas for new opportunities that change may produce. Because they are processes, they are describable and teachable. Leveraging change as an opportunity for creativity greatly reduces the negatives that can arise from personal feelings about change and the subsequent emotional intensity.

Change is inevitable. It's always a challenge, but we can control the way we respond to it and how well we set the stage for others to deal with it. If you are leading and managing change of any kind, start by grounding yourself and each player involved in the change process in an understanding of your mindsets and thinking preferences, and how that will affect your role

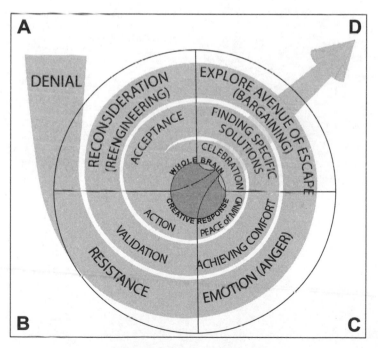

FIGURE 19-3 Dealing with change.

and effectiveness in the change process. When possible, look for opportunities to use change as a platform for new creative thinking. Doing so will provide a benchmark, common language, and frame of reference to guide people through the change process in a more predictable, successful, and, hopefully, somewhat less painful way.

SO WHAT?

> In a world in which the only constant is change, changing people's minds is a critical skill that is rife with challenges because of different mindsets.
> Making change happen requires understanding the mindsets and thinking involved.
> All change initiatives require the involvement and the thinking of everyone.
> When change happens successfully, it is because the brains behind the initiative were engaged, focused, aligned, and synergistic.
> When communicating change, visit all four quadrants of the Whole Brain Model to ensure that you are speaking to all of the mindsets involved.
> Change provides a natural platform for creative thinking, which can be leveraged as a positive outcome.

GLASBERGEN

"Each serving of Leadership Crunch cereal contains 12 grams of confidence, 9 grams of wisdom, 17 grams of patience, 11 grams of inspiration, 22 grams of motivation and 2 grams of sugar."

CHAPTER 20

How CEOs Think and Lead: Insights from Research on CEOs Around the World

CHAPTER HIGHLIGHTS

> Senior leadership competencies that will drive success in the twenty-first century are distributed across the four quadrants of the Whole Brain Model.

> An analysis of the thinking preferences of more than 9,300 CEOs around the world shows that today's CEOs demonstrate a primary preference for each of the four thinking quadrants, but some of those preferences are stronger than others.

> While there are some variations among CEOs across countries, as well as between male and female CEOs, overall the occupation continues to be multi-dominant.

> CEOs have a unique profile that, when leveraged, enables them to get the full benefits of the typical diversity found on their top team(s).

The pressure on this CEO and his leadership team was unrelenting. With all eyes on them as they neared the IPO deadline, stress was at an all-time high. The CEO, frustrated by where they were in the process, scheduled an offsite meeting to try to get to the bottom of the problem. This was a group of highly talented people with years of requisite functional experience, so how was it that they could be so siloed in their views of the business, especially when they were all so clearly interdependent? Even worse, their aversion to open debate and their lack of curiosity about one another made team interaction feel like torture. Adding to his irritation, the CEO could see and understand all of the various functional views—they were all obvious to him—yet the individual team members seemed blind to anything outside their own narrow perspective.

Every CEO we have ever worked with has shared a similar complaint. They tell us that while it's no problem for them to comprehend the intersection of the various functions across the organization, they realize, to their endless frustration, that this is an ability that most of the other people on their team simply don't have.

Maybe that's why, with the growing body of research and data we've collected over the years from organizations across the globe, we're often asked this one question in particular: "How do CEOs think?"

> To me, business isn't about wearing suits or pleasing stockholders. It's about being true to yourself, your ideas, and focusing on the essentials.
>
> —Sir Richard Branson

What makes CEOs different? What's the secret sauce? In fact, CEOs are an interesting breed. What's consistently true is that no matter what changes are taking place in the world—whether it's the economy, demographics, market trends, technological advances, new regulations, disruptions, catastrophic events, or other internal and external factors—the data reveal that CEOs are different from others in their mult-dominance. On average, they tend to have *strong preferences* across all four quadrants (a 1-1-1-1 average profile), more so than any other occupational group, even though they often come from a wide range of different functional backgrounds.

The multi-dominance of the CEO may explain the puzzlement that people often feel when they are trying to "psych out" the CEO. To an uninformed observer, multi-dominant preferences can appear both disarming and tough to pin down because of the wide array of interests, approaches, and "clues" that they provide. It also explains why CEOs as a group are so effective at the role they play in overseeing and leading teams composed of a myriad of different specialized functional leaders. In addition, it serves them well in synthesizing and distilling wide-ranging information for their own "bosses," the board of directors. Their multi-dominance provides them with the ability to translate ideas from the language of one quadrant or function to that of the next and then integrate it all in order to make decisions. This is a crucial skill when the time comes to take

> It's a matter of continuing to grow and transform, and it means that executives have to have extraordinary adaptability.
>
> —Warren Bennis

action: CEOs have to be able to advance facts and data toward conclusions *and* articulate concepts *and* incorporate the human factors into those concepts *and* synthesize many ideas into a few. The power to lead, engage, and communicate clearly with a variety of internal and external "tribes" in such a way that they work together effectively is the critical competitive work of the CEO.

Studies of the common traits of effective CEOs confirm the prevalence of this breadth of thinking within the top ranks. For example, Adam Bryant, author of *The Corner Office: Indispensable and Unexpected Lessons from CEOs on How to Lead and Succeed*,[1] found that CEOs consistently demonstrate:

- **Passionate curiosity.** They are alert and engaged with the world, and they want to know more (more D-oriented thinking).
- **Battle-hardened confidence.** This comes from *persistently* overcoming adversity (more B oriented).
- **Team smarts.** They have the ability to recognize the players the team needs and how to bring them together around a common goal (more C oriented).
- **An ability to be concise.** This is what Bryant calls a simple mindset (more A oriented).
- **A willingness to take risks when it is most difficult.** In other words, they exhibit fearlessness (more D oriented).

These represent a variety of traits that are rarely found in one individual, but they are typical among CEOs, with their breadth of available thinking.

Another study, by the executive search firm Russell Reynolds Associates,[2] examined survey responses from more than 3,700 executives, including 134 chief executives at large companies in North America and Europe. It determined that the top three traits separating CEOs from other leaders are a willingness to take calculated risks, a bias toward thoughtful action, and the ability to read people efficiently. The other six were forward thinking, optimistic, constructively tough-minded, measured emotion, pragmatically inclusive, and a willingness to trust.

Overall, most studies are consistent in that they cite as differentiating characteristics traits that span all four quadrants of the Whole Brain Model. What they reveal is that, in contrast to the many functional leaders who see the world in terms of this *or* that, CEOs more often see *and*. As complexity grows and changes hit business at an even faster pace, the nature of the CEO job—and increasingly, that of leaders at all levels—will increasingly demand this kind of "and" thinking.

In fact, when you look at the commonly cited twenty-first century leadership competencies, the need for breadth of thinking is no longer limited to the CEO role. Critical thinking, being able to anticipate change, dealing with ambiguity, and analytical thinking consistently show up. Variations of adaptability, innovation, change orientation, risk taking, and visionary thinking come up repeatedly. With globalization increasing, so is the need for greater cultural competencies and skills like interpersonal sensitivity, team and group management, self-management, and emotional intelligence. And finally, focus, execution, and managing priorities in a chaotic world are skills that every company needs now more than ever. When you organize these commonly cited competencies across the four quadrants of the Whole Brain Model (see Figure 20-1), it's obvious that all leaders need to be able to access and apply all thinking preferences and consciously shift their thinking depending on the needs of the situation. (For more on Whole Brain Leadership, see Chapter 14.)

Put It to Work

Whether or not you are already a C-level leader, it is useful to do a quick audit of your breadth of thinking as compared to the twenty-first century leadership competencies mapped against the Whole Brain Model in Figure 20-1. Select those that you feel you have already developed or are in the process of developing.

Next, select and prioritize those that are not as well developed, but that you know you will need. For the number one "missing" competency:

- Describe why this is important to you and your role in the future (D quadrant).
- Clarify what this competency means by writing out the specific behaviors you will need to demonstrate to show that you've acquired it (A quadrant).
- Think about whom you know that could serve as a mentor, inspiration, or resource for developing this competency (C quadrant).
- Explore where can you get specific skill development (for example, the training department, a local college or university, or online resources), and decide when you will get started (B quadrant).

Thinking Preferences of Twenty-First Century CEOs

CEOs seem to be better designed for the challenge of shifting their thinking from moment to moment. So how *do* they think? And to what extent do today's CEOs demonstrate an ability to think across the quadrants? Has their profile changed in comparison to what we found in a similar study that we conducted in the mid-1990s? We dug into the data to find out.

Critical Twenty-First Century Leadership Competencies

A

- Builds and maintains a focus on results
- Analyzes data, facts, & information effectively
- Breaks down and solves complex problems and business challenges
- Stays current on research to support evidence-based decision making
- Demonstrates global business acumen
- Possesses up-to-date financial knowledge and know-how
- Shows decisiveness and swift response time under pressure
- Leverages new technologies
- Possesses relevant technical know-how
- Thinks critically and concisely
- Demonstrates clarity of purpose
- Sets clear goals and accountabilities

D

- Develops and models vision
- Drives and embraces ongoing change
- Focuses on the future and long-term benefit despite urgent, short-term demands
- Takes appropriate risks
- Tolerates ambiguity and navigates effectively in an ambiguous world
- Thinks globally, understanding the big picture
- Builds a culture where creativity and innovation thrive
- Thinks strategically and anticipates change
- Creates a culture of learning from failure and promotes experimentation
- Challenges the status quo and seeks breakthrough solutions
- Creates alignment and integration across business units, functions, and processes
- Demonstrates adaptive thinking and sees problems as opportunities

- Demonstrates agility, in response to changing needs
- Models a balanced approach to their own development, continually building self-awareness
- Demonstrates resilience in response to ongoing changes and challenges
- Pursues and encourages lifelong learning

B

- Maintains order and organization in a volatile world
- Maintains singularity of focus when required
- Instills a sense of security in turbulent times
- Takes timely action, even when resistance and challenges are present
- Demonstrates consistency in thought and action
- Promotes quality and consistency
- Ensures execution amid chaos
- Drives constant, continuous improvement
- Manages conflicting priorities
- Demonstrates effective self-management
- Filters and prioritizes information
- Acts consistently according to ethics and principles

C

- Engages, inspires, and motivates others
- Recognizes, understands, and manages emotions
- Values diversity and builds relationships across cultures
- Empowers and develops others
- Develops trust by being open and authentic
- Collaborates and builds high-performing teams in a virtual world
- Promotes shared values and purpose
- Demonstrates social responsibility and is attentive to community and societal needs
- Creates and nurtures partnerships, coalitions, and social networks
- Provides feedback, listens, and communicates
- Shows empathy and a keen interest in customers
- Demonstrates social awareness and reads people and situations well

FIGURE 20-1 Critical twenty-first century leadership competencies based on a literature review. These are placed based on the primary emphasis of the competency by quadrant, with those in the center requiring all four quadrants.[3]

Analyzing data from our international database of CEOs, we looked at their preferences as a group, then drilled down further to see if there were differences among countries or between males and females, and finally, looked at how the data have changed since our last study. Here's what we found.

Our sample consisted of data on 9,300 CEOs who had completed the HBDI assessment between January 1, 2000, and May 31, 2014. These CEOs represent a variety of industries, including, but not limited to, life sciences, retail, architecture and engineering, social sciences, finance, technology, consumer packaged goods, and general business. Hailing from 76 countries, including Australia, Canada, Denmark, France, Germany, India, China, South Africa, and the United States, the CEOs ranged in age from 30 to 86, with an average age of 49. Of the group, 80 percent were male and 20 percent were female.

Overall, although the average shows strong preferences across all four quadrants, when we looked at the data more closely, the *strongest* preferences showed up for visionary thinking, with the highest overall average being in the D quadrant (see Figure 20-2).

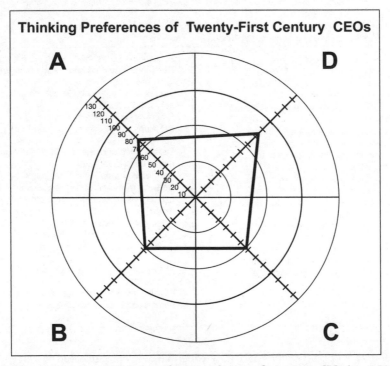

FIGURE 20-2 Average of thinking preferences of twenty-first century CEOs (n = 9,300).

One of the most powerful sections of the HBDI is the forced ranking of 16 work elements, which represent the types of tasks or activities that someone might have to do to perform his or her job (for example, problem solving, innovating, or teaching/training). The work element that was ranked by all CEOs (both male and female) as the work they do best was problem solving (see Figure 20-3), which does not come as a surprise in light of the varied responsibilities that CEOs carry. In today's environment, at the CEO level, this is more about managing dilemmas in an ambiguous and chaotic environment than about traditional problem solving.[4] In comparison to the similar CEO study that we conducted in 1996, this finding is consistent for males but represents a change for female CEOs, who had previously ranked organization as their number one work element.

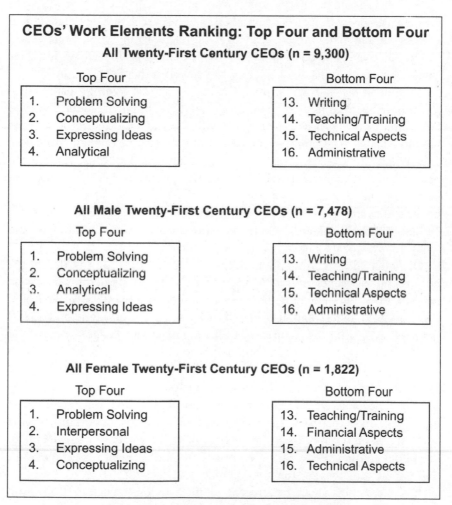

CEOs' Work Elements Ranking: Top Four and Bottom Four

All Twenty-First Century CEOs (n = 9,300)

Top Four	Bottom Four
1. Problem Solving	13. Writing
2. Conceptualizing	14. Teaching/Training
3. Expressing Ideas	15. Technical Aspects
4. Analytical	16. Administrative

All Male Twenty-First Century CEOs (n = 7,478)

Top Four	Bottom Four
1. Problem Solving	13. Writing
2. Conceptualizing	14. Teaching/Training
3. Analytical	15. Technical Aspects
4. Expressing Ideas	16. Administrative

All Female Twenty-First Century CEOs (n = 1,822)

Top Four	Bottom Four
1. Problem Solving	13. Teaching/Training
2. Interpersonal	14. Financial Aspects
3. Expressing Ideas	15. Administrative
4. Conceptualizing	16. Technical Aspects

FIGURE 20-3 Work elements: CEOs across the globe.

The element ranked second-highest by males and fourth by females is conceptualizing, up from the fourth-highest ranking overall in our earlier research. Conceptual thinking is the ability to understand a situation or problem by identifying patterns or connections and addressing key underlying issues.[5] This corresponds to today's need to see patterns and trends at a strategic level, and the ability to then generalize the business implications.

Expressing ideas ranked as third-highest for female CEOs (after interpersonal) and fourth-highest for males, a change from sixth and seventh place, respectively, in the previous study. When you consider the high visibility of today's CEOs as visionary communicators who need to be able to engage effectively with others and communicate new ideas, this work focus makes sense. The ranking of interpersonal as second for female CEOs versus sixth for males aligns with recent Zenger Folkman research[6] showing that women leaders outrank men in their ability to build relationships, collaborate, team, inspire, motivate, and develop others. The focus and preference for interpersonal interaction among female CEOs helps explain those data.

Analytical ranks third for male CEOs, in contrast to ninth for females. Often developed earlier in their careers, analytical thinking and the ability to break things down is useful in an age in which big data is emerging as a growing trend and critical thinking is an important part of the executive function. Clearly less preferred by females, analytical has dropped from fifth to ninth place among women compared to our earlier research. The bottom two for both male and female CEOs are administrative and technical aspects. These are activities that are most likely delegated to a large extent, although some degree of technical fluency and technological savvy is required to navigate today's world and understand the business landscape.

Of potential concern is the finding that teaching/training is among the bottom four elements (out of 16) for all CEOs. This data point mirrors the recent CEB study indicating that only 13 percent of organizations are looking closely to understand how they best learn.[7] This finding is potentially the most worrisome, as companies are facing huge knowledge gaps as these CEOs and a large wave of baby boomers who are currently in the leadership ranks begin to retire. While there's been plenty of talk about addressing the looming "leadership crisis," CEOs can't outsource this task entirely. They need to take an active role in mentoring, developing, and transferring their knowledge and expertise to the next generation and, most important, making sure that this is a top priority for the organization. The development side of the talent challenge is clearly before us, and CEOs must take the lead in making learning the new fuel for organizational growth.

It is interesting to note that, in general, the activities related to B-quadrant thinking ranked the lowest, although organization appeared in the top four for CEOs in Germany and China, possibly because of cultural differences. Of all of the B-quadrant characteristics, however, organization is ranked highest overall (in the eighth position), a change from the study we conducted in the 1990s, when it was number two for males and number one for females. The advent of technology and support systems that facilitate organization, along with the continued pressure to focus more on the big picture and global concerns, most likely contributed to this shift. As discussed in Chapter 14, this lower emphasis on B quadrant aspects is also consistent with the types of work that require the attention of leaders as they progress through the Leadership Pipeline developed by Ram Charan, Stephen Drotter, and James Noel.[8] As leaders progress up the pipeline to a senior level, the more tactical, B-quadrant aspects are delegated to other people in the organization and are gradually overtaken by a need for more strategic, "big-picture" D-quadrant thinking.

Our data show that, although *most managers* include problem solving in their top five, in contrast to CEOs, their top five also includes planning, organization, and/or implementation. Managers as a whole have either creative or innovating—both important twenty-first century competencies, in the *bottom five*. This not only highlights the differences between leading at the C-level and managing, but also shows that these managers will have to stretch outside their mental comfort zones and potentially draw on less-preferred thinking styles if they are to develop into successful leaders of the future.

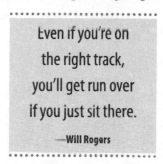

> Even if you're on the right track, you'll get run over if you just sit there.
>
> —Will Rogers

A Closer Look: Country-by-Country Differences

Does a CEO's cultural context affect his or her thinking preferences? Figure 20-4 shows the composite averages for both male and female CEOs from each of 12 countries that provided sufficient data to consider them representative. The similarities in the overall HBDI profiles indicate that there's a relatively uniform distribution of mental preferences for the CEO occupation worldwide. One noteworthy finding was that, on average, CEOs from Singapore appeared to favor the A quadrant more than CEOs from other countries did. The remaining quadrants were relatively similar across the 12 countries, confirming the consistency in breadth of thinking that we saw in the CEO study we conducted in the mid-1990s: wherever you are in the world, the role still requires a multi-dominant approach—and more so today than ever.

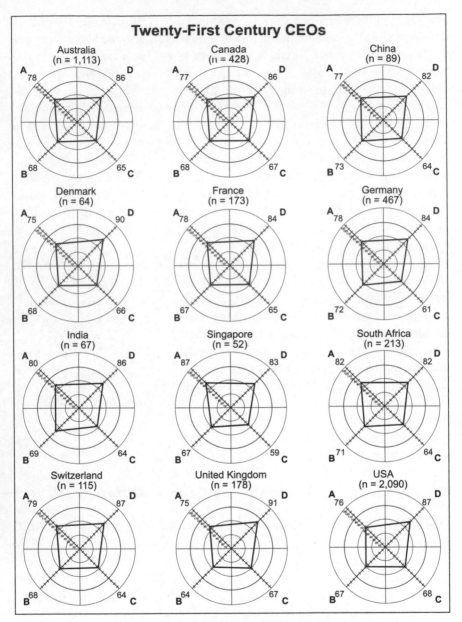

FIGURE 20-4 Average profiles of CEOs by country.

CEO preferences in the work elements section by country are fascinating. Consistent with our previous CEO research, in 11 of the 12 countries, problem solving is the universal choice as the top work element (for France, it is ranked 2). As mentioned earlier, in our current world, problem solving is no longer just a logical, cut-and-dried process. The multi-dominant profile tends to broaden the approach, making it more of a Whole Brain process than would naturally occur in profiles with less breadth.

Other elements that are at the top across the world include conceptualizing, expressing ideas, innovating, and analytical. However, unlike problem solving, there are country-by-country differences for each of these. For example, conceptualizing is ranked much lower than the overall average (it is internationally ranked second) for the European countries of France (where it is ranked tenth), Denmark (ranked seventh), and Switzerland (ranked fourth). And although expressing ideas is ranked third internationally, it's near the top of the list for some countries (for example, the United States, the United Kingdom, and Australia) and in the middle for others (for example, China and Singapore). Analytical is near the top for most countries, but the United States, the United Kingdom, and Australia all rank it at six or seven. These CEOs seem to place greater emphasis on strategic aspects (for example, conceptualizing and innovating) and people aspects (for example, interpersonal and expressing ideas) than on analytical aspects.

Innovating appeared in the top six in all countries except Germany, Switzerland, and China. Interestingly, in contrast, creative aspects ranked lower across the board, landing in the middle between the seventh and fourteenth position out of sixteen (the average was 9.5) for all countries except France (where it ranked fifth). This is consistent with our previous CEO study, which means that although innovation is ranked higher, we are not seeing an increase in the ranking for creativity—even though, according to IBM's most recent CEO study, creative thinking was cited among the top three traits sought out in employees.[9] One probable reason for this is that innovation feels less risky than creative thinking. Since innovation requires creative thinking, this presents an interesting leadership dilemma. (For more on creative thinking, see Chapters 21 to 23.) For CEOs, creative thinking is even more important today than it was in previous years, since it represents a very effective way to deal with change, which is now a given and happening at a faster rate than ever before. Today's CEOs also have to be able to lead and facilitate the typically diverse top team as well as set the tone for the open debate and creative contention necessary to generate the best possible ideas. Research by McKinsey has shown that top teams benefit from this diversity:[10]

> Between 2008 and 2010, companies with more diverse top teams were also top financial performers. That's probably no coincidence....
>
> The findings were startlingly consistent: for companies ranking in the top quartile of executive-board diversity, ROEs [returns on equity] were 53 percent higher, on average, than they were for those in the bottom quartile. At the same time, EBIT [earnings before interest and tax]

margins at the most diverse companies were 14 percent higher, on average, than those of the least diverse companies. The results were similar across all but one of the countries we studied; an exception was ROE performance in France; but even there, EBIT was 50 percent higher for diverse companies.

From our experience and through our research on team diversity, we know that it takes skilled, effective leadership to make those highly diverse teams so successful (see Chapter 12 for more on teams). With their breadth of thinking, CEOs are uniquely positioned to be able to take on this challenge.

In terms of work elements that are consistently ranked low, administrative is ranked in the bottom four in all countries and is last or second to last in 10 of the 12 countries, while technical aspects is in the bottom four (12 to 16) for CEOs in all 12 countries—consistent with our previous study. Again, we believe that these work elements represent work activities that are largely delegated to others rather than being carried out by the CEOs themselves. The drop in ranking for administrative, which was previously ranked between 9 and 12, is indicative of the probable impact of technology on eliminating much of the administrative burden on senior leaders. At the same time, though, with technical aspects currently being in the bottom four, some C-level leaders (for example, baby boomers or those less comfortable with new technology) may be relying on support staff to handle more complex technology-related needs.

Of great importance is the finding that teaching/training is in the bottom four on the list for CEOs in 11 out of 12 individual countries. Again, the need for the CEO to pay attention to the development needs of the top team, as well as to set the tone and priority in the culture for continued learning, reassessment, and growth, may be at risk if these organizations do not have a strong voice at the table driving learning, knowledge transfer, coaching, and development.

To see more specific data on each country, please visit www.wholebrain businessbook.com.

When you think about how globally integrated the economy and business are today, it's both fascinating and valuable to understand the similarities and differences in CEOs over this wide range of countries. Every business runs on thinking, and it starts with the CEO. Having a better understanding of the lens through which CEOs from different countries view the world, their work, and others allows you to have context for the decisions, direction, and general tone established by each CEO you interact with.

A Closer Look: Gender Differences in CEO Thinking Preferences

What about male versus female CEOs? As discussed earlier, differences do exist in the overall profiles. We found that in three of the four quadrants, there was a statistically significant difference: male CEOs showed a stronger preference for the A quadrant than did female CEOs, while females scored stronger preferences for the C and D quadrants than did their male counterparts (see Figure 20-5). The A and C differential is consistent with our overall HBDI database studies, although the higher D quadrant in females is unique to female *CEOs*.

Another section of the HBDI shows that female CEOs selected intuitive as the strongest general descriptor of themselves, with logical as the second, whereas males selected intuitive second and logical first. This, combined with the fact that more than two-thirds of both male and female CEOs agreed with the statement, "I rely on hunches of rightness or wrongness when moving toward a solution," and three-fourths agreed that "I can frequently anticipate the solutions to my problems," demonstrates how much all CEOs rely on their intuition, after having gathered all the facts, engaged with team members, envisioned the options, and looked at implications, to develop the best possible solution. This rings true given my experience, both as a CEO and working with them: when all else fails and no more input is available, the CEO often steps outside and draws a conclusion based on his or her brain's synthesizing everything it has processed, heard, and learned.

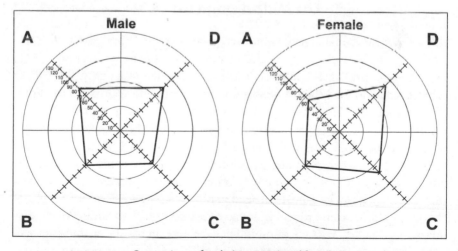

FIGURE 20-5 Comparison of male (n = 7,823) and female (n = 1,749) twenty-first century CEO thinking preferences.

More than two-thirds of the CEOs, both male and female, rated themselves as extroverts, while close to 13 percent described themselves as being down the middle—what's sometimes called "ambivert." Only 3 percent of females identified themselves as introverted compared to 18 percent of males. An interesting finding is that there is a significantly stronger C-quadrant score for extroverts, while the A-quadrant score is higher for introverts. Validating this shift is the placement of interpersonal as a work element for introverts—it is ranked eleventh out of sixteen, versus being ranked third for extroverts.

As the number of female CEOs continues to grow, and as the Zenger Folkman research has shown, the preferences of female CEOs do provide a potential advantage in the competency domains of emotional intelligence, engagement, collaboration, teaming, and coaching, all very important. However, it's important to note that these differences don't imply that one gender is better equipped to be an effective CEO. First, there was a large amount of individual variability—some males were higher in the C quadrant than the average female, and some females were higher in the A quadrant than the average male. Second, the twenty-first-century leadership competencies and CEO success traits are distributed across the entire Whole Brain Model. That means that all CEOs must be able to capitalize on their strong preferences *and* apply less-preferred styles based on changing and often unpredictable demands. Regardless of gender, ethnicity, age, and any other demographic or biological characteristic, all leaders today need to be *situationally whole* if they are to be successful.

The Multi-Dominant CEO

As we've seen consistently since we began keeping data on CEO thinking preferences, and as these more recent data confirm, on average, CEOs continue to have well-balanced profiles—a good sign when you consider what it takes to lead the top teams and an organization through the complexities and challenges of twenty-first-century business. Consistent with previous studies, CEOs with strong preferences for the A-quadrant analytical, technical, and financial aspects of leadership tend to least prefer the C-quadrant interpersonal and emotional aspects. Likewise, CEOs in this study who strongly prefer the B-quadrant safekeeping, administrative, and task-accomplishment aspects of leadership have a tendency to least prefer the D-quadrant strategic and innovative aspects of leadership. As we discussed in Chapter 3, a lack of preference for certain modes of thinking will have consequences for performance and effectiveness, just as a strong preference will (see Figure 20-6).

A Low preference in the A quadrant can result in leadership ineffectiveness such as:	Low preference in the D quadrant can result in leadership ineffectiveness such as: D
Possible reduced focus on analytical, legal, and technical aspects, as well as quantitative or financial aspects. At the C level, this could create serious challenges when it comes to essential functions such as critical analysis, financial savvy, the ability to understand and put complex data in context, and the need to focus on what's most important in a noisy world.	Possible reduced focus on vision, dealing with ambiguity, thinking strategically, synthesizing, and providing innovative, global, big-picture perspectives. In today's rapidly changing world, all of these are absolutely essential at the C-level in order to be effective and "see around corners," visualize alternative options, and scale at a global level.
Low preference in the B quadrant can result in leadership ineffectiveness such as:	Low preference in the C quadrant can result in leadership ineffectiveness such as:
Possible reduced task focus, ability to pay attention to critical details, and ability to effectively manage priorities, organization, and follow-through. C-level consequences include potential problems managing conflicting and changing priorities and tasks through to completion. B	Possible reduced interest in interpersonal aspects, building relationships, communication, cultural aspects, and facilitating team collaboration. This can inhibit a C-level leader's facilitative leadership effectiveness when it comes to artful management of the top team(s), as well as coaching and communication effectiveness and the ability to manage strategic relationships (internal and external). C

FIGURE 20-6 Examples of leadership obstacles stemming from low preference.

The Power of "And"

Most CEOs around the globe have both the burden and the advantage of taking the "wide view," one that encompasses all four quadrants. The prevalence of that multi-dominant profile at the top is great news because the role of CEO clearly requires it, especially given the focus on innovation that every company needs today. Those CEOs who do not themselves have this natural breadth of thinking must seek to develop it and/or partner with a complementary thinker or thinkers to expand their brain bandwidth. There are numerous examples in business of just such C-level partnerships. As Darrell K. Rigby, Kara Gruver, and James Allen wrote in their *Harvard Business Review* article "Innovation in Turbulent Times":[11]

> The world's most innovative companies often operate under some variation of a both-brain partnership. In technology the creative partner might be a brilliant engineer like Bill Hewlett and the business executive a savvy manager like David Packard. In the auto industry the team might be a "car guy" like Hal Sperlich—a major creative force behind both the original Ford Mustang and the first Chrysler minivan—and a management wizard like Lee Iacocca. The former track coach Bill Bowerman developed Nike's running shoes; his partner, Phil Knight, handled manufacturing, finance, and sales. Howard Schultz conceived the iconic Starbucks coffeehouse format, and CEO Orin Smith oversaw the chain's rapid growth.

They go on to mention Apple as the company with the best-known "both-brain partnership," with CEO Steve Jobs having played the role of creative director, shaping everything from product design and user interfaces to the customer experience at Apple's stores, while COO Tim Cook handled the day-to-day running of the business. Now Cook is leading the enterprise, surrounding himself with other complementary thinkers. These examples show how any leader can expand his or her thinking to live and operate successfully in the CEO's world of "and." The key, however, is recognizing both your preferences and your mental blind spots.

It is apparent that the occupation of CEO requires a discrete set of interests, preferences, and competencies that are generally consistent across country, cultural, and gender boundaries. That represents both an opportunity and a challenge for most CEOs. Each of us can become a situationally Whole Brain leader, but doing so starts with, and must be developed by *you*. For those of you who are already CEOs, and for those who aspire to become one, ask yourself: How well are you leveraging your thinking, and, just as important, the thinking of others? As a CEO myself, I know I cannot do it alone. As Justin Menkes stated in his *Harvard Business Review* article "Three Traits Every CEO Needs,"[12] "The best CEOs had been, and continued to be, distinguished by their ability to manifest the very best from their workforce."

So what about our frustrated CEO from the beginning of this chapter? The offsite turned out to be an eye-opening experience for everyone. As the team members learned about their individual and team HBDI Profiles, the data gave them a clear picture of the group's diversity. It was apparent that their thinking differences had been creating obstacles to the group's productivity and its ability to collaborate and engage in creative contention and debate. As each member of the team shared a personal "HBDI autobiography" story explaining his or her background and the context of his or her preferences, I saw the walls between them begin to fall. They realized that, in fact, they had more in common with one another than they had thought, and that the diversity available on the team was a resource that they could each use to expand his or her own thinking. That evening, the vice president of finance pulled me aside to say: "Now I get [the CEO's] frustration with me."

The next day, each member defined and shared what came to mind when he or she heard the word *conflict*. Most used negative language (anger, frustration, danger, and so on). The CEO waited until the end to share his view: "I think conflict is positive, and we need it on this team! It's an opportunity for me to take advantage of the differences I expect each of you to bring to the table." Suddenly the group members realized that they had wasted a lot of energy and shortchanged the collective value of the group by not learning to appreciate the differences that each of them brought. Now they were ready to do the work that was needed to become a "first team," focused on making the leadership team their primary focus rather than getting dragged down into the functional noise. After they discussed and agreed on Whole Brain group norms, the balance of the meeting focused on strategy—and was one of the best they had ever held. Most important, the CEO now knew that he had a team he could count on to perform at a high level as he headed into his time-consuming IPO prep.

And when that IPO turned out to be a huge success, it was clear that the CEO could not have gotten there alone. Now that he had the best brains in the company aligned with him, nothing would stop them!

> There are a lot of things that go into creating success. I don't like to do just the things I like to do. I like to do the things that cause the company to succeed.
>
> —**Michael Dell**

SO WHAT?

> CEO HBDI data confirm that the role is whole-brained by nature.
> The demands on CEOs today and the leadership competencies for the twenty-first century require a Whole Brain approach to the job.
> Much can be learned about the CEO's "secret sauce" by understanding male/female data, introversion and extroversion differences, and the discrete work elements, both globally and country by country.
> Despite rapid and ongoing change in the business environment and the broader world, the CEO profile has remained remarkably consistent over the years, a finding that demonstrates how important situational wholeness is for succeeding in the top job.

PART 4

Tapping into Breakthrough Thinking

"Thank you for calling Creative Business Seminars. If you'd like to become a more creative problem solver, press 1 without touching any part of your telephone."

CHAPTER 21

Increasing Business Creativity and Innovation— Head First

CHAPTER HIGHLIGHTS

> The brain is the source of creativity.
> Each of us has the mental diversity within us to be creative.
> Creativity and innovation are different, and both are important to business success.
> Each of the Whole Brain Thinking quadrants contributes to the creative process, but each does so in different ways.
> The degree to which you engage all the quadrants of the Whole Brain Model in the process is the extent to which the process will be successful.
> Compared to homogeneous teams, mentally diverse heterogeneous teams have a clear advantage in terms of the quality of their creative output.

"But *we* are the creatives!" exclaimed the lead executive of the ad agency team. Clearly, he was feeling somewhat threatened. The idea that we would put them in a room with their large consumer products client's brand team to learn creative problem solving *together* made them nervous. They were uncomfortable because they felt that the program was demystifying the "magic" of their creative process. Creativity was the domain in which they were the "experts," the area for which they were getting paid a lot. They were as yet unaware that the applied creative problem-solving process they would learn would go beyond their definition of "creativity."

The client insisted. The leaders had become frustrated by the infighting and lack of cohesion that were resulting in project overruns, which were costing the company a lot of money. They felt that by learning together, the two teams would be able to maximize the advertising investment being made for each product line. The brand team's problems would be better understood by the agency team, and the agency team's advertising recommendations would be more in line with the brand team's expectations.

Once the members of the agency team were convinced that they should attend the workshop we were delivering—and were willing to bring the brand team and the creative team together for the experience—it became evident that all the participants had something to contribute to the team's creative problem-solving process. The program focused on specific, real-time brand product problems, including analyzing the problem/opportunity, evaluating customer input, finding new ideas for effective positioning, looking at team communication and process issues, and dealing with technical and execution challenges. All the different processes across the mental spectrum were required to resolve those differing aspects of the problems successfully across the two collaborating teams.

> Senior men and women have no monopoly on great ideas. Nor do Creative people. Some of the best ideas come from account executives, researchers, and others. Encourage this; you need all the ideas you can get.
>
> —David Ogilvy

The ultimate outcome of the pilot session was a greatly enhanced team process, alignment of team objectives (which provided significant savings of money and time that had been wasted on "misfires"), and a genuine respect for the different perspectives that each of the team members brought to the table. The two teams that had not been able to work well together prior to the program were so engaged that they refused to end the workshop, and worked hours beyond the normal closing time in order to take advantage of this newfound motivation. A series of subsequent programs was rolled out over several years with similar results, demonstrating that creativity was indeed crucial for success *and available to all*—even those who didn't work for an advertising agency!

Years later, demand for creative thinking has never been stronger. It is being clearly articulated by business leaders as essential for driving growth and maintaining a competitive edge, and in a recent IBM CEO study,[1] creative thinking was cited as being among the top three traits leaders are seeking out in employees.

Particularly as the world grows more complex and the pace of change just keeps getting faster, we find ourselves looking for ways to unleash new perspectives and fresh thinking about our products, markets, internal challenges, and competitors. From developing new offerings to coming up with better ways to "do more with less," we need every bit of our creativity at work to discover new answers and see the opportunities that others might miss.

Yet there continues to be a lot of mystique around the creative process. Many people will shut themselves down, saying that they're "just not creative." In fact, once creative thinking is understood as a series of thinking processes that can be applied and learned, it suddenly becomes available to us all.

Creativity is part of the human condition. It is an important aspect of life from early childhood to old age. It takes many forms, from child rearing to learning languages, to arts and crafts, to cooking, to gardening, to composing, dancing, writing, problem solving, and inventing. These are just a few of the many aspects of life that help define the domain of creativity. Out of this list, the words *problem solving* and *inventing* strongly suggest a business application of the creative process. It is the business application of creativity that is the focus of this chapter.

In describing what creativity is and how it works, I often use the word *innovation* in partnership with *creativity*. The reason is that many businesspeople use the term *innovation* in place of *creativity* because they feel more comfortable with the former term. Actually, I believe that there are significant differences between creativity and innovation. I will present an argument that strongly suggests that business needs both, but that in terms of process, they are a bit different, and I will describe what those differences are.

Whatever you call it, if your competitors have the same products, the same markets, the same customers, and the same delivery systems as you do, unleashing the creativity of your organization can make the winning difference.

> Every single one of us is creative, and the greatest companies and the greatest cities are going to stoke that creative furnace burning inside every one of us.
>
> —Richard Florida

Unleashing Creativity

It is a foregone conclusion that business executives would like to unleash the creativity they are sure is locked up in their organizations. They talk about it in staff meetings, write headlines about it in the internal newsletters, and proclaim it as a company goal at the annual meeting. We hear it all the time: CEOs announcing, in one way or another, "What this company needs to do is to unleash the creativity of its employees."

But there are consequences, and the consequences of unleashing creativity are often not considered. For starters, unleashing creativity means that risks will have to be taken. Mistakes will be made, rules will have to be changed, and the status quo will be challenged. In fact, business assumptions will have to be reconsidered and leadership concepts will have to be altered. You can count on the fact that none of these results are what the leaders had in mind. All they wanted was the fruits of creativity, not the challenges to the status quo that are integral to the creative process.

The creative process is not "business as usual." It's like having 100 or 1,000 or 10,000 tightly wound springs suddenly releasing their energy into the organization at random. Those business leaders who recognize this tend to be fearful of it; those who do not tend to underestimate the power of creativity. In either case, they'll often try to manage and control it, but this approach won't be effective because it inhibits by design the natural flow of creativity. In order to cultivate creativity, you have to understand the process.

The Brain Is the Source of Creativity

Creative thought processes are the result of specialized mental modes that respond situationally to life's experiences. Idea generation is in fact a neural event. Neural transmitters streaming across the synaptic gap convey the electrochemical elements of an idea in formation. We are learning more every day about how ideas occur in our brains, but we know that they arise in specialized parts of the brain that, through massive interconnections, can come in contact with other ideas and together form the basis of synergy.

> The only frontiers that can never be conquered are the creative frontiers of the mind.
>
> —Anonymous

Creative and innovative thinking work best when the brain is up to the challenge of increased synaptic activity. Whether you are feeling sharp or dull at any given moment can be due to the chemistry in your head. Some people refer to their bad brain days as, "I'm just not thinking straight today." Other times, the ideas and thoughts just keep coming, and you may think to yourself, "I'm really sharp today." And when you are really on top of things, you may feel not only tuned-up mentally, but also creative and smart.

This is how it works. The brain is an electrochemical organ. Neurotransmitters are the chemical agents that cause synaptic transmissions to take place, which in turn produce electrical potentials, which, together with the chemical reactions, power the brain in its thinking processes. There are more than 100 neurotransmitters, such as serotonin, that stimulate synaptic transmissions. Each neurotransmitter has a matching receptor that's like a lock and a key. If there are no matching receptors, then the neuron-to-neuron synapse will not take place. When the synaptic transmission does not take place, we are less sharp. When those transmissions do take place, we have the potential for being smart and creative. The greater the synaptic activity, the more likely it is that ideation will take place.

In order for its chemistry to work, the brain must be properly fed. What we eat and drink fuels not only our bodies but our brains as well. There are so-called smart foods and drinks that purport to stimulate our mental activity by fueling the neurotransmitters that are the basis of synaptic interaction. Choline, for example, is a precursor for the neurotransmitter acetylcholine. Studies have shown that increasing the consumption of raw beef liver, broccoli, cauliflower, spinach, hard-boiled eggs, codfish, milk, wheat germ, chicken, grapefruit, peanuts, and almonds (among other things) can boost your choline levels. Research is ongoing as to whether consumption will have a long-term positive impact on memory and cognitive function, but the bottom line is clear: the greater the flow of neurotransmitters, the greater the synaptic activity.[2]

> The creative person is, in any case, continually working at it. His mind is shuffling his information at all times, even when he is not conscious of it.
>
> —Isaac Asimov

Sleep is also important if our brains are to operate for peak creativity. The adage of "sleeping on it" has been scientifically validated. Studies by Dr. Jan Born[3] at the University of Lübeck in Germany (reported in *Nature,* January 2004) demonstrated that memories are restructured in the first four hours of the sleep cycle, enhancing memory and creativity.

The detailed inner process of synergy among all the different specialized areas of the brain that takes place naturally is a key characteristic of both creative and innovative thought. Although these two processes have a lot in common, they have individual uses, which we will discuss in this section.

Whole Brain Creativity and Innovation

Over the years, many descriptions of creativity have referred to it as what is often called a "right-brained" process. The model of applied creativity and innovation I will describe here is a process that, from concept to completion, takes advantage of all the brain's specialized modes. When researching creative processes for the programs I created at GE, I found that the stages defined by Graham Wallas[4] fit my vision of a Whole Brain creative-thinking process. The specialized characteristics of each quadrant and of each mode of the Whole Brain Model are applied in various combinations as the process takes place. A missing quadrant or mode will tend to stall or even shut down the entire process. In order to apply Wallas's original concept to my own,

I added two elements, which are necessary if the process is to be successful and complete. They are *interest* and *application*. Interest gets the process off the ground, and application ensures that the ideas aren't left up in the air but are implemented to solve real problems.

The elements of the expanded process as I apply it are as follows: interest, preparation, incubation, illumination, verification, and application (see Figure 21-1).

Interest is critical to engaging in the creative process. Without it, you can't really get started. It is quadrant-neutral and can emerge for a wide variety of reasons. For example, it may start with an urge to solve an issue, curiosity, the desire to deal with a human need, or an intriguing technical challenge. As obvious as this may seem, interest provides the necessary fuel for the process to get initiated.

The second stage of the process is *preparation*. This step requires gathering information, analyzing the facts, and chronological sequencing of those facts into accurate statements of the problem.

Consider this situation: you work for a company that records concerts and other live entertainment, and it has been looking for new applications to give it a competitive advantage. You just can't get excited about finding more

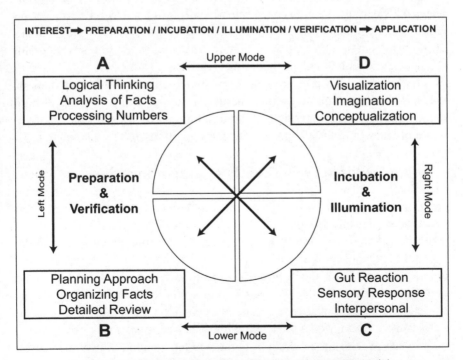

FIGURE 21-1 Whole Brain creativity and innovation iterative model.

ways to dress up the on-screen graphics, but you're intrigued by this challenge. For the last couple of days, you've been thinking about your music fanatic nephew who lives in a small town and rarely has the opportunity to experience a concert live and in person. You have the interest and therefore a strong motivation to tackle this problem: a method of filming and recording concerts that replicates as closely as possible the sights, sounds, and feelings of being there in person.

In the preparation stage, the definition of the exact problem to be solved needs to be stated. Let's say it is, "How to create an interactive, immersive online entertainment experience so that those who can't attend the live event will have a great experience." An analysis of this population's needs would have to be made, along with an assessment of how new technology and ways of filming and recording the events would address these needs better than what is currently available. The preparation phase requires delving into more A- and B-quadrant thinking approaches.

The next phase of the process involves *incubation*. This is where the brain, now having a problem to work on and being motivated by personal interest, processes that problem in both conscious and unconscious ways that allow the brain's natural problem-solving processes to be engaged. This incubation stage of the creative process clearly draws more on C and D types of mental activities, making use of intuitive and conceptual understanding to bring potential solutions up to a conscious level. It often works best when we are totally disengaged from the task at hand and are relaxed or tinkering with something else.

Continuing with our example, after you've defined the problem and collected the facts, you let all this information simmer, so to speak. This is where your brain makes connections as you attend a few live shows and soak up the surround sound at a 3D movie. You are not consciously looking for solutions in this stage; you are simply going about your day in a relaxed manner. Sometimes incubation can take a few hours, and other times you will continue to incubate as the preparation process continues. This creative problem-solving process does not happen in a neat, chronological manner. An iteration between stages is often necessary before ideas begin to emerge.

The next stage is called *illumination*, which is frequently referred to as the aha! or eureka! event in the creative process. This is where ideas suddenly pop into our minds as potential solutions, sometimes as an accompaniment to the theta brain waves that we experience while we are daydreaming. The illumination stage integrates all the aspects of the creative process that took place in the interest, preparation, and incubation stages. And through integration, synthesis, and synergy, ideas present themselves in response to everything that has happened along the way.

Let's go back to the virtual concert experience project. You've been experimenting with different methods, but you're not making much progress. Getting frustrated, you decide to take a break and play with your flight simulator program. Once you've crashed for the last time, you go to bed and fall into a dreamy state. You dream about your nephew playing with the flight simulator program. Then you notice that he's not in the flight simulator but moving throughout the stadium of the concert you attended last week. He takes his place near the front, with the crowd chanting all around him as the amplifier crackles and the music seems to vibrate up through his chest. Then you wake up, with fractured memories of this dream. All of a sudden it clicks. You grab a piece of paper and jot down fragmented thoughts and notes. In a minute your mind is racing, trying to figure out how you can apply these thoughts to the process of filming and recording a virtual concert.

> Without this playing with fantasy, no creative work has ever yet come to birth. The debt we owe to the play of imagination is incalculable.
>
> —Carl Jung

The next stage that is needed is *verification*, which requires a hard-nosed, objective review of the potential solution in relation to the facts of the original problem. Does this new idea have any relationship to the original problem that you were attempting to solve? Verification is necessary, since the idea-generating activity that results from the illumination process can come up with all manner of potential ideas, some of which have no relationship at all to the problem at hand. They may, in fact, be solutions to problems that have not yet been defined. So a critical assessment of the appropriateness of the potential solution has to take place before that potential solution can be applied. Once again, you'll need to draw more on A/B processes that take particular advantage of the critical, diagnostic, and analytic capabilities of the A quadrant.

Now that you have some potential solutions, you need to critically assess their relationship to the problem. Is a particular solution feasible? Will it truly improve the virtual experience? Or does this concept lend itself to a totally different application? You think this solution will work for your needs, but you have to check it out.

Once a solution has been verified, *application* is the next step in the process. This is actually a Whole Brain process in its entirety, but it starts with more of a B-quadrant-oriented focus on implementation, with some analysis from the A quadrant, interaction with the "customer" in the C quadrant, and taking into account the big picture and whole application process in the D quadrant. As you attempt your initial applications, you may need to revisit the verification process. Does the potential solution fit the original problem, and is the application viable? Does the thing work? What do you need to do to make it work? And when you finally get it to work, does the idea solve the original problem?

As an example of a process that emerged during the illumination stage and didn't pass the verification process for the problem that the developer was trying to solve, consider a specific adhesive developed by 3M. In trying to create an adhesive that was very thin but extremely strong, the developer created a glue that was easily applied, but wasn't permanent enough to be what the company was looking for. Later on, a 3M colleague, Art Fry, had been in church for choir practice, grappling with a regularly occurring problem with his hymnbook: Fry would bookmark his hymnbook with pieces of paper, but by Sunday morning, they would have fallen out. Art had a moment of illumination. Here was the perfect application for this faulty adhesive: a nonpermanent way to stick memos to hymnals—or anything else! Voilà! The birth of Post-it Notes.[5] Even though this particular adhesive didn't meet the requirements for the original application, another aha! moment pointed to a completely different application that could easily have been discarded. The next process step, application, brought the Post-it Notes product we know today to the world of additional uses.

It is important to note that, although the description just given goes through the process steps sequentially—from interest to preparation to incubation to illumination and, finally, to application, as shown in Figure 21-1—in reality, the process is much *messier*, iterating back and forth across the quadrants, like zigzag lightning, engaging the whole brain. This zigzagging path is more of a true reflection of how the brain works, as shown metaphorically in Figure 21-2.

Diagnosing this creative process leads to only one overarching conclusion: *all quadrants and modes are involved, and the degree to which all of the brain contributes to the process is the extent to which the process is successful.* Leaving out a critical step or an essential mental process will adversely affect the viability of the creative solution or idea.

While these are completely natural processes and often take place without our really being aware of the steps and sequence, creativity can be greatly enhanced if we understand the process and engage in it in a conscious way. For this reason, creativity, which *can* be taught, *should* be taught. Our experience is clear: creativity will be unleashed with greater efficiency and success when an individual or group *has been trained in*

> Good ideas are not adopted automatically. They must be driven into practice with courageous patience.
>
> —Admiral Hyman Rickover

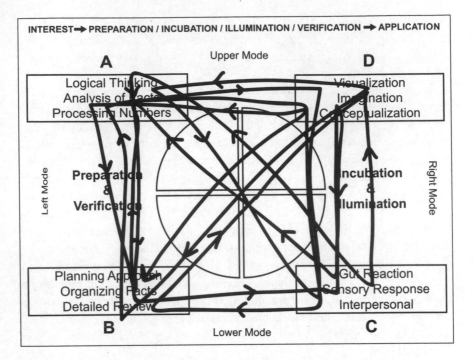

FIGURE 21-2 The messy Whole Brain creativity and innovation iterative process in reality.

the creative process. Through that understanding, everyone knows that he or she has a way to contribute to the process, and, more important, there is a far greater sensitivity to the climate required for the process to take place in order for the fragile nature of idea generation to thrive.

Riding the Brain Waves for Better Results

Another way to improve your creative outcomes is to understand the role that brain wave states play, as you can apply this knowledge to optimize each phase of the process.

Although every brain is unique, all brains are electrochemical. Electrical brain waves supply a convenient measure of the brain's operating status at any given time. Just as we are a coalition of the four thinking selves (rational, safekeeping, feeling, and experimental), we are equipped with five brain-wave states: *gamma, beta, alpha, theta,* and *delta* (see Figure 21-3), each one specialized for a particular kind of neural activity. The more we understand these brain wave states, the more we are able to consciously engage in them to enhance our thinking. Brain wave states are defined by electrical frequencies, measured in cycles per second (cps) or hertz (Hz). To best leverage your brain

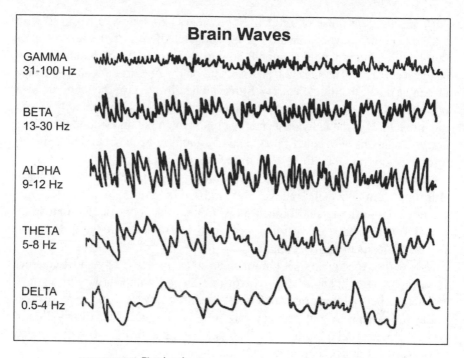

FIGURE 21-3 Five key brain waves common to all human beings.

for creative thinking, it is important to know and recognize the different brain wave states and recognize when and how they occur most frequently for you.

Beta represents the aroused, alert state. The frequency ranges between 13 Hz and about 30 Hz. The higher the number, the more aroused or alert the brain state is. When you are brainstorming, you are most like to be in beta, which may or may not be the most opportune time for you to generate ideas. If you get a lot of ideas when you are interacting with others, this may be a prime creative brain state for you.

Alpha represents the absence of arousal. This is a calm, meditative state and is defined by brain wave frequencies of 9 to 12 Hz. When we are in deep contemplation or idea incubation, we are likely to be in an alpha state. Many people experience aha! moments and insights in this more relaxed state, especially when they are showering, exercising, or listening to music.

The next state, *theta*, represents a very open, free-flow creative state. The brain-wave frequencies for theta are 5 to 8 Hz. For many people, the shift into theta occurs naturally as they fall asleep or wake up in the morning. You may find that you have a lot of ideas, often fleeting, at that time.

The *delta* brain wave state represents deep, dreamless sleep. The frequency range for delta is 0.5 to 4 Hz. Many people describe waking up in the morning with an idea or a sense of an idea. Some years ago, we were working with DuPont engineers who were struggling with a challenge on the factory floor that had them completely stumped: how to stop hoses from collapsing. The solution came from an idea that an associate on the line brought up based on a dream he'd had the night before: a Slinky! The Slinky gave the team the idea of putting a coil in the hoses to prevent collapse, and this immediately solved the problem. Had the individual and the organization not understood the power and mechanisms of Whole Brain Creativity and thus been open to listening to a "crazy" idea about a Slinky, they might still be stuck!

Finally there is the *gamma* range, which was discovered more recently. Running from above 30 Hz to as high as 100 Hz, gamma is the fastest frequency. While there is still much more to uncover about the gamma state, initial research shows that gamma waves may be connected to learning, memory, and information processing.

My early experiments with brain wave states measured by an EEG (electroencephalograph) and a Mind Mirror that displayed the activity by right or left hemisphere demonstrated that all of these brain waves are typically present at any given time, but that they vary greatly in terms of the distribution of beta, theta, and delta brain waves. When a person is fully alert and engaged in performing a task, a high percentage of that person's brain waves will be in the beta range. The more intense and the more alert you are, the higher the frequency of those beta waves. At the other end of the spectrum, an individual who is deeply asleep will have the highest percentage of his or her brain waves in delta, and the deeper the sleep, every 90 minutes the coalition of brain waves shifts to include an increasing amount of theta waves. It is these theta waves that introduce some of the fantasy trips and "movies in the head" that take place during REM (rapid eye movement) dreaming.

Put It to Work

- Take a moment to think of the times when you get your aha! moments, insights, and ideas.
  - When does that typically happen?
  - Where are you?
  - What are you doing?
- Our research has shown that for most people, this occurs when they are waking up in the morning, going to sleep, in the middle of the night, showering or bathing, listening to music, relaxing, driving, exercising, walking, or doing any activity that does not require intense mental concentration (for example, yard work, doing the dishes, or talking with others). For others it occurs when interacting with people or ideas.

- Once you have an idea, how often have you forgotten it?
- What do/can you do to combat that?
- Once an idea emerges from alpha or theta, you have only 10 seconds of memory before the idea vanishes. Here are some ways you can capture it before it's gone:
  - Write it down (always have a small notepad with you).
  - Record it on your phone, tablet, or voice mail.
  - Say it out loud.
  - Imagine a picture of it in your mind or any other association.
  - Start an idea journal, either digital or on paper, and have that available to you to at all times. That will allow you to take advantage of your natural creativity. Make sure to write down all ideas, even if they do not yet make sense. You can work with them later to see how you can best use them.

The types of ideas that occur to you when you are not always working on the problem may be your best thinking! Remember the DuPont employee who dreamed of a Slinky? Had he not captured that idea and held onto it, the company might still be trying to solve the collapsing hose problem. Brain wave research conducted by creativity researchers, including me, suggests that there is a close alignment between the brain wave states just described and the stages of the creative process: interest, preparation, incubation, illumination, verification, and application.

The findings are as follows:

Interest is a general state of alert consideration of a problem situation. The brain state is most frequently beta.

Preparation for applying the creative process to a specific problem situation involves beta at the higher frequencies: more intense, more purposeful, more applied.

Incubation of a problem situation following preparation takes place in alpha, with the lower-frequency, high-amplitude brain waves producing the best results of contemplation—it may even touch theta.

Illumination, which is often described as the aha! stage of the process, takes place for most people in alpha or theta. This is the stage where the potential solution presents itself in the form of an idea, which, as described earlier, sometimes occurs at 2:00 a.m., or in the shower, or while commuting to work. There is a lot of new research on "the moment of insight," confirming that there seems to be a resting state prior to the aha!. Note: the idea may still be somewhat "raw" or unformed (like the

Slinky was for the DuPont employee). You may need to hold on to the idea as you move to the next stage to see if it really solves the problem at hand.

Verification returns the mental process to beta and is the stage when an alert evaluation of the potential solution is considered in relation to the original problem. This is generally high-frequency beta.

Application is the final stage of the process and continues as an aroused beta-level activity.

> The intuitive mind is a sacred gift and the rational mind is a faithful servant. We have created a society that honors the servant and has forgotten the gift.
>
> —Unknown

The creative process I have just described takes advantage of the four quadrants of the Whole Brain Model and the brain wave states that are involved in a conscious processing of the discrete stages of creativity.

Following the Creative Selves Model

As I said earlier, Graham Wallas's model naturally correlates with a Whole Brain creative process. In the Creative Selves Model, the quadrant descriptors reflect the principal aspects of how each "self" across the quadrants typically shows up in the Whole Brain Creativity process: the problem-finding self for A, the implementing self for B, the idea-sensing self for C, and the idea-finding self for D (see Figure 21-4).

It is well documented that Albert Einstein imagined himself riding on a beam of light as a prelude to conceiving the theory of relativity. Einstein considered his gift for fantasy much more important to his thinking repertoire than the more rational and organized modes of thought. He felt that he'd really had only two "big" ideas in his entire life, and that he had spent many years either preparing them or confirming their validity. For him, the acquisition of knowledge, facts, data, and statistics was simply preparation for the intuitive process from which his epochal ideas emerged.

Einstein didn't set up his fantasies; he simply experienced them, captured them, and took action as a result. The connection occurred in the subconscious and manifested itself through a mental process that "speaks" metaphorically in fantasy or dreams. Most of the time we can't plan this; it just happens. But we can help it happen more often by learning to tap our dreams and fantasies, and by having a capture system ready to record the

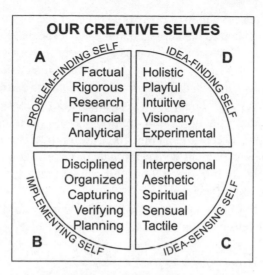

FIGURE 21-4 The creative selves model.

resulting ideas. (See the "Put It to Work" activity earlier in this chapter for ways to capture your ideas.)

Mental Diversity and Synergy

I have mentioned before that individuals are not single entities, but rather a coalition of four selves—a self-contained team. The diversity within an individual provides the basis for synergy. A rational idea juxtaposed with an intuitive thought can produce a new idea through synergistic interaction. When someone is working alone, this may require some stretch, but it is doable and effective. When more than one person is involved, the diversity of mental preferences that exists naturally can significantly enhance both individuals' creative potential. Therefore, teams that are assembled to deal with creative problem situations should be formed on the basis of diversity of thinking preferences. Our experience has shown that there is a clear advantage to having all four thinking modes represented on a team (heterogeneous) rather than those with similar preferences (homogeneous). This is not an untested theory; it is a popular and successful technique that we have employed extensively for more than three decades. (See Chapter 12 for more on the creative problem-solving power of Whole Brain teams.)

It isn't that a homogeneous team can't come up with a creative solution. The fundamental problem is that homogeneity leads to quick consensus. The members of the team think alike. They are on the same mental wavelength, so there is little confrontation of opposing concepts and ideas. No matter how much time is allocated to the homogeneous team, especially one with strong A or B preferences, it will typically come back early with a workable solution. The team members will say that taking more time to consider the problem would be a waste of time and counterproductive. They've already gotten the "best answer" available, and they did it quickly. Early consensus can be an advantage, but not in the domain of creativity and innovation. The absence of continued interaction results in missed opportunities. In a direct comparison of homogeneous solutions with heterogeneous ones, the quality of creative team output is clearly in favor of the heterogeneous teams. I would estimate the advantage at over 80 percent.

Considering this clear advantage, why in the world would anybody who's looking for a creative solution form a team that's not a heterogeneous, diverse group?

Among the reasons are:

1. The people in charge aren't aware of the advantage.
2. They don't have a way of assessing the thinking styles to assemble such mentally diverse teams.
3. They don't know enough about the creative process to understand the significance of diversity.
4. They can't be bothered with these kinds of theories.

One immediate way you can increase the creative output of your work is to partner with diverse thinkers, in pairs and in groups. Be diverse by design!

Creativity and Innovation: Similarities, Differences, and Why Business Needs Both

The term *innovation* has become confused with and synonymous with *creativity* in recent years. I think of creativity and innovation in both similar and in differentiated terms. They are both mental. They both add value. They both involve process. They both have elements of the other embedded in them, but there are significant differences that those who apply these processes need to know in order to optimize the added value that each can contribute.

I see creativity as being grounded in originality. The process starts with a bare desk, an empty notebook, an unrecognized beginning. Remember such inventions as the lightbulb, television, or telephone? These are all examples of *new* creations. In sharp contrast, I think of innovation as having a beginning that is grounded in already-invented products or processes. Therefore, I see innovation as building on existing, already-created concepts, ideas, processes, and devices. Innovation, then, is more in the nature of elaboration and extension, building upon the existing results of previous creative activity. Both processes can come up with new and novel ideas, but the needed elements of originality are missing from the process of innovation.

An obvious example is the iPod. MP3 players existed before the iPod was created, but the form and user interface of the iPod was a significant innovation beyond the idea of an MP3 player. Another example might be an original piece of music that exists in the form of melody and accompaniment. Up to this point in the process, we are dealing with a product of creativity. When a music arranger elaborates on the original melody and accompaniment and develops a full-blown orchestral arrangement, this is a product of innovation. The original creative element of the finished product is there in its entirety, but now it has been given additional value in the form of an arrangement that brings in additional instruments and additional musical patterns woven around the original melody.

If a business limits itself to just the "innovation track," it is basically restricting its future to elaborations and extensions of its (or others') current and past products. For most businesses, this is not enough to allow the company to prosper and differentiate itself, and, in fact, not enough for it to survive the ever-present creative competition.

When you consider that most businesses need to continuously elaborate on and extend their existing product lines as well as create new ones, using both creativity and innovation is clearly an advantage. This requires a new way of thinking about both and being very clear about what you mean when you use the terms. Innovation occurs largely within the existing paradigm of a product or a process, whereas creativity can be in a totally different paradigm. Since it is not bound by the past, it is entirely original, with a starting point that is based upon a new need or a new problem to be solved. Creativity can be a fresh concept or a breakthrough idea resulting from experimentation or just playing around. In any case, creativity and innovation both require Whole Brain Thinking, and the four stages of the process apply to each when we are looking for ideas—whether new ways to do what we are already doing or a completely new thing to do!

SO WHAT?

> The brain is the source of creativity, as it is of all mental processes.

> Because of a general lack of understanding of creative work and creative people, many management decisions regarding jobs and people are counterproductive. Everybody loses—the employee, the manager, and the company.

> Creative and innovative thinking work best when the brain is up to the challenge of increased synaptic activity.
> You can better tap into your most creative time of the day by paying attention to your brain states and capturing the ideas that result.
> Heterogeneous teams will produce greater creative output than homogenous teams.
> Innovation and creative thinking both require and benefit from a process that draws on Whole Brain Thinking.

© Randy Glasbergen
glasbergen.com

GLASBERGEN

"I want you to find a bold and innovative way
to do everything exactly the same way
it's been done for 25 years!"

Getting Business Results from Creative Thinking

CHAPTER HIGHLIGHTS

> Just as creativity exists in every individual, creative potential exists in every organization.
> To unleash the full creative potential in an organization, leaders and managers have to make it "safe" for everyone to think creatively and provide a platform that allows people's contributions to be heard.
> All good ideas should be either applied or saved and rewarded in some way—none should be wasted.

What's Holding Back Creativity in Business?

The senior leader of a Fortune 100 company had delivered a clear directive: "We need new ideas to change the culture here so that people will see we're serious about innovation."

Looking to increase the quantity and quality of new ideas to improve results at one of the company's regional plants, this leader had formed a team and given it the task of changing the creative climate at the plant. The team was excited about the challenge and dove in with full force. One of its proposals included designing a "creative space" where employees could go to change their perspective and mental state away from the day-to-day "noise," find resources to stimulate their creativity, meet with others for idea generation, and get their creative juices fired up or recharged. The team members had studied this concept and found data to substantiate its effectiveness—especially

311

in cultures where people found it very difficult to shift their thinking at their workspace. I was asked to help in the design.

The team had very little budget, but it was able to locate a mostly unused room that, with a little freshening up, would do the trick. Team members eagerly rounded up volunteers to clean and repaint the room and solicited donations internally and from friends and family for creative objects and furniture to decorate it. I was so impressed with the creativity this team was generating to get this project done, with so little budget, that I happily donated a painting I had painted of a local forest to contribute to the "space." Once the room was complete, it had a delightful array of comfortable chairs and seating options, books, music, and creativity-inspiring objects such as materials for creative modeling, toys, interesting artifacts, and crafts. The team members held an inaugural ceremony featuring a dedication by the senior management sponsor, and buzz and excitement abounded about how this location was truly committed to changing the culture. After all, here was a tangible sign that creative ideas were encouraged!

A month later, I made a trip to the plant, anxious to visit the room and see how it was going. Much to my surprise, the door was locked and there was no one in sight. I sought out the team lead, and he looked at me with frustration in his eyes as he told me: "It's our SOP. Our standard operating procedures don't allow us to leave the creativity room open, and the procedure for requesting the key is so cumbersome that no one is using it! I've tried to get an exception for the room, but they claim we can't do that. The worst part is, this is sending a strong negative message to the organization: 'We have it, but you can't use it.' It's awful! I almost wish we'd never done it now."

As silly as it sounds, one of the biggest barriers to creativity in business is the day-to-day culture, the existing norms of that business.

The Stumbling Blocks: Are They All in Our Heads?

"More than rigor, management discipline, integrity, or even vision—successfully navigating an increasing complex world will require creativity." This quote from IBM's 2010 Global CEO study, which surveyed 1,500 CEOs from 60 countries and 33 industries, made it crystal clear: creativity is a business requirement in today's world. Since then, CEOs have continued to make speeches proclaiming a "fresh commitment to new ideas and more creativity" and urging an entrepreneurial approach to business. But has much really changed? We talk about emulating the Steve Jobses of the world, studying the latest new technology innovators, hiring those who can come up with clever solutions, or creating breakthrough new products that will transform entire markets and industries.

So why are the results so consistently disappointing?

There are a number of reasons, but first and foremost, these CEOs are calling for more risk-oriented, nontraditional, disruptive, D-quadrant-style thinking, while, given the stress of today's environment, the management organization is even more likely to be thinking in rational, safekeeping, risk-avoidance, and stewardship terms—primarily A- and B-quadrant-oriented thinking. They may latch onto a concept like Design Thinking because it represents the "latest and greatest," and they may find the process and structure appealing, but that's where the real *adoption* ends because the culture is just not ready. The requisite risk taking and nonlinear connecting points are too far outside their comfort zones, or, as we saw in the previous example, other cultural norms and procedures take precedence. As a result, companies usually end up applying dollars that were supposed to be allocated to creative efforts to shoring up the existing product line rather than exploring something that is truly new. Any change that does happen is incremental rather than breakthrough.

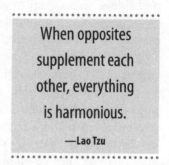

When opposites supplement each other, everything is harmonious.

—Lao Tzu

The frustrated CEO asks: "What must I do to get new thinking from my people? I tell them what I want, but nothing changes!" The managers appear to understand, and they applaud sincerely, but this is too much of a risky-feeling mental stretch for them to implement, especially in the current environment. Many of them have been hired, trained, and rewarded for operating in an A/B environment, and now, when they're being exhorted to bring in their C/D thinking preferences as well, they don't know how to respond effectively. They feel uncomfortable and insecure when they are operating in modes that they neither trust nor understand. And for those who are more naturally inclined to think this way—often those who are rising up through the ranks and who view the world from a younger generational perspective—the challenge is daunting in a different way. Unless they're working for a company like Google, where "Googlers" are still encouraged to spend 20 percent of their time on projects of their own interest (although the company has added more guidelines in recent years), these employees find that they hit a wall when they try to pitch a new idea to the layer of management they report to. So they ask themselves, "How do I actually pursue creative thinking in a culture that is so unwilling to listen to new ideas, an environment that is so hard to change, with leaders who don't get it?" Going forward, this new generation will be less prone to join or stick around in an environment that does not meet their creative needs. The lesson for organizations is clear: to continue to attract and retain the talent you need if you are to remain successful, it's essential that you have a full commitment—at all levels—to creative thinking and the value it brings to the business.

Second, in most business contexts, the creative process is often thought of and labeled as problem solving. Although the application of creative thinking to problems has value, culturally it means that an issue has to be judged to be a problem—something negative—in order to evoke a creative response. People forget that defining and meeting a need may have more to do with seeing an opportunity (a plus) than with defining a problem (a negative).

Compounding the issue, most people think of problem solving as what has been incorrectly labeled a "left-brain" process—orderly and straightforward, a step-by-step analysis and application of logic. That view of the process takes off the table a wide array of enormously effective C- and D-mode techniques and activities, such as having empathy, modeling, simulating, doodling, drawing on intuition, thinking metaphorically, and synthesizing (combining things to create something new with worth that far surpasses the total of what each idea could be worth separately)—C- and D-oriented techniques that produce the visions and thinking that power truly innovative contributions.

Another common stumbling block is that creativity often gets relegated to (or is viewed as) the domain of a particular function or individuals. It's what the people in R&D or marketing do, or perhaps product development. This is also true of the term *innovation*, which is considered the lofty domain of a select few, perhaps those in R&D, not a required thinking skill for all. (See Chapter 21 for more on the differences between innovation and creativity.)

Creativity and innovation exist and need to be cultivated in every corner of our organizations. The problem is that they are often hidden and even discouraged. We need to make it safe and provide a platform for those contributions to be heard—whether they're coming from IT, human resources, finance, sales, or management. A "fail fast, fail cheap" approach helps make it acceptable for people to pilot ideas, to test things ... and to fail safely.

> **An essential aspect of creativity is not being afraid to fail.**
>
> **—Edwin Land**

And finally, although leaders ask for creativity and say that they value it, in the do-more-with-less world where there never seems to be enough time or resources to get things done, creativity becomes viewed as a nice-to-have, the "fluff," or work that can happen only outside office hours, not the "real work." The irony? Do-more-with-less is a condition that's screaming out for creativity. Imagine how much more we could ultimately get done if we sanctioned that creative time!

So what can we do about this? We need the climate, champions, and support for creativity as a key ingredient for business success.

Creating the Right Climate

Some years ago, we conducted an HBDI thinking preference study of more than 5,000 employees across a broad range of divisions and functions within a large chemical company. The company was struggling to do more with less and felt that a lack of innovation had become pervasive. The HBDI data revealed that although "creative" ranked fifth out of twenty-five characteristics as a key descriptor for employees when they described how they see themselves in general, it ranked fifteenth out of sixteen as a work element! In other words, creativity wasn't the problem; creativity *on the job* was the problem. The company was hiring people who saw themselves as creative, but clearly, the climate of this company did not support creative and innovative thinking, so it was most likely that creative pursuits were happening outside of work.

A plan was put in place, driven by the CEO and senior management, to very visibly shift the culture using training, performance systems, and consistent messaging. A critical component of the success of this initiative was the internal champions who kept it going deep inside divisions across the globe. Such champions already exist in every company we have worked with; however, they typically are not highly visible if the culture is one that thwarts innovation. The steps in the box that follows will help you find and get the most out of the creative process champions in your organization.

Ten Steps for Establishing Creative Process Champions and Whole Brain Problem-Solving/Opportunity-Finding Teams

1. Arrange for senior management sponsorship.
2. Solicit and identify interested candidates.
3. Invite the candidates to learn about their thinking preferences by administering the HBDI assessment.
4. Gauge the breadth of their existing creative process expertise and the degree of alignment between their thinking preferences and the mentality of the creative processes in which they have expertise. If the level of existing expertise is inadequate or too limited, arrange for the needed training and development to help them achieve mastery of a broader array of creative processes. Note: It is not necessary to limit the creative processes to the quadrants of greatest preference—your ultimate objective is to have a broad selection of preferences and creative processes available on the team.

5. Arrange and get buy-in and support from direct reporting management for the creative process champions to be given temporary assignment to a creative process problem-solving team.
6. When a major opportunity where new thinking is needed or a tough challenge or problem occurs, select from the pool of creative process champions a group of five or six who represent a composite Whole Brain group with the mix of expertise that would optimize the solution to that major problem or opportunity.
7. Arrange for meetings between the creative process champions and the owner(s) of the problem or opportunity to gather data and define scope, timelines, and so on. Make sure that the owner(s) are available to consult with the team during the process to answer additional questions or provide needed information.
8. Let the role of leader be determined by the team. If there is a "problem or opportunity owner," make sure that person is part of the team. The team may want to have that person serve as the team leader, if it's appropriate.
9. Provide the team with a dedicated time, space and tools (both online and other) to apply its creative mastery. Include an online shared workspace as well as a physical meeting location that has a full spectrum of resources, including creative materials to support model making and experimentation with alternative solutions.
10. Make it easy for the team to communicate its solution recommendations to the senior management problem or opportunity owners if they are not members of the team.

Here are some additional considerations to take into account in creating a climate that will support the creative process, particularly when heterogeneous teams are involved:

- Creativity needs to be free of too much control and overscheduling. This requires a culture of trust and flexibility.
- Creativity is an inefficient process from a productivity standpoint. It may feel "messy." This is normal. The more you structure it, the faster you shut it down.
- Creative results cannot be guaranteed on demand. Build this into your planning.
- Mistakes will be made. Create a safe environment that focuses on learning from them instead of punishing for them. Mistakes and the learning from them is an essential part of the creative process.

- Interpersonal relationships may be stressed by the creative contention. Prepare those who are involved by helping them understand the importance of thinking diversity and skills to best handle it.

It is essential that the manager who is in charge of a creative team first establish a climate that encourages diversity of thinking, tolerates ambiguity, and is flexible in terms of schedule, outcomes, and personal behaviors. This climate must allow for a fundamentally messy process to take place in an otherwise orderly organization. When traditional business approaches to encouraging innovation don't work, management has been known to take a chance on nontraditional ones. Generally speaking, these approaches are outside the regular corporate system, so in many cultures, a special place must be found for them within a facility that allows people to be authentic in their work habits (such as flexible work hours and/or relaxed dress codes, if that is not already the norm), and that visibly differs from the daily work habits and facilities of the parent organization.

An idea can turn to dust or magic, depending on the talent that rubs against it.

—**Bill Bernbach**

Put It to Work

Resist the temptation to fall back on brainstorming as the only tool in your creative toolkit; it rarely provides needed results. Try this exercise to expand your creative toolkit:

- Review the creative processes in Figure 22-1, and look for two or three processes that you have never tried before, but that sound intriguing.
- Take the initiative to find out more about those processes (for example, search online).
- Now think of a challenge you have at home or at work. Apply the first process, then the second.
  - What did you learn?
  - How do the results of the different processes differ from one another?
  - How were the experiences different from your usual approach to creativity?
  - Was the process uncomfortable or comfortable for you? Do you notice a correlation with your comfort zones of thinking?
- Every time you have a challenge, try another process. Involve others, too. You'll discover that it can really be fun to engage in creative thinking when you have some fresh tools in your toolkit.

I can guarantee that this approach really works. We have worked with several organizations using an accelerated process called Whole Brain Hackathons to get the best possible solutions as quickly as possible, drawing on an array of processes across the Whole Brain Model. (For more information on how to set up Whole Brain Hackathons, contact us or visit www.wholebrainbusinessbook.com.)

Universe of Creative Processes

A-QUADRANT

Assumption Reversal
ATAR Model
Attribute Listing
BionicsConstructive Controversy
Five Whys
Force Field Analysis
Kepner-Tregoe Process
Mathematica
Method 6-3-5
Pareto Analysis
POV Madlibs
Problem Definition (How Might We)
Reengineering
Reverse Brainstorming
TRIZ
Value Thinking Analysis

MULTI-DOMINANT

Applied Creative Thinking Process
CPSI Process
Design Thinking
Disney Creativity Strategy
Mind Mapping
Olsen DO IT Model
Pugh Method
Simplex Method
Six Thinking Hats Method
Storyboarding
TLC (Tempting-Lacking-Change)
Whole Brain Creativity Process
Whole Brain Problem-Solving
Walk-Around

D-QUADRANT

Crawford Slip Method
Creative Materials
Doodling & De-Doodling
Dreaming & Guided Imagery
Free Association
Incubation-Theta State-Free Flow
Intuition (Solution Ahas)
Lateral Thinking
Magic Wand Thinking
Mess Worksheet
Metaphoric Thinking & Modeling
Play
Provocation Technique
Sketching & Modeling
Solution After Next
Synectics
Visual Thinking & Visualization
What-If Process

Checklists (Senses, Human needs, etc.)
Delphi Method
Force Fitting
Idea Evaluation Model
Kano Model
Interview Preparation
Morphological Analysis
NAF (Novelty, Attractiveness, Feasibility)
Operational Analysis
Plan-Do-Check-Act (PDCA) Cycle
Scamper
Stepladder Technique
Sticking Dots
The Improver
The Selector
Betterment Time Line Principle
Trigger Concept

Brain Writing
Charrette Procedure
"Chilling Out" & Relaxing
Crowdsourcing
Empathy Mapping
Interactive Brainstorming
Intuition (Feeling Ahas)
Kinesthetic Modeling
Meditation & Sensory Processing
Nominal Group Technique
People Design Principle
Reframing Matrix
Rolestorming & Fresh View Process
Storytelling
Symbolic Metaphors
Whole Brain Team Process
World Cafe

B-QUADRANT

C-QUADRANT

FIGURE 22-1 Categorizing 82 creative processes in terms of the Whole Brain Model.

Managing the People Responsible for Creative Work

Even though applied creativity is by its nature a Whole Brain process, some of the visible behavior characteristics of people who need to be part of the process are consistent with C/D thinking, particularly D-quadrant qualities. People doing this type of creative work often have a low tolerance for rules and regulations and resist being closely supervised on the basis of detailed step-by-step processes. They are more inclined to break rules than to make rules. They are more likely to take risks and experiment. Therefore, the job of "managing" this kind of thinker is always a challenging one. It requires a mixture of trust in the process, patience, encouragement, and realistic goals.

The job of many managers, however, is to run a "tight ship" by monitoring quality, maintaining consistency, and providing the structure and control that minimizes variability. The differences between these two approaches are so sharply defined that we are dealing with oil and water. When creative thinking is part of the job description, leaders, managers, and supervisors need to be sensitive to the conditions under which the creative process can be most productive. The best way to lead and manage those who are responsible for creative thinking is to be clear about the objectives and deadlines from the start and then manage them with some distance. Placing too many rules and conditions on the individuals will inhibit the natural flow that is necessary to creativity. Although it may seem inefficient to incubate ideas or potential solutions, it actually takes less work and time when you create a safe environment.

The styles that are typical of a technical supervisor/manager may be perilous to the creative solution. When managing a creative person or team, steer away from:

1. Too much close supervision or micromanagement, which stifles the free flow of unusual ideas.
2. Strict adherence to procedures that will inhibit people's ability to pursue the natural free flow associated with creative thinking. (Remember the locked creativity room at the beginning of this chapter?)
3. Application of quantitative performance measures too early in the process, before there are enough data to measure.

Even though applied Whole Brain Creativity requires some of these more A/B-oriented disciplines in order to define, follow through, and implement creative ideas, those on the creative team will often ultimately perform these steps themselves because of their self-motivation. If you state the desired outcomes at the beginning, there should be no need for close supervisory techniques. By striking a balance between firm project control and a totally open-ended and undefined process, the manager in charge of the creative team can promote productivity instead of hampering it. What's essential is

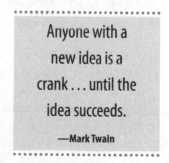

Anyone with a new idea is a crank ... until the idea succeeds.

—Mark Twain

having the conversation up front and making sure that both parties clearly understand and buy into it.

It is important to emphasize this point, because our HBDI database indicates that the thinking-style norm for lower- and middle-level managers, while more multidominant than in the past, is still more strongly left-mode, A/B-oriented than C/D-oriented. Therefore, the management styles of this population tend to go against the grain of what is needed in the early stages of the creative process. Typically, it is only at the higher levels of the organization that creativity and innovation become legitimized. It is at these higher levels that you might find leaders who are themselves creative champions and who begin to encourage and even sponsor creative behavior. Because many of the processes inherent in creativity and innovation typically conflict with the mental preferences of operational managers, supervisors, and the culture at large, both leaders who attempt to change an embedded culture like this and rising potential creative champions feel as if they are running into a brick wall. In this case, some sort of company-wide creativity campaign may be required.

> Creativity and innovation are about finding unexpected solutions to obvious problems, or finding obvious solutions to unexpected problems. We should use our creativity to provide better businesses and solutions rather than constantly trying to disrupt what people are doing.
>
> —Rei Inamot, Chief Creative Officer, AKQA

Changes that would allow the creative and innovative potential of the organization to be unleashed would first require a top-down, company-wide culture-changing educational program that provides needed understanding to everyone in the organization, including managers, supervisors, and plant managers, as well as knowledge workers and frontline production workers. Several of our clients have created award programs, videos, and case examples to prove the worthiness of pursuing creativity and innovation. And in parallel with that, I would suggest an educational program that reveals the nature and source of creativity and innovation and how everyone can pursue it and contribute through application. You do not have to be Google to have company-specific initiatives and programs that designate time and resources for

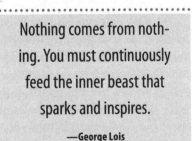

> Nothing comes from nothing. You must continuously feed the inner beast that sparks and inspires.
>
> —George Lois

new ideas, but you must be clear about how each individual can contribute. Until individuals understand who they are and why they do the things they do and the way they do them, creativity will remain a mystery, and the resulting thinking and ideas that are so critical to sustaining a competitive advantage in today's environment will remain out of the company's reach.

Generating and Managing "Killer" Business Ideas: A Case Study

Several years ago, the Australian arm of global liquor giant Brown-Forman, manufacturer and marketer of some of the best-known spirits in the world, including Jack Daniel's Tennessee Whisky and Southern Comfort, came to our colleagues in Australia with a challenge: although the company had a robust process in place—dubbed "ideation"—to generate new marketing ideas, the ideas it was producing were typically only one step removed from what it was already doing. They were good ideas, but they weren't, as the representatives put it, "killer" ideas. They told our team that they wanted not just to start thinking outside the existing continuum but also to learn to think *way outside* their comfort zones to make their ideation process even more effective.

This was a highly energized group with a relatively broad spectrum of HBDI Profiles, as one would expect, although there was an overall bias toward the C- and D-quadrant preferences. Michael Morgan of Herrmann International Asia describes some of the process he used with the team.[1]

This approach to "ideation facilitation" is rooted in Whole Brain Creativity and goes well beyond what many companies refer to as "brainstorming." Although the process is carefully planned, with specific, closely managed steps, the participants don't necessarily notice this. They quickly get caught up in the spirit of a sometimes zany and wacky, but at all times highly stimulating exercise. Importantly, each of the steps is rooted in Whole Brain Thinking to ensure that people understand their own and others' thinking preferences and therefore work together better and more creatively.

For Brown-Forman, we had to address some very clear needs and generate ideas around some very specific business issues. We had to help the company define and if necessary redefine its objectives in more creative ways and then take it through a process of idea generation, verification, and prioritization.

My basic philosophy in taking people through this process is that the human brain is absolutely useless in coming up with ideas, but is brilliant at making connections. If someone has you sitting in a blank room and says, "Give me 20 ideas on how to decorate a birthday cake," most people would struggle to come up with five, and none of them would be what you'd call "breakthrough." However, if I said, "Come up with 20 ideas on how to decorate a birthday cake, and here is a book of *Ripley's Believe It or Not*[2] stories that I want you to look through to get some ideas," we would end up with the most amazing cake with all sorts of things jumping out of it.

It is the same as saying to a group of people, as happens far too often in corporate life, "Go away and brainstorm for 20 minutes and come up with ideas on how to solve this problem." Most people will attempt to obey the instruction. but they generally won't come up with stunning ideas. That is why our idea generation techniques are designed to stimulate people to find different ways to define issues and challenges and then to come up with ideas by making connections.

In addition, I've found that people often rush into idea generation and end up solving the wrong problem. An example I use is, "Oh, dear, the lightbulb has gone out. But I can't reach the light." However, if we looked at it another way ("The light is too far away"), we would be more likely to come up with ideas about how to make the light closer—for instance, having it attached to an extendable cord like a Venetian blind so that we can pull it down when we need to. In other words, by redefining the problem and then making connections, we can become far more creative. In a business context, the challenge, "How can we increase sales?" may well become, instead, "How can we help customers buy more?"

As a means of helping the Brown-Forman team come up with more creative definitions of the problem, I used a technique called "Who? Do? What?" A lot of people find it difficult to come up with wacky ideas, especially if they are logical, rational, and sequential. If they have a wacky thought, most people tend to edit it out. "You can't have a purple cake," they say subconsciously.

So if you want people to have wacky ideas, you must give them a process. And such a process has to appear to be logical to get them out there. Our "Who? Do? What?" is a very logical process that can help people generate hundreds of ideas.

An example could be: How can we increase sales? (Who = We; Do = Increase; What = Sales.)

If we just say, "Come up with lots of ideas for increasing sales," the results will often be boring. However, if we use a whiteboard or butcher's paper table headed up by "Who? Do? What?," we can generate lateral thinking by getting the group members to come up with all types of "whos" (we, customers, suppliers, teenagers, policemen, Bugs Bunny ... whoever comes to mind).

Then we get them to fill in the "Do" column, and they may come up with "increase, decrease, accelerate, explode, eradicate, eat, drink, and party." And then the "Whats"—sales, profits, turnover, carrots, fast cars, and so on. By getting them to randomly connect the items in the three columns, we get them to make a whole heap of wacky connections. And, out of those connections, ideas start to spring.

Some other techniques for helping people break out of their comfort zones include:

- **Magic wand thinking.** Ask *what if* I had a magic wand and was able to solve this problem with no constraints on what the solution might look like or how "off the wall" it might be. What would that solution look like?
- **TLC.** To turn crazy ideas into actionable solutions, ask: What's Tempting about this idea? What's Lacking? What could I Change to make it work?

At Brown-Forman, a huge number of wacky ideas were whittled down into some killer breakthrough ideas, including one that culminated in the decision to form the Jack Daniel's V8 Supercar team, which quickly became the sport's number one merchandise seller. The brand was soon experiencing double-digit growth along with increased awareness, popularity, and loyalty.

Looking for the Positive Deviants

Is the answer you're looking for already there and you just aren't looking for it in the right places? The concept of positive deviance was pioneered in the early 1990s, based on the observation that solutions can be found and change can grow from within if we seek out and learn from the "positive deviants" in our organizations—those people who behave differently or use different approaches and strategies that allow them to find better solutions to problems that their peers continue to struggle with, even though they're all facing similar challenges.

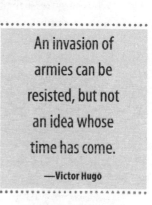

An invasion of armies can be resisted, but not an idea whose time has come.

—Victor Hugo

While it might seem as if it would be easy to identify the uncommon behaviors, this isn't something that we are likely to do without conscious effort. As explored in the discussion about change in Chapter 19, mindsets are a powerful thing. We're guided by those mental maps that are based on our prior experience and knowledge, and this can prevent us from looking around for other options and ideas that might help us solve our problems.

But let's say that the out-of-the-ordinary behavior sticks out like a sore thumb, and you just can't miss it. The next challenge is recognizing its value. Throughout this book, we've talked about the mental defaults that can become traps and blind spots. For example, we know that people tend to hire, value, and reward the thinking that is most similar to their own. This makes it especially challenging to recognize positive deviance and take advantage of the often ingenious solutions that might be playing out right under our noses.

In their book on the subject, *The Power of Positive Deviance*,[3] Richard T. Pascale, Jerry Sternin, and Monique Sternin reiterate this point: "As a problem-solving process, this [positive deviance] approach requires retraining ourselves to pay attention differently—awakening minds accustomed to overlooking outliers, and cultivating skepticism about the inevitable 'that's just the way it is.' "

Using a Whole Brain approach as part of the deliberate process of identifying positive deviance will give you the best odds of finding, understanding, valuing, and then applying the solutions that may already be working on a smaller scale, hidden in plain sight within your organization.

Action Steps for Increasing Creative Potential and Business Yield

1. **Challenge assumptions.** When we are dealing with a problem situation, instead of accepting what somebody tells us or how the problem is stated in writing, or even how we define the problem ourselves, it is creatively healthy to challenge the basis of these statements by questioning the facts upon which they are based or the premise upon which they are based. Our assumptions are often the filters through which we perceive the problem situation. When these are challenged, important new understandings are often revealed. A problem well stated is a problem half solved. There are specific techniques you can learn for better problem definition. Start by asking "How do I_____in order to _____?"

2. **Recognize your mental defaults.** Perhaps it is because we get "stuck" that we sometimes call creative thinking "out-of-the-box thinking." Clearly we appear to have an intuitive sense that each of us needs to break out of our natural thinking processes, to "get out of our own box." Understanding the nature of your thinking preferences, ideally using an HBDI Profile, which shows the different degrees of preference across the four quadrants, provides a new definition of the mental boxes or boundaries we may have created for ourselves.

   In fact, as we discussed in detail in Chapter 19, we each have a set of mental defaults, where we go almost unconsciously when we are faced with a decision or challenge. Once you know what these defaults might be, however, it is much easier to predict and define what your boundaries will be and thus the areas that will be a challenge for you to see differently.

3. **See in new Whole Brain ways.** A client was challenged because its packaging of large light fixtures caused costly breakage. Not only were the costs of the packaging and breakage skyrocketing, but the materials used were difficult to recycle. The team members were sure that they had thought of every possible solution, but using Whole Brain Creativity techniques to get "out of their box," they devised the idea of packaging the fixtures in garbage cans, which could then be resold. The recycling problem was solved, while costs—and breakage— dropped significantly, all because they were able to see the issue in a new Whole Brain way.

The Problem-Solving Walk-Around (see Figure 22-2) deliberately examines a problem (or opportunity) from the perspective of the four quadrants: the logical, rational A quadrant; the organized, procedural B quadrant; the interpersonal, emotional C quadrant; and the experimental, holistic D quadrant. Since most of us have our favorite way of looking at things, based on our thinking preferences, this walk-around technique provides an easy way for us to be facilitated to seeing in new ways.

A	D
• Having a technical perspective • Checking the numbers closely • Examining things critically • Concentrating on fixing it • Calling in an expert • Analyzing in depth • Doing research	• Getting excited, maybe impatient • Generating lots of "crazy" ideas • Looking for new perspectives • Breaking the rules to solve • Looking at 'the big picture' • "Sleeping on it" • Brainstorming
• Making a plan • Minimizing the risk • Taking first things first • Organizing the information • Focusing on time and timelines • Searching for overlooked details • Considering steps to be completed **B**	• Talking it out • Building a team • Calling a friend for help • Listening to own intuition • Getting emotionally engaged • Considering own values/ feelings • Persuading those involved to help **C**

FIGURE 22-2 The Whole Brain Problem-Solving Walk-Around.

4. **Make connections.** A high percentage of creative ideas is the result of synergy occurring between two thoughts or perceptions, especially when they cross quadrant boundaries. Making connections between them can stimulate synergy, which will increase the yield of fresh, new ideas. Some of these connections take place naturally, but seeking out different perceptions and forcing a connection between them can often yield creative results. Doing this is, in fact, a distinctly creative process.

5. **Take risks.** Those among us who have a D-quadrant preference often enjoy risk taking and make use of this creative step naturally. Others of us who have preferences in the other quadrants need to overcome our resistance to risk taking. The way to do that is to practice taking small risks on purpose until you achieve a comfort level. In this way, you become more comfortable with risk taking so that it can become a tool in your creativity toolkit. We also need to create cultures of experimentation in our organizations where it is OK to take a risk—and potentially fail, with a focus on learning from those failures for new insight.

6. **Seize upon a chance.** Many people who consider themselves already creative are opportunistic as they engage in a problem-solving or opportunity-finding situation. Their past experience has demonstrated that taking a chance pays off. Others of us who would like to be more creative need to add this, as well as risk taking, to our toolkit. With a little practice, we can improve our responsiveness to creative opportunities. In most cases, we are dealing with a dynamic, rather than a static, issue—changing situations somewhat similar to a highway roundabout, where cars are entering into and exiting from a circular roadway. We've all experienced the frustration of being behind someone who doesn't respond to an opening in the traffic pattern and remains stuck in place. They are too safekeeping, or security-minded, or fearful that they can't maneuver their car quickly enough to fill in

> Creativity is just connecting things. When you ask creative people how they did something, they feel a little guilty because they didn't really do it, they just saw something. It seemed obvious to them after a while. That's because they were able to connect experiences they've had and synthesize new things.
>
> —Steve Jobs

an open space in the traffic. Seizing upon a chance in a potentially creative situation is analogous. We have to take a calculated risk in order to take advantage of an opening that will allow us to move forward toward a creative solution. The consequences of not seizing a chance are that we are stuck in our own mental traffic jam and there is no creative outcome or business benefit.

Put It to Work

It may be helpful to gain a new perspective on a problem by viewing it from a different mode of thinking.

Using the worksheet template in Figure 22-3, on a piece of paper, ask yourself how this problem would appear to a person viewing it from the A, B, C, or D-quadrants. Refer back to Figure 22-2 for prompts for each quadrant.

Capture your responses in each quadrant. See what new insights toward a solution you might gain from "walking around" your problem.

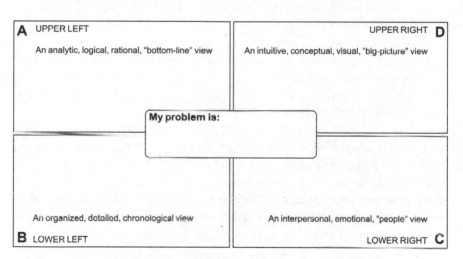

A UPPER LEFT	UPPER RIGHT **D**
An analytic, logical, rational, "bottom-line" view	An intuitive, conceptual, visual, "big-picture" view
My problem is:	
An organized, detailed, chronological view	An interpersonal, emotional, "people" view
B LOWER LEFT	LOWER RIGHT **C**

FIGURE 22-3 A problem-solving walk-around worksheet.

Bridging the Gap Between the Different Thinking Tribes for Great Creativity

Given the generally left-mode, A/B-oriented preferences of the business community, it's not surprising that there is some skepticism about creativity and the creative process from the perspective of bottom-line, traditional, rational thinking. For some businesspeople, a more creative approach can take on the image of crazy tangents, impractical ideas, and generally weird behavior. But there are rational explanations for this seemingly "odd" behavior, and it is important for organizations to understand this so that it can be considered acceptable and thus be legitimatized.

> I used to think anyone doing anything weird was weird. Now I know that it is the people who call others weird that are weird.
>
> —Paul McCartney

1. What business calls thinking is different from what a more creative community calls thinking. The different preferences of the creative community engage parts of the mental process that are more expansive, free-flowing, aesthetic, experimental, and risk-oriented—not the usual processes for most business communities.
2. Members of a more creative community are stimulated by different kinds of work. They have different values and different priorities. They like to have a variety of stimuli, and thus they may get frustrated or even bored by the more structured, nuts-and-bolts work activities that many traditional businesspeople find stimulating.
3. The classic business community is smart in one way, and the more creative community is smart in other ways. And while these different kinds of smartness should be complementary, they are often misunderstood and end up being mutually antagonistic.

This combination of thinking preferences, types of smartness, differing values, and differing priorities contributes to what is, in many businesses, an arm's-length relationship between those who are more interested in viable, yet more traditional business approaches and those who are looking for new, more innovative, and more creative approaches. As a result, it often turns into a situation of "us" and "them." The sad part is that it doesn't have to be. The loss of potential synergy is enormous and costly.

How do you bridge the divide between those who like to spend all day batting around ideas and relying on their "hunches" and those who prefer a clear, step-by-step process and structure? The first step is to give them an understanding of how they each think (for example, using a tool like the HBDI) so that people can learn about their own preferences with a focus on *application in terms of solving real business challenges*—not just a "feel-good" exercise. Then bring them together to understand their *thinking* differences, identify the value in them, and learn how they can complement each other and add value to the business. Provide them with tools that they can use to leverage those differences, and let them get to work on a real challenge. Once they see that the results they get together will almost always outperform those that they get separately, it becomes a very different conversation, and a very different culture.

There is often common ground that you can build on. Our colleague Chuck McVinney[4] shared a great example of results that came from "bridging the gap" in a midsized company that had a problem between two major teams, one that was more C/D-oriented—they were designers and purchasers of innovative products—and the finance and administrative team, whose role included keeping people compliant with budgets. Neither team really "got" the other, and the result was a meager 30 percent compliance with the planned budget and procedures.

When their HBDI Team Profiles were analyzed, Chuck noted that both teams had one element in common in spite of their differences: they both scored high on teaching and training. We know from our research that different thinking preferences lead to different teaching and learning preferences (see Chapter 11). So in a program set up to address the compliance problem, the finance team was asked, "What do you mean by teaching?" The team members replied that they taught employees about their systems and procedures, how to be compliant, how to fill out the forms, and similar activities. Those on the design team were then asked how they preferred to learn. Their answers included activities like discovery and dialogue—certainly not the "information download" that the finance team was doing, in effect telling them what to do.

The result was that those on the design team felt as though the finance team was like a police force, wanting to control everything. Once the members of the finance team understood this, they redefined the way they taught compliance, involving the members of the design team as contributors to the education process. Compliance went up to 80 percent almost immediately.

How do you define the thinking culture of your company in terms of the Whole Brain quadrants? How many people are using old processes to fix new problems? How do your hiring, development processes, performance measures, and leadership approaches impede or support creative thinking? Here is the good news: the late W. Edwards Deming wrote that 94 percent of quality issues were caused by the system—and not the workers.[5] This is a prime opportunity for improvement that anyone in the organization can directly affect.

SO WHAT?

> Without a climate and a culture that support creative thinking, organizations will miss out on their full creative potential and the resulting business benefits.
> Whole Brain teams made up of creative process champions who are experts in a particular creative process can be assigned to solve major problems by applying multiple processes to the solution.
> There is a universe of creative processes that can be used as a resource to help teams leverage their breadth of thinking.
> To move from incremental to truly breakthrough solutions, we have to build in strategies for overcoming the natural resistance between the different mental tribes in the organization—only then can the resulting synergies emerge.

© Randy Glasbergen
glasbergen.com

"You see clutter. I see an environment that encourages the random juxtaposition of disparate elements for the potential generation of creativity born of chaos!"

Want Enterprise-wide Innovation? Make Creativity a Core Competency for Every Job Across the Business

CHAPTER HIGHLIGHTS

> Complex new problems and business realities require more creative solutions, which in turn require leaders who are committed to supporting the development of competencies in creative thinking across the organization.

> The creativity that we all have experienced in our youth can be reclaimed by adults in a business context, but it has to be nurtured.

> Jobs are often typecast as "creative" or "noncreative," when the reality is that all roles can benefit from some level of creative thinking.

> Specific strategies are required to affirm creative thinking, build a climate in which creativity will flourish, and develop creativity as a legitimate core competency required for everyday work.

"How does an improvisation class or a cooking competition help someone handle complex project delivery in a global environment?" This was a question that the facilitators at the global hotel company IHG had to be prepared to answer as they began training and development around the new "IHG Way" of managing projects.[1]

Although IHG had a team of experienced project managers in place, the group was struggling to deliver projects in the IHG environment. Their work was complex, but even more problematic was the clash of thinking that was making it difficult to carry projects through to completion. Project management typically relies on rigorous, incremental thinking, with processes and tools designed to match, but the project managers at IHG were dealing with a service-oriented culture filled with people who preferred to get things done through collaboration, relationship building, and free-form communication. It's a culture that aligns well with the organization's stated goal of creating "Great Hotels Guests Love," but it was presenting a challenge for the project managers, who were used to the more A/B, analytical, and structured work processes that are the hallmark of traditional project management systems.

As Crystal Snoddy, IHG's head of global delivery excellence, put it, "The project managers were trying to succeed in a creative environment, and they didn't have the tools to do it."

So the company set out to change that. Among the many tools and methods that IHG has since provided to its project management teams are Whole Brain Thinking and the Whole Brain Model, which are embedded throughout the company's project management approach. In fact, the first thing that stands out when you open IHG's project management toolkit is that it looks nothing like any conventional project management process you'll find. Its striking design, method cards, discovery cards, and color-coded materials filled with infographic-style visuals communicate the same information, but in a dramatically different way.

Beyond the immediate visual difference, the tools themselves are different, designed to appeal to all four thinking preferences and to help people who may not be naturally inclined toward creative thinking to get more comfortable with exploring, idea generation, and seeing problems in new ways.

These tools help build confidence, but it's the training that accompanies the process that really pushes people outside their comfort zones. To set the stage for shifting their thinking, the very first activity that participants are asked to do is to draw a picture. Later come the improv workshop and the "Iron Chef" competition. Although the initial reaction usually ranges from a reluctance to try—and potentially fail—to outright resistance, the facilitators encourage people to "just go with it," and a funny thing happens: participants begin to realize not only that they *can* do it, but that this journey outside their comfort zones is helping them be more successful and productive in their project work. As one team member said, "Before coming to this team, I was never a visual thinker, and now I draw everything!"

> Everyone is born a genius, but the process of living degeniuses them.
>
> —R. Buckminster Fuller

As children, we are all naturally creative, but we begin to lose that spark as we gain self-discipline, learn language, accept our parents' discipline, and obey society's rules. A global study conducted by Adobe in 2012[2] revealed that a whopping 75 percent of people think that they're not living up to their creative potential. Our data on more than 1.5 million adults in our current HBDI database indicate that only 42 percent think of themselves as being creative. This leaves 58 percent who apparently do not think of themselves as being creative.

I believe the same would also be true of the general business population. What happens to the more than half of our business employees who don't think that they're creative? What happens to the other almost half who think that they are creative, but probably not nearly as creative as they could be? What happens to those who think that they are creative, but not at work? If they were creative as children, the chances are good that they can reclaim much of what they lost during the maturing process. It's a little bit like riding a bike. Once you experience success, you can reclaim that success even after 20 or 30 years. All you need is permission, encouragement, and the right circumstances.

A prime reason that many people have temporarily lost their creativity is that they didn't feel that they had *permission* to be creative. Well-intentioned parents, teachers, and bosses behaved in ways that partially or even totally shut down these people's natural creativity as children, adolescents, and their employees. I resisted my own natural creativity for half my life—at least any public demonstration of it. The parental values that were handed down to me were along the lines of, "Do it right the first time." At least, that is how I interpreted what my family was saying to me, so it was easy for me to have a fear of failure. If there was any risk of failure, I tried things out in private. It was only when I was faced with a midlife medical crisis that I was able to see

> Imagination grows by exercise, and contrary to common belief, is more powerful in the mature than in the young.
>
> —W. Somerset Maugham

how silly and self-defeating this behavior was. I had provided myself with an excuse for failing in public, but that never really happened. In the domain of art, I discovered that the public rewarded *trying* to be an artist to a far greater degree than it punished poor execution of the finished art. I found that the rewards outweighed the risks to such an extent that my activity level soon gave me the practice that I needed to overcome the skill deficits of a beginner.

It's critical to recognize that getting creative doesn't need to be so difficult that you waste half your life wondering whether you are good enough to even start. I am confident that most adults can reclaim their creativity because I did so myself, and I have witnessed thousands of others who were in the process of doing so. Lost creativity can be reclaimed, particularly among business employees who function in an organization with leaders who are motivated to take action. And to stay ahead of change, I believe that this is not just a personal imperative, but a business one as well. Enterprise-wide innovation can happen only when creativity is nurtured and developed at the individual level so that it can be developed as a core competency that is valued in the enterprise.

In order to understand how this may be accomplished on a large scale, let's look at what it takes to make this possible:

1. **Attitude**. A significant aspect of adult creativity is that more than half of adults don't think they have it. Yet 75 percent think that they are not living up to their potential, so somehow we must convince them that they were naturally creative as children and that they can regain enough of that early creativity to be usefully creative as adults. I use the strategy of *personal affirmation* as the primary method of accomplishing this. Since people tend to equate drawing with their early creativity, and since most of them lost what they thought were their natural drawing skills at about age 10, when they acquired a significant language capability, one successful approach I have used is to affirm them by demonstrating that they can draw again. When we teach people the basics of how to draw, we find that a very high percentage of them (80 to 90 percent) actually can. They are then confronted with indisputable evidence of a regained capability. Included in this group are some adults who claimed that they could never draw even as children. Nevertheless, relatively simple techniques can be used to provide a stunning affirmation. As the IHG example shows, this helps people get over a major mental hurdle that they may have about whether they are creative or not.

   A second potential area of affirmation is in the ability to visualize in your mind. Again, this is a natural mode of childhood. Just recall how you, as a child, once played with toy soldiers, baby dolls, forts, dollhouses, kitchen sets, construction models, or empty cardboard boxes. We got lost in these fantasies and were able, through our natural ability to visualize, to make real castles out of simple blocks, forts out of blankets, or operating rooms out of plastic toys. This is another domain where affirmation is readily available. Individuals who claim that they can no longer do this discover that they can, and the success level with typical business groups is again over 80 percent and may be as high as 90 percent. When confronted with indisputable evidence of success, participants are hard-pressed to deny this capability. They can then build on it to develop other ways of being creative.

2. **Technique.** There are specific techniques for achieving these affirmations. Dr. Betty Edwards (who I collaborated with 30 years ago), the author of *Drawing on the Right Side of the Brain*[3] and *The Artist Within*,[4] describes in detail the precise steps in the "learning how to draw" process. There are hundreds of experts throughout the world

who can facilitate Betty's techniques. Dan Pink, author of *A Whole New Mind*,[5] described how this approach affected him:

A few years ago, I took a five-day drawing class in New York City—Betty Edwards' "Drawing on the Right Side of the Brain"—that changed my life. I entered the class a complete ignoramus on matters visual. By week's end, I was somewhat less of an ignoramus because, to my amazement, I had begun learning how to see. These insights don't require a week-long class, of course; others look to something as non-threatening as doodling to get started.

Many adults claim that they used to be able to write rather creatively, but can no longer do so. Books such as Gabriele L. Rico's *Writing the Natural Way*[6] and Ann Lamott's *Bird by Bird*,[7] along with a plethora of websites and writing groups, provide specific techniques for opening up people to their natural latent creative writing ability. That's a specific path toward affirmation. There is nothing quite as persuasive as being impressed by your own creative "stuff," whether it is prose or poetry.

Another technique for providing affirmation of creative expression is that of "modeling" a problem situation. You can build creative models out of such materials as paper towel rolls, wood blocks, Styrofoam packing, old washing machine parts, dowels, used tennis balls, shoe boxes, feathers, and string, using these creative materials to assemble a three-dimensional metaphorical model of a problem or a situation. Through this hands-on experience of creating something visual, natural imaginative ideas surface and are applied to the evolving model. Insights about the situation emerge as you access thinking that you would not normally process if you were just talking about the issue. The resulting models represent such strong physical evidence of people's ability to think creatively (when they didn't think they could) that participants will describe the models to their coworkers and family with great pride and often actually take them home to show them off. Even though this is not about "art," there is a strong sense of accomplishment when the insights are so powerful.

Participants in one high-level series of workshops on strategic thinking felt that their models of the company and its relationship with key customers were so significant that they incorporated photographs of them into official strategic planning reports.

3. **Tools.** First on the list of tools is the creative process itself. By providing individuals with a take-away process that they can independently apply, we can give self-described "noncreatives" a golden key that unlocks

their own closed door of creativity. In Figure 22-1, in the previous chapter, I identified 82 discrete creative processes that can be selected and applied by people with any mental preference in the four-quadrant model. Through specific training and practice, affirmations lead to individuals becoming creative champions of a particular process that suits their thinking style.

I forged the thunderbolts. She fired them.

—Elizabeth Cady Stanton
on Susan B. Anthony

4. **Teams and pairs.** Many individuals who have lost their creativity have also lost their confidence in their ability to regain it by themselves. While creativity is a very personal process, it also can be very lonely. Pairing up two or more people can be positively reinforcing. Building a team of individuals who are in various stages of creative reclamation can be very mutually supporting and also very exciting. Through team activity, individuals can model stages of the creative process to one another in ways that greatly facilitate creative growth. It's very hard to resist the momentum of successful creative group involvement. As the IHG example shows, people who are encouraged to "go with it" tend to get caught up in the process, and before they realize it, they have demonstrated their own creativity. It is thrilling when they do, and it's hard for them to deny that they did it.

5. **Climate.** In order for any of this to happen, there must be a climate that provides permission, support, and reward for creative behavior. For many people who lost their early creativity, this is a crucially needed reversal of what turned them off in the first place. Many of them didn't feel that they had permission. They didn't feel that they had any support, and sometimes they were even punished for their attempts at being creative. This is where business managers must demonstrate their own understanding of creativity by metamorphosing into creative managers. Their goal should be to become creative champions.

   If creativity is a specific business goal, then to achieve that goal, the people in charge must understand the opportunity they have to assist their employees in the process of reclaiming the natural creativity of their youth. Managers who do so are also unleashing the creative potential of the organization, and this means that everything will now be different. The more managers become champions of creativity, the more likely it is that the corporate goal of "going creative" can be achieved.

   The track record of success is our own more than three decades of business application of this Whole Brain approach to reclaiming creativity in the workplace with organizations around the world.

Creativity Is a Core Competency for
Every Job Across the Business

Business leaders can talk creativity all they want, but until there is some permission granting and empowering going on, individuals will be leery of taking a risk. This is especially true for those who are concerned about job security and performing well at creativity. However, most jobs, even those that require repetition, will benefit from unleashing more creative mindsets. You may not consider your job creative, and neither may your boss, but the following is an example of how jobs can be typecast unnecessarily.

During the course of my 35 years with General Electric, I held a number of jobs that were officially "creative" and a number that were not. The tunnel vision of corporate structures lent credence to the idea that only certain jobs in certain departments were creative. For example, I worked for a while in General Electric's General Engineering Laboratory as a developmental engineer. Although I was a physicist and thought like a physicist, I was called an engineer and needed to think like an engineer. Because this was a developmental engineering laboratory, I needed to think like a developmental engineer, and that meant that I had to *invent* things. I needed to be creative, although the word *creativity* was never mentioned. It was not part of GE's official language back in those days. Meanwhile, other people in the laboratory who were not development engineers were *not* considered "creative."

I recall vividly one of the wonders of the laboratory facility. It was a self-service stockroom, filled with every electronic and mechanical gadget, device, or part that you could imagine. It was like an inventor's flea market. But the only people who had access to this resource were developmental engineers; in other words, only those who were officially "creative" could benefit from this facility, even though there were at least three times as many "noncreative" people supporting the developmental activities.

Well, this seemed odd to me at the time, and viewing it from the perspective of so many years later, such a policy was not only ridiculous, but obscene. In point of fact, every job in the organization was, to a certain degree, creative. Some jobs had creativity implied in the job title, such as developmental engineer, while others who directly supported those positions were called technicians; they did the bidding of the developmental engineers and were thought of as

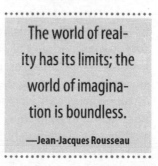

The world of reality has its limits; the world of imagination is boundless.

—Jean-Jacques Rousseau

noncreative because of their subordinate position. In retrospect, the hourly-rated toolmakers in the laboratory's machine shop had to be extremely creative in translating the developmental engineering sketches into experimental hardware. The nonexempt administrative staff, whose members translated the technical dictation of the development engineers and tried to make sense out of the notes on paper napkins drawn in the cafeteria, had to be actively creative in order to survive the nearly impossible role that they played.

Even in my own organization, it would be quite difficult to identify a job that did not have some element of creativity in it. However, in those long-ago times, GE's culture was like an iceberg: the small part above the water line was visibly creative, while the main body of the iceberg beneath the surface represented the huge, unrecognized, and invisible domain of creativity. It seems odd that so many people could be blind to the obvious in such a smart company. But, as Henry Mintzberg[8] reminds us, "People seem to be smart and dull at the same time." GE is a vastly different company today, but many organizations still have vestiges of this tunnel vision.

If we now pull back from this microscopic view and look at business and industry through a wide-angle lens, we will find hundreds, thousands, and probably millions of employees whose job title and description are officially deemed "noncreative." Yet many of these jobs have opportunities for creative functioning. These creative job elements are not visible to management. Creative performance is neither encouraged nor rewarded when it occurs. Incredibly, in fact, creative initiatives are often grounds for punishment.

Some companies ignore the creative capabilities of existing employees and outsource their creative needs to consulting organizations that employ individuals who are "officially" creative. I have some personal expertise here because my creative capability was overlooked for 20 years until I "officialized" myself by becoming a professional artist. In so doing, I took advantage of the fact that management wouldn't understand the difference between artistic creativity and business creativity.

As I write this, I'm thinking about the hundreds of thousands of individuals with enormous creative potential who are assigned to officially noncreative work. Translated into Whole Brain Thinking terms, this means that a lot of very imaginative C- and D-quadrant-oriented people are assigned to A- and B-quadrant work that feels relatively tedious to them. Most of them have demonstrated that they can do the work, but as in the iceberg example, most of their capability and motivation lie below the water line. In many cases, it's painful for these people to go to work in the morning because only a small portion of their job assignment represents the kinds of activities that stimulate them (see Figure 23-1). *Most* of their job is made up of work that they actively dislike, but, largely for economic reasons, they are sufficiently motivated to perform that work at an acceptable level ... that is, until another opportunity comes along that allows them—and their company—to fully leverage their strengths and talents.

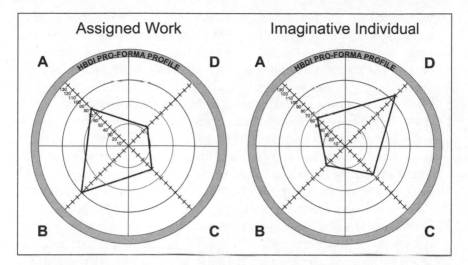

FIGURE 23-1 Pro-forma comparison profiles of assigned work and imaginative individuals.

Let us turn now to people who are not so imaginatively driven, but who have been assigned to work that has a high creative content. This is another form of misery, but not as long-lasting, since their obvious lack of performance reveals the mismatch early in the job cycle (that is, of course, if supervisors and managers are able to see what is happening). I can't visualize too many things that would be more painful than to be expected to produce creative results on schedule if using your imagination is not your idea of fun. However, I am reminded that for some people, having to squelch your imagination is equally painful. In both cases, this is a lose-lose-lose situation: it's lose for the employee, it's lose for the manager, and it's lose for the company. Once the notion of Whole Brain Creativity is understood, organizations can find ways to have everyone contribute to the creative process, but to do so in ways that are congruent with their preferred approaches.

Igniting the Creative Spark . . . and Saving $100,000

Ted Coulson and Alison Strickland,[9] leading creativity experts, tell this story about Karen Gammon, an administrative assistant who participated in a creativity workshop that they conducted at DuPont. Karen revealed that she was not fulfilled in her job and that she felt she had more to offer than the position allowed. During the workshop, she decided to do something about her office in the Richmond, Virginia, plant. She wanted to clean it up, repaint it in colors that she liked, and turn it into a showplace. That night, she called her husband, who was head of the maintenance union at the plant, and asked him to get the paint she wanted and remove the furniture from the office so that she could paint it when she got back the next weekend.

She did exactly what she planned to do, and the place looked great. As she started to move her stuff back into the office, however, it dawned on her that she didn't need this piece of furniture, and she didn't need that piece—as a matter of fact, she didn't need most of the "stuff" that had crowded her office. She told the story to her colleagues, who decided that they also didn't need a lot of their office stuff. Karen's creative solution was to have an office "yard sale." People came from all corners of the plant and acquired what they needed and contributed what they didn't need. The result was impressive: $100,000 saved for the company; a major charitable gift by DuPont to the city of Richmond, Virginia; a whole lot of great-looking offices; and a group of very pleased and fulfilled staff members. Some time later, motivated by her creative affirmations, Karen decided to change careers. She entered art school and progressed rapidly to become an independent, skilled, self-employed professional artist. It is really never too late to try your creative wings.

Creative Courage

Many people do creative things without giving a second thought to the courage it takes to deal with the consequences. But particularly in business, it's more common for people to be afraid to try because they're afraid to fail and suffer the very real consequences that are either an explicit or an implicit part of the organizational culture.

Assume for a moment that you have developed a highly creative solution to a longstanding problem in your company. However, some influential people feel that your solution is laughable, impractical, and, in fact, weird. It's totally off the wall, and you are ridiculed for even suggesting such an outlandish approach to a serious problem. The idea is rejected out of hand.

Or maybe you've come up with what you know is a groundbreaking innovation that could catapult your company ahead of the competition. Yet the powers that be don't have the stomach for any potential failure. If you can't guarantee them a 100 percent success rate, they don't even want to consider it. Conversation over.

This is where courage is required. It takes a lot of guts to stand up for your creative idea in the face of severe criticism from the security-minded, safekeeping traditionalists. There is never a lack of naysayers ready to throw cold water on any ideas that deviate from the norm. A whole language has been developed to kill creative ideas (see Figure 23-2). It is likely that all of us have heard these kinds of idea killers, and maybe inadvertently used them ourselves.

Put It to Work

Review the list in Figure 23-2, and put an X next to those you have said yourself and those you have heard others say.

- *How might you respond to one of those idea killers to keep from squashing potential creativity?*

1. Don't be ridiculous.
2. We tried that before.
3. We've never done it before.
4. It costs too much.
5. That's beyond our responsibility.
6. It's too radical a change.
7. We don't have time.
8. We're too small for it.
9. That will make other equipment/products/departments obsolete.
10. That's not practical.
11 Management will have a fit.
12. Let's get back to reality.
13. That's not our problem.
14. Why change it? It's still working okay.
15. You're two years ahead of your time.
16. We're not ready for that.
17. It isn't in the budget.
18. Can't teach an old dog new tricks.
19. Top management will never go for it.
20. We'll be a laughingstock.
21. We did all right without it.
22. Let's put together a team to study it.
23. Has anyone else ever tried it?
24. Are our competitors doing it?

FIGURE 23-2 Attitudes that kill creative ideas.

No one is saying that you can't comment on or critique ideas. One simple technique to keep from rejecting an idea out of hand, though, is to always replace "but …" as your reaction with "and how might we …?" In this way, you're adding on versus decimating.

Here's an example:

Instead of:

That idea is interesting, but because of budget constraints, I don't think it will work.

Try:

That idea is interesting, and since we know our budget's limited, how might we get creative with our resources so we can get quicker buy-in?

• *Try this at your next meeting, and encourage those you work with to change their language as well.*

The high-ranking VP-level idea killers I have personally experienced seemed to wear the scalps of dead creative proposals with great pride. On one occasion, I was presenting a creative proposal to a senior vice president heading up a roomful of managers whose approval was required, when he asked the following question at the end of my presentation: "Ned, is what you are recommending something that our leading competitors are doing?" Even though that was totally beside the point, I had to answer, "No." He responded, "Well, that does it for me," and he stood up and left the room. Without a word, everybody else stood up and also left the room.

I was blindsided. I was taken by surprise and was unable to spontaneously counter his idea-killing comment. That incident could have terminated several weeks' worth of creative effort that my task force had put in, but I was so convinced of the soundness of the proposed solution that I made a conscious decision not to cave in, even though this guy was a powerful senior vice president. With the help of the task force members, I prepared and sent to him a written *restatement* of the proposed creative solution, and ended it by saying, "As you well know, this is an industry-wide problem, and if our competitors got wind of what we propose to do, they would immediately steal our solution and get ahead of us with our key customers." To my surprise, I got a note back from the senior

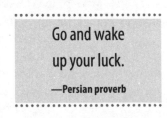

Go and wake
up your luck.
—**Persian proverb**

vice president that said, "I have reconsidered your recommendation, and I think you are right. Thanks for not giving up. I have told the Review Board that I am approving your recommendation." Now, you can argue that he didn't have the right to take unilateral action, but I elected not to use a killer phrase to stop him.

There will be times like this when you can challenge killer phrases by having the courage of your own convictions. People who use these idea-killing phrases enjoy a great deal of success. The phrases are so effective that they provide power to people who seek power. I have discovered that in most instances, there is no substance to these killer phrases. People who use them expect to be challenged, and when they are not, their suspicions appear to be correct, and they quickly claim victory. As a result of my own successful experience, I prepared myself not to be blindsided again, particularly by high-level officers whose primary weapon was their rank. I now came ready to deal with any idea-killing phrases that might be made.

The net result was a sharp increase in my creative-proposal batting average. If courage is involved, it comes from the worthiness of the creative recommendation, and it is supported by the success of applying this strategy of positive confrontation.

Finally, but in many ways most importantly, it's much easier to be courageous—and to get the benefits of creative courage—when you have committed leadership and a strong culture that support doing so. As leaders, we need to not only give permission for creativity, but also make it acceptable for people to fail. Promoting a culture of experimentation by creating safety around trying things out is the only way we can truly achieve enterprise-wide innovation. Think about it: most of us are dealing with entirely new challenges, completely unprecedented issues, and a future that's pretty much impossible to predict with any sort of accuracy.

The only way you learn to flip things is just to flip them!

—Julia Child, after flipping a pancake onto the floor on her television show

A "fail fast, fail cheap" approach helps make it acceptable for people to pilot ideas and test things out. Take a page from the world of IT development and build in prototyping and regular checkpoints to allow for future-proofing products and ideas along the way. Make sure you allow people to have small wins. Creativity researcher Teresa Amabile's Progress Principles have shown that you can increase and affirm creativity by celebrating the small milestones.[10] And as a 3M slogan so aptly states, never kill an idea, just deflect it.

SO WHAT?

> Many people who have creative potential are unaware of it and therefore lack the confidence and willingness to try to apply it.

> Even those jobs that are labeled noncreative require and benefit from some level of creative thinking.

> A high percentage of the ideas that are developed in an organizational setting are wasted. Leaders who want to encourage creativity need to be aware of this and actively campaign to change the culture from killing creativity to stimulating it, supporting it, and rewarding it.

> Key components of the successful application of corporate creativity programs are top management's recognition of the need for creativity to keep the organization competitive, an understanding of the creative process and its consequences, and the presence of one or more courageous and knowledgeable creativity champions to provide inspirational leadership and protective air cover.

> Moving from "but" to "and how might we" to avoid killing ideas will open people up to sharing more of their creative thinking.

PART 5

Personal Growth Through Whole Brain Thinking

"We're looking for someone who can stretch with the demands of this job. Are you flexible?"

CHAPTER 24

Stretching Your Thinking and Overcoming Mental Blind Spots

CHAPTER HIGHLIGHTS

> There are tools and techniques that anyone can apply to stretch beyond his or her mental defaults and think in new ways.

> Claiming mental space requires expanding your mental profile of preferences to include what is needed for the goal or the task.

> One way to unleash your personal potential is to develop and commit to new learning habits.

The leadership at Cornerstone Schools of Alabama has a complex job. As a nonprofit that serves low-income children, the school is funded entirely by donations, meaning that the leaders start each year with no money guaranteed—not even tuition. To earn the budget to run and manage the school, the development department depends heavily on the support of corporations, foundations, and local business leaders. Theirs is data-intensive, time-sensitive work that requires a relentless focus on the numbers and details to keep up with a fast-growing and traditionally underserved student population along with the stringent academic standards involved with maintaining the school's accreditations and its status as an International Baccalaureate World School.

Considering all this, it's not surprising that the PR volunteer coordinator was in a challenging position and was driving everyone else on the team crazy. As talented as she was in relating to others, always being ready to pitch in and be flexible about helping out, when she was asked for the data, charts, and detailed information that the other team members needed, she *never delivered*. In fact, she didn't seem to be interested in the numbers at all. She was outgoing, friendly, and well spoken, but her operating style was best described as "all over the place." It had become a continual source of frustration for the rest of the team.

However, the executive director, Dr. Nita Carr,[1] saw the value that this person provided, and she wanted the others to see it, too. She brought in HBDI practitioner Bill Hart to conduct HBDI Profiles and facilitate a Whole Brain Thinking workshop to help all the team members understand how the team's diversity contributed to its mission.

There were plenty of "aha! moments" during the discussions. Although no one was shocked to discover this person's extremely strong preference for interpersonally oriented C-quadrant thinking, a lot of lightbulbs went off—the other members realized that they needed her unique strengths and perspectives to keep the community engaged and maintain the partnerships that were so essential to the school's ongoing viability. Dr. Carr was thrilled with the results.

So she was surprised when the PR coordinator showed up at her office the next day, visibly upset. She told Dr. Carr that she didn't want to be viewed as someone who had no interest in the numbers or in following processes. She felt that she had more to offer than what they were seeing of her, and she made a personal commitment: she would stretch herself and get more comfortable with her analytical A- and structured B-quadrant thinking modes. She put together her own development plan focused on building these skills.

> The best part of one's life is the working part, the creative part. Believe me, I love to succeed; but the real spiritual and emotional excitement is in the doing.
>
> —Garson Kanin, writer and director

"At one point, I had worried that she might be stuck, that I wouldn't be able promote her," Dr. Carr said. "But she totally turned it around. People's perceptions of her changed, too. And it was all her. She took the initiative."

As I've said throughout this book, your thinking preferences are just that— preferences. You're not limited to them. But how do you stretch outside your "mental defaults" and grow in new directions? This chapter will give you some practical ways to take the initiative and take charge of your own learning and development.

Claiming Your Mental Space

One of the best ways for people to help themselves move in any desired developmental direction is for them to "claim their own mental space." By this, I mean finding the energy to develop the required skills in those portions of the Whole Brain spectrum that need to be accessed if you are to fulfill your long-term goals successfully. A current example for me was the writing of this book—an important long-term goal. My least-preferred quadrant is the lower-left B, and even though I have developed a wide range of skills in that mode over the course of my career, to get this book finished, I had to "claim" even more of the mental B-quadrant discipline and attention to detail to meet my goal.

A colleague with strong preferences in the A and D quadrants recently did a similar exercise in claiming mental space in the C quadrant. Embarking on what he called an "empathy skill development track," he wanted to know what resources I could recommend in that regard. When I asked why this was a focus for him, he shared that both at work and at home, his lack of attention to and low level of sensitivity for emotional issues continued to be a problem for him. At home, it was affecting his relationship with his daughter and his wife. Although his values are strongly anchored in "family," he knew that his preferences and behaviors were getting in the way. In addition, a recent feedback session with his boss had highlighted a similar gap in his ability to manage and coach his direct reports with greater interpersonal sensitivity and skills. He embarked on the development journey with great motivation, using the Whole Brain model as a reminder that he *could* do it.

Another great example is an independent consultant I have known for years who decided that her low preference for the A quadrant was the primary reason that she was not getting her dissertation work completed. She had reached the phase of the work that required taking a deep dive into the collected data and performing statistical analysis; it was the final barrier to getting this life project completed. Once she understood that her low preference was part of the issue, she concocted a fun way to "mind hack" herself into developing energy and enjoyment for this critical work. She thought of it like a game and reached out to a mentor for moral support. Her dissertation was completed in two months.

And here's one more example: an associate told the story of how her lack of attention to detail was impeding her small business. Billing was delayed, important information was getting misplaced, and she found herself spending more time looking for things and catching up. This was her livelihood! She decided that this had to change. She found and hired an organizational consultant who helped her set up a visual, color-coded system with reminders and tracking that leveraged the technology she had available. They simplified the number of systems she had, and voilà! Everything began to work more smoothly, and her business grew as a result. Most of all, she felt enormous satisfaction from having conquered this "dragon" that was preventing her from accomplishing her goal.

Where do you want to put your mental energies and effort at this point in your life? How can you better use your mental potential to get where you want to go? Think first about a long-term goal that you want to achieve, either personal or professional (for example, become an artist, start your own company, invent a new product, get a handle on your financial future, or get that next big promotion). Tap into your own instincts to identify the thinking modes that you are currently not using, and perhaps actively resisting, but that you need to access in order to achieve your developmental priorities. This is about charting your mental path. A tool to aid in this process is the Claiming My Mental Space exercise (see Figure 24-1).

In completing the exercise, you have used your increased understanding of your thinking self, developed by reading this book, along with the possible missing critical thinking elements that you need to access in order to be fully productive in the situation you have in mind. These elements most frequently occur in an area of lesser preference. This means that there is a gap between how we prefer to think and the portions of the thinking spectrum that have to be added in order to accomplish a goal or a task, but that are not now an active preference for you personally. What can you do about that?

Figure 24-2 shows my personal profile, along with a profile of the shift in mental space that I needed in order to write this book. As I mentioned earlier, the writing of a book required more mental space than is typically available

1. Write down your long-term goal.
2. Think about what is getting in your way. Use this chart to identify any key thinking elements that may be required, and are currently missing, potentially preventing you from successfully accomplishing your goal.
3. Note which quadrant(s) you need to "claim" by intentionally accessing that "mental space" to pursue the missing elements needed in order to achieve your goal.
4. Outline the steps necessary to get started.

A	D
• Analyzing issues and data	• Seeing trends and the signs of coming change
• Gathering facts	• Recognizing new possibilities
• Understanding how things work	• Tolerating ambiguity
• Arguing and debating rationally	• Integrating ideas & concepts
• Critical thinking and analysis	• Simultaneous processing of different input
• Forming and understanding theories	• Challenging established processes and policies
• Measuring precisely	• Synthesizing unlike elements into a new whole
• Problem solving logically	• Inventing innovative solutions to problems
• Financial analysis and decision making	• Problem solving in intuitive ways
• Technology savvy, understanding technical elements	• Seeing "the big picture"
• Working with numbers, statistics, data, and precision	• Being playful, artistic, and/or creative
• Brief, clear, and succinct communication	• Taking risks and being more entrepreneurial
• Other:_____	• Other:_____

Key Elements That, if Missing, May Prevent Your Success

B	C
• Finding overlooked flaws	• Recognizing interpersonal difficulties
• Approaching problems practically	• Anticipating how others will feel
• Standing firm on issues	• Intuitively understanding how others feel
• Maintaining a standard of consistency	• Picking up nonverbal cues
• Providing stability	• Engendering enthusiasm
• Reading fine print	• Persuading, conciliating
• Organizing and keeping track of info or data	• Coaching, mentoring, teaching
• Developing detailed plans and procedures	• Expressing and sharing openly with others
• Articulating in a clear and orderly way	• Understanding emotional elements
• Keeping records straight	• Considering values
• Consistently following through	• Active listening (without interrupting)
• Being on time	• Attentive to others' (internal, external) needs
• Other:_____	• Other:_____

FIGURE 24-1 The claiming my mental space exercise.

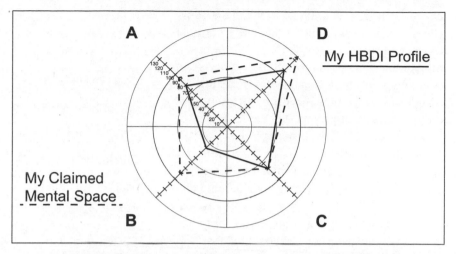

FIGURE 24-2 The mental space the author claimed when writing this book.

to me under ordinary day-to-day circumstances. The implications were clear. In order to write this book in accordance with the book proposal that the publisher had accepted, and to deliver a manuscript complete with illustrations and graphics and do so within the allowable budget and on time, I would have to substantially supplement my normal profile of A- and D-quadrant preferred thinking with a substantial amount of additional B-quadrant mental activity. Furthermore, to accomplish my goals, I would have to consciously and deliberately claim not only my everyday mental space, but this new, enlarged mental space required by the task at hand.

You will notice that I not only increased the stretch from my normal profile in the D quadrant, but also added a significant amount of mental space in the B quadrant. This is where the procedural and production aspects of book development are located. It's where the signed contract takes precedence and where due dates need to be met as committed. This is where writing discipline is located and where much of the editorial work needs to take place.

Alas for those that never sing, but die with all their music in them.

—Oliver Wendell Holmes, Sr.

A good personal example of how I applied this exercise to the writing of this book is that I committed myself to the discipline of writing each morning, seven days a week, until the initial writing phase was completed. The habit that I formed over the months of applying this discipline now allows the editing, rewriting, illustrating, and quote selection processes to take place each morning, seven days a week. This illustrates the point that once I had fully claimed the mental space, it provided the basis for a significant increase in my overall capability. As a result of claiming this space, I have acquired a habit that greatly increases my productivity, not only on this book project, but in the everyday accomplishment of my business tasks.

> Creative activity could be described as a type of learning process where teacher and pupil are located in the same individual.
>
> —Arthur Koestler

As I think is already clear, the kind of mental space I am talking about is not something that your boss or your spouse or your parents can give to you. For this new space to work for you, it must be *owned* by you, and there is only one good way that I know of to own it, and that is to personally claim it.

Jump-Starting Your Own Personal Development

When it comes to initiating your own development, I have pondered the question of how to begin for many years. It doesn't need to be so difficult that you waste half your life wondering whether you are good enough to even start. For many people, that, in itself, is a huge barrier. Since getting started on mental development is such a personal issue with many variables involved, a rank-ordering of my considered answers on the best place to start is difficult, but high on the list has got to be *affirmation*, which we touched on in Chapter 23. Attempting something that you have always wanted to do and then *doing it successfully* is an affirmation that can convince even the most practiced skeptic that he has what it takes to succeed. In my case, learning how to draw, sculpt, visualize, and use creative materials were techniques that allowed me to achieve in areas that I had never thought possible. I've seen this work time and again with other people, too. They were convinced that they could not do certain things, and so they avoided even trying. When they were guided into attempting these things and discovered that they could succeed, they were confronted with their own accomplishment. Whether it is taking up a new hobby, learning a new skill, or embarking on any new learning endeavor, find ways to engage in activities that provide affirmation along the way. Often it helps to break things down into small milestones so that you can achieve "small wins" on the path to affirmation.

A key to affirmation is finding *facilitation* of the activity that leads to affirmation. For example, for a person whose mental space is blocked as if by an insurmountable brick wall, facilitation is a ramp up to *a door in that wall*. It is helpful to think of being "blocked" as only a temporary kind of disability that can be overcome through understanding. Through skilled facilitation, a person can uncover natural capability and have that ability developed and released in very effective ways. Think for a minute about a coach who can facilitate ability in a youngster who is batting a ball or ice skating or drawing a likeness. Amateur athletes use coaches throughout their careers; professional teams use coaches on a full-time basis; professional golfers and opera singers rely on coaches. The same approach works with a businessperson or any other individual who needs coaching or

> I want to grow. I want to be better. You grow. We all grow. We're made to grow. You either evolve or you disappear.
>
> —Tupac Shakur

mentorship to facilitate his or her movement toward a new skill or ability. Such coaching, mentoring, or facilitation is available from many sources. However, the motivation must come from the individual who is seeking to grow.

Along with affirmation and facilitation comes *permission*, which we just touched on in the exercise of claiming your mental space. Many of us hang back until we think we have permission. By that I mean permission to try, permission to take a risk, permission to experiment, and, most especially, permission to fail. I have discovered that this permission is very hard to come by. We are reluctant to give ourselves permission, and what's surprising is that we are often prone to decline the permission that has been granted to us by others. For me, there was a certain inherent shyness that came to the surface when a chance to be creative was offered. It is all too easy to turn down the invitation and not seize the opportunity. For this reason, permission must be overt. It must be obvious. It must be without strings or consequences, and in this regard, the hardest permission to come by is the permission that we give ourselves. In fact, to help learners get past self-denial and the fear of failure, I would encourage them to hang a formal certificate on their wall giving them permission to claim their own mental space (see Figure 24-3). This applies to anything where the fear of failure prevents us from moving forward.

By *mental space* I mean the both the physical and the psychological space that allows, gives permission for, and encourages personal development to take place. For example, some forms of development demand a certain amount of private *physical space* to allow people to engage in the activity and still feel "safe." Taking learning risks might be too messy and too long-lasting to be done on the kitchen table, in front of the TV, or on your desk at work. So you need your own dedicated area where you can do what you need to do without possibly interfering with other people's workspace, without getting in the way

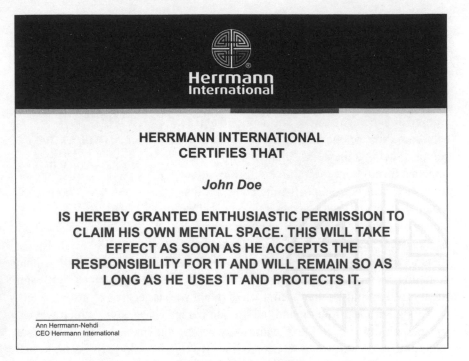

FIGURE 24-3 A sample "Claim Your Mental Space Certificate" for claiming your own mental space.

of your everyday tasks, and where you have the freedom to do what might feel like "weird stuff" to you, especially in the beginning.

After physical space, the next space to consider is the *psychological space* we all need when privacy is essential to our feeling safe during the process, and where personal risks can be explored before they are committed to publicly. *And* where we are simply comfortable enough to eliminate the self-generated ogres that tend to get in the way of the learning process.

Finally, there is the stretch to the new *mental space* that needs to be claimed, as we discussed earlier.

I encourage you to create your own declaration of granting yourself permission to claim your mental space. (Visit www.wholebrainbusinessbook.com to download a certificate.) Keep it in your workspace, within your line of sight. That way, whenever you become unsure that you have your own permission or the organization's permission, you can refer to your "official certification of permission" as documentation that you have what it takes to behave in new ways. Claiming your mental space implies that it is a priority. It is more than just a personal urge; it is actually legitimate work.

Unfortunately, there are many business cultures that consider learning activities to be something other than work. Instead of being on task, these activities are thought of as a loss of focus and a deviation from assigned work. For these reasons, the priority that I am alluding to needs to be held not only by the person who is attempting to learn, but also by those people who manage that individual. In a workplace environment, to be most effective, this sense of priority has to be established simultaneously by the individual and his or her manager.

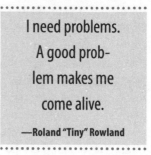

> I need problems. A good problem makes me come alive.
>
> —Roland "Tiny" Rowland

Along with affirmation, facilitation, priority, and permission, I recommend creating a *portfolio of personal accomplishments*. Successful artists have a portfolio of their prize-winning work. Authors have a shelf of books. Photographers have a portfolio of pictures. Businesspeople have a résumé or curriculum vitae that lists their accomplishments. Businesspeople can also assemble a portfolio of their new learning accomplishments. This can include such things as certifications, ideas submitted to the suggestion system, accomplishments as a member of a task force, or documented new solutions submitted to management. It won't take long to accumulate an impressive body of work that represents your learning journey. In surveys I have conducted, I have discovered that more than a third of the thousands of people responding have a "body of work" suitable for documentation, *much of which may have been developed outside of the workplace*. I think it is revealing to note that most of these people never thought in terms of a body of work until I asked the question. Recognizing that a personal body of work exists is a major affirmation of one's ability. I could tell from the brightness of the respondents' eyes and the broad smiles on their faces that these individuals felt very good about their accomplishments over the years. I have kept a portfolio of my accomplishments, and I find it personally inspiring to review this growing body of work. It is, in fact, a very real affirmation that reminds me to give myself permission to "go for it" again.

Acquiring Personal Learning Habits

Developing stretch or learning habits is another helpful way to unleash your personal potential. During the 15 years that art was my second professional occupation, I developed a habit that contributed in a major way to my artistic success and productivity. I typically painted a picture a week and completed a sculpture every two months. I discovered that at any given time, I had in my mind four or five compelling scenes or subjects for my next painting or sculpture. The problem was making a choice among a number of very desirable subjects. I would usually start a painting on Saturday morning and finish it for framing a week later, typically on Sunday afternoon. On one occasion, at the beginning of this highly productive period, I decided to make the decision about the subject of the next painting *before I left the studio* after finishing the current painting. After signing the paint-

> **Man's mind, once stretched by a new idea, never regains its original dimensions.**
>
> —Oliver Wendell Holmes, Sr.

ing that I was working on and removing the watercolor paper from the art table, I would think for a few minutes about the subjects that intrigued me at that moment. In a few minutes of contemplation, I was able to sort out the one that was of primary interest, and then, working rapidly with my pencil, I would commit myself to that as the subject of my next painting. I would often commit myself more completely to that chosen subject by brushing in a color wash in the places appropriate to the final scene. I would then set that new watercolor paper aside and complete the matting and framing of the work I had just finished.

What happened next strongly confirms the stage of the creative process that is called *incubation*. We know that our brains are working all the time, and this is proof: between the time I committed myself on paper and the next time I could work in my studio, I found myself painting that picture in my mind. By the time I returned to the painting, several days might have passed, or even most of the week, but I was able to quickly complete the preliminary sketch that was the initial phase of the painting and then block in the main elements of the scene, with almost complete confidence that what I was doing would be part of the finished painting. This technique worked so well for me that it became an absolute unwritten rule that I would always start the next painting before I left the studio. Tangible evidence of the success of this strategy was that I won prizes (60) and sold paintings (400) at an increasing rate.

I applied the same discipline to my sculpture, but since the processes are so different, I couldn't commit myself with a few lines on paper; instead, I had to make a miniature in clay of what I intended to sculpt on a larger scale. Again, the same thing happened. I was able to make progress subconsciously by working through the design of the finished piece in my mind as I went about my other business. This is a key characteristic of the brain. If you present your mental self with a situation, your mind can work on that situation unconsciously and effortlessly during other activity or sleep, so that as you reengage with the task in question, you have made progress toward its solution. I have used this habit now for about 30 years with great success. You can, too!

A new habit that I acquired while writing this book is writing or recording my ideas every morning, seven days a week, on topics of interest that come to mind. Before I go to sleep, as I contemplate the next morning's writing, I present myself with subject alternatives. When I wake up, I spend 15 minutes in a theta state that is conducive to my creative process, which positions me to engage the subject that I'm interested in. When I go to my private place, the subject presents itself to me in a manner that I can respond to with great ease and comfort.

Another measure of the success of these strategies is that I never "lost" a painting or a sculpture, and I never "lost" a topic. In other words, in each case, I completed what I started out with in a form that I could frame, display, or publish. You can easily apply this process to anything you want to work on or learn. Just get started!

> Many people know how to work hard; many others know how to play well; but the rarest talent in the world is the ability to introduce elements of playfulness into work, and to put some constructive labor into our leisure.
>
> —Sydney J. Harris

Put It to Work

- Take a moment to pick something that you would like to learn in order to expand your own potential—whether in your personal life or at work.
- Use the Claiming My Mental Space exercise to explore what will be required for you to take this on mentally.
- Identify the specific action steps it would take for you to do this over the next two months.
- Plot the action steps on your calendar, noting small milestones along the way, and make a commitment to making it happen.
- Think about who might be a resource to help facilitate your process. If this would be helpful, consider finding a buddy to engage with you on this journey.
- Make sure to give yourself permission to go for it and celebrate once you are finished.
- Now make a new commitment to the next learning you will engage in; like the brushstroke on my blank canvas, this will get you on your way.

Read through the following suggestions to help get you started.

Unleash Your Full Brainpower

Unleashing your full thinking potential can be uncomfortable, whether you are a highly structured thinker who needs to experiment and take more risks, or a highly imaginative person who needs the discipline and organization to be more productive with your time.

Fortunately, brain research supports the fact that you *can* stretch and overcome your mental blind spots. It starts with making your thinking work for you rather than being trapped by it. Here are some tips for putting your Whole Brain to work:

1. **Get used to being uncomfortable.** Discomfort is a sign that your brain is engaged and learning. As the business environment becomes more challenging and diverse, with new generations and increased globalization being added to the mix, your initial reaction may be to see the negative in all this complexity. Instead of wanting to avoid those who make you uncomfortable, recognize the opportunity they offer to help you stretch your perspectives. Hire and enlist them. They can become your biggest assets. Instead of avoiding domains that make your head spin, embrace them. Make it a personal challenge to work through the discomfort to new understanding.
2. **Challenge your assumptions.** The brain is very efficient, and it will "fill in the blanks" for you when you're looking for a solution. But when you're trying to see something in a different way or find a new way of doing things, the quick leap to conclusions can ultimately be a trap. When you begin to make an assumption, flip it around. Ask yourself, "What if this were *not* true?"
3. **Embrace the unknown.** It is your ally, not your enemy. The known may be your worst enemy. Change presents a great opportunity for new thinking, but only if we deliberately and consciously take advantage of it.
4. **Optimize your toolkit.** Use your own thinking preferences to determine the tools that work for you. If you're a highly visual thinker, a linear, spreadsheet-style planning tool may make the task of getting organized even more difficult for you. If the techniques and processes aren't helping, look to your thinking preferences for clues and help on how you can find or create a more workable solution for you.
5. **Lighten up.** Unconventional approaches free the brain and stimulate new ideas and perspectives. Find ways to jolt your thinking and have fun with it.
6. **Make it a mental habit.** Decide what you want and go for it, working at it daily if possible, making your desired future outcomes a reality.

SO WHAT?

> Claiming your mental space allows you to chart your mental path and use your thinking potential to take you where you want to go.

> A good way to start the release of hidden potential is to experience the *affirmation* of success, and this can be greatly *facilitated* through *coaching* or *mentoring*.

> For many people, the key to accessing locked-up potential is the granting of *permission*, not only by others such as the boss, but also, hardest of all to achieve, by themselves.

> The difference between success and failure, particularly in work that requires new learning, is often the personal discipline and commitment that we provide. By identifying a needed discipline(s) and making a habit of it, we help guarantee a successful professional outcome.

> Stretching your thinking and seeing beyond your mental blind spots can be an uncomfortable process, but it will make you more engaged, informed, and able to succeed in an ever more complex world.

I'M ALWAYS LOOKING FOR WAYS
TO BREAK THE RULES AND
DO THINGS DIFFERENTLY.
THAT'S THE KEY TO
MY SUCCESS!

CHAPTER 25

Entrepreneurial Thinking: What It Is, Why You Need It, and How to Develop It

CHAPTER HIGHLIGHTS

> Many people seek to become more entrepreneurial as a way of expanding their options, whether inside their organization or in an effort to "go it on their own."

> Those who think they have what it takes to make it on their own often need some reassurance and support to ensure that they are on the right track.

> The typical entrepreneur's profile is strongly oriented to D-quadrant thinking. What if your preferences are different?

> "Intrapreneurs" are entrepreneurs functioning inside an organization.

A colleague, Russell Means, started a very successful legal practice by involving retired lawyers in the Florida city where he set up his first practice. As a young person who had never set up a business, he found an enormous pool of successful people who were energetic, smart, and available. Russell was able to take advantage of several hundred years of accumulated experience in launching his legal practice. The level of competence that these highly experienced people provided was beyond his ability to pay for, but because of their circumstances and his need, he got a dollar's worth of ability for ten cents.

No matter how you do it, if you want to start a business, you need to know your own strengths and limitations and find ways to fill in the business gaps so that you don't become another statistic in the annual report of business failures. At a bare minimum, most entrepreneurs should line up a CPA and a lawyer whom they trust, and pledge to listen to them. Trust your instincts, but take their advice. Every step along the way, seek out the expertise you need to complement your own.

Many people aspire to go out on their own, and in today's environment, a move to become an entrepreneur may be the most desirable or only option. But it's one thing to know that you want to "make the leap"; it's something else entirely to know whether you have what it takes. Understanding your preferences and using a Whole Brain approach will significantly improve your chances of success. It will also help you understand the entrepreneurial mindset—a key factor for making any start-up or brand-new initiative successful.

> The entrepreneur is essentially a visualizer and an actualizer. He can visualize something, and when he visualizes it, he sees exactly how to make it happen.
>
> —Robert L. Schwartz

Beyond the typical application involving a new business venture, entrepreneurial thinking is also at the heart of many corporate initiatives that champion an innovative mindset and seek to emulate the creative and boundary-breaking energy that many start-ups produce. Because of the nature of the work, these kinds of projects require people to behave like "intrapreneurs," all within a corporate culture that may or may not be ready for or open to it.

Whether you are considering an intrapreneurial approach or going out on your own, looking at what we know about entrepreneurs can help you better understand entrepreneurial thinking and what it might mean for you.

How Do Your Thinking Preferences Compare to the Average Entrepreneur's?

You've got this terrific idea. You think it will work, but you need some reassurance that you are on the right track and an affirmation that you've got what it takes. There are numerous experts who can help you get your act together—financial experts, business process experts, and motivational psychologists, not to mention friends, neighbors, and family. Many of them have written books on the subject or offer workshops or webinars and often include motivational phrases such as "go for it." What I have to offer is not in competition with any of these sources, but it is one of the first things that you should explore.

I believe it is essential for someone who is contemplating starting a business or who is, in essence, being asked to become an intrapreneur inside a business to know what his or her thinking preferences are and the potential influence of those preferences on the person's entrepreneurial business behavior.

A strong D-quadrant primary preference—a high average score (92)—is characteristic of all entrepreneurs in our global database (both technical and nontechnical, male and female). *Nontechnical* male entrepreneurs also have a primary preference in the A quadrant (70). In contrast, the female norm for nontechnical entrepreneurs is slightly more balanced, but with an even stronger D quadrant (97) combined with a C-quadrant primary preference. Not surprisingly, *technical* entrepreneurs (both male and female) have higher A-quadrant scores, but still maintain that very strong D-quadrant score, which clearly defines the entrepreneurial mindset. A study conducted by Huefner, Hunt, and Robinson, looking at a comparison of four scales predicting entre-preneurship, confirmed the consistency of a high D-quadrant preference for entrepreneurs.[1]

Look more closely at the HBDI data, and you'll discover that the work elements ranking for all entrepreneurs reinforces their unique profile, showing the top six most-preferred to be, in descending order, problem solv-ing, expressing ideas, innovating, conceptualizing, interpersonal, and creative. This is distinctly different from the managerial data discussed in Chapter 20, where innovating and creative appear *in the bottom five*. Even for CEOs, inno-vating is lower, landing in the fifth spot, and creative is even lower, at ninth. This highlights the difference between entrepreneurs, who have a consistently high average preference in the D quadrant, and other key leaders.

So if you're an entrepreneur with the typical profile, the high average D-quadrant preference, combined with the work element preferences for inno-vating, conceptualizing, and creative, implies that you have ideas, concepts, and a vision of the future. You are also better suited to deal with risk and ambiguity, and probably are pretty optimistic about your chances for success (see Figure 25-1). These characteristics are what fuel an entrepreneur's energy, drive, and strong focus on the vision and the dream, often sustaining him or her when the going gets tough and the inevitable challenges arise in the start-up pro-cess. From a business perspective, however, the dark side of the entrepreneur's profile implies that he or she has (1) only a moderate level of interest and probable capability in the ratio-nal, analytic, and financial domain; (2) perhaps some knowledge of but not much energy for or even skill in business planning and details; and (3) limited perspective in recognizing that cer-tain other people may have to be involved in the

> You're going to fail, probably many times. But that's okay—In fact, it's essential. Very often, the differ-ence between success and fail-ure is simply perseverance.[2]
>
> —Arianna Huffington

venture. At the extreme, a typical entrepreneurial mentality is often: "Legal advice costs money I don't have, and since this is a low-risk venture, I don't believe I'll need a lawyer *or* a financial expert *or* a business planner *or* a human resource mentor."

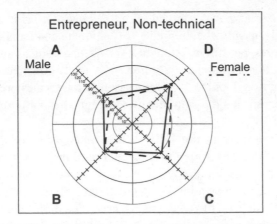

Entrepreneur, Non-technical

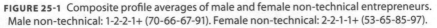

FIGURE 25-1 Composite profile averages of male and female non-technical entrepreneurs. Male non-technical: 1-2-2-1+ (70-66-67-91). Female non-technical: 2-2-1-1+ (53-65-85-97).

Our research and the study of successful entrepreneurs shows that you *do* need to supplement your strong preferred modes with additional interests and needed competencies—never forgetting the critical importance of those areas that may not be in your sweet spot, like legal or financial advice if you have a typical entrepreneurial profile.

If, on the other hand, you do not have a strong preference for the visionary, risk-oriented D quadrant, other challenges are likely to emerge.

Suppose your HBDI Profile is more oriented toward the B quadrant and its safekeeping thinking preferences (2-1-2-2)—the opposite of an entrepreneur's typical profile (see Figure 25-2). Case in point: Sarah had been persuaded by others that her idea was too good to pass up, so she went for it. But her preferences put up challenges. Along with her traditional and conservative approach to life, she was very focused on safety, security, and details to the point of wanting to have everything perfectly lined up and predictable. As a result, she wasn't able to have the big-picture view, a long-range vision that could serve as her guiding star. She struggled at every step along the path, and because she was so concerned about control and possible risk, her health started to suffer.

Sarah did not realize or see with clear objectivity that she would be "riding the brake" throughout her business's birth and infancy stages, creating enormous delay and frustration along the way. Ideally, Sarah needed to partner with a complementary thinker, an entrepreneur whose vision, enthusiasm, and risk orientation could carry her through the first few years of her business journey, but she ended up so frustrated and out of energy from trying to get everything "just right" prior to launch that she ended up dropping the project altogether.

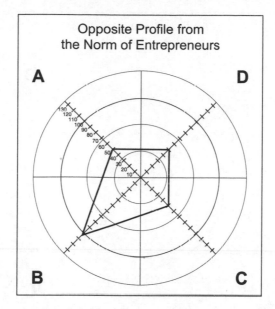

FIGURE 25-2 An atypical HBDI profile for an entrepreneur: The 2-1-2-2 profile.

Roxie, on the other hand, has a strong preference for the interpersonal C quadrant (2-2-1-2) (see Figure 25-3) and enthusiastically wanted to start her own consulting business. Roxie *loves* people, and her profile confirmed what she already knew: she really didn't know much about business, she'd never been good at organizing and planning, and her new business idea was much more of an urge than a concept—she had kind of "felt" that the business could be a real success. Roxie was an HBDI practitioner who had a very strong intuition that she could make a go of it, but she also recognized from her knowledge of Whole Brain Thinking that when she compared her profile to that of the occupational norm for an entrepreneur, there were significant differences. She knew that it would be risky for her to attempt to launch her business given her nonbusiness mentality, so she joined forces with a group of other consultants in her area, and as a result, they all benefited from the greater breadth of thinking and the support system that they needed to be successful.

Bryson, with a strong A-quadrant, technical-oriented preference (1-2-2-2), knew that he had a tiger by the tail (see Figure 25-4). A technical whiz, he had a business idea that was surely a winner. The logic of it was overwhelming. Bryson had analyzed the need and diagnosed the market potential, and he had a good handle on the needed finances. What he lacked was a solid business plan and a timeline for the new product's development. Missing the big-picture

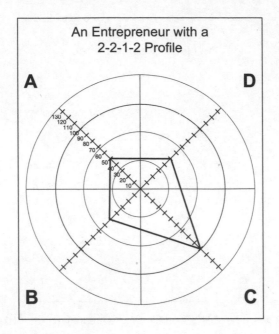

FIGURE 25-3 An entrepreneur with a strong C-quadrant orientation: The 2-2-1-2 profile.

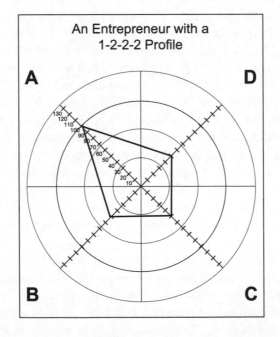

FIGURE 25-4 An A-quadrant entrepreneur with a 1-2-2-2 profile.

concept of where his proposed business could really go, Bryson's view had been extremely narrow, with essentially a tunnel-vision focus on just trying to get this thing built. But the weakest link in his business experience had to do with people: he simply wasn't interested in this critical aspect, and he felt it every time he needed to make a pitch or try to sell someone on the idea—people just weren't as interested in all the technical aspects as he was! Bryson ultimately got involved with the local start-up community, where he was able to build a team and get good advice on how best to get his product off the ground.

All of these aspiring businesspeople went for it, in spite of the predictable consequences of their particular coalition of mental preferences. The quest to have their own business was so strong that it overrode many of the inadequacies they might have felt along the way.

Since the statistics on business failures are so frightening, I believe that people who want to start their own business need to be absolutely objective about their own mental capability to undertake such a risk. So the first order of business is to understand themselves. The second order of business is to supplement their areas of low preference—which most frequently represent their lowest levels of established competence—by aligning with or bringing in people to provide those competencies. I've said it since Chapter 1: every business runs on thinking, and I'm convinced that starting and running a successful business is a Whole Brain activity. As my colleague Michael Morgan of Herrmann International Australia likes to say: "You can be in any business you like, but successful business requires Whole Brain Thinking." All four of the examples here needed to supplement their single-quadrant primary preferences with the other three.

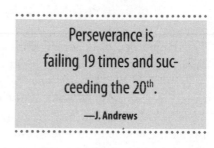

> **Perseverance is failing 19 times and succeeding the 20th.**
>
> —J. Andrews

> **The freedom to fail is vital if you're going to succeed. Most successful people fail time and time again, and it is a measure of their strength that failure merely propels them into some new attempt at success.**
>
> —Michael Korda

Imagine for a moment a four-person volleyball team in which only one of the players is really skilled in the game, while the other three are generally familiar with volleyball, but have played it only once or twice. This is an analogy or metaphor for the four selves (see Figure 3-1) that make up our mental capabilities. The business world requires four skilled players on each team. Without all four, not only are the chances of winning greatly decreased, but even staying in the game becomes a critical question.

You can supplement the three less-skilled players on your "team" in many ways. If your financial assets allow, you can hire them. One or two could be family members, or you can get the needed input from established contacts, such as bankers and lawyers. But there is another possible source. Remember Russell Means? Russell was successful because he understood his strengths and potential blind spots and planned around them, creatively using retired resources. What is most important is finding that breadth of thinking, no matter how and where you do it.

Thinking like an Entrepreneur

The unique nature of entrepreneurial thinking has been consistent over the last several decades. It is interesting to compare the current HBDI data analysis showing a very strong preference for D-quadrant thinking (2-2-2-1+) with the data from a study I conducted more than 30 years ago of 70 entrepreneurs who had attended the School for Entrepreneurs at the Tarrytown House and were participating in a reunion led by its founder, Bob Schwartz[3] the consistency of high D-quadrant preference among entrepreneurs is astounding. It is seldom that an occupational group has such a clearly defined norm. In my initial study, what struck me most was that all the profiles were within five or ten points of each of the quadrant scores making up the average. In interviews with these people, I discovered that almost all of them were currently successful, but that they *had failed at least once during their entrepreneurial career.*

> Entrepreneurship is business behavior resulting from a specialized form of thinking greatly influenced by an individual's D-quadrant mental preferences.
>
> —Ned Herrmann

Could aspiring entrepreneurs who have their strongest primaries in the A, B, or C quadrants succeed in an entrepreneurial venture? Based on all of our entrepreneurial research to date, I would have to say that these people would not be the best choice, as they would need to stretch far beyond their natural preferences in order to undertake a true entrepreneurial venture. This is not to say that someone with such a profile, especially if it is combined with a low D-quadrant score, could not make it, but it is clear to me that to succeed in a *true entrepreneurial situation* dealing with high-risk new products and unknown markets, it takes a very strong D-quadrant thinking preference to achieve the level of success that is funda-mental to entrepreneurial behavior. For those who don't naturally think that way, they must have a very strong motivation and drive to "up the D-quadrant game," something that is often accomplished by partnering with another entre-preneur and/or hiring one early in order to be truly entrepreneurial. Other alternatives might include joining an existing small business, own-ing a franchise, or scaling back the risks with a less ambitious business plan.

This explains what is often referred to as the "entrepreneurial bug." Entrepreneurs are inter-ested in the adventure, in the pursuit, in the chase of a business venture that has never actu-ally been launched in this unique way. It is not just the thrill of the investment risk; it is the need for the spirited chase of the personal dream. For

> My biggest moti-vation? Just to keep challeng-ing myself. I see life almost like one long University education that I never had—every day I'm learning something new.
>
> **—Sir Richard Branson**

these reasons, the strong, overriding D-quadrant mentality is almost essential to playing the role to the hilt (see Figure 25-5). No other strong quadrant pref-erence provides the needed ingredients for entrepreneurial behavior.

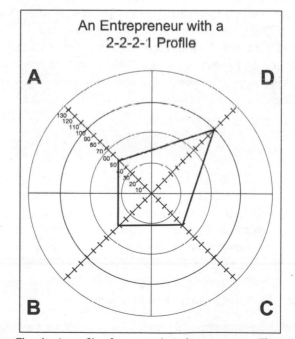

FIGURE 25-5 The classic profile of a non-technical entrepreneur: The 2-2-2-1 profile.

Of course, there are significant consequences to unleashing that behavior based upon a very strong, often single primary preference in the D quadrant. It would be typical of this mentality to want to continue "to entrepreneur," even though it was time to change gears and focus on building and delivering the product. This is frequently a fatal consequence of D-quadrant thinking that is not appropriately moderated by contributions from the A, B, and C quadrants. Entrepreneurs need to be smart enough to be aware of their own obsession and also to seek out objective advice and counsel regarding their stewardship of the entrepreneurial enterprise.

International management consultant Ichak Adizes describes the life cycles of a business from its "infancy" to its achieving of "prime."[4] As discussed in Chapter 15, during these growth stages, through infancy and adolescence, entrepreneurial thinking is almost always the key mentality required for success, but as the business matures and begins to enter a state of optimization and stability, the leadership style must change and the "obsessive" entrepreneurial behavior must stop, or the business will suffer and ultimately fail.

Most entrepreneurs are capable of shifting their mental processes if they become alert to the need to do so. The HBDI includes strong primaries (1), secondaries (2), and even low tertiaries (3). (For more information, refer to Appendix A in the back of the book.) Once they understand that their HBDI Profile also includes secondary preferences, they can shift by intentionally and *situationally* engaging those secondary preferences (and the resulting competencies) as the need for their primary entrepreneurial focus declines in the business. This requires a wake-up call of reality from their team, advisors, or consultants to effect the midcourse correction that they need to make in order to survive infancy and adolescence and achieve mature success. Even then, such a shift takes tremendous energy and focus for most entrepreneurs.

Put It to Work

Use the checklist provided in Figure 25-6 to think through whether or not you, a colleague, a friend, or a family member is ready to start up a business. If you are already started or have a small side business, use the checklist to ensure that you have all of your bases covered for the best results possible.

Engaging that team of diverse thinkers is critical. Here's one of the ways our colleague Joseph Kayne, former director of the Miami University Institute for Entrepreneurship and current CEO of the Imagine It Project, would highlight the importance to his students:[5]

At Miami University we used the HBDI to reinforce the value of diverse thinking preferences in an entrepreneurial venture. One exercise which drove this point home was class discussion around the question, "What would a new business look like if the entire senior management had a blue preference? Green preference? And so on." Regardless of the quadrant preference, students quickly realized a single-preference management team would be highly dysfunctional.

Whole Brain Checklist as You Consider a Start-Up Business

A Financial and Technology	Brand and Strategy D
• Do you have a business plan that specifies financial and operational goals by quarter and year? • What funding do you have/will you need for the first 12 months, assuming you get the revenue as you start? • How well can you understand and manage numbers? Who will help you? How do you avoid losing money? • What technology platforms do you need to build and maintain your bottom line (accounting, CRM, etc.)? • What products and services will you sell and at what margin? Distributor? Franchise? Consulting?	• What is your value proposition? Elevator speech? • Where do you want your business to be in three years? How will you get there with time/resource constraints? • What is your strategy for your personal brand so people know about your business? • In what ways can you WOW your customers with new marketing, offerings, and innovative ideas? • How can you use social media and technology (e.g., website) to build your brand quickly?
• What do you need to have in place to start your business (products, people, office space, equipment, clients, business name, corporate structure, legal, etc.)? • What is your marketing plan? How much time will you spend on marketing per week? • What and how will you deliver to customers and at what cost? How will you track those activities? • What systems and support do you need to ensure timely follow-through and execution? • What administrative support do you have? Should you have?	• How will you sell? How good are you at selling? • How can you best leverage the "relationship" credibility that you have with existing contacts to build customers? • What networks or associations can you join? • How can you reach out, build rapport, and stay in touch with contacts, customers, and prospects using social media and online connections? • Who can you partner with to help you grow your business and provide emotional support?
B Planning and Infrastructure	Sales and Customers C

FIGURE 25-6 Whole Brain Start-Up Checklist. Do you have what it takes?

In working with an entrepreneur who was so obsessed with his dream that he couldn't see it *not happen*, I found that the most effective way to demonstrate what was missing—and needed—for success was to help him understand how, without good counsel, financial issues could prevent him from achieving "the dream." We then arranged for a CPA he trusted to conduct a financial audit and share the results with all the key players in the enterprise. After reviewing the audit results, he developed a

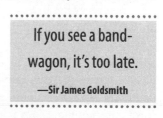

If you see a bandwagon, it's too late.

—Sir James Goldsmith

revised entrepreneurial statement of business objectives and passed it to all key personnel for their annotated comments. Next, working with the CPA, I helped the entrepreneur diagnose the audit results and the statement of business objectives using the four-quadrant model, testing for viability in each quadrant. With the help of the CPA and the team, we came to terms with each of the nonviable aspects of the business and then prepared a newly revised statement of business objectives that all concerned considered financially viable. This felt like a painful process at the time, but it provided an essential reality check that ultimately saved the business. It struck me at the time how little preparation most entrepreneurs really have as they embark on their journey.

Then, some years later, I was invited to attend Cornell University's Entrepreneurship and Personal Enterprise Celebration honoring M. Arthur Gensler as Cornell's Entrepreneur of the Year. I was surprised and pleased to discover that Cornell University had launched, with strong support from a group of inspired, entrepreneurially oriented alumni, a university-wide Entrepreneurship and Personal Enterprise (EPE) program. I was also intrigued to see a relatively large number of students from the College of Agriculture and Life Sciences, the Cornell Hotel School, and the Johnson Graduate School of Management in attendance, demonstrating that entrepreneurship can exist across many disciplines. The focus on entrepreneurship at Cornell continues today through Entrepreneurship at Cornell (ECA) and a wide range of programs and initiatives across all the colleges at Cornell.

The heart and soul of EPE depended on its advisory council of Cornell graduates, all of whom have a successful track record as entrepreneurs. They served as visiting faculty members and contributors to events like the one I participated in and had a direct interface with the students, who came from many colleges and schools throughout the university. It's an approach that is widely used in other programs today.

This integration of the active input from successful entrepreneurs with the academic aspects of entrepreneurial management and the essential business skills for successful personal enterprise into one multidiscipline program is, I believe,

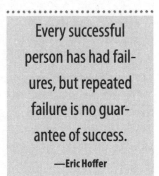

Every successful person has had failures, but repeated failure is no guarantee of success.

—Eric Hoffer

key to their success. Many schools have MBA programs and business courses, but until recently, it was rare to find schools that offered both undergraduate and graduate entrepreneurship programs like Cornell, Miami University in Ohio, Belmont University in Nashville, the University of St. Thomas in Minneapolis, Babson University in Boston, and the many, many others that now exist. Today, owing perhaps in part to the economy and in part to the changing interests and motivations of the new generations entering the workforce, entrepreneurship is one of the fastest-growing majors in the United States. In addition, "start-up institutes" and business incubators are popping up in cities across the world with the purpose of educating entrepreneurs and helping them establish and grow their businesses. What a break for the aspiring entrepreneur! I would love to go back to school and acquire the skills that I missed completely and had to learn the hard way. These programs make a real contribution to business education, and the HBDI is built into a number of them as a core component of the self-understanding required to navigate the entrepreneurial journey effectively.

Do You Really Want to Own a Business, or Are You Looking for Intrapreneurship?

For many people, the idea of being an entrepreneur often turns out to be more appealing than the reality of it. The term *entrepreneur* conjures up the image of an independent person with a unique product or service idea that is developed and brought to market by the wits, skill, energy, and risk taking of that highly motivated person. Many such businesses fail, although some, like Lazarus, rise from the ashes of defeat and ultimately succeed. In the Tarrytown School entrepreneur study, I learned that most of that group, even though they were now successful, had experienced failure one or more times. This is a typical trait of entrepreneurs and implies a level of motivation to succeed that overrides trouble along the way and is often so strong that it could be described as an obsession. They have caught the "entrepreneurial bug" and usually will not be satisfied until the business idea has been fully explored. The typical entrepreneur is almost always working outside of any formal company organization, unless it's a company that he or she personally owns. If that's the case, the entrepreneur has freedom of action that doesn't exist inside an organization—freedom to take risks without justifying them and to fail without the usual organizational consequences. But what about those who wish to be or need to be entrepreneurial inside an organization? Today, "entrepreneurial thinking" is showing up more frequently on desired leadership competency lists. In just one example, a large, global multinational's competency list recently specified, "Lead with an entrepreneurial mindset."

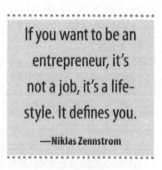

If you want to be an entrepreneur, it's not a job, it's a lifestyle. It defines you.

—Niklas Zennstrom

The word *intrapreneur* was coined by Gifford Pinchot III,[6] who was associated at the time with Robert Schwartz at the Tarrytown School for Entrepreneurs. By *intrapreneur*, Pinchot meant an individual who was functioning in an entrepreneurial way *within* an organization. The concept is great, but the intrapreneur's circumstances are very different because, unlike the entrepreneur, the intrapreneur is tied to an organization that has a climate, culture, leadership, policies, budgets, audit procedures, *and* supervising management. In every sense, it almost always reeks of political complexity and fear of risk, and it often has a bureaucracy. Catching the entrepreneurial bug and going it alone is not often possible under these conditions. In most cases, the reality is that others who have managerial decision-making authority are also involved in the intrapreneurial project. The true classic entrepreneur would never buy into this situation. The conditions are too limiting for freedom of action, and freedom of action is a requirement for entrepreneurialism.

If the organization wants to develop a climate that supports risk taking and freedom of action, then the process might work. However, my experience tells me that in order for the intrapreneur to be able to function in an entrepreneurial manner, his or her mentality and that of the sponsor need to be in very good alignment. My personal belief is that it takes a high-level champion who thinks like an entrepreneur to create intrapreneurial protective "air cover." We don't have a thinking preferences norm for intrapreneurs because this is not an occupational title. If it were, I have reason to believe that the norm for intrapreneurs would be generally similar to the profile for entrepreneurs, so the opportunity for organizations is to find these thinkers and provide them with the air cover they need if they are to survive.

However, I *do* see a catch-22. Most entrepreneurs don't want to have anything to do with constraining structures or bureaucracies. They don't want to have anything to do with people looking over their shoulder. They don't want to have anything to do with externally imposed financial constraints. In general, they don't want to have anything to do with rules, procedures, policies, audits, and strict reporting relationships.

Years ago, I talked to Gifford Pinchot at length about his concept of intrapreneurship and argued the points that I've just made. His idea is very appealing, of course, and under the right circumstances, it can be applied successfully. And when it succeeds, it is wonderful. Resources do exist. The League of Intrapreneurs[7] is one example, providing tips, support mechanisms, and ideas for intrapreneurs.

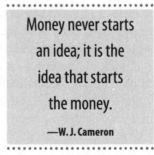

Money never starts an idea; it is the idea that starts the money.

—W. J. Cameron

Under the right circumstances, it is possible to have successful intrapreneurs. I was an intrapreneur within GE for five years before I left the company and became an entrepreneur. Much of what I have described in this book, including the Whole Brain concept, the Herrmann Brain Dominance Instrument, and their application to teaching, learning, creativity, and innovation were all developed while I was an employee of General Electric.

During the high-risk developmental phase of this technology, I was given the necessary air cover by my direct boss, Lindon Saline, and his financial manager, Dave Dickson, and also by the senior vice president and the CEO. However, there were several high-level managers, including another senior vice president, who felt that what I was doing was not in any way aligned with General Electric's business operations and was therefore inappropriate. Because of the air cover my champions provided me, along with my own wits and ingenuity and the quality of my ideas, I not only survived but succeeded. In a win-win arrangement, I partnered with GE through the infancy stage of my entrepreneurial endeavors and the starting of my own company, with GE sending participants to my creativity workshops, a process that benefited the organization's ongoing efforts to build creative problem-solving skills. GE also used me as a consultant in the area of cognitive diversity as I made the transition out of my role.

While I love the idea of intrapreneurship, there are potentially severe personal consequences from playing that role or serving as a champion for others. It takes good ideas, high motivation, guts, and a thick skin—a true entrepreneurial spirit. A golden parachute also helps!

Building Entrepreneurial Thinking as a Core Competency

For organizations that truly wish to encourage entrepreneurial thinking, the challenge is no less daunting. First, they need to make sure that they understand what entrepreneurial thinking actually entails and not just pay lip service to it. Creating a clear definition is the first step. Next, it is crucial that they focus on the outcomes they hope it will produce: new product ideas, additional opportunities with customers, internal process improvement ideas, and so on. Then it is vital that they put in place the necessary thinking skills—through training and development as well as through project work that allows those skills to be applied. Many companies try hiring people who bring an entrepreneurial mindset with them, but the risk is that if the company lacks the requisite climate, those hires will leave in frustration. Another approach is to seek out those employees who may be natural entrepreneurs but are using those skills outside of the organization and provide them with the air cover they need to bring their ideas inside.

Finally, and most important, doing a full audit of what is really required in terms of climate and leadership to support those efforts is essential! Entrepreneurial thinking is available—but be careful what you ask for! Once it is unleashed, it has terrific power.

SO WHAT?

> People who start businesses need to know their own strengths and weaknesses first so that they can then seek out complementary skills in internal or external advisors.
> Many entrepreneurs share a common profile, with a strong preference for D-quadrant-oriented, visionary, risk-driven thinking.
> The dark side of that profile is that the other three quadrants of needed business interests and competencies are usually inadequate or missing.
> Business is a Whole Brain activity. Therefore, the chance of start-up success increases when interest and competency in all four quadrants are available in the leadership role.
> Those who are interested in being internal entrepreneurs, or intrapreneurs, can succeed, but they require air cover by a senior champion and a very strong motivation to successfully navigate the cultural roadblocks they are likely to encounter along the way.
> Organizations that seek to build entrepreneurial thinking as a core competency should make a commitment to build the climate and leadership willingness to support it, or it will not succeed.

"The computer says I need to upgrade my brain to be compatible with the new software."

CHAPTER 26

Breaking Down the Barriers to Whole Brain Growth

CHAPTER HIGHLIGHTS

> When it comes to growth, people change when there is a reason for them to do so, and most of us have about a 70 percent chance of changing if the conditions are right.
> Whole Brain Thinking can help change be positive for all concerned.
> While other people are involved in the change process, self-motivation is often the key to successful change.

As much as I know about the need to stretch mentally, I, too, had to face a challenge. As I went through the process of increasing my use of technology and computers, I became more aware of the walls that I had built up over the years. When it came to making more effective use of the technology tools that I had available, these walls got in the way. I had become so accustomed to my way of working and was so sensitive to avoiding systems that required me to learn a different language, rules, and processes that I found myself becoming exasperated by operating systems that required you to follow, in detail, the platform's proprietary process steps. If you didn't know the next step and did not comply, you'd be stuck—so I'd find myself either just sitting there or ending up someplace I hadn't expected to be. It was maddening. I would become irritated, even incensed, by the often counterintuitive processes that were required in order to perform seemingly straightforward tasks. Once I had mastered one of these tasks, it seemed that I then had to change to a new operating system! It all seemed like too much effort! Over the course of nearly 60 years, I had erected walls that prevented me from building the facility I needed and wanted in my technology usage. I was trying, in essence, to speak in a language I'd never learned.

One night I observed my grandchildren, Chris, Karim, and Selim, doing their homework on their computers. They weren't bothered at all by the technology—in fact, it was helpful to them. I suppose a major reason is they had had neither the time nor the inclination to build walls before they started learning how to use the various systems they interacted with. Because they had never known another way, they did not have the annoyance of learning a new way to get the results they were looking for, and so there was no fear or irritation getting in the way of their accomplishing their task. From texting to social media to new apps and devices, it was all intriguing and miraculous, and they quickly adapted to and adopted them.

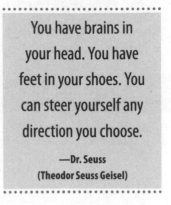

You have brains in your head. You have feet in your shoes. You can steer yourself any direction you choose.

—Dr. Seuss
(Theodor Seuss Geisel)

One conclusion is that walls are a great deal easier to build than they are to tear down. But walls are not likely to be built at all if the pathway to successful outcomes is magical, intriguing, and fun. It's clear that the newest technical pathways that emerge almost every day are much more readily available to children than they are to adults. That's why children can program a brand-new phone without hesitation, while we get frustrated, and may even give up, especially if it is a different operating system than we are used to. I would surmise that much of the world's adult population is easily frustrated by the counterintuitive procedures that are built into so many of the products they try to use. Children, on the other hand, have not developed barriers to making these new, often complex, but useful devices work. Apparently, to children and young adults, the means justify the ends. For many adults, the means prevent the ends from ever happening. Whether it is tackling a new type of tablet, learning how to fly a drone, or installing a high-tech new remote smart system for your home, it all requires learning—and that means change.

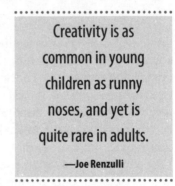

Creativity is as common in young children as runny noses, and yet is quite rare in adults.

—Joe Renzulli

Can People Change?

Can people change? Yes. But it's not always easy, as we discussed in Chapter 19. Most of us are largely a result of what's happened to us. Converting that to percentages, it is my belief, from years of pondering this issue, that on the average, about 70 percent of who we are is the result of nurture—what we have experienced—rather than nature. Of course, in the final analysis, it must be both nature and nurture. But if my theory is right, most of us have about a 70 percent chance of changing *if the conditions are right*. Even if you consider what much of the current academic thinking on nature versus nurture suggests—a 50/50 split—that is still a message of hope! There are many circumstances under which the conditions for change can be right. Here is a list of what I think are the most important instigators for change:

1. The individual wants to change.
2. The individual's job changes radically.
3. The individual becomes a parent.
4. The individual undergoes a significant values shift because of a life-changing experience.
5. The individual experiences significant learning.
6. The individual loses a job and must find a new one.
7. The individual is being mentored or coached.

This is just a sampling of the many reasons why people might change. But for this section, let's look just at businesspeople and the role that Whole Brain Thinking can play in bringing about needed change in several common business situations.

> Nothing in progression can rest on its original plan. We might as well think of rocking a grown man in the cradle of an infant.
>
> —Edmund Burke

When Overcoming Mental Blind Spots

There are plenty of developmental opportunities offered throughout the world. There are resources that will provide almost anything that you might want, from technical training to creativity training, leadership training, empathy training, organization development, and other types of business training across all functions. Essentially, whatever your need is, there will be books, blogs, apps, videos, other online content, programs, or activities available. A first step in the process is that individuals need to be motivated to seek out these materials and find the time and energy to experience them.

In my own case, I revealed a lower preference in the C-quadrant feeling area, so I took five weekend seminars offered by the Esalen Institute, located in Big Sur, California. These experiences helped me become comfortable in my own skin with my feelings and more effective in my interpersonal relationships. They allowed me to become less inhibited and more open and imaginative. Not only was I a better person for it, but I was more effective in my work.

I think most people instinctively know when they have a deficit in their array of thinking options, and I also believe that many people want to fill that deficit with useful forms of mental processing. For many people, it's uncomfortable to be "incomplete." Often this feeling of incompleteness can be partially satisfied through marriage or partnership, where we seek out a partner who complements us. But for those of us who truly want to develop ourselves, the feeling of completeness is internal. For example, like me, there are people who may realize that they are avoiding dealing with emotional issues; they aren't letting their feelings come to the surface in a relationship, in a conversation, or in a business situation. I became so intrigued with the techniques and processes used by the Esalen Institute that I talked about those experiences with my family, my business associates, and my direct reports. They were all fascinated. In retrospect, I discovered that my talking about emotions, feelings, and interpersonal relationships had helped break down the walls that had been built up during my adolescence and went a long way toward freeing me from those self-imposed and self-limiting beliefs and constraints.

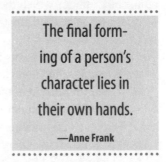

The final forming of a person's character lies in their own hands.

—Anne Frank

When High Unemployment, Downsizing, or Layoffs Occur

Being downsized or laid off is another issue that all too many businesspeople are facing during these times of downturns, reorganizations, and organizational flattening. Under those circumstances, or perhaps straight out of school, suddenly you are in the job market, and the particular job for which you have the most skills is not one that other companies are seeking to fill. This is when an objective understanding of your mental preferences, competencies, and mental options becomes not only a key to self-awareness, but also a key to finding the next job. The self-understanding that can come from knowing your thinking preferences allows you to map your current qualifications and also to locate your areas of needed competencies. When these needed competencies are in mental alignment with your existing competencies and preferences, you have a clear path to achievable self-development. When the opportunities you are trying to pursue are not in alignment with your existing preferences and competencies, great motivation is required to acquire them, and the likelihood of expert-level success is substantially reduced.

I recall the story of a woman who had been laid off from her job as an HR partner. The role had changed—it had become strategic, and thus out of alignment with her preferences and skills, which were much more tactical—to such an extent that her performance was marginal and her job fulfillment unacceptable. We all know people who've experienced this. But the trauma of being laid off can turn out to be an opportunity—to find work that is a much better fit and can ultimately lead a person to greater success and substantially more job fulfillment and personal satisfaction.

Our experience demonstrates that the likelihood of this happening is greatly improved if the person knows his or her preferences and the associated strengths and weaknesses as they translate into job capabilities—the person can then pursue the strengths with renewed confidence. A process developed by our partners in France called Snapshot (Photo-Competences) was originally developed for a large corporate assessment center that sought to provide better guidance for employee development. It builds off the individual's HBDI preference data, comparing it to the HBDI job profile and the HBDI proforma profile of the person's desired growth path. This is particularly useful when you're at a point in your life where the door is open to becoming more aligned with the work that stimulates you most, and you are seeking development opportunities that are in alignment with those preferences. This strategy breaks the nonaligned cycle of the past, in which you may have ended up in work you didn't really like to do and from which you derived little satisfaction. Life is too short to perpetuate this mismatch.

When New Learning Takes Place

Another key basis for change is experiencing a significant new learning. Take the all-too-common case of a person who has never managed before and has been promoted into a management position because of his or her technical competence rather than his or her management qualifications. This happens all the time in sales and other functions. In the case of TJ, a combination of excellent management education and mentoring enabled him to become a knowledgeable, skilled management practitioner. He knew that a significant change was taking place, and his most important feedback came from his direct reports, his peers, and the leader to whom he reported. The combined learning from academic courses, mentoring, and coaching transformed him from someone who managed by instinct to someone who now understood the work of managing and had developed the skills to perform the role effectively. In addition to a measurable shift in TJ's thinking, there was also an

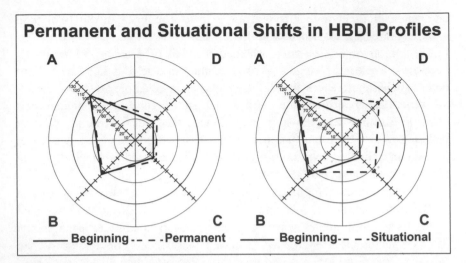

Permanent and Situational Shifts in HBDI Profiles

FIGURE 26-1 HBDI Profiles: Two types of change. Permanent and situational shifts in profiles.

essential new capability, that of being situationally responsive to daily managerial requirements.

I am describing two different kinds of change. One is a relatively permanent shift in preference toward the quadrant direction of the learning enlightenment. This is possible, but it requires a shift in values, so it's less frequent. The second aspect of change is the increased flexibility of responding for brief periods of time via mental domains that are not primary preferences but are now more available situationally as the work requires (see Figure 26-1).

When Values Shift

Next, consider an individual who has undergone a significant shift in values. The cause might have been recovering from a major illness, escaping a serious accident, having a child, or losing a dear friend or a spouse. Whatever the reason, the person has been affected so significantly that his or her values are now different. A specific example is when my daughter Ann had her children. Having these young and fragile new family members suddenly shifted her focus to a caring, stable, and more traditional approach to life. Her worldview had changed significantly, and because of that, so did her HBDI Profile and behavior.

Value shifts at this level can change the way people think and therefore change what they want to do and how they want to do it. Most of us can cite personal examples of people we know or have read about. My point is that these changes do happen—sometimes unplanned—and they usually show up as a dramatic change in the person's profile. How to put these shifts in values, interests, and priorities to work is a question that is worth considering. (For more on the relationship between values and thinking preferences, download the bonus chapter, "Your Hidden 'Owner's Manual': A Whole Brain Approach to Personal Values," at www.wholebrainbusinessbook.com.)

When a values shift causes a job mismatch, corrective action is called for. It is up to the individual to take that action. I am convinced that most of us know more about our jobs than anybody else, including our managers, and most of us have a great deal more freedom of action than we have thus far claimed. Therefore:

1. Where we have freedom of action, we should make changes in our job to bring it into better alignment with our current mental preferences and those activities that both stimulate us and fulfill the job requirements.

2. Where we don't have freedom of action, we should bring the proposed changes to the attention of our manager and persuade him or her that it's in the best interests of all concerned to make them.

3. If we are the manager, we should make use of our own freedom of action to foster those changes by encouraging our employees to better align themselves with their work and by granting them the freedom to act more independently in making those adjustments.

> There was an old man who began an orchard upon his retirement. Why plant trees? They told him he would never live to see a mature crop. He planted anyway and he has seen them blossom and has eaten their fruit. We all need that type of optimism.
>
> —Deng Ming-Dao

I see this as a win-win-win scenario: it's a win for the person, it's a win for the manager, and it's a win for the company because a better-aligned employee is going to be more productive and more fulfilled on the job. This is what managers are supposed to do anyway. But by taking advantage of change, we are finding ways for the employees to help managers achieve their bottom-line goals.

Put It to Work

As we discussed in Chapter 19, our mindsets will get in the way of growth and any needed change; unless they are addressed correctly, they will stop any change from taking place. Applying Whole Brain Thinking is a good way to start breaking down the walls around your mindset, to better enable you to change. Start by thinking about some of the walls you've built over the years, walls that need to come down in order for you to grow.

Define and analyze it. What are these walls, and what mindset(s) do they come from? (A quadrant.)

- What is the current mindset that is shaping your thinking and creating these walls?
- What are some of the recent decisions you've made that might have been influenced by this mindset, and that would have been better served by another approach?
- In what specific ways do these walls represent a barrier to change for you?

Challenge it. Why are you holding on to this mindset, and why haven't you let go of it? (D quadrant.)

- What are the potential blind spots that this mindset and these walls create?
- Have these walls become self-fulfilling prophecies? How can you change your mindset around them to see things differently?
- What will be your biggest fears and challenges in breaking down the walls?
- What will be your greatest opportunities and wins if you explore a new mindset?

Sense it. How do I and others feel about it? (C quadrant.)

- How do your feelings and emotions support and fuel this mindset?
- How is your current mindset different from those of other people who do not seem to have these walls?
- Who can you talk with to gain greater confidence and clarity concerning the situation at hand?
- Who can help you look at things differently from the way you normally do, mentor you, and provide needed affirmation and support in this situation?

Develop a plan. Am I ready to change, and, if so, how? (B quadrant.)

- What would it take for you to change this mindset and break down these walls?
- What are some low-cost, low-risk ways of getting started to test what this change will be like?
- How will your preferences affect the process and make this easier or harder? How can you leverage or mitigate those effects?
- What are some of the other mindsets and approaches that you have seen work for others that you might adopt and use in the process?
- What will success look like? When and how will you get started?

As the Greek philosopher Heraclitus said, "Nothing endures but change." It is the one thing that we can absolutely predict will happen. This cannot be more true than in the world of business. The good news is that through an understanding of how you and others think, and with the application of Whole Brain Thinking, you can ride the wave of change to greater levels of success: for you, for your team, and for your organization. It's up to you.

SO WHAT?

> Resources for facilitating change are available around the world. These include schools, developmental institutes, courses, books, online resources, MOOCs and webinars, and mentors and coaches.
> Changes that bring individuals into better alignment with their work are often win-win-win: a win for the individuals, a win for the manager, and a win for the company.
> When motivated, individuals can and should develop skills in areas of lesser preference in order to be more effective and deal with their blind spots.
> Whole Brain Thinking provides a good starting point for breaking down the barriers to change.

Afterword

"On Mondays, I get ready to plan my week.
On Tuesdays, I plan my week. On Wednesdays,
I revise my plan for the week. On Thursdays, I put
my plan for the week into my computer. On Fridays,
I think about starting my plan for next week."

"This stuff works."

It's the comment that we hear almost daily from practitioners, business-people, learning professionals, and others. It works.

While advances in technology and new discoveries about the brain are continuing at an incredibly rapid pace, the point that matters most is this: How can you apply what we know about the brain and business to make a difference in the way you manage your attention, approach your work, communicate, solve problems, and lead? Because, without application, there's not much business value.

So how *will* you apply what you've learned? After all, you're the only one who can decide how to better leverage your own brain and the thinking that others provide. Each chapter in this book included a "Put It to Work" section. That's a great place to start. You can also go online to www.wholebrainbusinessbook.com to find additional activities and resources that expand on and supplement what you've learned here, Another way to tap into and build collective intelligence is to connect with other readers on the book's LinkedIn, Facebook, Twitter, and Pinterest pages to find ways they are applying Whole Brain Thinking, and to share your own.

It's up to you. Think about the key points you learned in this book and decide how *you* will apply them to get better business results:

- **Recognizing, adapting, and applying all of the thinking resources available within you, your team, and your organization.** This will increase your capacity!
- **The relationship between preferences, competencies, job satisfaction, work alignment, and performance.** Understanding this will help you better manage your own performance and that of others.
- **The consequences of both your preferences and the areas that you least prefer.** Watch for those blind spots!
- **The benefits of cognitive diversity and what it takes to leverage it.** How are you leveraging it on your teams?
- **How thinking preferences affect your communications, management style, work processes, and interactions—as well as your effectiveness with people who think like you and those who think differently.** The bottom line is that when you connect with someone in the way that best suits that person, you gain speed and effectiveness. Who doesn't need more of that?
- **The thinking patterns of leadership and why situational wholeness is so critical in today's complex world.** In what ways can you better stretch your thinking to be the best leader you can be? Start today!
- **Your own creative potential and that of those you work with.** There are thinking processes involved in getting business benefit from creativity. Why wait? You can benefit from untapped potential and get better engagement!
- **Your ability to stretch, build skills, learn, and grow even in the areas that are uncomfortable for you.** Only you are in control of this, and your brain is your secret sauce. What can you do every day to taste that growth and build your brainpower?

This book has given you a lot to think about but, more important, a lot to do.

Your journey begins here. Get started now putting Whole Brain Thinking to work—because it works.

www.wholebrainbusinessbook.com

Profile Scores and Preference Codes

PREFERENCE CODE: This consists of four numbers placed in order of the quadrants: ABCD. The terms "Primary, Secondary, and Tertiary" are used to designate the 1 (prefer), 2 (use), and 3 (use least) zones of the profile grid.

	A	B	C	D
Preference Code:	1	3	2	1
Profile Score:	83	32	60	110

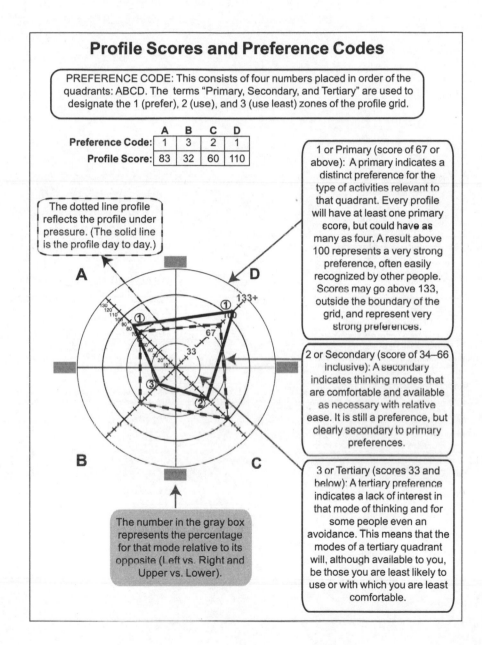

1 or Primary (score of 67 or above): A primary indicates a distinct preference for the type of activities relevant to that quadrant. Every profile will have at least one primary score, but could have as many as four. A result above 100 represents a very strong preference, often easily recognized by other people. Scores may go above 133, outside the boundary of the grid, and represent very strong preferences.

The dotted line profile reflects the profile under pressure. (The solid line is the profile day to day.)

2 or Secondary (score of 34–66 inclusive): A secondary indicates thinking modes that are comfortable and available as necessary with relative ease. It is still a preference, but clearly secondary to primary preferences.

3 or Tertiary (scores 33 and below): A tertiary preference indicates a lack of interest in that mode of thinking and for some people even an avoidance. This means that the modes of a tertiary quadrant will, although available to you, be those you are least likely to use or with which you are least comfortable.

The number in the gray box represents the percentage for that mode relative to its opposite (Left vs. Right and Upper vs. Lower).

Notes

Chapter 2

1. R. W. Sperry, "Bridging Science and Values: A Unifying View of Mind and Brain," *American Psychologist* 32, no. 4 (1977).
2. R. E. Ornstein, *The Psychology of Consciousness* (New York: Harcourt Brace Jovanovich, 1977).
3. P. D. MacLean and V. A. Kral, *A Triune Concept of the Brain and Behaviour* (Toronto: published for the Ontario Mental Health Foundation by University of Toronto Press, 1973).
4. http://www.humanconnectomeproject.org/.
5. http://www.whitehouse.gov/share/brain-initiative.
6. D. Goleman, *Emotional Intelligence* (New York: Bantam Books, 1995); D. Goleman, *Working with Emotional Intelligence* (New York: Bantam Books, 1998); D. Goleman, *Social Intelligence: The New Science of Human Relationships* (New York: Bantam Books, 2006).
7. C. M. Christensen, M. B. Horn, and C. W. Johnson, *Disrupting Class: How Disruptive Innovation Will Change the Way the World Learns* (New York: McGraw-Hill, 2008).

Chpater 4

1. C. Heath and D. Heath, *Made to Stick: Why Some Ideas Survive and Others Die* (New York: Random House, 2007).
2. B. Keysar, S. L. Hayakawa, and S. G. An, "The Foreign-Language Effect: Thinking in a Foreign Tongue Reduces Decision Biases," *Psychological Science* 23, no. 6: 661–668, January 1, 2012.
3. F. Herzberg, *One More Time: How Do You Motivate Employees?* (Boston: Harvard Business Press, 2008).
4. D. H. Pink, *Drive: The Surprising Truth About What Motivates Us* (New York: Riverhead Books, 2009).

Chapter 5

1. D. Leonard and S. Straus, "Putting Your Company's Whole Brain to Work," *Harvard Business Review*, July/August 1997.
2. E. Lumsdaine, M. Lumsdaine, B. J. Clark, and M. Luhrs, *Creative Problem Solving: Thinking Skills for a Changing World* (New York: McGraw-Hill, 1994).
3. A. W. Woolley, T. W. Malone, C. Chabris, A. Pentland, and N. Hashmi, "New Study by Carnegie Mellon, MIT and Union College Shows Collective Intelligence of Groups Exceeds Cognitive Abilities of Individual Group Members," press release, October 2010.

Chapter 6

1. Henry Mintzberg, "Plan on the Left, Manage on the Right," *Harvard Business Review*, July/August 1976.
2. Howard Gardner, "Frequently Asked Questions—Multiple Intelligences and Related Educational Topics," 2014, http://howardgardner.com/faq/.
3. D. Goleman, *Emotional Intelligence* (New York: Bantam Books, 1995); D. Goleman, *Working with Emotional Intelligence* (New York: Bantam Books, 1998); D. Goleman, *Social Intelligence: The New Science of Human Relationships* (New York: Bantam Books, 2006); D. Goleman, *Ecological Intelligence: How Knowing the Hidden Impacts of What We Buy Can Change Everything* (New York: Broadway Books, 2009).

Chapter 7

1. J. Hunt, J. P. Garant, H. Herman, and D. J. Munroe, "Why Are Women Underrepresented Amongst Patentees?," *Research Policy* 42, no. 4: 831–843, May 1, 2013.

Chapter 8

1. J. Gray, *Men Are from Mars, Women Are from Venus: A Practical Guide for Improving Communication and Getting What You Want in Your Relationships* (New York: HarperCollins, 1992).

Chapter 9

1. D. H. Pink, *Drive: The Surprising Truth About What Motivates Us* (Edinburgh: Canongate, 2010).
2. G. M. Bellmann, *Getting Things Done When You Are Not in Charge*, 2nd ed. (San Francisco: Berrett-Koehler Publishers, 2001).

Chapter 10

1. A. H. Maslow, "A Theory of Human Motivation," *Psychological Review* 50, no. 4: 370–396 (1943).

Chapter 11

1. A. de Boer, P. du Toit, D. Scheepers, and T. Bothma, *Whole Brain Learning in Higher Education: Evidence-Based Practice*, Chandos Learning and Teaching Series (Oxford, UK: Chandos Publishing, 2013).
2. F. Coffield, and Learning and Skills Research Centre, *Learning Styles and Pedagogy in Post-16 Learning* (London: Learning and Skills Research Centre, 2004).
3. C. S. Dweck, *Mindset: The New Psychology of Success* (New York: Random House, 2006), https://web.stanford.edu/dept/psychology/cgi-bin/drupalm/cdweck; A. Herrmann-Nehdi, "In Practice, Learning Lessons from IBM," *Chief Learning Officer* 9, no. 6 (2010), http://www.clomedia.com/.
4. Lewis Lubin, executive coach, president of Lubin Executive Coaching, Berkeley, CA, "The Importance of Coaching New Leaders," *Career Convergence*, February 2010, https://www.right.com/thought-leadership/articles-and-

publications/the-importance-of-coaching-new-leaders-ndcas-career-convergence-web-magazine.pdf.

5. Lynne Krauss, chief innovation officer, BBTD Services Inc., Brain Based Training & Development, http://www.bbtdinc.com/About_Us.html.

6. M. Elkind, Mindtech, Inc., http://www.mindtech3.com/home/home.html.

Chapter 12

1. Charles DeRidder and Mark A. Wilcox, "How to Improve Group Productivity. Whole Brain Teams Set New Benchmarks," Herrmann International Case Study, http://www.herrmannsolutions.com/balance-of-thinking-improves-team-effectiveness/.

2. J. R. Katzenbach and D. K. Smith, *The Wisdom of Teams: Creating the High-Performance Organization* (Boston: Harvard Business School Press, 1993).

3. Fred Keeton, vice president of external affairs and CDO at Caesars Entertainment, http://www.diversitybestpractices.com/person/fred-keeton; http://www.diversityjournal.com/319-fred-keeton-caesars-entertainment-corp/.

4. D. Leonard and S. Straus, "Putting Your Company's Whole Brain to Work," *Harvard Business Review*, July/August 1997.

Chapter 13

1. Tiffany McMacken, senior manager, sales training and development, Purdue Pharma.

2. D. H. Pink, *To Sell Is Human: The Surprising Truth About Moving Others* (New York: Riverhead Books, 2012).

3. Dr. Tony Alessandra, professional keynote speaker, Alessandra & Associates Inc., http://www.alessandra.com/tahome.asp.

4. Chuck McVinney, owner, McVinney & Co., Facilitating Executive Teams, http://www.mcvinney.com/index.html; Charles Leiserson, professor of computer science and engineering, Massachusetts Institute of Technology, http://web.mit.edu/professional/short-programs/courses/engineering_leadership_skills.html.

5. "Kinect Adventures: Product Development for a Whole-Brain World," Herrmann International Case Study, 2013, http://www.herrmannsolutions.com/kinect-adventures-product-development-for-a-whole-brain-world/.

6. "How Telecom New Zealand Used Whole Brain Thinking to Turn Call Centers into Customer Loyalty Generators," Herrmann International Case Study, 2012, http://www.herrmannsolutions.com/saving-time-and-money-at-telecom-new-zealands-call-centers/.

Chapter 14

1. R. Charan, S. J. Drotter, and J. L. Noel, *The Leadership Pipeline: How to Build the Leadership-Powered Company* (San Francisco: Jossey-Bass, 2001).

2. CLP India, "Powering Growth Through a Culture of Whole Brain Thinking," Herrmann International Case Study, 2013, http://www.herrmannsolutions.com/clp-india-powering-growth-through-a-culture-of-whole-brain-thinking/.

3. Rich DeSerio, "How IBM Develops Managers for a Complex World," Herrmann International, 2013, http://www.hbdi.com/brainbytes/nov_13.html.
4. M. Morgan, http://www.herrmannsolutions.asia/au/content/about-us.
5. T. J. Peters and R. H. Waterman, In Search of Excellence: Lessons from America's Best-Run Companies (New York: Harper & Row, 1982).

Chapter 15

1. http://www.sba.gov/sites/default/files/FAQ_March_2014_0.pdf.
2. "Cookie Time: How Whole Brain Thinking helped Cookie Time Renew Its Recipe for Success," Herrmann International Case Study, 2010–2015, http://www.herrmannsolutions.com/cookie-time-whole-brain-thinking-drives-a-business-and-cultural-transformation/.
3. A. H. Maslow, "A Theory of Human Motivation," *Psychological Review* 50, no. 4: 370–396 (1943).

Chapter 16

1. H. Mintzberg, "Plan on the Left, Manage on the Right," *Harvard Business Review*, July/August 1976.
2. Chuck McVinney, owner, McVinney & Co., Facilitating Executive Teams, www.chuckmcvinney.com.
3. Ayn Fox, founding coach, Empower Parties, http://www.empowerparties.com/Ayn-Fox-bio.aspx.

Chapter 17

1. Ann McGee-Cooper, founder and partner, Ann McGee-Cooper & Associates, http://amca.com/; Duane Trammell, president and COO, Ann McGee-Cooper & Associates, http://amca.com/.
2. Paul Gustavson, president, Organization Planning and Design, Inc., author of *Running into the Wind. The Power of Living by Design*, and *A Team of Leaders*: P. Gustavson and A. Von Feldt, *Running into the Wind: Bronco Mendenhall: 5 Strategies for Building a Successful Team* (Salt Lake City, UT: Shadow Mountain, 2012); T. Ward and P. Gustavson, *The Power of Living by Design* (n.p.: FriesenPress, 2013); P. Gustavson and S. Liff, *A Team of Leaders: Empowering Every Member to Take Ownership, Demonstrate Initiative, and Deliver Results* (New York: AMACOM, 2014).
3. HBDI practitioners Robert Webber, Colin Pidd, and David Clancy, "Westpac Bank and Challenge Bank: A Whole Brain M&A Process," Herrmann International Case Study, 2010–2015, http://www.herrmannsolutions.com/westpac-bank-and-challenge-bank-a-whole-brain-process-yields-mergers-acquisitions-success/.
4. Ibid.

Chapter 18

1. D. Myburgh, E. Seville, and C. Webb, "Effective Decision Making and the Disaster Recovery Phase," *Business Continuity and Resiliency Journal* 1, no. 4 (2012), Continuity Central.http://www.herrmannsolutions.com/articleeffective-decision-making-in-the-disaster-recovery-phase/.

Chapter 19

1. A. Deutschman and E. Miller, *Change or Die: The Three Keys to Change at Work and in Life* (New York: Regan, 2007).
2. Cynthia Radford, principal, GreenLeaf Consulting International, leadership development consultant, http://www.greenleafconsulting.com/aboutcynthia.htm.
3. D. Kahneman, *Thinking, Fast and Slow* (New York: Farrar, Straus and Giroux, 2011).
4. M. Holloway and M. Merzenich, "The Mutable Brain," *Scientific American*, 2003.
5. C. S. Dweck, *Mindset: The New Psychology of Success* (New York: Random House, 2006), https://web.stanford.edu/dept/psychology/cgi-bin/drupalm/cdweck.
6. Chuck McVinney, owner, McVinney & Co., Facilitating Executive Teams, www.chuckmcvinney.com.
7. E. Kübler-Ross (1926–2004), psychiatrist, and pioneer in near-death studies; author of *On Death and Dying* (New York: Macmillan, 1969).

Chapter 20

1. A. Bryant, *The Corner Office: Indispensable and Unexpected Lessons from CEOs on How to Lead and Succeed* (New York: Times Books, 2011).
2. D. Stamoulis and E. Mannion, "Making It to the Top: Nine Attributes That Differentiate CEO's," *In Touch with the Board,* Russell Reynolds Associates, 2014, http://www.russellreynolds.com/content/making-it-top-nine-attributes-differentiate-ceos.
3. Boyatzis, R. E. (2008). Competencies in the 21st century. *Journal of Management Development*, 27, 5-12. doi:10.1108/02621710810840730.

   Boyatzis, R. E., & Saatcioglu, A. (2008). A 20-year view of trying to develop emotional, social and cognitive intelligence competencies in graduate management education. *Journal of Management Development*, 27, 92-108. doi:10.1108/02621710810840785.

   Boyatzis, R. E., Stubbs, E. C., & Taylor, S. N. (2002). Learning Cognitive and Emotional Intelligence Competencies through Graduate Management Education. *Academy of Management Learning & Education*, 1, 150-162. doi:10.5465/AMLE.2002.8509345.

   Dreyfus, C. (2008). Identifying competencies that predict effectiveness of R&D managers. *Journal of Management Development*, 27, 76–91.

   Goleman, D. (2006). *Social intelligence: The new science of human relationships*. New York, NY, US: Bantam Books.

   Goleman, D. (1995). *Emotional intelligence*. New York, NY, England: Bantam Books, Inc.

   Johansen, B. (2012). *Leaders make the future: Ten new leadership skills for an uncertain world*. Oakland, CA: Berrett-Koehler Publishers.

   Loew-Arth, B. (2011, November 3). *Developing 21st Century Leaders Who Make a Difference*. Retrieved from http://www.ere.net/wp-content/uploads/2011/11/developing_leaders.pdf.

   Perrin, C., Blauth, C., Apthorp, E., Daniels, S., Marone, M., Thompson, J., ... Moran, L. (2010). *Developing the 21st-century leader: A multi-level*

analysis of global trends in leadership challenges and practices. Retrieved from
http://www.achieveglobal.com/resources/files/AchieveGlobal_21st_Century_
Leader_Report.pdf.

Tett, R. P., Guterman, H. A., Bleier, A., & Murphy, P. J. (2000). Development
and content validation of a 'hyperdimensional' taxonomy of managerial competence. *Human Performance*, 13, 205-251. doi:10.1207/S15327043HUP1303_1.

Williams, H. W. (2008). Characteristics that distinguish outstanding
urban principals: Emotional intelligence, social intelligence and environmental adaptation. *Journal of Management Development*, 27(1), 36-54.
doi:10.1108/02621710810840758.

Yukl, G., Gordon, A., & Taber, T. (2002). A hierarchical taxonomy of leadership
behavior: Integrating a half century of behavior research. *Journal of Leadership
and Organizational Studies*, *9(1)*,15-32. doi: 10.1177/107179190200900102.

4. "The CEO's Greatest Challenge: Managing Paradoxes for Sustained Competitive
Advantage," *Chief Executive*, May 26, 2010, http://chiefexecutive.net/the-ceos-
greatest-challenge-managing-paradoxes-for-sustained-competitive-advantage.

5. "Conceptual Thinking," *Psychology Wiki*, http://psychology.wikia.com/wiki/
Conceptual_thinking.

6. J. Zenger and J. Folkman, "Are Women Better Leaders than Men?," *Harvard
Business Review*, March 2012.

7. B. Kropp, executive director, Corporate Executive Board, in a presentation at the
2014 Neuroleadership Conference.

8. R. Charan, S. J. Drotter, and J. L. Noel, *The Leadership Pipeline: How to Build
the Leadership-Powered Company* (San Francisco: Jossey-Bass, 2001).

9. http://www-935.ibm.com/services/us/en/c-suite/ceostudy2012/.

10. T. Barta, M. Kleiner, and T. Neumann, "Is There a Payoff from Top-Team
Diversity?" *McKinsey Quarterly*, April 2012.

11. D. Rigby, K. Gruver, and J. Allen, "Innovation in Turbulent Times,"
Harvard Business Review, June 2009, https://hbr.org/2009/06/
innovation-in-turbulent-times/ar/1.

12. J. Menkes, "Three Traits Every CEO Needs," *Harvard Business Review*, May 2011,
https://hbr.org/2011/05/three-traits-every-ceo-needs/.

Chapter 21

1. http://www-935.ibm.com/services/us/en/c-suite/ceostudy2012/.

2. http://lpi.oregonstate.edu/infocenter/cognition.html#choline.

3. J. Born and U. Wagner, "Memory Consolidation During Sleep: Role of Cortisol
Feedback," *Annals of the NY Academy of Science* 1032: 198–201, 2004, PMID:
15677410.

4. G. Wallas, *The Art of Thought* (New York: Harcourt, Brace and Company, 1926);
the Wallas Stage Model of Creativity.

5. http://www.cnn.com/2013/04/04/tech/post-it-note-history/.

Chapter 22

1. Brown-Forman, Herrmann International Case Study, 2009–2015, http://www.hbdi
   .com/brainbytes/extras/HI_BrownForman_WholeBrainCreativity.pdf.
2. Ripley Entertainment, Inc., & Miles Kelly Publishing, *Ripley's Believe It or Not*
   (Orlando, FL: Ripley Publishing, 2004).
3. R. T. Pascale, J. Sternin, and M. Sternin, *The Power of Positive Deviance: How
   Unlikely Innovators Solve the World's Toughest Problems* (Boston: Harvard
   Business Press, 2010).
4. Chuck McVinney, owner, McVinney & Co., Facilitating Executive Teams, http://
   www.mcvinney.com/.
5. W. E. Deming, *The New Economics for Industry, Government & Education"*
   (Cambridge, MA: Massachusetts Institute of Technology Center for Advanced
   Engineering Study, 1993).

Chapter 23

1. "Transforming Project Delivery at InterContinental Hotels Group (IHG),"
   Herrmann International Case Study, 2012, http://www.herrmannsolutions.com/
   transform-project-management-with-whole-brain-thinking/.
2. Rupal Parekh, "Global Study: 75 percent of People Think They're Not Living Up
   to Creative Potential," *Advertising Age,* April 23, 2012, http://adage.com/article/
   news/study-75-living-creative-potential/234302/.
3. B. Edwards, *Drawing on the Artist Within: A Guide to Innovation, Invention,
   Imagination, and Creativity* (New York, Simon and Schuster, 1986).
4. B. Edwards, *Drawing on the Right Side of the Brain: A Course in Enhancing
   Creativity and Artistic Confidence* (Los Angeles: J. P. Tarcher, Inc., New York:
   distributed by St. Martin's Press, 1979).
5. D. H. Pink, "Pencil as Power Tool," 2011, http://www.danpink.com/2011/02/pencil/.
6. G. L. Rico, *Writing the Natural Way: Using Right-Brain Techniques to Release
   Your Expressive Powers* (Los Angeles: J. P. Tarcher, 1983).
7. A. Lamott, *Bird by Bird: Some Instructions on Writing and Life* (New York:
   Anchor Books, 1995).
8. H. Mintzberg, "Plan on the Left, Manage on the Right," *Harvard Business
   Review,* July/August 1976.
9. Ted Coulson and Allison Strickland, owners, Applied Creativity, Inc.; T. Coulson
   and A. Strickland, *Wow! How Did They Think of That?: The Principles of
   Creativity* (Seminole, FL: Applied Creativity Inc., 2000).
10. "Amabile and Kramer's Progress Theory," Mind Tools, 1996–2015, http://www.
    mindtools.com/pages/article/progress-theory.htm.

Chapter 24

1. Bill Hart, board member and HBDI practitioner, and Dr. Nita Carr, executive
   director, Cornerstone Schools, http://www.csalabama.org/.

Chapter 25

1. J. Huefner, H. K. Hunt, and P. Robinson, "A Comparison of Four Scales Predicting Entrepreneurship," *Academy of Entrepreneurship Journal* 1, no. 2: 56–80, 1996.
2. Arianna Huffington, "Great Advice," Tory Burch Foundation, 2013, http://www.toryburchfoundation.org/get-inspired-great-advice/getinspired-advice-AriannaHuffington,default,pg.html.
3. G. Pinchot and R. Pellman, *Intrapreneuring in Action: A Handbook for Business Innovation* (San Francisco: Berrett-Koehler, 1999).
4. I. Adizes, *Corporate Lifecycles: How and Why Corporations Grow and Die and What to Do About It* (Englewood Cliffs, NJ: Prentice Hall, 1988).
5. Dr. Joseph Kayne, http://www.imagineitproject.com/.
6. Gifford Pinchot III, http://www.pinchot.com/.
7. http://www.leagueofintrapreneurs.com/.

Index

About the Authors

Ann Herrmann-Nehdi

Ann Herrmann-Nehdi is CEO of Herrmann International. The company's primary subject matter expert, she applies the principles of Whole Brain® Thinking to her varied responsibilities, including research and development, leadership, strategic consulting, ongoing research, learning design, and speaking engagements.

Herrmann-Nehdi has worked with many hundreds of organizations of all sizes and industries around the world, helping them leverage their cognitive diversity and increase their thinking agility to improve profitability, leadership, productivity, innovation, and overall business results.

A thought leader in her field, she has been featured in media outlets such as *Business News Daily, Chief Executive Magazine, Chief Learning Officer Magazine, HR Executive Magazine, Investor's Business Daily, Management Today, T+D Magazine, Training Journal*, and *O The Oprah Magazine*, and has contributed chapters to many books on the topic of Whole Brain Thinking and Learning. A sought-after, powerful speaker, she has delivered hundreds of featured keynotes and programs for domestic and international groups.

Herrmann-Nehdi's ultimate goal is to help thinkers better understand how they think so that they can learn and interact more effectively, find greater fulfillment, and get better results in everything they do. Through Herrmann International's global offices and the thousands of HBDI® practitioners around the world, millions of individuals and their teams—including nine out of ten of the Fortune 100 and prominent universities such as Stanford, MIT, Vanderbilt, and INSEAD—have applied the Whole Brain system to improve performance.

Ned Herrmann

Ned Herrmann, who founded Herrmann International in 1981 and was the originator of Whole Brain Thinking, first pioneered the study of the brain in the field of business while working as manager of General Electric Corporation's Management Education at Crotonville.

Herrmann's work has been featured in the *Harvard Business Review, Business Week, Scientific American, Discover, USA Today, Training*, and *Reader's Digest*, among many other national and international publications.

In 1988 he published his widely acclaimed book, *The Creative Brain*, tracing the scientific and historical roots of his innovative Whole Brain Thinking approach. In 1995 McGraw-Hill published the first edition of *The Whole Brain Business Book,* creating a new benchmark in the arena of mind research and its applications to business.

Herrmann viewed the Whole Brain Model as a metaphor for an organizing principle of how the brain works, and as clients and practitioners around the world demonstrate every day, the exponential applications of one simple model have created a system that can improve virtually all aspects of personal and work performance.

Now what?
How will you achieve better thinking?

Many references are made throughout the book to resources you can use to get better results from Whole Brain® Thinking. To access these resources, as well as bonus material and tools you can use, or if you are interested in discovering your HBDI® Profile, please visit www.wholebrainbusinessbook.com.

To learn more about the HBDI® and the Whole Brain® Thinking System, please visit www.HerrmannSolutions.com or contact us at info@hbdi.com.

Better Thinking. Better Performance. Better Results.

We help individuals, teams, and organizations understand and apply Whole Brain® Thinking to achieve their desired results.

We invite you to connect with us:

(icon)	The Whole Brain Blog	www.hbdi.com/blog
(icon)	Twitter	@herrmannintl
(icon)	LinkedIn	linkedin.com/company/Herrmann-International
(icon)	Facebook	www.facebook.com/pages/Whole-Brain-Thinking-HBDI-Fan-Page
(icon)	YouTube	www.youtube.com/user/herrmannintl